A BASIC DICTIONARY OF
SYNONYMS AND ANTONYMS

A BASIC DICTIONARY OF SYNONYMS AND ANTONYMS

Laurence Urdang

ELSEVIER/NELSON BOOKS
New York

Library of Congress Cataloging in Publication Data

Urdang, Laurence.
  A basic dictionary of synonyms and antonyms.

  First published in 1978 under title: The basic
book of synonyms and antonyms.
    1. English language—Synonyms and antonyms.
  I. Title.
PE1591.U7   1979   423'.1   79–4064
ISBN 0–525–66604–4

Published in the United States by Elsevier/Nelson Books, a division
of Elsevier-Dutton Publishing Company, Inc., New York. Published
simultaneously in Don Mills, Ontario, by Thomas Nelson and Sons
[Canada] Limited.

Printed in the U.S.A.   First Edition
10 9 8 7 6 5 4 3 2 1

How to Use This Book—
A Word of Caution

Anyone who knows language well will acknowledge that there is no such thing as a *true* synonym. That is, there are words that can be substituted for other words, but they almost never have exactly the same meaning in the same context.

To understand this, it is important to recognize the difference between *denotation*, which is the meaning of a word in a given context for most speakers of the language, and *connotation*, which is the meaning of a word in a given context together with its associations. Thus, a denotation of *home* is "where a person resides"; the connotation of *home* may include such emotional overtones as "warmth, comfort, affection, good food," and so forth.

Another reason why words that are often called synonyms are not always interchangeable is that language functions at different levels, some more formal, others less formal. For example, *residence* may be a perfectly suitable synonym for *home* in certain formal contexts, but in less formal writing it would be out of place. *Maternal, paternal,* and *fraternal,* though technically synonyms for *motherly, fatherly,* and *brotherly,* cannot be said to carry the same connotations. Therefore, one must be very careful in selecting a "synonym" for a word, because in addition to providing variety of expression, the synonym must also be appropriate to the kind of writing one is engaged in.

A third caution in selecting the proper synonym should also be observed. Many words in English—most of the common ones—have a great many senses, some of them quite different from others. For example, *curious* can mean either "inquisitive, prying" or "odd, peculiar," depending on how it is used. In some uses, its meaning can be ambiguous. In the sentence "A squirrel is a curious animal," the meaning could be either "inquisitive" or "odd." It is important to note that in this book we have tried to separate common meanings and to provide

v

example sentences that show the sense distinctions clearly. Also, we have tried to group together the synonyms for each sense in such a way that any of the words listed can be substituted for the entry word in the examples given. However, this doesn't always work, partly because the connotations of synonyms are not always the same and partly because not all of the words in a given list behave exactly the same way in a sentence.

Here, for instance, is the way the entry for *curious* appears in the book:

curious   *adj.*   **1.** inquiring, inquisitive, interested; nosy, prying: *If you weren't so curious about things that didn't concern you, you wouldn't get into so much trouble.* **2.** peculiar, odd, strange, unusual, queer: *There was a curious animal with a red plume and a white tail and blue fur sitting on the fence.*

In actual usage, one could substitute "inquisitive" or "nosy" for *curious* in the example sentence without making any change at all, and the denotations would remain close to that of the original. However, the sentence "If you weren't so inquiring about things . . ." would be awkward, and the substitution would not be proper: it would be better to use "inquiring" in a phrase like "If you didn't have such an inquiring manner about things . . ." Similarly, if "interested" is chosen, the sentence would have to be changed to "If you weren't so interested in things . . . ," because one does not use "interested about" in English. Thus, the example sentence should be looked upon as a guide that is subject to interpretation and variation, depending on the synonym selected. In most cases, it will probably serve well as a sample context, but caution should be exercised.

Antonyms

The user of this book will see that many of the entries include a short list of antonyms at the end, and a word or two might be helpful concerning them. First, it will be seen that the antonyms are keyed to a particular set of synonyms (where more than one set occurs), either by number or by part of speech.

Second, the antonym lists are rather brief, and there are two reasons for this. One is that there may be only one common antonym for the entry word; for example, the antonym for *entrance* is "exit." There may be other antonyms for *entrance*, but "exit" is the most useful one. Another reason is that the antonyms, in many cases, have their own synonyms, and repeating all of them would be wasteful of space: that is, the antonyms given under an entry should be used as cross-references, and the user should look up the main entry for the antonym given in order to find synonyms for it, many of which would be associated antonyms for the original word.

For example, the antonyms listed under *enemy* are "friend, colleague, cohort, ally." Of these, only "cohort" has no entry in this book, because it is not among the basic words of English. But if the user looks up the other words, their synonyms will provide these antonyms for *enemy*:

ally . . . associate, friend, partner.
colleague . . . associate, co-worker; collaborator.
friend . . . companion, acquaintance, crony, chum, mate.

From among these the user can make a choice that best suits his need.

A Word About Style

It is not always simple to make fine distinctions among meanings of words, for the meaning of a word is the sum total of all of the instances of the word's use in the language. It can easily be seen that it would be impossible to record every use of every word in any language. Even the largest dictionaries available can barely scratch the surface of the meanings of words. Consequently, the compiler of a dictionary must rely on conventional use and must interpret, as best he can, the most useful way in which to present the information gathered. To provide the information in this dictionary in a concise, usable form, we have taken certain shortcuts. In some cases, where a group of synonyms properly belong together but have characteristics that are slightly different, either as to level of usage, appropriateness, or the grammatical or syntactic contexts in which they are found, they have been separated, within the same numbered set, by a semicolon.

An example of this can be seen in the entry for *curious*:

curious *adj.* **1.** inquiring, inquisitive, interested; nosy, prying.

Here, "nosy, prying" have been separated from the rest because they are less formal words and because their meaning is slightly different, even though they belong in the same group as the other words in the set.

Another example occurs at *colleague*:

colleague . . . associate, co-worker; collaborator.

"Collaborator" has been separated from the others because it frequently has the connotation of one who works with another to do evil, though it can also have the simple meaning of "co-worker."

A Final Word of Caution

The best use of this dictionary is to remind the user of words he cannot think of when they are needed. It is intended as a guide to commonly used words in English, and those are almost always the most expressive. Much larger (and much more expensive) synonym books are available, but they often confuse the user by providing long lists of complicated, often rare words without giving any indication of how appropriate the words may be in simple, straightforward writing. Besides, they do not provide example sentences that illustrate the words in familiar contexts.

Synonyms and antonyms are sought by those who wish either to add variety to their writing or to find help in selecting alternative ways of expressing themselves. Used with good judgment, this book should yield both results.

LAURENCE URDANG

Essex, Connecticut
June, 1977

A BASIC DICTIONARY OF
SYNONYMS AND ANTONYMS

✌₰ A ₰✌

abandon *vb.* **1.** leave, quit; desert, forsake: *The captain was the last to abandon the sinking ship.* **2.** give up, surrender: *The castaways never abandoned hope that they would be found. adv. phr.* **with abandon** freely, unrestrainedly, without restraint, control, inhibition, *or* constraint: *Whenever his parents were not at home, he behaved with wild abandon.* **ant.** join, engage, unite, embrace, retain.

abandoned *adj.* wicked, depraved, evil; immoral: *Her abandoned behavior caused a lot of trouble.* **ant.** righteous, virtuous.

abbreviate *vb.* shorten, abridge, cut, reduce, condense: *They abbreviated the long novel for publication as a paperback. The name "United States" is often abbreviated to "U.S."* **ant.** lengthen, extend, augment.

abbreviation *n.* cut, shortening, condensation: *The abbreviation for "United States" is "U.S."*

able *adj.* **1.** capable, qualified, fit, competent: *People are able to speak a language.* **2.** talented, skilled, clever, skillful: *She is an able mathematician.* **ant.** unable, incompetent.

abnormal *adj.* unusual, uncommon, odd, peculiar, queer; strange, weird: *They thought he was abnormal because he put salt on his grapefruit.* **ant.** normal, average, usual.

abode *n.* See **dwelling.**

abolish *vb.* end, obliterate, erase, put out, eliminate: *Slavery has been abolished in almost every nation.* **ant.** establish.

abominable *adj.* hateful, loathsome, bad, terrible, awful, nasty, unpleasant: *They lived in abominable conditions of poverty.* **ant.** admirable, fine, noble.

about *prep.* **1.** concerning, relating to, involving: *The book was about pirates.* **2.** near, close to, around, almost, approximately: *The blouse is about my size. adv.* **1.** nearby, around, close, close by: *There's a ghost about at midnight!* **2.** nearly, almost: *It is about four o'clock.*

above *prep.* over, higher than, superior to: *His house was* *above hers on the hill. The admiral is above the lieutenant in every navy.* **ant.** below, under, beneath.

abreast *adv., adj.* alongside, beside, side by side: *The boys walked down the street three abreast.*

abridge *vb.* shorten, cut, abbreviate, abstract: *Many of the dictionaries we use today have been abridged from larger books.* **ant.** expand, extend, increase.

abroad *adv.* **1.** overseas: *She studied abroad last year.* **2.** broadly, publicly, widely, in all directions, in all places: *The news was made known abroad that they were to be married.* **ant. 2.** privately, secretly.

abrupt *adj.* **1.** sudden, short: *He came to an abrupt stop at the door.* **2.** short, curt, blunt, brusque, hasty, rude: *When I asked where she had been, she became very abrupt and asked me to leave.* **3.** steep, sudden: *The road made an abrupt descent to the valley.* **ant.** gradual.

absence *n.* want, need, lack: *The absence of any affection made him yearn for his family.* **ant.** presence, existence.

absent *adj.* **1.** away, not present, out, off: *I was absent from school on Monday.* **2.** missing, lacking, nonexistent: *Common sense was clearly absent from their decision.* **ant.** present.

absent-minded *adj.* forgetful; inattentive, wool-gathering, day-dreaming: *He is getting so absent-minded that he almost went out without his shoes.* **ant.** alert, attentive.

absolute *adj.* **1.** perfect, whole, complete, unqualified, total: *The court had absolute proof that he had committed the crime.* **2.** total, complete, unlimited, limitless, unrestricted, arbitrary, tyrannical, dictatorial: *The dictator assumed absolute power.* **ant.** partial, limited, fragmentary, incomplete.

absolutely *adv.* definitely, positively, really, doubtlessly: *Is she going to the party? Absolutely!* **ant.** uncertainly, doubtfully.

absolve *vb.* acquit, exonerate, free from blame *or* responsibility (for), excuse, forgive, pardon, clear: *The boys were absolved of the charge of stealing books.* **ant.** accuse, charge.

absorb *vb.* **1.** consume, occupy: *The film absorbed their attention completely.* **2.** suck up, sop up, take in *or* up: *A sponge absorbs water.* **ant. 2.** leak, drain.

absurd *adj.* foolish, ridiculous, preposterous, laughable, silly: *The belief that the earth is flat is today regarded as absurd.* **ant.** sensible, sound, reasonable.

abundance *n.* plenty, copiousness, ampleness, profusion: *There is an abundance of water in the oceans.* **ant.** scarcity, want, dearth, absence.

abundant *adj.* plentiful, abounding, copious, profuse: *An abundant harvest means that there will be enough food for everyone.* **ant.** scarce, rare, uncommon, absent.

abuse *vb.* **1.** misuse, misemploy, misapply: *The king abused his power by making the people pay high taxes.* **2.** mistreat, maltreat, hurt, harm, injure: *It was cruel of the children to abuse their kitten by keeping it in a cage.* **3.** scold, upbraid; berate, reproach: *The teacher was wrong to abuse Billy in front of his classmates.* *n.* misuse, misapplication, misemployment, mistreatment, maltreatment: *The puppy suffered the boys' abuse without whimpering.*

accept *vb.* **1.** receive, take: *She accepted the gift with thanks.* **2.** admit, allow, consent to: *He accepts criticism from anyone but his father.* **ant.** refuse, reject, ignore.

accident *n.* mishap, misadventure, misfortune, mischance, disaster, calamity, catastrophe: *Three men were knocked unconscious in the accident at the factory.* *n. phr.* **by accident** unintentionally, accidentally: *I spilled the sugar by accident.*

accommodate *vb.* **1.** aid, assist, help: *The natives accommodated us with food and water for three days' journey.* **2.** provide for, house, serve, hold: *The restaurant cannot accommodate more than 35 people.* **ant.** **1.** inconvenience.

accompany *vb.* escort, go with, join, attend: *Two of my best friends accompanied me on the trip.* **ant.** abandon, leave, forsake.

accomplice *n.* confederate, accessory, assistant, associate, partner (in crime): *The police accused the bank teller of being the robber's accomplice.*

accomplish *vb.* do, complete, achieve, fulfill, perform, finish, realize: *It was amazing how much the mayor had been able to accomplish in his two-year term.* **ant.** fail.

accord *vb.* **1.** agree, concur: *The description that the witness gave of the attack accorded with that of the victim.* **2.** award, grant, reward with, give: *When the sergeant was killed in action, he was accorded an officer's burial.* *n.* agreement, concord: *The governments reached an accord regarding offshore fishing rights.* **ant.** *n.* disagreement, difference, quarrel.

account *n.* **1.** explanation, report, history, description, recital: *John gave an account of what had happened to him over the weekend.* **2.** story, tale, anecdote, narration, narrative: *We were frightened by the old man's strange account of the cave.* **3.** record, balance sheet, ledger, book: *According to the store's account, we owe them $52.* *vb.* explain, give an explanation *or* reason for, make *or* give excuses for: *The teacher asked Maria to account for her absence from school.*

accurate *adj.* precise, correct, exact, right, true: *Newspapers don't always print an accurate report of an incident.* **ant.** inaccurate, inexact, mistaken, wrong.

accuse *vb.* blame, charge, incriminate: *An innocent man was accused of the crime.* **ant.** absolve, clear.

accustomed *adj.* (usually fol. by **to**) used to, familiar with, comfortable with; in the habit of: *I am accustomed to your singing in the shower. He is accustomed to having bacon and eggs for breakfast.* **ant.** unfamiliar, strange.

achieve *vb.* **1.** do, perform, complete, accomplish, reach, realize: *Only after much hard work are most of us able to achieve our goals.* **2.** attain, gain, acquire, secure, procure: *The candidate achieved victory in the election after a hard campaign.* **ant.** fail.

acid *adj.* **1.** sour, tart, vinegar-like: *Lemons have an acid taste.* **2.** sardonic, sarcastic, bitter, biting: *Because of his acid wit, few people would associate with him.* **ant. 1.** sweet, bland, mild.

acknowledge *vb.* **1.** agree to, admit, allow, concede, accept, grant: *After a fierce battle, the general finally acknowledged defeat.* **2.** accept, receive, express thanks *or* gratitude for, thank for: *The prizewinner gratefully acknowledged the award.* **ant.** deny, refuse, reject.

acquaintance *n.* associate, colleague, companion: *I wouldn't say that he's a friend of mine—just an acquaintance.*

acquire *vb.* obtain, procure, secure, get, gain, appropriate: *On his grandmother's death, he acquired her collection of rare books.* **ant.** lose, forfeit.

acquit *vb.* excuse, forgive, exonerate, find not guilty: *After a long trial, he was acquitted of the crime.* **ant.** condemn, sentence.

act *n.* **1.** deed, achievement, action, accomplishment, feat, exploit: *He received a medal for an act of bravery.* **2.** law, decree, statute, judgment: *The senate voted on the crime-prevention act.* **3.** performance, routine, skit, turn:

a balancing act. *v.* **1.** do, perform, operate, function: *The crowbar acts as a lever.* **2.** perform, play, impersonate: *He acts Hamlet very well. She acts the part of the vampire in the film.*

action   *n.*   **1.** movement: *His actions are not graceful.* **2.** battle, fight, fighting, combat: *He saw action on the western front.*

active   *adj.*   **1.** energetic, vigorous, industrious: *He's 80 but still active.* **2.** busy, occupied, engaged: *Mrs. Robinson is active in many charitable organizations.* **ant. 1.** lazy, lethargic, inactive.

actual   *adj.* real, true, genuine, certain: *Although she had a cold, the actual reason she didn't come was that she didn't want to.* **ant.** unreal, pretended, fake, bogus, false.

acute   *adj.*   **1.** severe, piercing, sudden: *I have an acute pain in my toe.* **2.** sharp, keen, quick, perceptive, discerning, intelligent: *A human's eyesight is not as acute as that of an eagle. She is an acute critic of the modern theater.* **ant. 1.** mild, bland. **2.** insensitive, obtuse.

adapt   *vb.* conform, suit, modify, adjust, fit: *Primitive peoples find it difficult to adapt to modern life.*

add   *vb.*   **1.** increase, supplement, augment: *Add this painting to your collection.* **2.** total: *Adding the numbers in this column gives exactly 312.* **ant.** subtract, remove, withdraw.

address   *n.*   **1.** location; residence, home, abode, dwelling; place of business, office: *Please let me have your address so that I can write to you. I'll visit your office if you give me the address.* **2.** speech, lecture, oration, presentation: *The president's address lasted three hours.* *vb.* **1.** speak to, talk to, accost: *Don't ever address me that way in public.* **2.** concentrate on, pay attention to: *You should address yourself to the problem at hand and avoid rambling.*

adequate   *adj.* sufficient, enough; satisfactory, fit, suitable: *There isn't adequate food to feed so many people. The quality of the radio reception was adequate for hearing the code signals.* **ant.** inadequate, insufficient.

adhere   *vb.*   **1.** cling, stick, hold; cleave: *The new tape will adhere to anything.* **2.** be attached, be faithful, be devoted: *She adheres to the ideas she had as a child.* **ant. 1.** separate, loosen.

adherent   *n.* supporter, follower: *He's an adherent of a new Christian sect.* **ant.** defector, renegade, dropout.

adjacent *adj.* near, next (to), close (to), neighboring, nearby: *The two houses are adjacent. The shop is adjacent to the library.* **ant.** apart, separate, distant.

adjoining *adj.* close to, near, near to, next, next to, touching, bordering: *The house adjoining ours is vacant. My father waited in an adjoining room.* **ant.** separate, distant, remote.

adjourn *vb.* suspend, postpone, put off; defer, delay: *We adjourned the meeting until next Friday.* **ant.** assemble, convene, begin.

adjust *vb.* **1.** set, regulate; change, alter; repair, fix: *I adjusted the clock so it would run on time.* **2.** arrange, settle: *We adjusted our spending to our income.* **3.** adapt, suit, fit, accommodate: *Betty quickly adjusted to the new school schedule.*

administer *vb.* **1.** manage, direct, supervise, oversee; rule, govern; conduct, control, superintend; administrate: *The high school was administered by Dr. Jonas.* **2.** dispense, mete out, deal out, give out, distribute: *The magistrate administers justice in a police court.* **3.** give, provide, contribute, *or* distribute aid, help, assistance, medicine, *or* treatment: *The doctor administered the vaccine to the villagers.*

administration *n.* **1.** management, direction, conduct, supervision: *The new foreman's administration of the plant emphasized safety.* **2.** executive, government: *This administration was voted into power by seventy per cent of the people.*

admirable *adj.* excellent, fine, worthy, praiseworthy: *Bill did an admirable job in organizing the team.* **ant.** contemptible, despicable, sorry.

admiration *n.* wonder, awe, pleasure, approval, esteem: *The critics looked upon the new sculpture with admiration.* **ant.** contempt, disdain, disrespect.

admire *vb.* revere, esteem, venerate; like; find praiseworthy *or* desirable: *We all admired Alice's improvement in swimming.* **ant.** dislike, loathe, detest, hate.

admission *n.* **1.** entrance, access, admittance; ticket, pass: *The boys charged ten cents for admission to the hockey game.* **2.** confession, acknowledgment: *Her admission of guilt resulted in a suspension of two days from school.*

admit *vb.* **1.** confess, acknowledge, own: *Bob admits that he ate all the candy.* **2.** let in, allow to enter: *When we*

showed them our pass, we were admitted to the theater.
ant. 1. deny. **2.** obstruct, reject.

admittance *n.* entrance, access, admission: *To gain admittance backstage, you have to be in the cast.*

admonish *vb.* **1.** warn, caution, advise against: *The teacher admonished Jimmy to stop talking in class.* **2.** reprimand, rebuke, censure, reprove: *Afterward, the teacher had to admonish him for making faces.* **ant.** praise, glorify.

ado *n.* fuss, trouble, bother, to-do, bustle, flurry, activity, commotion, stir, excitement, upset, hubbub, confusion, tumult, turmoil: *There was much ado in the government when they found out about the wiretapping.* **ant.** quietude, tranquillity.

adolescent *adj.* teen-aged, teen-age, young, youthful, immature: *Why do so many adults act in such an adolescent way?* *n.* teen-ager, youth, young person: *And why do so many adolescents act like little children?* **ant.** *adj.* adult, grown, mature.

adore *vb.* love, idolize, worship, revere, venerate; respect, honor, esteem: *Cornelia adored her children and did everything to make them happy.* **ant.** despise, hate, loathe.

adorn *vb.* decorate, ornament, beautify, enhance, embellish: *The elephants in the parade were adorned with the most elaborately embroidered cloths.* **ant.** strip, bare.

adroit *adj.* skillful, clever, adept, dexterous, ingenious, expert: *Old Bill is still adroit enough to do these beautiful and intricate carvings.* **ant.** clumsy, awkward, oafish, graceless.

adult *adj.* mature, of age, full-grown: *An adult grizzly bear can reach a height of more than nine feet.* *n.* man, woman, grown-up: *This ticket admits one adult and one child.* **ant.** *adj.* immature, infantile.

advance *vb.* **1.** proceed, progress, move, bring, *or* go forward: *The armies advanced toward one another.* **2.** further, promote: *These treaties will advance the cause of peace.* *n.* **1.** progress, forward movement, advancement, improvement, promotion: *Advances in many industries have been brought about by advances in technology.* **2.** promotion, improvement, upgrade, upgrading, rise: *His advance to the presidency of the company depended on his skill as an administrator.* **ant.** *vb.* **1.** retreat, withdraw, flee. **2.** retard, obstruct. *n.* **1.** retreat, retardation, withdrawal.

advantage *n.* **1.** favor, vantage, edge: *Because of his height, Roger has the advantage when trying out for the basketball team.* **2.** profit, gain, benefit: *Marrying the boss's daughter was to his advantage, for he's been made president.* **ant.** disadvantage, hindrance, loss.

adversary *n.* opponent, antagonist, foe, enemy, contestant: *George's adversary in the boxing match was the biggest man he'd ever seen.* **ant.** friend, ally.

adverse *adj.* **1.** unlucky, unfortunate, unfavorable: *Adverse business conditions made him decide to close the shop.* **2.** contrary, opposite, opposing, opposed: *Adverse winds delayed the plane two hours.* **ant. 1.** beneficial, favorable.

adversity *n.* trouble, misfortune; distress, calamity, disaster, catastrophe: *The adversities of war left many millions of people homeless and penniless.* **ant.** happiness, benefit.

advertisement *n.* commercial, poster, blurb, publicity, billboard, want ad, flyer, brochure, bill, handbill, throwaway: *The advertisement in buses and in newspapers and magazines created a huge demand for pretzels.*

advice *n.* **1.** counsel, recommendation, guidance, suggestion, opinion: *If you take my advice, you'll finish school before looking for a job.* **2.** admonition, warning, caution: *The policeman's advice was to walk home only on well-lit streets.*

advisable *adj.* prudent, sensible, wise; proper, suitable, fit, fitting: *The principal didn't think it advisable for the younger students to dissect animals.* **ant.** inadvisable, ill-considered, imprudent.

advise *vb.* **1.** counsel, recommend, suggest: *Her father advised her to go out with friends of her own age.* **2.** warn, caution, admonish: *I was advised not to swim in the lagoon because of the sharks.* **3.** inform, notify, acquaint: *The premier was advised of the treachery of the generals.*

advocate *vb.* support, recommend, argue *or* plead in favor of: *The biologists advocate preservation of national forests.* *n.* supporter, promoter, upholder: *Advocates of spelling reform in English have a long fight ahead of them.* **ant.** *vb.* oppose. *n.* opponent, foe, adversary.

affect *vb.* **1.** modify, alter, change, transform: *A change in the speed limit affected everyone's driving habits.* **2.** impress, stir, move, touch: *The death of Jennie's kitten affected her deeply.*

affection *n.* liking, fondness, attachment, friendliness, warmth, tenderness: *The teacher's affection for her stu-*

dents showed in her many acts of kindness. **ant.** dislike, aversion, antipathy.

affectionate *adj.* fond, tender, attached, warm, loving: *Suzy's new puppy is so affectionate!* **ant.** cold, distant, unfeeling.

affirm *vb.* **1.** declare, state, assert, say: *She affirmed that she was at the movies last night.* **2.** confirm, establish: *The Senate affirmed the nomination of the new Secretary of State.* **ant. 1.** deny, disclaim.

affliction *n.* **1.** trouble, distress, grief, misfortune: *Poverty is the affliction of millions of people.* **2.** pain, suffering, misery; sickness, ailment: *In his old age, headaches became a serious affliction.* **ant. 1.** benifit. **2.** relief, easement.

afraid *adj.* frightened, fearful, scared, terrified: *Liza was afraid to go into the cave alone.* **ant.** confident, courageous, bold.

age *n.* era, time, period, epoch: *The last ice age ended about 20,000 years ago.* *n. phr.* **of age** mature: *When you become of age, you will have the right to vote.* *vb.* mature, ripen, grow old: *I think this wine has aged long enough.*

aged *adj.* old, elderly, ancient: *That aged gentleman is almost 100 years old.* **ant.** young, youthful.

aggravate *vb.* intensify, worsen, make worse *or* more severe, heighten: *His illness was aggravated by the lack of heat in the room.* **ant.** ease, relieve, soothe.

aggressive *adj.* **1.** attacking, pugnacious, ready to fight, offensive: *Her aggressive manner irritated so many people that no one wanted to spend time with her.* **2.** active, vigorous, energetic, enterprising, determined: *We need an aggressive governor, not one who is too shy to act for us.* **ant.** passive, shy, timid, withdrawn.

agile *adj.* active, nimble, graceful, lively, light on one's feet, spry: *An agile dancer, Marie had studied ballet for many years.* **ant.** clumsy, awkward, inept.

agitate *vb.* **1.** shake, jar, shake up, toss, disturb: *If you agitate the bottle, you'll stir up the sediment at the bottom.* **2.** stir up, excite, disturb: *Her speech on equal rights for women agitated many in the crowd.* **ant.** calm, soothe.

agony *n.* pain, suffering, torment, torture: *After the accident, Peter was in agony for a week.*

agree *vb.* **1.** settle, concur, harmonize, unite: *The members of the committee could not agree on where the party should be held.* **2.** assent, consent, yield, concede: *He agreed to leave the room so that his parents could talk in private.* **ant. 1.** disagree, argue. **2.** refuse.

agreeable *adj.* friendly, cooperative, pleasing, pleasant: *I like being with George because he's so agreeable.* **ant.** disagreeable, quarrelsome, contentious, touchy.

agreement *n.* **1.** treaty, pact; deal, bargain, contract, understanding, arrangement: *An agreement was reached between the union and the company.* **2.** settlement, accord, concord: *There was basic agreement on the terms of the pension contribution.* **ant.** disagreement, discord, misunderstanding.

aid *vb.* help, assist, support, back: *Unless you all aid me, I cannot win the election.* *n.* help, assistance, support, backing: *Without his aid I couldn't have climbed to the top of the mountain.* **ant.** *vb.* impede, obstruct, hinder. *n.* obstacle, hindrance.

ailing *adj.* sick, ill, sickly: *The ailing president knew that he wouldn't live much longer.* **ant.** well, hearty, hale.

ailment *n.* sickness, illness, affliction, disease: *The doctor diagnosed Donald's ailment as indigestion from eating too much ice cream.*

aim *vb.* **1.** point, direct: *Aim a little below the bull's eye when firing a rifle at a target.* **2.** try *or* strive for: *Some of us aim at perfection, but only a few ever achieve it.* *n.* **1.** purpose, goal, target, object, objective: *My aim in life is to be a really good doctor.* **2.** direction, sight, sighting: *His aim was so poor that he missed the target completely.*

air *n.* **1.** atmosphere: *The envelope of air is kept close to earth by gravity.* **2.** manner, appearance, character, look, attitude: *He has an air about him that gives everyone the impression that he thinks he's just wonderful.* *vb.* **1.** ventilate: *We really ought to air out the room to get rid of the smell.* **2.** display, publicize, expose, reveal: *The principal gave the students the chance to air their complaints against the teacher.* **ant.** *vb.* **2.** hide, conceal.

alarm *n.* **1.** fright, fear, dismay: *They greeted the news of the accident with alarm.* **2.** siren, bell, gong: *The fire alarm could be heard two miles away.* *vb.* frighten, scare, terrify, startle: *The nurse was alarmed by Jane's temperature.* **ant.** *vb.* calm, soothe, comfort.

alarming *adj.* shocking, appalling, daunting: *The warden had an alarming lack of consideration for the prisoners.* **ant.** soothing, comforting, calming.

alert *adj.* **1.** watchful, attentive, vigilant, keen, wide-awake, observant: *The alert watchman gave the alarm when he* *found the broken window.* **2.** quick, lively, active, spirited, bright: *Dick's alert mind understood at once where the error was in the calculation.* *n.* alarm, warning: *When they smelled smoke, they sounded the alert.* **ant.** *adj.* listless, dulled, sluggish, logy.

alien *n.* foreigner, immigrant; stranger: *In some countries, aliens become eligible for citizenship after one year.* *adj.* foreign, strange; nonnative: *The spaceship landed the explorers on an alien planet.* **ant.** *adj.* familiar, commonplace, accustomed.

allay *vb.* quiet, soothe, calm, lessen, lighten, soften, moderate: *Mother's anxiety was allayed when we phoned her and told her we were safe.* **ant.** arouse, worsen, intensify.

allege *vb.* declare, affirm, state, assert: *The boy that the policeman alleged to be the thief was completely innocent.* **ant.** deny.

allegiance *n.* loyalty, faithfulness, duty, obligation: *I pledge allegiance to the United States.* **ant.** disloyalty, treachery.

alley *n.* lane, byway, footway: *The back door of the shop opens onto an alley.*

alliance *n.* **1.** relation, interrelation, relationship, interrelationship; marriage, intermarriage: *The alliance between the two families was established when Pamela and Henry were married.* **2.** association, connection, combination: *The alliance between biology and psychology is well established.* **3.** agreement, treaty, pact; union, league: *The Triple Alliance was among Germany, Austria-Hungary, and Italy.*

allot *vb.* distribute, divide, deal out: *Each of the children was allotted his fair share of dessert.*

allow *vb.* **1.** permit, let: *My mother won't allow me to go out until my cold is better.* **2.** grant, cede, concede: *Allow me one more chance to prove I can run faster than Glenn.* **3.** set aside *or* apart, provide for: *We didn't allow enough time to drive to the station and missed the train.* **ant.** **1.** forbid, prohibit.

allowance *n.* **1.** allotment, grant: *When Larry was seven, his father gave him an allowance of ten cents a week.* **2.** discount, deduction: *The shopkeeper gave us an allowance of 25 per cent because the box wasn't full.*

ally *n.* associate, friend, partner: *England and America were allies against Germany in the Second World War.* *vb.* **1.** associate, join, unite: *The countries were allied by the treaty.* **2.** unite, unify, combine, connect, join: *If we ally* *ourselves with them, we could be much stronger than if we remain alone.* **ant.** *n.* enemy, foe, adversary.

almost *adv.* nearly, somewhat: *Almost every house on the block is new.* **ant.** absolutely, completely.

alone *adj.* lone, apart, separate, isolated: *Robinson Crusoe was alone until he found Friday. adv.* solely, solo, solitarily; exclusively: *She sang alone at the graduation ceremony.* **ant.** *adv.* accompanied, together.

aloof *adj.* distant, uninvolved, uninterested, withdrawn, separate; disdainful: *Her aloof attitude won few friends for her.* **ant.** friendly, outgoing, cordial, warm.

also *adv.* too, as well, besides, furthermore, moreover, further: *They stole not only the chairs but the table and carpet also.*

alter *vb.* change, modify; vary; adjust: *The landscape was altered by the building of the housing project.* **ant.** keep, preserve.

alteration *n.* change, modification, difference, adjustment: *After the tailor made the alterations, the dress fit me perfectly.* **ant.** preservation, maintenance.

altercation *n.* argument, controversy, dispute, quarrel: *The police were called when an altercation broke out between the truck drivers.*

alternate *vb.* interchange, rotate: *In order to be fair, the teacher alternated the children at the head of the line.* **ant.** fix.

alternative *n.* choice, selection, option; possibility: *In "The Lady or the Tiger," the hero is given a difficult set of alternatives.*

although *conj.* even though, though, even if, in spite of (the fact that), despite, notwithstanding: *Although Marie wished very much to go, she had to study for a test.*

altitude *n.* height, elevation: *Our plane was flying at an altitude of 37,000 feet.* **ant.** depth.

altogether *adv.* entirely, completely, wholly, quite: *He was altogether too rude to his father. n. phr.* **in the altogether** nude, naked, stripped: *After the night football game, the whole team went swimming in the altogether.*

always *adv.* forever, everlastingly, eternally, ever, forevermore: *Jennie will always be the teacher's pet.* **ant.** never, rarely.

amateur *n.* novice, nonprofessional, tyro, beginner: *When it came to repairing watches, Jimmy was obviously an amateur. adj.* unprofessional, nonprofessional: *The amateur* *theater group put on an excellent performance.* **ant.** professional.

amaze *vb.* astonish, astound, surprise, stun, dumbfound: *The magician's tricks amazed the audience.* **ant.** bore, tire, disinterest.

ambiguous *adj.* unclear, uncertain, vague, deceptive: *When asked if he had broken the vase, Paul gave an ambiguous reply.* **ant.** clear, unmistakable, certain.

ambition *n.* eagerness; yearning, longing, desire: *Her ambition to become a doctor made her study hard.*

amend *vb.* improve, better: *After the teacher spoke with him, Fred amended his ways and behaved very differently.* **ant.** worsen.

amiable *adj.* friendly, amicable, good-natured, outgoing, agreeable, kind-hearted, kind, pleasant: *Don's amiable manner has won him many friends.* **ant.** disagreeable, ill-tempered, cross, captious, touchy.

amid *prep.* amidst, surrounded by, among, amongst, in the middle of: *It was difficult to find the flowers amid all the weeds.*

amiss *adv.* improperly, wrongly, astray, awry: *We knew that something had gone amiss when Barbara didn't come to school for three days.* *adj.* improper, wrong, faulty: *Something is amiss in the wiring of our house—the lights always flicker.* **ant.** *adv.* properly, correctly, rightly. *adj.* right, correct.

among *prep.* amid, in the middle *or* midst of, surrounded by: *Among the crowd I could pick out my parents, my uncle, and my cousin.*

amount *n.* quantity, measure: *There was only a small amount of sugar in the box.* *vb.* add up, total, aggregate: *At last count, those opposed to the plan amounted to less than a majority.*

ample *adj.* **1.** spacious, large, great, roomy: *The ample truck could hold all of our belongings.* **2.** liberal, abundant, plentiful: *There was ample food for everyone.* **ant.** **1.** cramped, confined. **2.** insufficient, inadequate.

amplify *vb.* enlarge, extend, broaden, develop, expand: *Asked to amplify his remarks, the teacher gave many examples of the kinds of problems he faced.* **ant.** restrict, confine, narrow, abridge.

amuse *vb.* entertain, please, charm, divert: *Oscar's parents hired a magician to amuse the children at the party.* **ant.** bore, tire.

amusement *n.* entertainment, pastime; diversion; enjoyment, recreation, pleasure: *For amusement, we used to watch TV.* **ant.** boredom, tedium.

amusing *adj.* entertaining, pleasing, pleasant; funny, comical: *Harvey helped us pass the time by telling amusing stories.* **ant.** boring, tiring, tedious.

analysis *n.* examination, investigation, separation: *The analysis of the blood sample confirms that George is healthy.*

analyze *vb.* examine, investigate, separate, take apart; explain: *The scientist was able to analyze the question and answer each part.*

ancestral *adj.* inherited, hereditary: *Lord Cummings lives on his ancestral estate near London.*

ancestry *n.* lineage, descent, line, family, house: *Chauncey's ancestry is royal.* **ant.** posterity.

anchor *vb.* fasten, fix, pin: *We anchored the bookcase to the wall. The boat was anchored in the harbor.* **ant.** loosen, free, detach.

ancient *adj.* antique, old, aged, old-fashioned, primitive: *There may be ancient cities buried beneath the sands of the Sahara.* **ant.** new, fresh, recent, current.

anecdote *n.* story, tale, narrative, account: *The old miner used to entertain us with anecdotes of the wild west, from when he was a young man.*

angel *n.* seraph, cherub, archangel: *Hark! the herald angels sing!* **ant.** devil, demon.

anger *n.* wrath, fury, rage, indignation; displeasure, exasperation: *We felt anger at the unfair way that Herb had been treated.* *vb.* enrage, infuriate, arouse, nettle, exasperate, inflame, madden: *Jean's mother was angered at her refusal to help with the housework.*

angry *adj.* furious, mad, inflamed, irate, wrathful: *All the townspeople were angry when they learned that the mayor had stolen public funds.* **ant.** happy, content, tranquil.

anguish *n.* pain, suffering, misery, distress, torment, agony: *The anguish of losing her kitten was almost more than Connie could bear.* **ant.** joy, ecstasy, pleasure.

animate *vb.* enliven, vitalize, invigorate, stimulate: *Her animated conversation made Amy a welcome guest at parties.* *adj.* alive, lively, vital, vigorous: *Rocks are not animate beings, but mice are.* **ant.** *adj.* inanimate, dead.

annex *vb.* add, attach, join, append: *Poland was sometimes annexed to Russia and sometimes to Germany.* *n.* addition; supplement, extension: *All of the x-ray equipment was moved to the hospital annex.*

announce *vb.* proclaim, declare, report, publish, publicize: *The president announced his resignation.* **ant.** suppress.

announcement *n.* notice, declaration, message, commercial: *The first announcement was made on the radio, the second was sent through the mail, and the third appeared in the newspaper.*

annoy *vb.* bother, irritate, irk, pester, harry, harass, disturb: *He was annoyed by the children whenever he tried to read.* **ant.** comfort, soothe, please.

annually *adv.* once a year, yearly: *The almanac appears annually.*

answer *n.* reply, response, retort, rejoinder: *His answer to her question was a nod.* *vb.* reply, respond: *She answered him with a shake of the head.* **ant.** *n.* question, query, inquiry. *vb.* ask, question, inquire.

antagonism *n.* hostility, enmity, opposition, conflict, animosity: *The antagonism between the candidates often caused them to insult one another.* **ant.** friendliness, geniality, cordiality.

antagonist *n.* adversary, opponent, rival; enemy, foe: *Sir Launcelot's antagonist was dressed entirely in black armor.* **ant.** friend, ally.

anticipate *vb.* expect, foresee, forecast: *Because we had anticipated our parents' permission, we were all ready to go.*

antique *n.* objet d'art, rarity, curio: *The auctioneer sold the antiques to the collector for a huge sum.* *adj.* old, ancient, early; antiquated, old-fashioned, out-of-date, passé: *Legally, antique furniture must be not less than 100 years old. An antique car cannot be that old, though.* **ant.** *adj.* new, fresh, recent.

anxiety *n.* uneasiness, distress, worry, foreboding, apprehension: *Anne's mother was filled with anxiety when she didn't come home for dinner.* **ant.** peacefulness, placidity, calmness, tranquillity.

anxious *adj.* worried, troubled, concerned, uneasy, apprehensive, fearful: *We were all anxious about Suzanne when we heard she was in the hospital.* **ant.** peaceful, tranquil, calm.

anyway *adv.* anyhow, nevertheless, in any case: *Anyway, after the way you talked to me, I wouldn't go if you paid me!*

apologetic *adj.* regretful, sorry: *Ethel was very apologetic for what she had said, so she was forgiven.* **ant.** unrepentant.

apology *n.* explanation, plea, excuse: *Roger offered no apology for painting his name on the wall.*

appall *vb.* horrify, shock, dismay; frighten: *The authorities were appalled at the treatment prisoners received in the county jail.* **ant.** please, edify.

apparel *n.* clothing, clothes, attire, garb, garments, robes, dress: *The beggar's apparel was neat and clean, though tattered and torn in some places.*

apparent *adj.* **1.** plain, evident, clear, obvious, transparent, understandable: *When we found the book in Cora's desk, it was apparent who had taken it.* **2.** seeming: *Although the gray mare had been the apparent winner of the race, the photo showed the real winner to be the brown one.* **ant. 2.** real, actual, evident.

appeal *n.* **1.** request, plea, petition, entreaty: *The annual appeal for contributions resulted in huge donations this year.* **2.** attraction, draw: *The cartoon has much more appeal than the main feature film.* *vb.* **1.** request, plead, petition, entreat, beseech: *The university appealed to the millionaire for financial support.* **2.** attract: *Frankly, that color doesn't appeal to me at all.* **ant.** *vb.* **2.** repel, repulse.

appear *vb.* **1.** seem, look: *Although that animal may appear wise, it is really very stupid.* **2.** emerge, arise; turn up, arrive: *Just when we were sure he wouldn't come, he appeared.* **ant. 2.** disappear, vanish, evaporate.

appearance *n.* **1.** look, mien, aspect: *From his appearance, I'd say he hasn't slept for days.* **2.** arrival, presence: *Her appearance at the party wearing a long dress was a surprise to us all.* **ant. 2.** disappearance, vanishing.

append *vb.* add, attach, supplement: *The publisher appended his comments to the manuscript of the novel.*

appetite *n.* hunger, craving, thirst, desire: *He has an appetite for learning that cannot be satisfied.*

applaud *vb.* praise, approve (of), acclaim: *Bill's mother applauded his decision to go to college.* **ant.** disapprove, criticize, condemn, denounce.

applicable *adj.* usable, fitting, suitable, proper, fit, appropriate, suited: *The statement you made about boys just isn't applicable to girls.* **ant.** inapplicable, inappropriate.

apply *vb.* use, utilize, employ, make use of, put to use: *The* *teaching methods used in grade school probably wouldn't apply to high school.* **ant.** neglect, ignore.

appoint *vb.* **1.** assign, nominate, name, designate, elect, establish, place: *He was appointed to the committee by the chairman.* **2.** determine, settle, fix: *If you appoint a time, I'll meet you at the office.* **ant. 1.** dismiss, discharge, fire.

appointment *n.* **1.** engagement, meeting, rendezvous: *I made two appointments for ten o'clock, so please change one of them.* **2.** assignment, designation, position: *Her appointment as head of the school board was widely applauded.* **ant. 2.** dismissal, discharge.

appreciate *vb.* **1.** prize, value; be grateful for: *What child really appreciates what his parents do for him?* **2.** recognize, understand: *I don't think that Marshall fully appreciates the dangers of swimming alone.* **ant. 1.** scorn, depreciate, undervalue.

apprehend *vb.* **1.** arrest, catch, seize, capture: *The police apprehended the burglar while he was trying to pick the lock of the shop.* **2.** understand, perceive, grasp: *When she graded his examination paper, the teacher knew that Ben had not apprehended Chapter 15 at all.* **ant. 1.** lose.

apprehension *n.* **1.** uneasiness, worry, fear, fearfulness, misgiving, dread, anxiety, anticipation: *When the police officer asked to speak to his father, Philip was filled with apprehension.* **2.** arrest, capture, seizure: *The apprehension of the fugitive at the top of the bridge tower was dramatic.* **ant. 1.** composure, self-assuredness, confidence.

apprentice *n.* learner, beginner; amateur; recruit: *An apprentice to a carpenter once had to spend ten years learning his trade.* **ant.** master, professional.

appropriate *adj.* fitting, proper, suitable: *Her blue jeans were not appropriate clothing for school.* *vb.* assign, apportion, authorize: *The town council appropriated $20,000 for road maintenance and repair.* **ant.** *adj.* inappropriate, unfit, inapt.

approve *vb.* **1.** praise, commend, appreciate: *I approve neither of borrowing nor of lending money.* **2.** authorize, sanction, endorse, confirm: *The budget committee approved plans for an increase in teachers' salaries.* **ant. 2.** disapprove, deny.

apt *adj.* **1.** proper, suitable, fitting, appropriate, fit, suited:

Before dinner, the speaker offered some apt comments on the undernourished peoples of the world. **2.** likely, disposed, liable, prone, inclined: *If you criticize him, he's apt to tell you to jump in the lake!* **3.** bright, clever, alert, intelligent, receptive: *When Rosemarie applies herself, she makes an apt student.* **ant. 1.** unfit, ill-becoming, unsuitable. **2.** unlikely. **3.** slow, retarded, dense.

aptitude *n.* gift, talent, knack, faculty; ability: *Nicole has always shown a remarkable aptitude for becoming a great cook.*

argue *vb.* **1.** debate, discuss: *We argued for an increase in time for lunch, and we won.* **2.** dispute, disagree: *My parents never argued about what they wanted for dinner.* **ant. 2.** agree, concur.

argument *n.* **1.** discussion, debate, dispute, controversy; disagreement: *There was a big argument at the restaurant about whether chocolate ice cream is more fattening than vanilla.* **2.** reason, ground, grounds, proof: *José's argument was that Cuba was still better off under Castro than it had been under Batista.* **ant. 1.** agreement, harmony, accord.

arise *vb.* emerge, originate, appear, spring up: *The problem arose when the students refused to do their homework.*

aristocrat *n.* nobleman, noble, peer, lord: *The aristocrats were once very cruel to the peasants.* **ant.** commoner, peasant.

arouse *vb.* awaken, stir, activate, animate, excite, stimulate, fire: *His strange behavior at the bank teller's window aroused my curiosity.* **ant.** calm, settle, soothe.

arrange *vb.* **1.** place, order, put in order, group, distribute; array: *Before we arranged the furniture in the bedroom, we laid down the rug.* **2.** organize, plan, prepare: *The travel agent arranged all of my hotel reservations.* **ant. 1.** disarrange, disturb, disorder.

arrangements *n. pl.* plans, preparations: *All the arrangements have been made for the King's visit.*

array *vb.* **1.** clothe, dress, attire; adorn: *Penny came into the room arrayed in her best clothes.* **2.** arrange, order, lineup, distribute: *The soldiers were arrayed along the front line in full battle dress.* *n.* **1.** order, arrangement, lineup: *The troops are in battle array.* **2.** display, arrangement, exhibit: *The array of diamonds in the jeweler's window took her breath away.* **ant.** *n.* **1.** disarray, disorder, disorganization.

arrest *vb.* **1.** take into custody, seize, apprehend, catch, capture, take prisoner: *The police arrested the burglar as he was trying to escape through the window.* **2.** stop, check, stay; delay, hinder, slow: *We arrested the growth of the plant by withholding water.* **3.** attract, engage, capture: *A small scratch near the lock arrested the detective's attention.* *n.* **1.** seizure, capture, detention, custody, apprehension, imprisonment: *The arrest of the judge was reported on the front page.* **2.** halt, check, stoppage; delay, hindrance: *Any arrest in the development of a child can have serious results.* *n. phr.* **under arrest** imprisoned, in custody, incarcerated: *The Queen placed Sir Walter Raleigh under arrest.* **ant.** *vb.* **1.** release, free. **2.** activate, encourage, stimulate.

arrival *n.* coming, advent: *Her arrival was met by cheers from the crowd.* **ant.** departure, leaving.

arrive *vb.* **1.** come, reach: *We arrived in Rome at six-thirty in the morning. He arrived at the right decision.* **2.** succeed, attain success: *Donald finally felt he had arrived when they presented him with the medal.* **ant.** **1.** leave, depart.

arrogance *n.* insolence, pride, haughtiness: *David's arrogance made him unpopular in the class.* **ant.** humility, humbleness, modesty.

arrogant *adj.* proud, haughty, insolent, prideful; scornful: *Young man, your arrogant attitude won't endear you to people around here!* **ant.** humble, modest.

art *n.* skill, aptitude, craft, dexterity, ingenuity: *The art that Patrick's father brings to his carvings is recognized by great collectors.*

artful *adj.* tricky, cunning, clever, deceitful: *The fugitive tried an artful ruse by doubling back through the woods.* **ant.** artless.

artificial *adj.* **1.** unnatural, synthetic, man-made, manufactured, not genuine, unreal: *Can't you tell artificial flowers from real ones?* **2.** false, pretended, unnatural, feigned, fake, faked, fraudulent: *Betty's sympathy for my problem was entirely artificial—she really didn't care.* **ant.** real, genuine, authentic.

artist *n.* painter, sculptor, water colorist; actor, actress, singer; designer: *Many artists in Europe are supported by the governments.*

artless *adj.* simple, naive, innocent, natural, open, frank, honest, sincere; candid, truthful: *Alexa's artless attempt* *to help a friend got her more deeply involved in the crime.* **ant.** artful.

ascend *vb.* rise, mount, climb *or* go upward: *The smoke ascended from the chimney. Bernard ascended the stairs so he could look down on the crowd below.* **ant.** descend.

ashamed *adj.* embarrassed, shamefaced, abashed, humiliated: *Tom was ashamed at the way he was dressed—in red velvet with lace trim.* **ant.** proud.

ask *vb.* **1.** question, inquire of, seek information (from), put a question (to): *Della asked people on the street if they knew where the bus stopped.* **2.** demand, request, charge, expect: *Alan complained that the shop was asking too much for the pair of sandals.* **3.** invite, call in: *Marie asked all of her friends to her party.* **ant. 1.** answer, reply.

asleep *adj.* sleeping; inactive, dormant: *Everyone was asleep when Philip came home last night.* **ant.** awake, alert.

aspect *n.* **1.** look, appearance: *The gloomy aspect of the mountains through the fog depressed the hikers.* **2.** point of view, viewpoint, attitude, view, outlook: *If you look at the problem from another aspect, you might understand what I mean.* **3.** phase, side, part, feature: *But I haven't considered that aspect of the situation.*

aspire *vb.* yearn (for), wish (for), hope (for), desire: *George aspires to become a doctor when he grows up.*

assail *vb.* attack, assault, set upon: *The farmers assailed the cowboys with sticks and stones. The critics assailed the playwright with sarcasm.*

assault *n.* attack, onslaught: *The cavalry could not withstand the assault of the trained mountain troops. vb.* attack, assail; charge: *The woman told the police that the tall man had assaulted her.*

assemble *vb.* **1.** meet, convene, collect, gather: *The class assembled in the auditorium to listen to the principal.* **2.** put together, connect, manufacture: *The manager told us that they could assemble an entire car in 30 minutes.* **ant. 1.** scatter, disperse. **2.** disassemble.

assembly *n.* congress, parliament, legislature, council: *The State Assembly met to consider the budget.*

assent *vb.* agree, consent (to); allow, concede, accede (to): *When Janet asked her father if she could go to summer camp, he assented. n.* consent, agreement, approval, permission: *I'll have to ask my parents' assent if I want*

attempt *vb.* try, seek: *The football team attempted to win every game. n.* try, effort, undertaking, endeavor, trial: *After three attempts, Jonathan finally jumped over the fence.* **ant.** *vb.* achieve, accomplish. *n.* achievement, accomplishment.

attend *vb.* **1.** go to, frequent, be present at: *The entire family attends church.* **2.** care for, serve, tend, wait on: *The waitress attended to our order first.*

attendant *n.* servant, waiter, valet, footman: *The millionaire had three attendants with him at all times.*

attention *n.* observation, heed, alertness, care, consideration: *The class turned their attention to the teacher at the door.* **ant.** inattention, absentmindedness, preoccupation.

attentive *adj.* **1.** observant, alert, heedful: *Unless you agree to be more attentive when I speak, I shall ask you to leave.* **2.** thoughtful, kind, polite, considerate, courteous: *Larry was always a very attentive father and husband.* **ant.** inattentive, absentminded, preoccupied.

attire *vb.* dress, clothe, apparel: *The beggar was attired in rags n.* dress, clothing, clothes, apparel: *Blue jeans are not appropriate attire for a dinner dance.*

attitude *n.* view, regard, position, manner, disposition, deportment: *I don't like your unfriendly attitude toward old people.*

attorney *n.* lawyer, attorney-at-law; (in England) barrister, solicitor: *Only a qualified attorney is permitted in the court at this time.*

attract *vb.* draw, invite, win: *The crowd's attention was attracted to the man juggling the eight oranges.* **ant.** repel, repulse.

attractive *adj.* appealing, alluring, pleasing, charming: *Henry behaved differently whenever an attractive girl came into the shop.* **ant.** unattractive, plain, homely, ugly.

attribute *vb.* assign, credit, ascribe: *She attributed her nervousness to the importance of the interview. n.* characteristic, quality, property: *One of Beth's chief attributes is her patience.*

austere *adj.* **1.** stern, severe, hard, harsh, firm, strict, stiff, inflexible: *The austere look on the teacher's face told the children that he would tolerate no nonsense.* **2.** plain, simple, unadorned, severe: *For the first few years, the lives of the pilgrims were very austere.* **ant.** **1.** lenient, permissive, soft. **2.** luxurious, fancy, opulent.

austerity *n.* severity, harshness, strictness: *Few pioneers sur-*

vived the austerity of life on the frontier. **ant.** comfort, luxury.

authentic *adj.* **1.** genuine, real: *Unless it is at least 100 years old, it isn't an authentic antique.* **2.** true, reliable, trustworthy, accurate, authoritative: *The witness testified that the signature on the will was authentic.* **ant.** fake, bogus; imitation, counterfeit.

author *n.* (of a play) playwright, dramatist; (of a poem) poet; (of a novel) novelist; (of a musical composition) composer; (of words to a song) lyricist, songwriter; (of a biography) biographer; writer, creator, originator: *She received the award for being the author of the best biography of the year.*

authority *n.* **1.** jurisdiction, authorization; permission, sanction, approval: *You have no right to go into that room without the proper authority.* **2.** command, rule, order, control, power: *The library is under the authority of the librarian.*

authorize *vb.* **1.** empower: *She wasn't authorized to use that typewriter.* **2.** allow, permit, sanction, approve: *The committee authorized the purchase of new playground equipment.* **ant. 2.** prohibit, forbid.

automatic *adj.* **1.** self-moving, mechanical: *The spinning cycle on this washing machine is automatic.* **2.** uncontrolled, uncontrollable, involuntary, unconscious: *The circulation of the blood is automatic.* **ant. 1.** manual, hand-operated. **2.** deliberate, intentional.

automobile *n.* car, motor car, auto; jalopy; (*Slang*) heap, wheels: *You can't drive an automobile to the city because there's no place to park.*

avail *vb.* benefit, help, serve; profit: *Dishonesty avails us nothing.* *n.* help, benefit, use, advantage, profit: *Attempts to persuade her to stay after she felt insulted were to no avail.*

available *adj.* obtainable, accessible, at hand, ready, handy: *A mechanic wasn't available at midnight, so we had to leave the car until morning.* **ant.** unavailable, unobtainable.

average *adj.* normal, common, typical, ordinary: *I never understood why 'C' was considered an average mark for school work.* *n.* mean; median: *The average of all meat prices rose 10 per cent last year.* **ant.** *adj.* atypical, abnormal.

aversion *n.* dislike, distaste; abhorrence, disgust, loathing, hatred: *I have an aversion to boiled eggs, to horror movies, and to people who talk all the time.* ant. liking, affinity, attraction.

avoid *vb.* elude, evade; shun: *For two years the murderer managed to avoid capture.* ant. meet, confront, encounter, face.

award *vb.* bestow, give: *She was awarded first prize in the essay contest. The father was awarded custody of the children.* *n.* prize, reward, payment, medal: *An award will be given to the employee who offers the best idea.*

aware *adj.* conscious, informed, mindful: *When Margaret lied about breaking the mirror, she was aware of the consequences.* ant. unaware, unconscious.

awe *n.* respect, wonder, fear, admiration: *At the hospital, all the nurses were in awe of the doctors.* ant. scorn, contempt.

awful *adj.* dreadful, terrible, abominable, bad, poor, unpleasant: *The concert was so awful that everyone left in the middle.* ant. wonderful, delightful.

awkward *adj.* 1. clumsy, graceless, unskillful, sloppy, ungraceful, ungainly, crude: *In an awkward attempt to reach the sugar, Everett spilled the milk pitcher.* 2. inconvenient, unwieldy, unmanageable: *From that awkward position, I was unable to turn the bolt.* ant. 1. graceful, deft, elegant, skilled, skillful.

back *vb.* support, help, assist, second, aid; endorse, ratify, stand by, approve; finance: *The investors agreed to back the new company with $1 million.*

background *n.* experience: *At only 18, Phoebe doesn't have the background needed for this job.* *prep. phr.* **in the background** unobtrusive, inconspicuous: *Millie always kept her personal feelings in the background.*

backward *adv.* rearward: *He walked into the room backward.* *adj.* **1.** rearward: *Looking over her shoulder, Suzanne gave him a final, backward glance.* **2.** slow, underdeveloped, retarded: *Some of the students were backward in their mathematics skills.* **ant.** *adv.* forward. *adj.* **1.** forward. **2.** precocious.

bad *adj.* **1.** evil, immoral, wicked, corrupt, sinful, depraved: *The people considered the dictator to be a totally bad man.* **2.** rotten, contaminated, spoiled, tainted: *Eight people were poisoned by the bad meat at that restaurant.* **3.** harmful, injurious; unfavorable: *Eating too much candy is bad for your teeth.* **4.** poor, defective, inferior, imperfect, substandard, faulty: *The picture tube is bad in this TV set.* **5.** improper, inappropriate, unsuited, unsuitable: *The paintings by amateurs are usually bad examples of art.* **6.** upset, sorry: *We all feel bad when a pet dies.* **7.** sick, ill, out of sorts; suffering: *I felt bad after eating all that popcorn.* **8.** disagreeable, unpleasant, uncomfortable: *Because of the storm, we had a bad flight from Chicago to New York.* **9.** cross, nasty, unpleasant, unfriendly, irritable, disagreeable, irascible, short-tempered: *When Sam heard about who was coming for dinner, it put him into a bad mood for the rest of the day.* **ant.** good.

baffle *vb.* mystify, puzzle, confuse, frustrate, bewilder: *Although I asked a simple enough question, I was completely baffled by his reply.* **ant.** enlighten, inform.

bag *n.* sack, poke: *A full bag of groceries can be heavy.* *vb.* catch, snare, trap: *The hunter bagged three rabbits.*

bait *n.* lure, enticement: *Many fishermen use worms for bait.* *vb.* **1.** lure, entice, entrap, captivate, ensnare: *Enid baited her boyfriend with her good cooking.* **2.** tease, torment, worry, pester, badger, heckle: *The audience baited the politician by asking him about his record.*

balance *n.* equilibrium: *The acrobat was able to balance easily on the wire. vb.* **1.** weigh, compare, evaluate, contrast: *When you balance the advantages against the disadvantages, I'd say we ought to go.* **2.** offset, counterbalance, make up for: *My reasons for staying balance my reasons for going, so I don't know what to do.*

balk *vb.* hesitate, stop; check: *The dog balked at jumping the stream.*

ball[1] *n.* sphere, globe, spheroid: *The pitcher threw the ball to second base.*

ball[2] *n.* dance, cotillion: *We were all invited to the masked ball given to raise money for charity.*

balloon *vb.* swell, enlarge, puff up *or* out: *The sail ballooned in the wind and the boat began to move.* **ant.** shrink, shrivel.

balmy *adj.* mild, gentle, soothing: *In Mexico we enjoyed balmy weather nearly every day.* **ant.** stormy, tempestuous.

ban *vb.* forbid, prohibit, disallow, outlaw: *Smoking is banned in the buses. n.* prohibition, taboo: *There is a ban on staying out in the streets after nine o'clock.* **ant.** *vb.* permit, allow.

band[1] *n.* group, company, society, association, body, crew, gang: *The band of converts established their own town out west. vb.* unite: *We had to band together for our own protection.*

band[2] *n.* strip, belt: *There was a narrow band of carvings around the base of the column.*

bandit *n.* outlaw, thief, robber, highwayman, hijacker, marauder, brigand: *Three bandits attacked the coach in the forest.*

banish *vb.* exile, deport, expel; dismiss: *Instead of executing him, the court banished Napoleon to Elba.* **ant.** embrace, receive, admit, welcome.

bank *n.* embankment, shore: *I swam to the edge of the lake and climbed out onto the bank.*

bar *n.* **1.** barrier, obstacle, barricade, obstruction, hindrance, impediment: *Peace should not be a bar to progress in science or business.* **2.** counter; saloon, cocktail

lounge, café: *The businessmen met at the bar before
going in for dinner. vb.* prevent, obstruct, hinder, impede, stop, deter, prohibit, block: *All those who were not
members of the club were barred from entering.* **ant.** *n.*
1. encouragement, aid. *vb.* permit, allow.

barbarian *n.* savage, brute, boor, ruffian: *The manager of
the theater called the police because the boys were acting
like barbarians. adj.* savage, rude, primitive, uncivilized,
uncultured, crude, barbaric, barbarous: *A barbarian tribe
never before seen was discovered in the Philippines.* **ant.**
adj. cultivated, civilized, tasteful.

barber *n.* hairdresser, coiffeur: *The barber restyled Vincent's
hair to make him look less bald.*

bare *adj.* **1.** nude, naked, unclothed, uncovered, undressed:
*In many European countries, small children run about
bare on the beaches.* **2.** plain, unfurnished, empty, barren: *The room was entirely bare.* **3.** mere, scarce: *Robinson Crusoe was marooned with just the bare necessities
of life. vb.* reveal, disclose, expose, publicize: *The district attorney bared the details of the political scandal.*
ant. *adj.* **1.** clothed, dressed, garbed. *vb.* hide, conceal,
disguise.

bargain *n.* deal, agreement, arrangement, contract: *I'll make
a bargain with you. I'll let you use my bicycle if you let
me use your wagon. vb.* agree, contract, arrange: *The
two farmers bargained until a fair agreement was reached.*

barren *adj.* sterile, unproductive, unfruitful, bare, childless:
*Michael soon realized that his wife was barren and that
he would never have a child.* **ant.** fertile, fruitful.

barricade *n.* barrier, obstruction, fence, enclosure: *The barricade prevented the horses from leaving the corral. vb.*
shut in, obstruct, block, bar: *We barricaded ourselves in
the cabin for protection against the wolves.* **ant.** *vb.* release, free, open.

barrier *n.* **1.** bar, barricade, fence, wall, railing, obstacle:
The barrier was opened to allow passengers through. **2.**
obstruction, hindrance, impediment, restraint, obstacle;
limit: *Neither the mountains nor love of home was a
barrier to the tribe's traveling great distances.* **ant.** **2.**
encouragement, aid, assistance.

barter *vb.* trade, exchange: *He bartered three bushels of
corn for a baby pig.*

base¹ *n.* bottom, support, stand, rest, foundation: *The base
of this column is carved from marble. vb.* found, estab-

lish: *A careful scholar bases his theory on sound exami-nation of the evidence.* ant. *n.* top, peak, pinnacle.

base² *adj.* **1.** low, immoral, bad, evil, depraved, wicked, mean, selfish: *Anyone who would allow a kitten to starve is really base.* **2.** cheap, tawdry, worthless, poor, debased, (of coin) counterfeit: *The clasp on your brooch didn't last long because it was made of base material.* ant. **1.** noble, exalted, virtuous. **2.** refined, valuable.

bashful *adj.* shy, timid, sheepish, modest, coy, shamefaced, ashamed: *Carl was too bashful to tell Gloria that he loved her.* ant. self-assured, immodest, arrogant.

basic *adj.* main, chief, essential, fundamental: *The detec-tive's basic reason for being at the scene of the crime was to question the witnesses.* ant. subordinate, subsidiary.

basis *n.* foundation, base, ground, essential: *The only basis for her behavior is jealousy.*

batter *vb.* beat, pound, hit, strike: *The boxers were batter-ing each other with repeated blows.*

battle *n.* **1.** fight, combat; war, warfare: *Her only son was killed in battle.* **2.** conflict, action, campaign, fight: *After the battle, each side looked after its wounded and buried its dead.* *vb.* fight, struggle, strive against: *Battling great odds, the team finally won.*

beach *n.* strand, sands, shore, seashore, coast: *Every sum-mer, we rent a cottage at the beach for a week or two.*

beam *n.* **1.** girder, cross-member: *The main beams of the roof are being eaten by termites.* **2.** ray, pencil, gleam: *The beam shone through the slit to light up the golden statue in the crypt.* *vb.* shine, gleam, glisten, glitter: *When the moon beams on the water it looks like a silvery path.*

bear *vb.* **1.** carry, support, hold up: *The columns bear the weight of the roof.* **2.** carry, transport, convey: *Beware the Greeks bearing gifts!* **3.** endure, stand, suffer, abide, tolerate: *I cannot bear to hear a baby crying.* *vb. phr.* **1. bear on** relate to, affect, be relevant (to), be connected (with): *What you do in school bears very much on how well you do when you graduate.* **2. bear out** substantiate, confirm, prove: *My prediction was borne out by your losing the key on the first day.* **3. bear up** endure, carry on, keep up: *I just don't see how Martha can bear up under the strain of caring for 15 children.* **4. bear with** forbear, be patient with; tolerate: *Please bear with me until I can straighten the problem out.*

bearing *n.* **1.** posture, carriage; manner, behavior, deportment, conduct: *The girl's regal bearing made everyone notice her when she walked into the room.* **2.** reference, relation, application, connection: *What you think has no bearing on what we ought to do.* **3.** direction, course, position: *It took a few minutes with the chart to get our bearings.*

beast *n.* animal; brute, monster: *She persuaded her lawyer that her husband had acted like a beast.*

beat *vb.* **1.** hit, strike, pound, batter, thrash: *When we came into the yard, Jan's mother was beating the carpet.* **2.** throb, pulse, pulsate: *I can feel my heart beating if I put my hand here.* **3.** defeat, conquer, overcome: *The home team beat the visitors 3–2. n.* **1.** stroke, blow: *Three beats on the divan will be the signal.* **2.** throb, pulse, pulsation, tattoo, rhythm: *The beat of the jungle drums could be heard for miles.*

beautiful *adj.* pretty, lovely, handsome, attractive: *You don't have to be beautiful to become a movie star, but it helps.* **ant.** homely, unattractive, plain, ugly.

beauty *n.* loveliness, comeliness, attractiveness: *There is a beauty in the wilderness that cannot be matched in the city.* **ant.** homeliness, plainness, ugliness.

because *conj.* since, as, for, for the reason that: *He refused to come into the room because he wasn't properly dressed.*

become *vb.* **1.** grow, change, *or* come to be: *When I told him what his friend had said, he became angry.* **2.** suit, befit, be appropriate *or* attractive to: *The green dress becomes you, but I don't care for the red one.*

beg *vb.* **1.** ask, request, entreat, beseech, petition, solicit, implore: *Kathy begged her mother to be allowed to go to the party.* **2.** panhandle: *Many cities do not allow people to beg in the streets.*

begin *vb.* **1.** start, commence; initiate; inaugurate: *Don't begin until everyone is ready.* **2.** originate, create, arise: *The practice of working five days a week didn't begin until the later 1940s.* **ant.** **1.** stop, end, finish, terminate.

beginner *n.* amateur, nonprofessional, apprentice: *Beginners in the printing industry must train for many years.* **ant.** professional.

beginning *n.* **1.** start, outset, commencement, emergence, initiation, inauguration: *At the beginning of a new enterprise everyone works very hard.* **2.** origin, source, rise, birth, creation: *The beginning of modern scientific* *thought can be traced to the 16th century.* **ant.** ending, finish, termination.

behalf   *n.* part, support, interest, aid: *He spoke to the judge on behalf of his client.*

behave   *vb.* act, conduct oneself, deport oneself: *The prisoner was allowed to work in the library because he had behaved so well.* **ant.** misbehave, rebel.

behavior   *n.* conduct, deportment, manners: *The children's behavior was so bad that the teacher kept them after school.* **ant.** misbehavior, rebelliousness.

behind   *prep.* in back of, at the back *or* rear of: *The playground is behind the school.* **ant.** before.

belief   *n.* **1.** view, opinion, conviction, creed, credo: *His belief is that all aspirin is alike.* **2.** faith, trust, confidence, assurance: *Nothing could shake his belief that his parents were the most wonderful people.*

bend   *vb.* **1.** curve, bow, deflect: *You could never bend that steel bar with your bare hands.* **2.** stoop, kneel, crouch, bow: *Martin bent to look through the grating in the sidewalk.* **3.** submit, yield, bow, stoop, agree: *The foreman had to bend under the pressure from the president.* **4.** subdue, suppress, oppress, influence, cause to yield, submit, *or* bow: *The president was accustomed to bending all the staff to his will.* **ant. 1.** straighten.

beneficial   *adj.* good, advantageous, helpful, useful, profitable, wholesome: *Fresh air and sunshine are beneficial.* **ant.** unwholesome, disadvantageous.

benefit   *n.* service, favor, help, support, good, profit, advantage: *Dick won't do anything unless it's for his own benefit.* *vb.* help, aid, support, profit, serve: *Every time you help someone else you benefit yourself.* **ant.** *n.* disadvantage.

benevolent   *adj.* humane, good, kind, well-wishing, kindly, kind-hearted, well-disposed; generous, open-hearted, liberal, charitable: *Benevolent graduates donated money to the college for the new library.* **ant.** malevolent, mean, cruel, evil.

bent   *adj.* **1.** crooked, curved: *The lock was so crude we could open it with a bent nail.* **2.** determined, resolved, set, decided, firm: *Although I tried to discourage him, Jim was bent on sailing across the ocean alone.* **ant. 1.** straight.

beseech   *vb.* beg, implore, ask, entreat: *I beseech you to consider your parents before getting into trouble.*

besides *adv.* furthermore, moreover, in addition, further: *You may not go out to play because it's raining and, besides, you haven't finished your homework. prep.* in addition to, except for, other than: *Besides me, there's no one else who cares about winning the game.*

bestow *vb.* give, confer, present, award: *The critics bestowed their highest honor on the playwright.* **ant.** withhold, withdraw.

bet *vb.* wager, lay *or* put (money), gamble: *I never bet on a horse race in my life. n.* wager, stake, ante, pledge: *Madam DeTour placed a three-dollar bet at roulette and won.*

betray *vb.* **1.** deliver, be treacherous *or* disloyal: *The traitor betrayed the location of the arsenal to the enemy.* **2.** reveal, expose; display, show, exhibit: *Although she seemed very angry, her smile betrayed her real feelings.* **ant.** safeguard, protect, shelter.

better *vb.* improve: *I could better my tennis game if I practiced more.* **ant.** worsen.

bewilder *vb.* confuse, puzzle, perplex, mystify, overwhelm: *When we came out of the dark cave, we were completely bewildered as to our whereabouts.* **ant.** enlighten, clarify.

bewitch *vb.* enchant, charm, captivate: *The giant bewitched the children into believing that he was a midget.*

bias *n.* prejudice, tendency, inclination: *The executive has a bias in favor of hiring only friends. vb.* influence, prejudice, bend, warp: *The politician's opinion was biased because he had received gifts from the manufacturers.* **ant.** *n.* impartiality, fairness.

bid *vb.* **1.** command, order, direct: *When the principal bids you to stand, you are expected to get to your feet immediately.* **2.** greet, say, wish: *I bid you good day, sir.* **3.** offer, tender, propose: *Mother bid only three dollars for the chair at the auction, but she got it. n.* offer, proposal: *I made an unsuccessful bid of two dollars for the lamp.*

bide *vb. phr.* **bide one's time** wait, remain, delay: *I'm going to bide my time until another sale is announced.*

big *adj.* **1.** large, great, huge, immense, enormous, gigantic, tremendous: *If it has 37 rooms, I'd certainly agree that it's a big house.* **2.** important: *The big event of the year was the Christmas party.* **3.** generous, kind, outgoing, bighearted: *It was very big of you to let us use your pool.*

bill *n.* invoice, statement, charge, account: *Please send me a bill for the broken window.*

bind   *vb.* **1.** tie, fasten, band: *Don't bind that bundle of clothes too tight because they'll tear.* **2.** obligate, oblige: *He was bound by the contract.* **ant. 1.** loosen, free, untie.

bit   *n.* scrap, particle, fragment, speck, drop: *May I have just a bit more sugar in my coffee? n. phr.* **bit by bit** gradually, slowly: *Bit by bit, Jim saved enough money to buy a bicycle.*

bite   *vb.* nip; gnaw, chew: *They say that barking dogs don't bite, but let someone else prove it. n.* **1.** nip, sting: *A dog bite is more serious than a mosquito bite.* **2.** morsel, mouthful; snack: *May I have a bite of that hot dog?*

bitter   *adj.* **1.** acrid, harsh, biting: *If you chew aspirin instead of swallowing it whole, it leaves a bitter taste in your mouth.* **2.** distressing, distressful, painful, grievous: *I had the bitter experience of studying hard but failing the examination.* **3.** painful, stinging, piercing, biting: *The day was bitter cold.* **4.** hostile, hated, severe, vicious: *The citizens of the two countries were bitter enemies.* **ant. 1.** sweet, bland.

black   *adj.* **1.** dark, sooty, inky, ebon, swarthy: *The black man stood in the doorway.* **2.** soiled, dirty, filthy, stained: *When he finished repairing the car, he was black from head to toe.* **3.** gloomy, dismal, sad, depressing, dark, somber: *The day of the financial panic is known as Black Friday.* **ant. 1.** white, light-skinned. **2.** clean, pure, pristine. **3.** bright, cheerful.

blame   *vb.* reproach, condemn, criticize: *The taxi driver was blamed for causing the accident. n.* responsibility, guilt, fault: *Before you place the blame on me, you'd better find out the facts.* **ant.** honor, credit.

blank   *adj.* **1.** empty, unmarked: *The application was blank except for where Michael had filled in his name.* **2.** uninterested, expressionless: *A sea of blank faces greeted the teacher on the first day of school. n.* void, area, form, vacancy: *Just fill in the blanks with the correct information, please.* **ant.** *adj.* **1.** filled. **2.** animated, alert.

blaze   *n.* flame, fire; holocaust, inferno: *The firemen fought a three-alarm blaze on Brady Street. vb.* burn, flare, flare up, flame, shine: *The fire was blazing in the hearth when we arrived for the Christmas party.* **ant.** *vb.* dwindle, die.

bleach   *vb.* whiten, blanch; pale: *The blue jeans were bleached pale blue by the sun. n.* whitener: *Don't use so much bleach in the laundry.* **ant.** *vb.* darken, blacken.

bleak *adj.* **1.** bare, desolate, barren, windswept: *The bleak landscape offered no shelter.* **2.** depressing, cheerless, gloomy, dreary: *The financial future of the company was bleak after the fire.* **ant. 2.** hopeful, cheerful, promising.

blend *vb.* mix, intermix, intermingle, mingle, commingle, combine: *Before pouring the batter into the baking dish, you should blend all the ingredients thoroughly.* *n.* mixture, combination, compound: *That pipe tobacco smells like a mild blend.* **ant.** *vb.* separate, divide.

blight *n.* epidemic, disease, sickness, affliction: *The blight killed off the entire crop.* *vb.* damage, ruin, harm, destroy: *His career was blighted by his poor school record.*

blind *adj.* **1.** sightless, unsighted, purblind: *A blind person's hearing is often very acute.* **2.** unaware, unknowing, unconscious, ignorant, thoughtless, unthinking: *Irena was blind to the fact that no one really liked her.* *n.* screen, shade, curtain, cover: *The sun is in my eyes; please pull down the blind.* **ant.** *adj.* **1.** sighted, seeing. **2.** clearsighted, knowing, discerning, aware.

blink *vb.* **1.** wink: *The light blinked on and off. She blinked when you shone the light in her eyes.* **2.** flicker, twinkle: *The stars are blinking in the black sky.*

bliss *n.* happiness, joy, gladness, ecstasy, rapture: *They have lived in married bliss for 25 years.* **ant.** misery, unhappiness, torment.

block *n.* obstacle, obstruction, impediment, hindrance, blockade: *The police stopped every car at the road block, looking for the escaped men.* *vb.* stop, obstruct, impede, retard, hinder, blockade, check: *The fallen trees blocked our passage to freedom from the narrow canyon.* **ant.** *n.* aid, advantage. *vb.* aid, assist, forward, promote.

blood *n.* **1.** gore, bloodshed, murder, slaughter: *Cain had his brother's blood on his hands.* **2.** lineage, heritage, ancestry: *The Prince of Wales is of royal blood.*

bloody *adj.* bloodthirsty, cruel, inhuman, pitiless, ruthless, murderous, ferocious: *The revolution of the peasants stopped forever the king's bloody reign.* **ant.** gentle, kind.

bloom *n.* flower, blossom: *My new roses are growing with huge blooms.* *vb.* flourish, blossom, flower: *Rose of Sharon blooms in September in this part of the country.* **ant.** *vb.* wither, shrivel.

blossom *n.* flower, bloom: *The cherry blossoms in Washington are beautiful in the spring.* *vb.* bloom, flower, flourish: *The century plant is so called because it is said to blos-*

som only once every 100 years. **ant.** *vb.* wither, shrink, dwindle, fade.

blot *n.* **1.** spot, stain, inkstain, inkblot: *I got that awful blot on my skirt when Ronnie spilled ink on me.* **2.** stain, blemish, taint, disgrace, dishonor: *The blot on his record harmed his career.* *vb.* **1.** spot, stain, spatter, soil: *You've blotted my book with your leaky pen!* **2.** dry, soak up, sponge up: *If you blot the ink it won't smear when you turn the page.* *vb. phr.* **blot out** eliminate, destroy, obliterate, erase, rub out, cancel: *I've blotted that terrible experience from my mind.*

blow¹ *n.* **1.** thump, hit, slap, rap, cuff, box, knock, stroke: *The boxer knocked his challenger out with a blow to the stomach.* **2.** shock: *The news of the death of her turtle was a terrible blow to Joanne.*

blow² *vb.* **1.** move, spread, drive: *The leaves started to blow down the street in the breeze.* **2.** whistle: *The siren blew at noon each day.* *vb. phr.* **blow up 1.** explode, detonate: *The spies blew up the bridge.* **2.** enlarge, inflate: *Blow up that balloon.*

blue *n.* azure, sapphire: *On a clear day, blue is the color of the sky.* *adj.* sad, gloomy, depressed, unhappy, dejected, melancholy: *I felt blue at the thought of leaving home.* **ant.** *adj.* happy, cheerful, optimistic.

bluff¹ *adj.* **1.** vertical, perpendicular, steep, precipitous, abrupt: *The cliff was bluff right down to the beach.* **2.** hearty, rough, open, frank, blunt: *The manager's bluff approach to people was basically good-natured and kind.* *n.* cliff, precipice: *We couldn't climb up the face of the bluff.* **ant. 1.** shallow, gentle, sloping. **2.** subtle, indirect.

bluff² *vb.* mislead, deceive, fool, pretend: *The gambler bluffed the others into thinking he had a good hand.* *n.* pretense, lie, fraud, fake, deceit: *Bill's tough manner is just a bluff—he's really a marshmallow inside.*

blunder *n.* mistake, error: *Telling Kitty about the party when she hadn't been invited was a stupid blunder.* *vb.* stumble: *I blundered into the lamp and knocked it over in the dark.*

blunt *adj.* **1.** dull, unsharpened, rounded, worn: *That blunt knife could hardly cut butter.* **2.** rude, crude, direct, impolite, abrupt, short, curt, brusque, gruff: *I don't invite Walter any more because his manner is too blunt.* *vb.* dull: *He blunted the ax on the rock.* **ant.** *adj.* **1.** sharp, keen, pointed. **2.** diplomatic, tactful.

blur   *vb.* stain, sully, obscure, dim, dull, confuse: *My eye-glasses were blurred by the fine mist. After she took the medicine, her senses were blurred and she couldn't drive her car home. n.* smudge, smear, stain, spot: *There was a blur of smoke on the horizon as the ship approached.* **ant.** *vb.* clarify, clear.

blush   *vb.* redden, color: *Whenever anyone told Irena how pretty she was, she blushed.*

boast   *vb.* brag, crow, exaggerate: *Nobody could stand being with Bill because he was always boasting about how great he was. n.* bragging, braggadocio: *Despite his boast, Bill was unable to jump across the stream.*

body   *n.* **1.** corpse, cadaver, carcass: *The body of the dead man was taken to the morgue. The body of the wolf was buried in the snow.* **2.** trunk, torso: *He had spots all over his body but none on his arms, legs, or head.* **3.** group, party, company, band: *We walked out of the meeting in a body.*

boil   *vb.* seethe, foam, bubble, simmer, stew: *The soup was boiling on the stove.*

bold   *adj.* **1.** brave, unafraid, fearless, intrepid, courageous, daring, valiant, heroic, gallant: *The four bold men stormed the machine-gun and captured it.* **2.** rude, disrespectful, insolent, impudent, shameless: *Richard was bold enough to answer back to the teacher.* **ant.** **1.** cowardly, fearful, timid, timorous. **2.** courteous, polite, deferential.

bond   *n.* **1.** fastening, fastener, rope, tie, cord, band: *The prisoner was unable to escape the bonds on his wrists.* **2.** connection, tie, attachment, link: *The bonds of friendship prevented me from telling the supervisor about Alice's taking three hours for lunch.* **3.** promise, promissory note, obligation, I.O.U.: *My word is my bond and everyone knows that I pay all my debts.*

bonus   *n.* reward, premium, gift, bounty: *The company will pay a bonus to all employees willing to work at night.*

book   *n.* volume, tome, publication, work; hardcover, paperback; novel, biography, text, workbook: *The library at the university contains hundreds of thousands of books.*

boom[1]   *vb.* **1.** reverberate, thunder, roar: *The huge guns boomed in the distance.* **2.** prosper, flourish: *The late 1960s were a time of booming prosperity: business was booming. n.* **1.** blast, roar, thunder: *I couldn't hear the* *music over the boom of the airplanes.* **2.** prosperity, rush: *Just before Christmas, there is always a big boom in toy sales.* **ant.** *n.* **2.** recession.

boom[2]   *n.* spar, pole: *The wind changed suddenly, causing the boom to swing around and hit me.*

booth   *n.* compartment, enclosure, stand, cubicle, box: *The telephone in the booth on the corner isn't working.*

border   *n.* **1.** frontier, boundary, limit: *We crossed the border between France and Italy.* **2.** edge, margin: *There was a border of blue flowers around the tablecloth.* *vb.* join, adjoin, edge, abut: *Maine is bordered by New Hampshire on the west and south and by Canada on the north.* **ant.** *n.* **2.** center, middle.

bore   *vb.* **1.** weary, tire: *We were all so bored by the movie that we almost fell asleep.* **2.** drill, hole, perforate: *This machine bores into the steel plate in 36 places at the same time.* **ant. 1.** interest, excite, arouse, captivate.

bosom   *n.* breast, heart: *The love in his bosom for his friend made him sympathetic.*

boss   *n.* manager, director, supervisor, employer, foreman: *My boss scolded me for being late again this morning.* **ant.** employee, worker, underling.

bother   *vb.* irritate, trouble, worry, disturb, annoy, vex, pester, upset, inconvenience: *It bothered me that I couldn't recall the name of the 17th President.* *n.* trouble, inconvenience, upset, distress, anxiety: *I never wanted to be a bother—I only tried to help.* **ant.** *n.* comfort, solace.

bottom   *n.* **1.** base, foot, depths: *I heard the bucket strike the ground at the bottom of the dried-out well.* **2.** underside: *The mark on the bottom of the cup shows the maker's name.* **3.** seat, buttocks, behind, rear: *Billy's mother gave him a sharp slap on his bottom for breaking the window.* **ant. 1., 2.** top, topside.

bough   *n.* limb, arm, branch: *The boughs of the tree are laden with fruit.*

bounce   *vb.* rebound, richochet, recoil: *The golf ball bounced on the ground, then against a tree, and ended up in the sand trap.*

bound[1]   *vb., n.* leap, jump, spring, bounce, skip: *The dog bounded along next to the car. With one bound Barbara had crossed the stream.*

bound[2]   *adj.* **1.** tied, trussed; shackled, fettered: *The prisoner was bound hand and foot.* **2.** sure, certain, destined;

required, compelled: *Suzie knew that her father was bound to say no when she asked him if she could go.* **ant. 1.** unfettered, free.

bound³ *adj.* on the way to, destined for: *This train is bound for Albuquerque.*

bound⁴ **n.** (usually **bounds**) boundary, limit: *Within the bounds of reason, there is no limit to how far you can push your imagination.*

boundary *n.* limit, bound, border, outline, margin, circumference, perimeter, edge, frontier: *The boundary between our properties is marked by a fence. There is a heavy black line marking the boundary on the map.*

bounty *n.* **1.** gift, generosity: *The settlers were grateful for the bounty from the earth.* **2.** reward, award, bonus, prize, premium: *The farmers' association offered a bounty of $50 for every dead wolf.*

bourgeois *adj.* middle-class, commonplace, ordinary, common, conventional: *Harvey's bourgeois upbringing made him wear a white shirt and a tie at all times.* **ant.** aristocratic, upper-class.

bout *n.* match, round, fight, contest, conflict: *The first bout was won by the challenger.*

bow *vb.* **1.** stoop, bend; yield, submit: *The porter was bowed down under the weight of the trunk. You ought to bow to the force of a stronger argument.* **2.** curtsey, salaam, kowtow, kneel: *Everyone bowed when the king came into the room.*

boy *n.* lad, youth, youngster; (*Informal*) kid: *The new family that just moved into the neighborhood has three boys.* **ant.** man, girl.

brace *n.* support, prop, stay, strut, bracket, crutch: *This wall ought to have a steel brace to hold it in place.* *vb.* support, prop, steady: *Brace yourself for some bad news.*

bracelet *n.* bangle, circlet, armband; (*Slang*) handcuff: *Anne wore a gold charm bracelet on her left wrist.*

brag *vb.* boast, swagger: *It's not good manners to brag about yourself.* **ant.** deprecate, depreciate.

braid *vb.* plait, wreath, weave, twine: *At the picnic, the girls braided daisies into their hair.*

brain *n.* (usually **brains**) intelligence, sense, common sense, intellect, reason, understanding: *Philip doesn't have the brains to come in out of the rain.* **ant.** stupidity.

branch *n.* **1.** limb, bough, shoot: *The branches on this tree grow very close to the ground.* **2.** offshoot, tributary: *The* *two branches of the stream join here.* **3.** division, part, subdivision, department: *The restaurant opened a new branch on the main road.*

brand *n.* **1.** kind, make, manufacture, trademark, label, trade name: *What brand of shampoo do you use?* **2.** stamp, mark, blaze: *The stolen cattle bore the brand of our ranch.*

brave *adj.* courageous, gallant, fearless, daring, valiant, valorous, intrepid, unafraid, heroic, bold: *The brave boys plunged into the icy stream to save the puppy.* **ant.** timid, cowardly, fearful, craven.

bravery *n.* courage, daring, valor, fearlessness, heroism, boldness: *This medal is given for bravery in the face of the enemy.* **ant.** cowardice, timidity, fearfulness.

brawl *n.* fight, melee, fray, fracas, riot, disturbance, dispute, disagreement: *The brawl in the dance hall brought the police in full force.*

brazen *adj.* bold, brassy, shameless, impudent, insolent, rude, immodest: *Because of his brazen manner to the teacher, Zeke's parents had to come to school.* **ant.** modest, retiring, shy, self-effacing.

breach *n.* **1.** break, rift, rupture, fracture, crack, opening, gap: *The explosion tore a breach in the wall big enough for the tank to pass through.* **2.** violation, breaking: *Her failure to deliver the merchandise by Monday was a breach of our agreement.* **ant. 2.** observation.

break *vb.* **1.** fracture, rupture, shatter, smash, wreck, crash, atomize, demolish: *When Jack sat on the antique chair he broke it into a hundred pieces.* **2.** violate, disobey: *I have no respect for those who break the law.* **3.** disintegrate, fall apart, collapse, splinter, smash, shatter: *The old vase might break if you looked at it!* *n.* **1.** crack, gap, opening, breach, rupture: *The water poured through the break in the dike.* **2.** suspension, stop, hesitation, interruption: *We all took a ten-minute break and then went back to work.* *vb. phr.* **1. break down** fail, falter, stop: *Our car broke down on the steep hill.* **2. break in a.** educate, train, initiate, prepare, instruct: *The foreman had to break in the new machinist.* **b.** invade, trespass: *The burglars broke into the bank at midnight.* **3. break off** interrupt, discontinue, stop, cease: *Roger broke off when Marie entered the room and didn't continue until after she had left.* **4. break out a.** start, initiate, begin, commence: *A riot broke out among the strikers.* **b.**

erupt: *Her face broke out from eating popcorn.* **c.** escape, flee, depart, leave: *Three prisoners broke out of the state prison last night.* **break through** penetrate, invade: *The platoon finally broke through the enemy lines.* **break up a.** divide, separate, split: *I see where Ellie has broken up with her boyfriend again.* **b.** disassemble, separate, divide, dismantle, take apart: *The principal insisted that the clique be broken up at once.* **ant. vb. 1.** mend, repair. **2.** obey.

breed *vb.* **1.** bear, conceive, beget, father, mother; create, produce, originate, generate: *The rancher bred prize cattle from stock he imported from Scotland.* **2.** rear, raise, nurture, bring up; educate, train, teach: *The Forsters' children are very well bred.* *n.* kind, sort, variety, species, strain: *The dogs on the farm were of mixed breed.*

breeze *n.* breath, air, zephyr, wind: *The sailboat moved out of the harbor in a light breeze.* **ant.** calm.

bridle *n.* curb, check, restraint, control, halter, hackamore: *The leather bridle for his favorite horse was studded with brass.* *vb.* curb, control, check, restrain, govern: *Walter would get along better with people if he could learn to bridle his temper.* **ant. vb.** loose, free, release.

brief *adj.* **1.** short, temporary, fleeting: *The life of some insects is so brief that it lasts only a day.* **2.** short, terse, concise, condensed, compact: *The brief reports did not leave time for any details.* *vb.* advise, teach, instruct: *The men were briefed before going into the meeting.* **ant. adj. 1.** long, extended, protracted. **2.** extensive, comprehensive, exhaustive.

bright *adj.* **1.** shining, shiny, gleaming, brilliant, sparkling, shimmering, radiant: *The marine had bright brass buttons on his uniform.* **2.** lively, cheerful, happy, gay, lighthearted: *Her bright personality makes her a pleasure to be with.* **3.** vivid, brilliant: *That bright-green dress becomes you very well.* **4.** intelligent, quick-witted, clever, keen: *The bright children were mixed together in class with the average ones to stimulate them.* **5.** promising, encouraging, favorable: *Bob seems to have a bright future in that new job.* **ant. 1.** dull, dim, lusterless. **2.** boring, dull, colorless. **4.** stupid, slow, backward.

brilliant *adj.* **1.** bright, splendid, radiant, shining, sparkling, glittering: *Mrs. Van Patten was wearing a brilliant diamond necklace.* **2.** talented, intelligent, gifted, ingenious:

That fellow George is a brilliant engineer. **ant. 1.** dull, lusterless. **2.** mediocre, second-rate.

brim *n.* edge, lip, rim, margin, border: *We stood at the very brim of the canyon and saw the stream far below.* **ant.** center, middle.

bring *vb.* carry, take, fetch: *Please bring that chair over here. vb. phr.* **1. bring about** cause, accomplish, effect: *The judge brought about a compromise between the two parties.* **2. bring around** *or* **round** convince, persuade: *If you argue enough, you can bring him around to your way of thinking.* **3. bring to** *or* **around** revive, restore: *It took 20 minutes to bring Vickie around after she had been knocked unconscious.* **4. bring up a.** rear, raise, nurture, educate, train, teach: *Netta's parents were away a great deal, so she was brought up by her aunt.* **b.** introduce, raise, propose: *Why did he bring up the question of her honesty?* **ant.** *vb.* withdraw, remove.

brink *n.* edge, rim, verge, margin, limit: *The car came to a stop just at the brink of the cliff.*

brisk *adj.* **1.** lively, active, animated, energetic, nimble, quick, agile, spry: *Every morning Harry would take a brisk walk in the park.* **2.** sharp, cool, stimulating, keen, invigorating: *On these November mornings the air can be very brisk.* **ant. 1.** slow, sluggish, lethargic. **2.** heavy, still, oppressive.

brittle *adj.* frail, fragile, breakable, weak: *These dry leaves are so brittle that they crumble right in your hand.* **ant.** flexible, elastic, supple.

broad *adj.* **1.** wide; large, expansive, extended, roomy: *The broad plain stretched out before them.* **2.** general: *In a broad sense, intolerance should be against the law.* **3.** extensive, wide, full: *He was appointed a judge because of his broad knowledge of the law.* **ant. 1.** narrow, constricted. **3.** limited, negligible.

broadcast *vb.* spread, distribute, send, transmit, announce, relay: *I told you that in secret and you shouldn't have broadcast it around town.*

broad-minded *adj.* tolerant, open-minded, unprejudiced, unbigoted, liberal: *Are your parents broad-minded about whom you select for your friends?* **ant.** narrow-minded, prejudiced, bigoted, petty.

brood *n.* litter, young, offspring: *The mother hen defended her brood of chicks from the kitten. vb.* ponder, think about, meditate on *or* about, consider, muse, reflect, deliberate: *The old man was brooding over the unfriendly things he had done in his youth.*

brook *n.* stream, rivulet, branch, run, rill, creek: *The trout swam in the brook just waiting to be caught.*

brother *n.* **1.** sibling: *Any son of my parents is my brother.* **2.** fellow man, kinsman; comrade: *All men are brothers.* **ant.** sister.

brow *n.* eyebrow, forehead: *The sweat stood out on his brow as he strained to lift the log.*

bruise *vb.* injure, hurt, wound, damage: *Hal was bruised on his arm when the mast fell against him.* *n.* black-and-blue mark, abrasion, contusion, injury, wound, damage, harm: *Beth suffered multiple bruises when she fell off her bicycle.*

brush *n.* **1.** broom, whisk, hairbrush, paintbrush: *I keep my brush alongside my comb.* **2.** bush, bushes, scrub, thicket: *We lost sight of the skunk when he ran into the brush.* **3.** encounter, meeting, affair, contact: *After he was released from prison, he never again had a brush with the law.*

brutal *adj.* cruel, mean, savage, pitiless, inhuman, barbaric, ferocious: *The brutal attack. on the bank teller by the robbers put him into the hospital.* **ant.** kind, kindhearted, gentle, mild.

brute *n.* beast, monster; savage, barbarian: *We caught the brute and put him into a cage.* *adj.* animal, savage, wild: *He picked up the two men using just brute strength and flung them away.*

bubble *vb.* froth, foam, seethe, boil: *The oil bubbled on the stove when we dropped in the potatoes for frying.*

bucket *n.* pail; can, canister, pot: *Fetch a bucket of water from the well.*

buckle *n.* fastening, fastener, clasp: *He wears a gold buckle on his belt.* *vb.* **1.** fasten, clasp: *Buckle your seat belt for safe driving.* **2.** bend, collapse, warp, yield, fail, give way: *The bridge buckled under the weight of the huge truck.*

buffet[1] *vb.* strike, beat, hit, slap: *The winds buffeted the house for three days.* *n.* blow, hit: *A quick buffet to the side of the head brought him to his senses.*

buffet[2] *n.* sideboard, server, cabinet, counter: *The food was set out on the buffet so that each person could help himself.*

build *vb.* construct, erect, put together, assemble: *In their spare time the children built doghouses and sold them to neighbors.* *n.* physique: *Kathy has the build of an athlete.* **ant.** *vb.* demolish, raze.

building *n.* structure, edifice; residence, house, office building: *The building near the corner of Main Street belongs to my father.*

bulge *n.* swelling, lump, protrusion, protuberance, bump: *The bulge at the side of the building looked dangerous.* *vb.* swell, protrude, extend: *As he blew air into the balloon, it began to bulge.* **ant.** *n.* depression, hollow.

bulk *n.* **1.** size, volume, magnitude: *The package wasn't heavy but its huge bulk made it difficult to carry.* **2.** majority, most, main part: *The bulk of my income comes from my salary.*

bulky *adj.* large, big, huge, clumsy, unwieldy, cumbersome, massive: *The crate was too bulky for one man to carry.* **ant.** delicate, small, handy.

bully *vb.* domineer, harass, intimidate: *You could tell that he was a coward because he was always bullying the smaller children.*

bump *vb.* knock, bang, collide with, hit, strike: *The first day he took out his new bicycle Alan bumped into a car.* *n.* knock, bang; collision, blow: *For trying to help the storekeeper, Jim was given a bump on the head by the thief.*

bunch *n.* cluster, group, batch, bundle, collection: *He picked a bunch of flowers for Mother's Day.*

bundle *n.* bunch; package, parcel, packet: *I tied the clothes into a bundle and brought it to the laundry.*

burden *n.* load, weight; worry, trial; trouble: *The donkey is a beast of burden. Concern about his father's health was too much of a burden for a child to manage.* *vb.* load, lade, weigh down, overload, oppress: *I don't want to burden you with my troubles.* **ant.** *vb.* disburden.

bureau *n.* **1.** department, office, division, unit, board, commission: *We all went down to the Labor Bureau to get our working papers.* **2.** chest, chest of drawers, dresser: *You'll find the keys in the top drawer of my bureau.*

burglar *n.* thief, robber, housebreaker: *The burglars escaped after stealing all of our paintings.*

burial *n.* funeral, interment: *I cried at the burial of my pet cat.*

burn *vb.* **1.** fire, combust, blaze, flame: *The fire burned for* *three days in the forest.* **2.** scorch, sear, char, set afire *or* on fire, consume: *The wooden carving was burned beyond recognition.*

burrow *n.* lair, den, hole, tunnel: *The rabbit ran back to his burrow before we could catch it.*

burst *vb.* explode, blow up, erupt: *The electric light bulb burst into a million pieces when I dropped it.* **ant.** implode.

bury *vb.* **1.** inter, entomb: *The men were buried for two hours by the avalanche.* **2.** hide, conceal, cover, secrete: *The book I was looking for was buried under the pile of magazines.* **ant.** disinter, raise.

business *n.* **1.** trade, occupation, commerce: *What business is your father in?* **2.** company, firm, concern; partnership, corporation: *After graduating from college, Victor went into his father's business.* **3.** affair, concern: *My personal life is none of your business.*

busy *adj.* active, occupied, engaged, employed, industrious, hardworking: *If you had six children, you'd be busy all the time, too.* **ant.** inactive, unemployed, indolent, lazy.

but *conj.* however, nevertheless, yet; on the other hand, though, still, although: *I wanted to go to the movies but it was too late. My sister went but I couldn't.*

buy *vb.* purchase; procure, obtain, get: *Did you know that we just bought a new house?* **ant.** sell.

by *prep.* near, at, close to, next to: *I like to walk by the river in the morning.*

ೞ C ೞ

cab *n.* taxi, taxicab, hack: *We took a cab home from the party.*

cabin *n.* cottage, hut; shack, shanty: *Would you like to spend a weekend at our cabin in the woods?*

cabinet *n.* council, committee, ministry: *The Prime Minister depends on the members of his cabinet for advice.*

café *n.* coffeehouse: *The sidewalk cafés in Europe are very popular.*

cagey *adj.* tricky, cunning, clever, cautious, wary, shrewd, evasive: *Bert always gives me a cagey reply when I ask him what he's doing.* **ant.** guileless, innocent, naive, straightforward.

calamity *n.* bad luck, misfortune, distress, trouble, hardship, reverse, catastrophe: *The farmers thought that the drought was a great calamity.* **ant.** boon, blessing.

calculate *vb.* **1.** figure, reckon, compute, tally, measure, determine; add, subtract, multiply, divide: *The clerk checked the total by calculating it on the adding machine.* **2.** estimate, judge, deliberate: *The company accountant calculated the cost of the new equipment.* **ant. 1.** guess, assume.

calculating *adj.* scheming, crafty, cunning, shrewd: *Because of his calculating manner, hardly anybody trusts Dick any more.* **ant.** ingenuous, simple, direct, guileless.

calculation *n.* computation, figuring, estimation, reckoning: *Your calculation of the interest rate on the loan is incorrect.* **ant.** assumption, guess.

calendar *n.* schedule, timetable, diary: *I don't see how I can fit that appointment into my calendar.*

call *vb.* **1.** call out, cry out, exclaim, shout: *I hear my name being called.* **2.** name, designate, term, label: *Her name is Catherine but they call her Sophie.* **3.** telephone, phone, ring, ring up: *Please call me when you arrive in town.* **4.** assemble, convene, collect: *We were called together for a meeting.* **5.** awaken, waken, wake, rouse, arouse: *They called us at five o'clock to start on the hike.* *n.* **1.** cry, outcry, shout, yell: *I heard the call of the hunters trying to find me in the forest.* 2. demand, need, occasion, claim: *The extra job puts a call on my spare time. vb. phr.* 1. **call on** visit, go (to) see: *I called on our new neighbors yesterday.* 2. **call up** telephone, phone, ring, ring up: *Please call me up tomorrow evening.*

calm *adj.* 1. quiet, peaceful, still, tranquil, mild, serene, smooth: *The sea became calm toward sundown.* 2. serene, cool, composed, collected, unruffled, level-headed, unexcited, detached, aloof: *Nella remained quite calm after I told her the bad news. n.* calmness, stillness, serenity, quiet; composure: *The wind and rain stopped suddenly in the calm before the storm struck. vb.* pacify, tranquilize, soothe: *When he learned that it had not been his son who had been in the accident, Bill calmed down.* **ant.** *adj.* 1. tempestuous, roiled, disturbed. 2. emotional, disturbed, excited. *n.* turmoil, upheaval, disturbance. *vb.* upset, excite, disturb.

cancel *vb.* 1. delete, cross out *or* off, erase: *My name was canceled from the list of Republicans when they discovered I was a Democrat.* 2. call off, void, rescind, set aside, recall: *I'm sorry, but I have to cancel our appointment for dinner tonight.* **ant.** 2. ratify.

candidate *n.* nominee, aspirant, applicant: *There were three candidates for the presidency of the senior class.*

canyon *n.* ravine, gully, gulch, gorge, arroyo: *The cowboys drove the cattle through the narrow canyon.*

capable *adj.* able, skilled, fit, skillful, accomplished, competent: *Laura is a capable pianist but she's not good enough to play in concerts.* **ant.** inept, incompetent, unskilled.

capacity *n.* 1. volume, content: *This silo has a capacity of only 10,000 bushels of wheat.* 2. ability, capability, aptitude, talent, faculty: *If he would only study harder, John has the capacity to be an A student.* **ant.** 2. incapacity, inability.

capital *n.* cash, money, assets, property, wealth, principal, resources: *My father started his business with capital of $2000. adj.* major, chief, first, primary, leading, important, principal: *St. Peter's Church is of capital interest to visitors to Rome.* **ant.** *adj.* trivial, unimportant, secondary.

captain *n.* 1. supervisor, commander, director, authority, leader: *The teacher appointed Eugene to be the captain* *of the group.* **2.** (of a ship) skipper, commander, commanding officer, master: *The captain ordered the lifeboats to be lowered over the side.*

captive *n.* prisoner, convict, hostage: *The hijackers kept the pilot as a captive while they demanded the money.*

captivity *n.* imprisonment, confinement, detention, custody; slavery, bondage: *Two men broke into the jail and released their friend from captivity.* **ant.** freedom, liberty.

capture *vb.* seize, take prisoner, trap, grab, nab, catch, arrest: *We set the trap to capture rabbits, but not one fell into it.* *n.* seizure, catching; recovery: *The escaped tiger avoided capture for three hours.* **ant.** *vb.* release, free, liberate.

car *n.* automobile, auto, vehicle, motorcar: *I have to drive the car to the service station for repairs.*

carcass *n.* body, corpse, cadaver, remains: *The desert was marked, here and there, with the carcasses of dead animals.*

cardinal *adj.* important, chief, principal, primary, prime, major, leading, essential: *My cardinal reason for coming was to see you.* **ant.** secondary, subordinate, auxiliary.

care *n.* **1.** worry, concern, anxiety, trouble: *Although his business was very bad, my father acted as though he didn't have a care in the world.* **2.** carefulness, attention, regard, concern, consideration: *Like many parents, Bob and Diane treated their first child with much more care than the later children.* **3.** charge, custody, protection, keeping, supervision, guardianship: *We left our dog in the care of the vet when we went away for a holiday.* *vb.* **1.** attend; consider, regard: *I don't care what you do with that eggshell.* **2.** watch, guard, keep, supervise: *Who's going to care for me when I'm old?* **ant.** *n.* **2.** indifference, unconcern.

career *n.* profession, occupation, job, vocation: *What career do you want to follow after you graduate? I want to be a doctor.*

careful *adj.* **1.** cautious, watchful, wary, guarded, vigilant: *You have to be careful of what you say when you're in church.* **2.** thorough, concerned, painstaking, meticulous: *I thought that Tim did a very careful job when he painted the railings.* **ant.** **1.** incautious, heedless. **2.** careless, messy, sloppy.

careless *adj.* messy, sloppy, unthoughtful, unconcerned, negligent, reckless, thoughtless, uncaring: *Even though his writing was very good, Stuart was careless about his spelling.* **ant.** careful, cautious, prudent, painstaking.

caress *n.* embrace, pat, kiss: *Under his mother's gentle caress, Billy was soothed enough to stop crying.* *vb.* pat, pet, stroke, fondle, coddle: *Dad took the photograph of Jennie while she caressed her kitten.*

cargo *n.* load, freightload: *The ship arrived with a cargo of coal.*

carry *vb.* bear, transport, move, transfer; take, bring: *The porter will help carry your luggage to the train.* *vb. phr.* **carry off** abduct, seize, kidnap, capture: *When the bandits attacked a village, they would often carry off all the girls.* **carry on 1.** continue, go on, proceed: *Please excuse the interruption: you may carry on with your conversations now.* **2.** misbehave: *Victor carried on so about being left behind that he was finally allowed to go.* **carry out** fulfill, complete, succeed, accomplish, win, effect: *The plan sounds good, but will they be able to carry it out?*

carve *vb.* cut, chisel, sculpt, hew, whittle, shape: *The huge statue was carved entirely by hand.*

case[1] *n.* **1.** instance, occurrence, example, happening, sample, illustration: *The detectives were investigating a case of murder.* **2.** action, suit, lawsuit, claim: *The prosecuting attorney opened the case for the state.*

case[2] *n.* container, crate, box, carton, chest; receptacle: *When he opened the case of wine, it contained only eight bottles, not twelve.*

cast *vb.* **1.** throw, hurl, fling, toss, pitch, sling: *To avoid being caught with the stolen bonds, Ezra cast them into the deep well.* **2.** direct, shed, impart: *The lamp cast a strange yellow glow about the room.* **3.** direct, turn: *Whenever her name was mentioned, Eliza cast her eyes downward in embarrassment.* **4.** mold, shape, form: *I cast this bronze statue in my own shop.* *n.* dramatis personae, players, actors: *There was a party for the entire cast after the first performance of the play.*

castle *n.* palace, mansion, chateau: *There are few noblemen who can still afford to keep castles.*

casual *adj.* **1.** chance, accidental, unintentional, unexpected, offhand, unplanned, spontaneous: *The whole trouble can be traced to their casual meeting in the garden.* **2.** informal, sport, sporty: *On weekends we wear casual clothes unless we expect company or go out.* **ant.**

1. planned, calculated, deliberate, premeditated. **2.** formal, dressy.

catalog, catalogue *n.* list, roll, inventory, record, directory; file; index: *The bookshop gave me a copy of the publisher's catalog.*

catastrophe *n.* disaster, calamity, accident, misfortune, mishap: *As far as his family was concerned, the loss of Arthur's job was a catastrophe.* **ant.** boon, blessing, triumph.

catch *vb.* **1.** seize, capture, take, grasp, grab, nab: *Did they catch the thief who stole your car?* **2.** hook, trap, snare, entrap, ensnare: *We caught two chipmunks in the trap but let them go after a while.* **3.** come down with, contract, succumb to: *You'll catch a cold if you don't wear your hat.* *n.* **1.** capture, arrest, seizure, apprehension: *The police made a few good catches when they raided the pool hall last night.* **2.** pin, clasp; bolt, latch: *The catch on the door is broken again.* **ant.** *vb.* **1., 2.** release, free.

cause *n.* **1.** reason, origin, creation, occasion, ground: *The cause of the accident was a broken brake lever.* **2.** aim, purpose, object: *We managed to raise $20 for the cause of orphans.* *vb.* occasion, give rise to, bring about, originate, effect: *His silly teasing shouldn't be enough to cause your anger.*

caution *n.* **1.** wariness, watchfulness, vigilance, heed, care: *Exercise caution when you approach that dog—he may be unfriendly.* **2.** warning, advice: *She gave me a caution about the broken stair.* *vb.* warn, admonish, forewarn: *The lifeguard cautioned us about the strong undertow.* **ant.** *n.* **1.** heedlessness, carelessness, incaution.

cautious *adj.* careful, watchful, wary; vigilant: *Morris was cautious in the way he approached Irene when she was in a bad mood.* **ant.** heedless, headstrong, indiscreet, foolish.

cave *n.* grotto, cavern, hole: *Bears hibernate in a cave during the winter.* *vb. phr.* **cave in** collapse, fall in: *Just as we were about to leave, the roof caved in and trapped us.*

cease *vb.* stop, end, put a stop *or* an end to, terminate: *I do wish that Ellie would cease her complaining.* **ant.** begin, start.

celebrate *vb.* honor, observe, keep, commemorate: *Labor Day is always celebrated on a Monday.* **ant.** ignore, disregard.

celebrated *adj.* famous, renowned, famed, well-known,

noted, illustrious, eminent; popular: *May I introduce the celebrated scientist, Albert Einstein.* **ant.** anonymous, unknown.

celebrity *n.* notable, dignitary, personage; hero, heroine: *If young people make a singer popular, he becomes a celebrity overnight.*

censure *n.* disapproval, criticism, reproach: *The Senate's vote for censure of the judge was unanimous.* *vb.* disapprove, criticize, condemn, reproach: *After the dishonest things the mayor did, the town council had to censure him.* **ant.** *n.* approval, praise. *vb.* praise, approve, applaud.

center *n.* **1.** middle, midst, inside, midpoint: *The center of the earth is said to be a sphere of molten iron.* **2.** focus, hub, heart, core: *The Grendel monument is at the center of the city.* *vb.* focus, direct, concentrate: *The attention of the crowd centered on the clown in the red costume.* **ant.** *n.* **1.** edge, brim.

central *adj.* **1.** middle, mid, focal, inner, halfway: *The chief's hut was central in the arrangement of the village.* **2.** principal, chief, dominant, basic, fundamental, necessary: *The central issue for the workers was more pay; increased pensions were secondary.* **ant.** **2.** secondary, auxiliary, side, incidental.

ceremony *n.* ritual, rite, service, formality: *When my uncle was to be sworn in as the new governor, we all attended the ceremony.*

certain *adj.* **1.** confident, sure, positive, assured: *After all he'd done for the town, his election as mayor was certain.* **2.** definite, particular, special: *It would not be wise for me to name certain people who were seen together at the party.* **ant.** **1.** doubtful, uncertain, questionable.

certainly *adv.* surely, absolutely, definitely: *Your mother certainly is very nice to all of your friends. Are you going to the party? Certainly!* **ant.** doubtfully, dubiously, questionably.

certificate *n.* document, credential(s), affidavit: *In our town, you cannot move into a new house unless it has been given a certificate of occupancy.*

challenge *n.* dare, threat: *The supermarket met the challenge of competition by reducing prices.* *vb.* dare, threaten: *Aaron Burr challenged Alexander Hamilton to a duel.*

chamber *n.* room, salon; cell: *The small chambers in the monastery were furnished very sparsely.*

champion *n.* hero, winner, victor: *The champion of the* *heavyweight boxers was Joe Louis. vb.* defend, support: *Jane Addams championed the cause of the poor.*

chance *n.* **1.** opportunity, possibility, prospect: *I'll tell you what you want to know if you'll stop talking and give me a chance.* **2.** luck, accident, fate: *You ought to make absolutely certain that he's coming and leave nothing to chance. adj.* accidental, casual: *A chance meeting at the club resulted in my getting the job.* **ant.** *n.* **2.** certainty, inevitability.

change *vb.* **1.** exchange, substitute, replace: *We changed our clothes before going out.* **2.** vary; modify, alter: *I wish you would change your mind and let us go swimming.* **3.** exchange, trade: *I have to change this dollar bill into coins to use in the telephone. n.* variation, modification, alteration: *Ellie had a change of heart and came with us.* **ant.** *vb.* endure, remain. *n.* endurance, steadfastness, immutability.

channel *n.* canal, duct, trough, way, runway, groove: *Mars was once thought to have many man-made channels on its surface.*

chant *n.* song, singing, hymn, incantation: *Certain kinds of chants have been used in church music for centuries. vb.* sing, intone, carol: *The children started to chant, "Kitty is a baby! Kitty is a baby!"*

chaos *n.* disorder, confusion, turmoil: *My sister's bedroom is always neat, but mine is in a state of chaos.* **ant.** tranquillity, order, organization, tidiness.

chaotic *adj.* disordered, confused, messy, disorganized: *We found the library files in a chaotic condition.* **ant.** ordered, organized, neat, systematic.

character *n.* **1.** personality, traits, features, characteristics: *The judge is a man of outstanding character.* **2.** quality, nature, disposition: *The cashier was of doubtful character so he was transferred to another job.* **3.** individual, eccentric: *That fellow is quite a character.*

characteristic *adj.* typical, unique, exclusive, distinctive, distinguishing, special: *All American flags, banners, and signals have the characteristic red, white, and blue. n.* character, feature, distinction: *A characteristic of the Pygmy people is their short stature.*

charge *vb.* **1.** price at, sell for: *They charge too much for service at the car mechanic's.* **2.** attack, assault, assail: *The cavalry charged up the hill at San Juan.* **3.** accuse, indict, blame: *Even though he had a perfect alibi, they* *charged Evans with robbery. n.* **1.** accusation, blame, indictment, allegation: *The charge against us was trespassing on private property.* **2.** care, management, custody: *The teacher left a monitor in charge of the class.* **3.** price, cost: *The charge for electricity increased this year.* **ant.** *vb.* **2.** retreat, flee. **3.** absolve, excuse, pardon.

charitable *adj.* kind, generous, liberal; considerate: *A really charitable person gives more than just money to help others.* **ant.** mean, petty, stingy, narrow-minded.

charm *n.* **1.** attractiveness, allure, enchantment; spell, magic, witchery: *When she used her charm on Rudolf, she could make him do anything she wanted.* **2.** amulet, good-luck piece, talisman: *The bearded pirate wore a strange charm on a chain around his neck. vb.* attract, enchant, lure, fascinate, captivate, bewitch: *When you were in India, did you see any men charming snakes?*

chart *n.* plan, map; diagram: *Using a sharp stick, he drew a chart in the sand showing where the gold was buried.*

chase *vb.* pursue, run after, follow, hunt: *The farmer chased us out of the cornfield. n.* pursuit, hunt: *At first, I ran after the thief alone, but two other people later joined in the chase.*

chaste *adj.* virtuous, pure, innocent, decent; virginal: *All nuns are supposed to be chaste.* **ant.** impure, worldly, sinful, immodest.

chat *vb.* talk, converse: *I chatted for a while with Mrs. Philbey about where she was going for her holiday. n.* conversation, talk: *During our chat, she told me she loved to go to the mountains.*

cheap *adj.* **1.** inexpensive, low-priced, low-cost: *Fresh fruit is cheaper when it's in season.* **2.** shoddy, inferior, poor: *If you buy cheap clothes, you rarely get good value.* **ant.** **1.** costly, expensive, dear. **2.** elegant, well-made.

cheat *n.* cheater, swindler, trickster, fraud, phony, charlatan, chiseler; crook, thief, confidence man, con artist, con man: *The man who offered to sell the Brooklyn Bridge was nothing but a cheat. vb.* swindle, trick, defraud, deceive, victimize, dupe, hoax: *The crook cheated me out of my life savings.*

check *vb.* **1.** stop, halt, arrest, block: *The tanks checked the advance of the enemy's soldiers.* **2.** control, curb; hinder: *This valve checks the flow of gas into the tank.* **3.** review, investigate, test, examine, compare: *Please check the inventory against this list. n.* **1.** control, curb;

hindrance, barrier, bar, obstacle, restriction: *Bill doesn't seem able to keep a check on his temper.* **2.** stub, counterfoil, ticket, coupon, receipt: *Don't forget to keep that check for your coat.* **ant.** *vb.* **1., 2.** advance, continue, foster, promote.

checkup *n.* (medical, physical) examination, medical *or* physical (examination): *I have my doctor give me a checkup every year.*

cheek *n.* impudence, impertinence, nerve, gall, effrontery: *She had the cheek to ask her mother her age.*

cheer *n.* **1.** approval, applause, encouragement: *After the coach's words of cheer, Bob went on to win the race.* **2.** glee, joy, mirth, gaiety, cheerfulness: *Be of good cheer: happiness is just around the corner.* *vb.* **1.** gladden, encourage, comfort: *The coach's words cheered us, and we won.* **2.** shout, yell, applaud: *The crowd cheered for the new champion.* **ant.** *n.* **1.** discouragement, derision. *vb.* **1.** discourage, sadden. **2.** boo, hiss.

cheerful *adj.* cheery, happy, joyous, joyful, gay, merry: *Alexa has a cheerful disposition that puts her friends at ease.* **ant.** sad, gloomy, morose, downhearted.

cherish *vb.* **1.** nurse, comfort, nurture: *I cherish the relationship I have with my brothers and sisters.* **2.** treasure, hold dear, value, prize: *She cherished the memories of her days at summer camp.* **ant.** **2.** scorn, undervalue, deprecate, disparage.

chest *n.* **1.** breast, bosom: *The little girl clasped the puppy to her chest.* **2.** box, trunk, coffer, case, casket: *The treasure chest contained rubies, pearls, diamonds, and gold.* **3.** (of drawers) dresser, cabinet, commode, chiffonier, chifferobe, bureau: *My father's cufflinks were on the chest.*

chew *vb.* bite, munch, gnaw; nibble: *The puppy has chewed up my slipper.*

chide *vb.* scold, criticize, admonish, reprimand, rebuke, reprove: *Victor's mother chides him for the slightest thing.* **ant.** praise, extol, commend.

chief *n.* leader, ruler, commander, boss, head: *The chief of the robber band was masked.* *adj.* leading, principal, main; head: *The chief reason for going to school is to learn something.* **ant.** *adj.* secondary, incidental, auxiliary, accidental.

chiefly *adv.* mostly, mainly, principally, especially: *We go* *out to the country chiefly on hot, sunny days in the summer.* **ant.** lastly, last.

childish *adj.* childlike, immature, babyish, infantile: *By the time you become a teenager, you must put away childish behavior.* **ant.** adult, grownup, mature, seasoned.

chill *n.* cold, coldness, coolness, cool: *You'll need a sweater in the chill of the evening. adj.* chilly, cool, brisk, frosty: *The nights in Vermont during October are quite chill.* **ant.** *n.* warmth, heat. *adj.* warm, heated, hot.

chirp *vb., n.* twitter, peep, tweet, warble, cheep, chirrup: *The birds were chirping happily in the trees. The chirps of the crickets and the birds woke me up.*

chivalrous *adj.* brave, valorous, noble; polite, courteous, gallant, gentlemanly: *Harry was always chivalrous when in the company of the ladies.* **ant.** rude, impolite, crude, uncivil.

chivalry *n.* nobility, knighthood; courtesy, gallantry: *The age of chivalry will never die as long as gentlemen continue to behave politely to women.*

choice *n.* selection, option, pick: *The saleslady offered us a choice of styles and colors. adj.* select, fine, rare, uncommon, valuable, precious: *The mare in the pasture is a choice example of the best horsebreeding.*

choke *vb.* strangle, throttle; gag: *When he resisted, the burglar tried to choke him. The pepper on that steak almost made me choke.*

choose *vb.* select, pick, decide between *or* on, settle on *or* for: *At the record shop, we had thousands to choose from. I chose an old jazz album.*

chop *vb.* mince, cut; hew, fell: *My mother asked the butcher to chop the meat for hamburgers. The woodsman chopped down the tree in ten minutes.*

chronic *adj.* continuing, persistent, continuous, lingering, perennial, sustained, constant, lifelong, permanent, unending, eternal, everlasting: *My aunt had a chronic illness that prevented her from getting out of bed.* **ant.** acute, fleeting, temporary.

chuckle *vb., n.* giggle, titter, laugh: *The teacher chuckled over the story that Marjorie had written. Every few minutes, he gave a little chuckle.*

circle *n.* **1.** ring; disk: *The magician drew a circle in the sand.* **2.** group, set, class, club: *In her circle of friends, everyone now chews gum. vb.* encircle, surround, round, enclose: *The road circled our farm.*

circuit *n.* orbit, circle, revolution; course, tour, journey: *The earth makes one circuit about the sun each year.*

circular *adj.* round, ringlike, disklike: *Most drinking glasses are circular.* *n.* advertisement, handbill, leaflet: *We received a circular in the mail advertising the sale at the department store.* **ant.** *adj.* straight.

circumference *n.* periphery, border, edge, perimeter: *The circumference of a square table that is two feet on each side is eight feet.*

circumstances *n. pl.* **1.** situation, conditions, facts, factors, grounds, background: *Among the circumstances that led to his punishment was the increased strictness of his parents.* **2.** means, assets, capital, income; class, rank: *Each year, after buying Christmas presents for his family, Christopher was in reduced circumstances.*

cite *vb.* quote, mention, refer to: *I cite the Holy Bible as the source of many of the expressions I use.*

citizen *n.* inhabitant, native, national, subject, denizen, dweller, resident: *The citizens of this country wish to be free.*

city *n.* town, municipality, metropolis; village: *Many people have moved from the cities to the suburbs during the last few years.*

civil *adj.* **1.** municipal, public: *Every citizen must do his civic duty.* **2.** polite, courteous, respectful, gracious, well-mannered: *Roger has always been very civil to me.* **ant.** **2.** impolite, rude, crude.

civilization *n.* culture, society: *Western civilization has much to learn from that of the Far East.*

civilize *vb.* cultivate, refine, polish, tame, teach, instruct: *Civilized people eat with a knife and fork.*

claim *vb.* **1.** demand, require, request, ask for: *After my grandfather died, my father claimed for himself all of the property along the river.* **2.** assert, state, maintain, insist, declare: *Donald claimed that he knew nothing about the theft of the statue.* *n.* **1.** demand, request, requirement: *The court ruled that the miner's claim was invalid.* **2.** title, right, interest: *I told you that Kitty has no claim to the brooch.*

clamor *n.* din, noise, shouting, uproar: *When the teacher announced another exam, there was such a clamor from the students that he canceled it.* *vb.* demand noisily, shout: *The girls in the audience clamored for the guitar* *player to come back on stage.* **ant.** *n.* quiet, serenity, tranquillity.

clan *n.* family, set, group: *The MacGregor clan has its own tartan.*

clarify *vb.* explain, clear, define: *I wish you would clarify what you are trying to tell me so that I can understand it.* **ant.** confuse, muddle, obscure.

clash *n.* **1.** clang, crash, clank: *The clash of armor could be heard for miles as the knights fought.* **2.** conflict, opposition, struggle, disagreement; collision: *There was a clash between those in office and those who sought to replace them.* *vb.* **1.** contrast, mismatch, conflict: *Your tie clashes with your shirt.* **2.** contend, conflict, disagree, interfere; collide: *Our points of view about what is right and wrong always clash.* **ant.** *n.* **2.** harmony, agreement, accord. *vb.* **1.** harmonize, blend. **2.** agree, match.

clasp *vb.* grasp, embrace, hug, clutch, hold: *Her father was so happy to find her safe and sound that he wept as he clasped her to him.* *n.* hook, catch, pin, fastening, brooch, buckle: *These two parts of the dress are held together by a silver clasp.*

class *n.* **1.** classification, rank, order, grade, division, sub-division, family, sort, kind, set, species, group: *I don't know whether this animal belongs in the fish or reptile class. The upper class doesn't have to work.* **2.** form, group, study group, grade, year, section: *Our class will graduate next spring.* *vb.* classify, rank, grade: *I wouldn't class you in the same category with your sister.*

classic *n.* masterpiece: *Paradise Lost is considered one of the greatest classics in the English language.*

classification *n.* **1.** category, order, class: *Into which classification should I put this book, science or philosophy?* **2.** arrangement, grouping, ordering, organization: *The librarian's classification of new books takes a great deal of time.*

classify *vb.* class, arrange, sort, order, organize, group, grade, index: *We were asked to classify these nations by the kinds of government they have. In the storeroom, the fabrics were classified by color rather than by kind of material.*

clause *n.* paragraph, article, condition, limitation: *According to the third clause of our contract, I am forbidden to work in the movies.*

claw *n.* nail, talon, hook: *The cat's claw caught in the cur-*

tain and tore it. vb. scratch, tear; rip: *The dog kept clawing at the door, trying to get in.*

clean *adj.* **1.** neat, tidy, clear, dustless, immaculate, unsoiled, unstained: *My mother made me scrub my room till it was clean.* **2.** pure, untainted, uncontaminated, purified: *Don't drink from a glass that isn't clean. vb.* **1.** dust, mop, vacuum, scour, scrub, sweep, wipe, wash, rinse, cleanse: *If you don't clean your room, you may not go out to play.* **2.** purify, decontaminate; sterilize: *All surgical instruments must be cleaned after every use.* **ant.** *adj.* dirty, soiled, impure, contaminated. *vb.* soil, dirty, pollute.

clear *adj.* **1.** plain, understandable, distinct, lucid, obvious: *I want to make the entire matter as clear as possible.* **2.** uncloudy, unclouded, bright, light; sunny, fair: *Water is a clear liquid. Saturday was such a clear day you could see for miles.* **3.** certain, sure, doubtless, obvious: *Alan's innocence was clear.* **4.** open, free, unobstructed, unblocked: *The road was clear early in the morning. vb.* **1.** empty: *Please clear the room so that it can be painted.* **2.** acquit, free, release, emancipate, let go: *The statements the murderer made about his other crimes cleared two men who had been arrested for them.* **3.** rid, loose, unloose, free, remove: *If they clear the channel of debris, we shall be able to sail the boat through it.* **ant.** *adj.* **1.** confused, muddled. **2.** overcast, cloudy, dark. **3.** dubious, questionable. **4.** obstructed, blocked, blockaded. *vb.* **1.** fill, clutter. **2.** implicate, involve. **3.** obstruct, block, blockade.

clearly *adv.* obviously, definitely, plainly, evidently, unmistakably, certainly, surely: *You are clearly not the kind of person we had in mind for this job.* **ant.** dubiously, questionably.

clerical *adj.* **1.** priestly, ministerial, churchly, pastoral, ecclesiastical; sacred, holy: *The bishop's other clerical duties did not prevent him from conducting services.* **2.** stenographic, secretarial: *After graduating from high school, Anne was lucky to get a clerical job in town.*

clerk *n.* **1.** office girl, file clerk, office boy, typist: *A clerk in the accounting department found an enormous error in bookkeeping.* **2.** salesclerk, saleslady, saleswoman, salesman, salesperson: *The clerk told me to take my purchases to another desk for gift wrapping.*

clever *adj.* **1.** bright, intelligent, shrewd, quick, talented, expert, gifted, smart: *A clever person could move ahead in that company.* **2.** skillful, adroit, dexterous, handy: *My brother is so clever with his hands that he finished a model airplane in two hours.* **ant. 1.** stupid, slow, backward, dull. **2.** clumsy, maladroit, inept.

client *n.* customer, patron: *If we don't have more clients, we'll have to close the store.*

climb *vb.* scale, ascend, mount: *The men started to climb up the mountain at dawn.* **ant.** descend.

clip *vb.* cut, mow, crop, snip: *They clipped my lawn too short.* *n.* fastener, paper clip, clasp: *Please put a clip on those papers to keep them together.*

cloak *n.* cape, mantle, wrap, shawl: *You'd better take your cloak—the evening is chilly.* *vb.* conceal, hide, cover, mask: *Her smile cloaked her real feelings about him.* **ant.** *vb.* reveal, show, display.

close[1] *vb.* **1.** shut, fasten, bolt, lock: *Be careful and make sure to close your doors at night.* **2.** end, terminate, conclude: *The speaker closed his remarks with a few compliments to the mayor.* **ant. 1.** open, unlock. **2.** begin, start.

close[2] *adj.* **1.** near, nearby: *If the market were closer to the house, I wouldn't have to walk so far to shop.* **2.** stuffy, unventilated, oppressive: *With the windows closed and the heater on, it feels very close in this room.* **3.** stingy, mean, mingy, tight: *Scrooge was certainly a close man with the penny.* **ant. 1.** far, distant. **2.** fresh, clear. **3.** generous, open-handed, charitable.

closet *n.* wardrobe, cabinet, cupboard; locker: *The weather here is so fine that my raincoat never leaves the closet.*

cloth *n.* material, fabric, textile, goods: *It required two yards of cloth to make this skirt.*

clothe *vb.* dress, apparel, garb: *The prince was clothed in garments woven with silver and gold.* **ant.** undress, strip.

clothes *n. pl.* garments, clothing, dress, garb, attire, apparel, costume: *Stanley comes home after school with his clothes torn and dirty.*

cloud *n.* **1.** haze, mist, fog: *The clouds made it a gloomy day for our picnic.* **2.** collection, mass: *The stagecoach rattled into town in a cloud of dust.* *vb.* dim, obscure, shadow: *The politician clouded the issue with his evasive answers.*

cloudy *adj.* **1.** dim, obscure, vague, indefinite, blurred, unclear, confused: *If your thinking is cloudy on a subject,* *you cannot write about it clearly.* **2.** overcast, clouded, sunless, gloomy; *It was a cloudy morning when we set sail for the island.* **ant. 1.** clearheaded, lucid, clarified. **2.** sunny, clear, brilliant, cloudless.

club   *n.* **1.** association, society, organization, circle, set: *There was a long waiting list for membership in the club.* **2.** cudgel, bat, stick, nightstick, blackjack: *The thieves were carrying clubs with which they threatened their victims.*

clue   *n.* hint, suggestion, trace, sign: *The detective found a clue that linked the night watchman to the theft of the bracelet.*

clumsy   *adj.* awkward, ungraceful, unskillful, bungling, bumbling, ungainly, inept: *The waitress was so clumsy that she dropped every tray on the way to the kitchen. The manager made a clumsy attempt to apologize for the rudeness of the saleswoman.* **ant.** graceful, adroit, skillful, polished, dexterous.

cluster   *n.* group, batch, bunch, clutch: *A cluster of flowers grew near the rock.* *vb.* group, gather, assemble, pack, crowd: *The students clustered about the bulletin board where the examination results were posted.*

clutch   *vb.* seize, grip, grasp, hold, grab: *The child clutched the doll to her. When I felt myself falling, I clutched at the stair handrail.*

coarse   *adj.* rough, crude, rude: *Burlap is a coarse cloth. People with bad manners are usually considered to be coarse.* **ant.** fine, refined, cultivated, genteel, suave.

coast   *n.* seashore, shore, shoreline, seaboard, beach: *We like to spend our vacations on the west coast of Florida.* *vb.* glide, ride; drift: *Pete came coasting down the hill on his sled. Some people just coast along through life letting nothing disturb them.*

coax   *vb.* wheedle, persuade, cajole, urge: *Why do mothers often have to coax children to eat things that are good for them?* **ant.** bully, force, coerce.

coincide   *vb.* correspond, agree, match, harmonize: *These two parts of the jigsaw puzzle coincide exactly. Our opinions coincide on how to treat naughty children.*

coincidence   *n.* chance, accident: *By coincidence, one of my classmates is the son of one of my father's classmates.* **ant.** plan, scheme, plot, prearrangement.

cold   *adj.* **1.** cool, chilly, chill; frigid, freezing: *Winter in Alaska can be very cold.* **2.** cool, chilly, unemotional, unfriendly, unfeeling, indifferent, heartless: *Susan's attitude toward her classmates was so cold that she had no friends at all.* **ant. 1.** hot, warm, temperate. **2.** friendly, warm, compassionate, outgoing.

collapse *vb.* fall, fail, drop: *The walls of the building collapsed during the fire.* *n.* failure, downfall, destruction: *The kingdom was doomed to collapse when the dictator overthrew the government.*

colleague *n.* associate, co-worker; collaborator: *The professor's colleagues honored him with a dinner.*

collect *vb.* **1.** gather, assemble, accumulate: *I used to collect seashells as a hobby, but now I collect stamps.* **2.** solicit, obtain, procure, secure, get, raise: *The Boy Scouts collected thousands of dollars for the poor in our town.* **ant. 1.** disperse, dispel, scatter.

collection *n.* accumulation, hoard, store, pile, aggregation: *There was a huge collection of dead leaves when the men finished raking.*

collide *vb.* crash, smash, strike, hit: *The car collided with the truck in front of the theater.*

collision *n.* crash, smash, smash-up: *There was a three-car collision on the highway in which six people were injured.*

color *n.* hue, shade, tone, tinge, tint: *I can't tell the color of your eyes through those dark glasses.* *vb.* tint, paint, tinge; decorate: *This room should be colored to match the carpet.*

colossal *adj.* enormous, huge, immense, gigantic: *The Merchandise Mart, in Chicago, is a colossal building. Phoebe told her mother a colossal lie.* **ant.** tiny, miniature, minuscule, microscopic.

combat *vb.* fight, battle, oppose, contest, struggle: *The economists seem to be unable to combat inflation effectively.* *n.* fight, battle, contest, conflict, war, struggle: *The two knights were locked in mortal combat.* **ant.** *vb.* surrender, yield, succumb.

combination *n.* **1.** blending, mixing, compounding: *The combination of flour and water makes a light paste.* **2.** blend, mixture, compound, composite: *Gunpowder is a combination of three simple ingredients.* **ant. 1.** separation, division.

combine *vb.* blend, mix; unite, join, connect: *If these ingredients are combined, a strong acid is produced. We must combine forces to fight the enemy.* **ant.** separate, divide.

come *vb.* **1.** approach, advance, near: *I want you to come* *here when I call you.* **2.** arrive, reach: *Dick came home late last night.* **vb. phr. come about,** happen, occur, take place: *The accident came about because you were driving recklessly.* **come around,** revive, recover, recuperate: *After the blow on his head knocked him out, it took ten minutes for George to come around.* **come to,** revive, recover: *Gene came to in a strange room.* **come upon,** discover, find: *Betty came upon an old cookbook in the attic.* **ant.** go, leave, depart.

comfort *vb.* soothe, relieve, console, ease, calm, cheer: *Whenever Victoria was upset, her mother was always there to comfort her.* **n. 1.** solace, consolation: *The comfort of knowing that you will stand by is all I need.* **2.** relaxation, rest, satisfaction, luxury, ease: *Because of her careful saving plan, the old lady was able to live in comfort.* **ant. vb.** upset, agitate, disturb, discompose. **n. 1.** uncertainty. **2.** discomfort.

comfortable *adj.* **1.** relaxed, easy, rested, contented, cheerful: *The teacher's friendly manner made us all feel comfortable.* **2.** restful, cozy, satisfying: *This is a very comfortable armchair.* **ant. 1.** uncomfortable, strained, tense, edgy.

command *vb.* order, direct, demand, decree, rule: *The principal commanded the children to appear in his office.* **n.** order, demand, direction, rule, decree, charge, authority: *By whose command was this ship sent into battle?* **ant. vb.** obey.

commence *vb.* begin, start, open: *The king gave the order that the festivities could commence.* **ant.** end, stop, terminate, finish.

commend *vb.* praise, recommend, applaud, laud: *The general commended the entire company for its bravery.* **ant.** blame, censure, criticize.

commendable *adj.* praiseworthy, deserving: *The actors turned in a very commendable performance.* **ant.** deplorable, bad, lamentable.

commendation *n.* praise, approval, recommendation; applause; medal, honor: *The highest commendation he received in the war was the Good Conduct Medal.* **ant.** condemnation, criticism, censure.

comment *n.* **1.** explanation, commentary, review, report, criticism, judgment: *Your comments on how the program succeeded will be helpful in planning one for next year.* **2.** remark, observation: *She made some offhand com-*

ment that I didn't hear. vb. remark, explain, observe, opine: *He commented that he thought the carpet might be a little bright for this room.*

commerce *n.* business, trade, marketing: *Interstate commerce in this country may slow down.*

commission *n.* **1.** committee, board: *The rent commission refused to allow any increases during the coming year.* **2.** order, command, permission, permit: *His commission as a second lieutenant came through today. vb.* appoint, delegate, authorize, commit, entrust, deputize: *I have been commissioned to bring you home.*

commit *vb.* **1.** entrust, delegate, empower, authorize, commission: *The association is committed to raising funds to help the blind.* **2.** do, perform, carry out: *The murder was committed by a person or persons unknown.*

commitment *n.* pledge, promise, duty, responsibility: *I have made a ʻcommitment to help you and I shall do everything I can.*

committee *n.* board, commission, council, bureau, delegate: *The executive committee meets on Wednesday, right after the finance and business committees submit their reports.*

commodity *n.* goods, merchandise, article, wares: *Wheat is one of the best export commodities of the United States.*

common *adj.* **1.** joint, communal, mutual, shared: *My neighbor and I have a common wall between our properties. Our common friend, Danny, invited us together.* **2.** customary, usual, regular: *This is a common garden variety of flower and not rare at all.* **3.** ordinary, natural, conventional, plain, commonplace, stale, trite: *The movie had rather a common plot.* **4.** ordinary, coarse, vulgar, low: *He was nothing but a common criminal.* **ant. 1.** separate, different. **2.** unusual, rare. **3.** distinctive, outstanding, extraordinary. **4.** refined, cultivated, genteel.

commonplace *adj.* ordinary, common, everyday, usual, undistinguished, frequent, run-of-the-mill, run-of-the-mine: *This is a commonplace piece of furniture, not the antique you promised to show me.* **ant.** unusual, distinctive, original.

communicable *adj.* catching, contagious, infectious, transferable: *The common cold is a highly communicable disease.*

communicate *vb.* **1.** impart, convey, transmit, reveal, disclose, divulge; advertise, publicize, publish: *The secretary communicated the President's comments to the press* *in his behalf.* **2.** transmit: *Disease can be communicated by using someone else's drinking glass.* **ant. 1.** conceal, withhold, dissemble.

communication *n.* **1.** transmission, announcement, disclosure, notification, declaration, publication: *The President often uses his press secretary for the communication of his ideas to the news media.* **2.** message, information, news, report, account, announcement, advice: *The secret communications between the governments were sent in code.*

community *n.* **1.** public, commonwealth, society, public: *The community felt that Victor was doing a good job as mayor.* **2.** town, village, city, township: *We moved to a small community south of Cleveland.*

compact *adj.* compressed, packed, tight, thick: *The soil was so compact that I was hardly able to force a shovel into it. n.* **1.** makeup box *or* case, vanity: *I lost my silver compact at the restaurant when I went to powder my nose.* **2.** agreement, treaty, contract, pact, covenant: *A trade compact was reached by the two countries.* **ant.** *adj.* loose, unconfined, sprawling, unfettered.

companion *n.* associate, comrade, mate, partner, colleague, friend: *When my daughter went to London, she took along Barbara as a companion.*

company *n.* **1.** business, firm, partnership, concern, house, corporation: *After all those years of hard work, Len was made president of a big paper company.* **2.** group, band, party, assembly, throng: *I told the company that had gathered at the steps why I thought they should obey the rules.* **3.** companionship, fellowship: *We have been members of the Royal Company of Silversmiths for generations.* **4.** guest(s), visitor(s): *Are you expecting company for dinner tonight?*

comparable *adj.* relative, alike, like: *The prices of hamburger and chicken are comparable today.* **ant.** different, unalike.

compare *vb.* **1.** contrast, match: *The teacher asked us to compare the invention of the telephone with any invention from before 1800.* **2.** compete, rival, vie: *Your beauty and hers cannot compare.*

comparison *n.* contrasting, likening, judgment: *How can you make a comparison between an apple and a banana?*

compartment *n.* section, division: *The ship was divided into a large number of watertight compartments.*

compel *vb.* force, coerce, drive, impel: *The robber compelled his victims to lie flat on the floor.* **ant.** coax, wheedle, cajole.

compensate *vb.* **1.** repay, remunerate, recompense, reimburse: *The insurance company compensated my father for the loss of the money.* **2.** balance, counterbalance, offset: *No amount of saying you are sorry could compensate me for the broken vase.*

compensation *n.* pay, remittance, wage, salary, earnings, settlement, payment, remuneration, repayment: *The rate of compensation for that kind of work is $2.50 per hour.*

compete *vb.* contest, vie, rival, oppose: *The grand masters were competing for the chess championship of the world.* **ant.** accord, reconcile.

competence *n.* ability, skill, capability: *Although she might not be very lovable, Phoebe's competence as a student is unquestioned.* **ant.** incompetence, ineptitude.

competent *adj.* capable, skillful, qualified, apt, able, proficient: *Ricky has become quite competent at swimming and has even won races.* **ant.** incompetent, inept, awkward, gauche.

competition *n.* rivalry, contest, tournament, match: *The competition in the sack race event will be limited to those under ten years of age.*

competitor *n.* contestant, rival, opponent: *You must defeat eight competitors to qualify for the finals in the tennis championship match.* **ant.** friend, ally, colleague.

complain *vb.* protest, grumble, moan, groan, fret: *I wish you would stop complaining about getting up so early.*

complement *vb.* complete, supplement: *That hat really complements your outfit—and I'm not just complimenting you!* **ant.** conflict, clash.

complete *adj.* **1.** whole, full, entire: *The complete chemistry set costs a great deal.* **2.** ended, over, finished, done, concluded: *The manuscript would be complete if the author could write the last chapter.* *vb.* finish, end, conclude, terminate; close: *I've completed all my homework for tomorrow.* **ant.** *adj.* unfinished, incomplete, partial. *vb.* begin, start, commence.

complex *adj.* complicated, involved, intricate: *This textbook on astronomy is much too complex for a sixth-grader to understand. A gasoline engine is more complex than a diesel.* **ant.** simple, uncomplicated, rudimentary.

compliment *n.* praise, honor, admiration, approval, commendation, appreciation: *She took it as a compliment when I told her she was too young to go to school.* *vb.* praise, honor, approve, commend, flatter: *I'd like to compliment you on your new dress, Diane.* **ant.** *n.* insult, aspersion, affront. *vb.* insult, affront, disparage.

compose *vb.* **1.** constitute, make up, go to make up: *There are thousands of minerals that compose the crust of the earth.* **2.** create, write, make up: *My sister composes popular songs in her spare time.*

composed *adj.* relaxed, calm, cool, untroubled, peaceful, serene, tranquil, quiet: *I can see from the way your hands are folded that you are quite composed.* **ant.** agitated, nervous, anxious, overwrought, hysterical.

compound *n.* mixture, combination, aggregate: *Water is a chemical compound made up of the elements hydrogen and oxygen.* *adj.* complicated, complex; combined, mixed: *Shawn suffered a compound fracture of his arm when he fell off the horse.* **ant.** *adj.* simple, uncomplicated.

comprehend *vb.* understand, grasp, perceive: *I could see from the boy's expression that he hadn't comprehended what I was telling him.*

comprehension *n.* understanding, perception, awareness: *The students hadn't the slightest comprehension of what the teacher had said.*

comprehensive *adj.* inclusive, broad, wide, complete, full: *At the end of the year, we must pass a comprehensive examination in each subject.* **ant.** partial, fragmentary, incomplete, limited.

compress *vb.* squeeze, compact, press, crowd, pack: *I've never seen nine people compressed into one telephone booth!* **ant.** stretch, spread, expand.

compulsory *adj.* necessary, required, unavoidable, obligatory: *Fastening your seat belt during takeoffs and landings in a plane is compulsory.* **ant.** optional, elective, unrestricted, free.

compute *vb.* calculate, reckon, determine, figure: *I have computed that it would have taken 300 years for this tree to have grown to this size.*

comrade *n.* companion, friend, associate: *We were comrades at school many years ago.*

conceal *vb.* hide, cover, secrete: *The murderer had a dagger concealed in his sleeve. I believe that you concealed your poor marks from your father.* **ant.** reveal, show, display, expose.

concede *vb.* admit, allow, acknowledge, yield: *After the policeman told him that three people had seen him at the lake, George finally conceded he had been there.* **ant.** deny, contradict, negate.

conceit *n.* vanity, egotism, self-esteem: *His high opinion of himself was due to conceit and not to any accomplishments.* **ant.** modesty, humility, humbleness, self-effacement.

conceited *adj.* vain, arrogant, proud, smug, self-important, egotistical: *She is so conceited about her new fur coat that no one can talk to her.* **ant.** modest, humble, self-effacing.

conceive *vb.* **1.** create, think(up), invent, imagine: *The prisoners conceived a clever plan to escape.* **2.** understand, perceive, grasp: *It is difficult to conceive why they chose purple wallpaper with pink polka dots.*

concentrate *vb.* **1.** focus, localize, condense: *The rays of light should be concentrated on one point by this lens.* **2.** ponder, center, meditate, scrutinize: *Please don't interrupt while I'm concentrating on my homework.* **ant. 1.** diffuse, scatter, disperse, dissipate.

concentration *n.* application, study, attention: *A lot of concentration is required to follow the plot of this book.* **ant.** distraction, confusion.

concept *n.* idea, notion, thought, theory: *I often wonder how the concept of arithmetic ever occurred to man.*

concern *vb.* **1.** interest, relate to, affect, touch, involve: *I don't see why what I had for breakfast should concern the Prime Minister of Uganda.* **2.** worry, trouble, disturb: *I'm concerned about my teenager's staying out past midnight.* *n.* **1.** interest, consequence: *International politics are of concern to everyone.* **2.** anxiety, worry, care: *My concern about the safety of children is not limited to that of my own.* **3.** business, firm, company, house, partnership, corporation: *Larry resigned from one company and started a concern of his own.* **ant.** *vb.* **1.** disinterest, bore, tire. **2.** soothe, calm. *n.* **1., 2.** disinterest, indifference.

concerning *prep.* about, regarding, respecting: *The defendant testified that he knew nothing concerning the disappearance of the jewels.*

concerted *adj.* joint, united, combined: *We made a concerted effort to persuade Frances to join our club.* **ant.** unorganized, individual, separate.

concession   *n.* yielding, admission, granting: *Although it was against the rules to admit anyone under 18, the owner made a concession and let us in.* **ant.** demand, insistence.

conclude   *vb.* **1.** finish, end, terminate, complete: *We concluded our dinner with a toast to the guest of honor.* **2.** arrange, settle, determine, decide: *The treaty was concluded when Japan agreed to stop whaling.* **3.** presume, assume, gather, understand, deduce: *I conclude from your comments that you do not like yogurt.* **ant. 1.** begin, start, commence.

conclusion   *n.* **1.** end, finish, termination, close: *In conclusion of these remarks, I should say that I once again welcome all of you to Old Siwash College.* **2.** decision, resolution, determination: *Don't jump to conclusions about Eddie just because he wears his shoulder-length hair in curls.* **ant. 1.** beginning, start, opening, commencement.

concrete   *n.* cement: *The airport runway is made of concrete.* *adj.* firm, definite, solid, precise: *I couldn't tell her any concrete reason for not wanting to go without insulting her, so I went.* **ant. 2.** vague, undetermined, amorphous.

condemn   *vb.* **1.** denounce, rebuke, blame: *You mustn't condemn a person just because he cannot do what you can do.* **2.** judge, doom, punish, convict, sentence: *The court condemned the man to ten years in jail.* **ant. 1.** praise, laud, extol, applaud. **2.** pardon, absolve, excuse.

condense   *vb.* reduce, abbreviate, shorten, abridge, concentrate, compress, digest, diminish: *This magazine condenses popular novels several hundred pages long into only a few pages.* **ant.** expand, enlarge, swell, increase.

condition   *n.* **1.** state, position, situation: *The doctor told me that I was in excellent physical condition.* **2.** requirement, necessity, provision, stipulation: *One of the conditions of employment in that restaurant is that you agree to turn over all tips to the management.* *vb.* train: *He was conditioned to perspire whenever they rang a bell.*

conduct   *n.* behavior, manners, deportment, actions: *Your conduct is not proper for an officer of the United States Navy!* *vb.* **1.** behave, act: *I thought that Philip conducted himself very well, considering he's only four.* **2.** lead, guide, escort: *Kathy got a job conducting tours of the United Nations Building in New York this summer.*

confer   *vb.* **1.** give, award, bestow, grant: *In his sixtieth year, the university conferred on him their highest honor.* **2.**

discuss, consult, deliberate: *Don't you think we ought to confer before announcing a hasty opinion by one person?* **ant. 1.** withdraw, retrieve.

confess *vb.* admit, acknowledge, grant, concede: *I confess I love you very much. The murderer confessed and the innocent man was released.*

confidence *n.* **1.** trust, faith, reliance: *My confidence in your abilities has always been justified by your accomplishments.* **2.** self-assurance, self-reliance, self-confidence, courage: *Many people would be more successful if they just had more confidence in themselves.* **ant. 1.** distrust, mistrust, doubt. **2.** shyness, modesty, diffidence.

confident *adj.* sure, certain, self-assured, self-reliant, self-confident, dauntless: *I was confident that we would win the championship.* **ant.** timid, uncertain, shy, self-effacing.

confine *vb.* limit, restrict, bound, hinder: *As a punishment, Marilyn was confined to her room for the rest of the day.* **ant.** release, free.

confirm *vb.* **1.** assure, verify, corroborate, substantiate: *I confirmed everything that she had told me.* **2.** validate, approve, ratify: *The higher court confirmed the lower court's findings.* **ant. 1.** deny, disclaim, disavow.

confirmed *adj.* habitual, established, chronic, regular: *I am a confirmed supporter of the Democratic party.* **ant.** infrequent, occasional.

conflict *vb.* oppose, clash, contend: *It seems obvious that your ideas about bringing up children conflict with mine.* *n.* **1.** fight, battle, struggle, encounter, engagement: *We must recognize the eternal conflict between right and wrong.* **2.** controversy, disagreement, contest: *I don't want to be caught in the middle of a conflict between political enemies.* **ant.** *vb.* agree, harmonize, concur, coincide. *n.* agreement, harmony, concurrence.

conform *vb.* **1.** comply, submit, yield, obey: *If you wish to remain a member of this club, you must conform to the rules.* **2.** agree, correspond: *The work you are now doing does not conform to our plan.* **ant. 1.** rebel. **2.** disagree, vary.

confuse *vb.* **1.** puzzle, perplex, bewilder, mystify, baffle, mislead: *The directions for putting the bicycle together confused my father.* **2.** mistake, mix up, jumble: *My aunt is often confused with my mother, whom she resembles closely.* **ant. 1.** enlighten, edify, illuminate, clarify. **2.** differentiate, distinguish.

confusion   *n.*   **1.** perplexity, bewilderment, uncertainty: *At first, there was some confusion among the actors as to where they should stand on stage.* **2.** disorder, mess, muss, turmoil, upset: *Your belongings are in such a state of confusion that I don't see how you can find anything.* **ant. 1.** enlightenment, understanding, comprehension. **2.** organization, tidiness.

congregate   *vb.* meet, gather, convene, foregather: *All of the teachers congregated in the lobby before going into the auditorium.* **ant.** disperse, scatter, dissipate, dispel.

congress   *n.* legislature, parliament, assembly: *Last year we attended the second annual congress of the new association.*

conjunction   *n.* junction, link, combination, connection: *The conjunction of the two opposing parties quickly resolved the issue.* **ant.** disconnection, separation, diversion, separation.

connect   *vb.*   **1.** unite, join, link, combine: *The front of our train was connected to the rear cars of the train in the station.* **2.** associate, relate: *Somehow, I failed to connect her quitting so suddenly with the disappearance of the vase.* **ant. 1.** disconnect, disjoin. **2.** dissociate, disassociate.

connection   *n.*   **1.** junction, union, link; bond, tie: *There was a loose connection that prevented the radio from working.* **2.** association, relationship, bond, tie: *I no longer have any connection with that company.* **ant. 2.** dissociation, disassociation.

conquer   *vb.*   **1.** succeed, win, gain, achieve: *The army conquered the fort in two days.* **2.** defeat, overcome, overpower, overcome, subdue: *It may be years before medicine will be able to conquer cancer. The small force conquered the enemy in hard fighting.* **ant. 2.** surrender, yield.

conquest   *n.* triumph, victory: *The conquest over infantile paralysis was gained only after many years.* **ant.** failure, surrender.

conscientious   *adj.* honest, upright, scrupulous, straight, straightforward, incorruptible: *Bob is a conscientious worker and will be very successful in whatever he does.* **ant.** irresponsible, careless, slovenly.

conscious   *adj.*   **1.** aware: *I suddenly became conscious of a slow, scratching sound at the window.* **2.** awake, sensible: *When Marilyn became conscious again after the blow on her head, she recognized her mother beside her.*

3. deliberate, intentional, purposeful: *I don't like him, so I make a conscious effort to avoid him.* **ant. 1.** unaware, insensitive. **2.** asleep, insensible, comatose. **3.** careless, indifferent, slack, negligent.

consent *vb.* agree, permit, allow, let, assent: *I consented to Laura's going to the movies with a friend.* *n.* permission, agreement, assent: *You have my consent to leave school early today.* **ant.** *vb.* refuse, dissent. *n.* refusal, dissent.

consequence *n.* **1.** result, outcome, effect, issue: *Eugene was rude in class and, as a consequence, was reprimanded by the teacher.* **2.** importance, significance, value: *Zeke's father is a man of some consequence in this town.* **ant. 1.** cause, impetus.

conservative *adj.* **1.** reactionary, right-wing, conventional: *The conservative members of the town council refused to allow men on the beach without tops for their bathing suits.* **2.** moderate, cautious, careful: *After the accident, Jed became a much more conservative driver.* **ant. 1.** liberal, radical. **2.** reckless, rash, adventurous, foolhardy.

conserve *vb.* preserve, keep, retain: *When I ask Alexa why she lies about in the sun all day, she says she's conserving her energy.* **ant.** squander, waste, use.

consider *vb.* **1.** study, think about, deliberate, reflect on, contemplate: *The committee agreed to consider Janet's request for an increase in salary.* **2.** think of, regard, look upon, judge, estimate: *Shirley had never considered Tom to be particularly good-looking.* **ant. 1.** ignore, disregard, disdain.

considerable *adj.* **1.** quite a lot, much, a great deal: *There was a considerable amount of snow last winter. The complaints from the public were considerable.* **2.** worthwhile, noteworthy, important, significant: *Dr. Einstein was a man of considerable accomplishments.*

considerate *adj.* kind, thoughtful, polite: *If you want to become a nurse, you must be considerate of others.* **ant.** inconsiderate, thoughtless, selfish.

consideration *n.* **1.** thoughtfulness, kindness, kindliness, concern, courtesy, politeness, sympathy, empathy: *It was Mark's consideration for other people that made him an outstanding social worker.* **2.** attention, thought, reflection, study: *I'll give that matter immediate consideration.* **3.** payment, fee, pay, compensation: *For a small consideration, the steward will serve your meals in your cabin.*

consistent *adj.* **1.** agreeing, compatible, harmonious: *Consistent with your wishes, I have asked that the meeting take place tomorrow.* **2.** regular, expected, faithful: *He might have been irresponsible about repaying debts to the bank, but he was always consistent about returning money to his friends.* **ant. 1.** contrary, opposed, antagonistic. **2.** inconsistent, erratic, eccentric.

consolation *n.* solace, comfort, sympathy: *It's been such a consolation to know that you were there when I needed you.* **ant.** discouragement, discomfort, burden.

console *vb.* solace, comfort, sympathize with: *When Kitty's dog died, her father consoled her by giving her a new puppy.* **ant.** disturb, upset.

conspicuous *adj.* noticeable, visible, clear, prominent, obvious, outstanding: *Steve made himself conspicuous by wearing a bright-green tie and a lavender shirt.* **ant.** inconspicuous, neutral.

conspire *vb.* plot, plan, scheme, intrigue: *The gang conspired to steal the car.*

constant *adj.* **1.** unchanging, fixed, stable, invariable, unchangeable: *The constant sunshine in the desert made me long for clouds and rain.* **2.** loyal, faithful, steadfast, true, staunch, devoted, steady, firm: *My constant companion during those years was Arthur.* **ant. 1.** irregular, off-and-on, periodic. **2.** occasional, infrequent.

constitute *vb.* **1.** make up, compose, form: *People once thought that all matter was constituted of four elements —earth, air, fire, and water.* **2.** found, establish, create, organize: *The courts are a duly constituted authority for dispensing justice.* **3.** delegate, appoint, commission, authorize: *My father was constituted ambassador to Ethiopia.*

constitution *n.* **1.** code, law: *The U.S. Constitution has been put to some severe tests during the last decade.* **2.** health, physique, vitality: *With your constitution, you should be able to eat anything.*

construct *vb.* build, erect, raise: *The prefabricated home was constructed in two days by four workmen.* **ant.** destroy, demolish, raze.

construction *n.* building, raising, fabricating: *The construction of this building is fireproof.*

constructive *adj.* helpful, useful, valuable: *After your constructive comments, I rewrote the paper and it got an "A."* **ant.** destructive, ruinous.

consult *vb.* confer, discuss, deliberate: *In the future, I think we ought to consult together about what we tell to the newspapers.*

consume *vb.* **1.** use, use up, exhaust, expend; eat, devour: *The people in this country consume more sugar than those of any other country.* **2.** destroy, devastate: *She had a consuming passion for Elvis Presley. The barn was quickly consumed by the flames.*

consumer *n.* buyer, user, purchaser: *When the wholesale prices increase, the consumer is the one who pays more in the end.*

contact *n.* touching, meeting: *The contact at this electrical connection is faulty.*

contain *vb.* hold, be composed of, include: *This clause in the contract contains the essence of the agreement. This cereal contains a lot of protein.*

contaminate *vb.* pollute, soil, dirty, corrupt, infect, poison: *The nearby sewer pipe contaminated our drinking water.*

contemplate *vb.* **1.** think about, consider, study, deliberate on *or* over, reflect upon: *Desmond was contemplating the outcome of the trial.* **2.** intend, plan: *Do you contemplate correcting your behavior?* **3.** view, look at, regard, observe: *Irene was contemplating her reflection in the mirror.*

contemplative *adj.* thoughtful, meditative, studious, pensive: *My uncle looked contemplative, so I didn't want to disturb him.* **ant.** indifferent, inattentive, thoughtless.

contemporary *adj.* **1.** contemporaneous, simultaneous, co-existing, coexistent: *Gilbert Stuart, the artist, was contemporary with George Washington, whose portrait he painted several times.* **2.** modern, up-to-date, fashionable: *The room was decorated in contemporary style.* **ant. 1.** antecedent; succeeding.

contempt *n.* scorn, disdain, malice: *Who can feel anything but contempt for a man who has betrayed the trust placed in him?* **ant.** admiration, approbation.

contemptible *adj.* low, base, mean, detestable, miserable: *Stealing money from the blind beggar was the most contemptible thing you've ever done.* **ant.** admirable, honorable.

contemptuous *adj.* scornful, disdainful, insolent, sneering: *The woman gave a contemptuous look at the man rummaging about in the trash can.* **ant.** humble, modest, self-effacing.

contend vb. **1.** combat, dispute, contest: *A teacher sometimes has to contend with students who misbehave.* **2.** claim, assert, maintain, argue: *The lawyer contended that his client was innocent.*

content adj. happy, satisfied, pleased, contented: *Sam wasn't content until he was sure that all the children were safe.* **ant.** dissatisfied, restless, discontented.

contest n. competition, match, tournament: *The seventh grade won the contest for the best traffic safety poster.* vb. dispute, oppose: *The miner contested the right of anyone to trespass on his property.*

continual adj. regular, consecutive, connected: *The hammering on the door was continual throughout the night.* **ant.** irregular, intermittent, occasional.

continue vb. **1.** persist: *If you continue in your present manner, you will be punished for it.* **2.** proceed, resume, recommence, renew: *The trial continued after an hour out for lunch.* **3.** endure, last, remain, stay: *After he was discovered to be dishonest, the manager realized he couldn't continue in his job.* **ant.** discontinue, stop, cease, interrupt.

continuous adj. uninterrupted, continuing, ceaseless, incessant, unceasing, constant, unending: *There was a continuous flow of water from the broken pipe.* **ant.** irregular, intermittent, sporadic.

contract n. agreement, bargain, pact; treaty: *The contract between the company and the union was signed yesterday.* vb. **1.** agree: *We contracted with our neighbor's son to mow the lawn each week.* **2.** diminish, reduce, condense, shrink: *The armadillo contracts into a little ball when it is threatened.* **3.** get, acquire, come down with: *I contracted a bad cold while out fishing.* **ant.** vb. **2.** expand, swell, enlarge.

contrary adj. **1.** opposed, opposite, disagreeing, conflicting, opposing: *If you say he should be released and I say he should be jailed, we obviously hold contrary opinions.* **2.** disagreeable, hostile, perverse, stubborn, headstrong: *If you agree with me, then why are you being so contrary?* **ant.** **1.** similar, like, complementary. **2.** obliging, agreeable, tractable.

contrast n. difference, distinction, disagreement: *There is a marked contrast between what you are saying today and what you said before.* vb. distinguish, differentiate, contradict, differ: *One of our exam questions was to con-*

trast the American Revolution with the Russian Revolution. **ant.** *n.* similarity, agreement, likeness.

contribute *vb.* donate, give, bestow, grant, provide, offer: *Every year I contribute money to charity. Eleanor contributes to her mother's support.* **ant.** withhold, deny.

contribution *n.* donation, gift, grant, offering: *A contribution to the church is deductible for tax purposes. Dick made no contribution to today's history class.*

contrive *vb.* **1.** invent, make, form, hatch: *We must contrive a plan to get even with those children who stole our bicycles.* **2.** maneuver, manage, arrange: *Despite visiting hours being over, I contrived to see my sister in the hospital.*

control *vb.* **1.** manage, direct, rule, dominate, command: *My uncle controls four companies.* **2.** check, restrain, curb, manage: *That woman couldn't control her children and they annoyed everyone in the waiting room. n.* **1.** management, direction, rule, mastery, command: *After buying large blocks of its shares in the stock market, Cawdry gained control of the zipper company.* **2.** check, restraint: *You will have to keep yourself under control if you want to sit in this theater.*

controversy *n.* dispute, argument, quarrel, debate, disagreement: *A controversy over the new teacher's appointment arose at the school board meeting.* **ant.** agreement, harmony, accord.

convenience *n.* **1.** availability, accessibility: *We all know the convenience of having a post office nearby.* **2.** assistance, help, aid, service, benefit: *When you live in the country, a car is a great convenience.* **ant. 2.** inconvenience.

convenient *adj.* accessible, handy, nearby, available, ready: *I always keep a fire extinguisher in a convenient place.* **ant.** inconvenient, awkward.

convention *n.* **1.** conference, meeting, assembly: *The political convention nominated Sarah's uncle for state senator.* **2.** custom, practice; rule, law: *The karate contestants followed the convention of bowing to each other politely before and after the match.*

conventional *adj.* everyday, common, usual, regular, habitual, accustomed, routine: *Our conventional arrangement calls for customers to pay on receipt of merchandise.* **ant.** unusual, extraordinary, exotic, bizarre.

conversation *n.* talk, discussion, chat, dialogue: *Please try to limit your phone conversations to five minutes' duration.*

converse *vb.* talk, chat, discuss, speak: *My mother and the principal conversed in such low tones that I couldn't hear what they were saying.*

convert *vb.* **1.** change, alter, transform, turn: *The alchemists tried to convert lead into gold.* **2.** win over: *I was converted from Christianity to Zoroastrianism, then to Taoism, Buddhism, and Shintoism by various teachers.*

convey *vb.* bear, carry, communicate: *"Disgust" doesn't convey my feeling toward her; perhaps "disappointment" would be more accurate.*

conveyance *n.* car, truck, van; train; plane: *By what conveyance other than the prairie schooner could the pioneers have traveled westward?*

convince *vb.* persuade, induce, assure: *You could never convince me that even a little fib isn't really a lie.*

cool *adj.* **1.** chilly; cold, frosty, wintry, icy, frigid: *The summer evenings are always cool in the mountains.* **2.** calm, composed, quiet, collected: *When everyone about her would get excited about something, Irena always remained cool.* **3.** unfriendly, distant, chilly: *After we broke her window with the baseball, Mrs. Thompson gave us a cool reception.* *vb.* **1.** chill: *You should cool the wine before serving it.* **2.** calm, quiet, moderate: *My enthusiasm for the job cooled when I found out how little it paid.* **ant.** *adj.* **1.** warm, hot, heated. **2.** excited, overwrought, hysterical. **3.** friendly, warm, outgoing. *vb.* **1.** warm, heat. **2.** excite, agitate.

cooperate *vb.* **1.** join forces, unite, combine: *If everyone cooperates, we can get the work done more quickly.* **2.** contribute, help, support: *We tried to get the mule into the barn, but it refused to cooperate.*

copious *adj.* plentiful, abundant, ample: *Copious supplies of grain were shipped from the Midwest last year.* **ant.** scarce, meager, scanty, paltry.

copy *n.* reproduction, imitation, facsimile, duplicate, likeness; carbon, print: *Please send me a copy of your article.* *vb.* reproduce, duplicate, imitate: *You ought to copy over your paper before handing it in—it's so messy.* **ant.** *n.* original.

cordial *adj.* friendly, polite, genial, affable, warm-hearted:

Even though she was very cordial, the lady in the blue house over there refused to buy an encyclopedia from me. **ant.** hostile, unfriendly, ill-tempered.

core *n.* center, kernel, heart: *Some people think that the core of the apple is more nutritious than the pulp.* **ant.** outside, surface.

corporation *n.* company, firm, business, conglomerate, organization: *Many of the large corporations in the U.S. are listed on the Stock Exchange.*

corpse *n.* body, cadaver, remains, carcass: *The corpse of an old man was found buried in the woods.*

correct *adj.* true, accurate, right, proper, precise, exact: *The only version that is correct is the one prepared by our own students.* *vb.* **1.** set right, rectify, emend; better: *The teacher corrected our papers before handing them back to us.* **2.** warn, caution, rebuke, admonish, punish: *Each time she said something they didn't like, her parents corrected her.* **ant.** *adj.* incorrect, wrong, inexact, erroneous.

correspond *vb.* **1.** match, compare, agree, coincide, fit, suit: *The two parts of this machine don't correspond.* **2.** communicate, write: *While I was away at school, I corresponded regularly with my brothers and sisters.* **ant.** **1.** diverge, differ, vary.

corridor *n.* hall, hallway, passage, passageway; foyer, lobby: *In the old days, you could leave your shoes in the corridor outside a hotel room and you'd get them back shined in the morning; today, you'd be lucky to get them back at all!*

corrode *vb.* eat away, erode, wear away: *Salt water—even the salt air near the seashore—causes brass to corrode.*

corrupt *adj.* **1.** dishonest, untrustworthy, crooked, treacherous, unscrupulous: *Before my uncle became mayor and cleaned things up, this town had the most corrupt officials you could find.* **2.** wicked, debased, low, evil, perverted: *The minister preached against all of the corrupt practices among some of the people.* *vb.* bribe, demoralize, degrade: *The gangsters used money, then threats, to try to corrupt the police chief.* **ant.** *adj.* **1.** honest, upright, scrupulous. **2.** pure, sanctified. *vb.* purify, edify, sanctify.

cost *n.* **1.** price, value, charge: *What is the cost of that puppy in the window?* **2.** sacrifice, loss, penalty, damage: *Risking the cost of our friendship, I must tell you that you are very mean to your mother.*

costly   *adj.* expensive, dear, high-priced: *Food becomes more costly every day.* **ant.** inexpensive, low-cost, cheap.

costume   *n.* clothing, dress, attire, clothes, garb, apparel: *For the school pageant, Sofia came in a costume made from peacock feathers.*

couch   *n.* sofa, davenport, settee, loveseat: *I sat on the couch in the living room while Penny left to get me some tea.*

council   *n.* committee, board, cabinet: *The town council has met to decide about new taxes.*

counsel   *n.* **1.** advice, opinion, guidance: *Your counsel in matters relating to marriage is meaningless, since you were never married.* **2.** lawyer, attorney, counselor: *If learned counsel will permit, I should like to cross-examine this witness.* *vb.* advise, guide: *He counseled me to remain quiet in court.*

count   *vb.* **1.** enumerate, number, reckon, total, compute, tally: *I counted 13 buns in the bag from the bakery—a baker's dozen.* **2.** amount to something, add up, figure: *Your score on the last test won't count because you copied the answers from a neighbor.* *n.* sum, total, number: *Take a count of the books on that shelf.*

countenance   *n.* **1.** face, visage, aspect, appearance: *I like to see the smiling countenances of my students each morning.* **2.** approval, support, encouragement, assistance: *I cannot give countenance for such activity.* *vb.* approve, support, favor, encourage, assist: *I refuse to countenance absence from school to watch a baseball game.* **ant.** *vb.* prohibit, forbid.

counteract   *vb.* offset, thwart, counterbalance, neutralize, defeat: *When you misbehave, you counteract any good feelings I had for you.*

counterfeit   *adj.* **1.** fake, false, fraudulent, spurious, false: *I thought we had become millionaires when the money was found, but it turned out to be counterfeit.* **2.** pretended, pretend, false, fake, sham: *Your counterfeit expression of love doesn't fool me.* *n.* forgery, imitation, fake: *This document is a counterfeit.* *vb.* **1.** forge, fake, falsify, imitate, copy: *The police found the men counterfeiting ten- and twenty-dollar bills in the basement.* **2.** pretend, sham: *At the funeral, those who were glad that George was gone counterfeited great sorrow.* **ant.** *adj.* genuine, real, authentic.

country   *n.* **1.** nation, state: *How many foreign countries have you traveled to?* **2.** farmland, forest, exurbia: *We* *gave up our apartment in the city and bought a house in the country.*

couple *n.* pair; team, brace: *A young couple just moved into the neighborhood. Hitch a couple of horses to the wagon.*

courage *n.* bravery, spirit, daring, fearlessness, valor, mettle, pluck: *It took a lot of courage for Jimmy, who is only ten, to jump into the swimming pool to save his six-year-old sister.* **ant.** cowardice, fearfulness, weakness.

courageous *adj.* brave, fearless, dauntless, intrepid, plucky, daring, heroic, valorous: *The courageous men who defended the fort against great odds were relieved to see the cavalry arrive.* **ant.** cowardly, fearful, timid.

course *n.* **1.** advance, progress, passage: *In the course of life it often becomes necessary to suffer hardship for the sake of others.* **2.** direction, way, bearing: *When I saw the Empire State Building, I knew we were on the wrong course for Miami.*

courteous *adj.* polite, well-mannered, gracious, respectful: *I don't expect people to bow and scrape, but they should at least be courteous.* **ant.** rude, impolite, discourteous.

courtesy *n.* politeness, graciousness, respect: *When I visited my friends in Sweden, they showed me every courtesy.* **ant.** rudeness, discourtesy.

cover *vb.* **1.** overlay, spread: *Please cover the furniture to keep the dust off.* **2.** conceal, hide; mask: *Miriam covered the scratch on the table with a lamp.* **3.** include, embrace: *The term "American" is used to cover all citizens of the United States.* *n.* **1.** lid, top, stopper, covering: *Evelyn couldn't get the cover off the jar.* **2.** shelter, protection, refuge: *During the thundershower, we sought cover under an overhanging rock.* **ant.** *vb.* uncover, expose, reveal.

coward *n.* milksop, milquetoast, dastard, cad: *He was such a coward that he was afraid to go outside alone even in daylight.* **ant.** hero.

coy *adj.* bashful, shy, timid, modest: *If you want another helping of food, don't be coy—just ask for it.* **ant.** bold, brash, forward.

crack *vb.* break, snap, split: *Just as Walter was looking at himself in the mirror, it cracked.* *n.* **1.** snap: *There was the* crack! *of the rifle and the rabbit lay dead.* **2.** break, flaw, split, fissure: *Be careful not to drink from the side of the glass with the crack in it.*

cracker   *n.* biscuit, wafer, saltine: *Cheese and crackers make a good midnight snack.*

craft   *n.*   **1.** skill, ability, talent, expertness: *Have you ever seen an expert cabinetmaker exercise his craft?* **2.** cunning, deceit, trickery, guile: *Charles used every bit of his craft to get Gennie to marry him.* **3.** handicraft, trade, occupation, profession: *The harpooner has not plied his craft for many years.*

crafty   *adj.* cunning, clever, shrewd, skillful, sly, tricky: *That crafty little beggar of a brother of mine knows how to steal affection although he's only three.* **ant.** guileless, gullible, open, naive.

cranky   *adj.* bad-tempered, short-tempered, cross, testy, irritable: *Many people become cranky when they are tired, or hungry, or both.* **ant.** good-natured, cheerful, happy.

crash   *vb.* shatter, smash, dash: *It was a miracle that you weren't even scratched when the car crashed into the wall.* *n.* smash, smashup: *Twenty people were hurt in the crash.*

crave   *vb.* desire, yearn for, want, long for, hunger for: *That little kitten craves affection.* **ant.** renounce, relinquish.

crawl   *vb.* creep, worm along: *I found the most beautiful caterpillar, crawling on the window.*

crazy   *adj.* mad, insane, lunatic: *You're crazy if you think I'm going to the party without Judy.* **ant.** sane, rational, lucid.

creak   *vb.* squeak: *The old iron gate creaked as we opened it.*

create   *vb.* **1.** originate, invent, beget: *The composer created a new piece to honor his parents on their anniversary.* **2.** make, form, construct, design: *The early pioneers created farms and homes out of the wilderness.* **ant.** destroy, abolish.

credible   *adj.* believable, conceivable: *The police found the suspect's story credible, so they released him.* **ant.** incredible, unbelievable, inconceivable.

credit   *n.*   **1.** belief, trust, faith: *How can anyone place any credit on what you say when they know how you lied in the past?* **2.** honor, merit, recognition: *Philip and Peter deserve a lot of credit for taking care of their aged mother.* **3.** repute, reputation, name, standing, rank: *My credit is good enough at the bank to get a loan for a new car.* *vb.* **1.** believe, accept, trust: *Even though I credit* *your explanation of the flat tire, you shouldn't have been out so late.* **2.** attribute: *The museum experts credited the painting to my grandfather.* **ant.** *n., vb.* discredit.

creditable *adj.* praiseworthy, worthy: *The high school band gave a very creditable performance during the intermission.* **ant.** discreditable, dishonorable, shameful.

creed *n.* belief, credo, doctrine, faith: *No one should be discriminated against because of race, color, or creed.*

creek *n.* stream, brook, rivulet, spring: *After a heavy spring rain, this creek turns into a raging river.*

crime *n.* wrongdoing, misconduct, wrong, offense; infraction, violation, misdemeanor, felony: *Possession of narcotics by unauthorized people is a crime.*

criminal *adj.* illegal, unlawful, felonious: *Maltreating a child is a criminal offense.* *n.* crook, gangster, lawbreaker, outlaw, felon, convict, culprit, offender, delinquent: *The escaped criminals were being sought by the police of three states.*

cripple *vb.* maim, injure, hurt, damage: *The fall from the second-story window crippled him for life.*

crisis *n.* emergency, climax: *The doctor said that my aunt had passed the crisis and would get better quickly. There was a crisis at the bank when they found that $50,000 was missing.*

critic *n.* **1.** judge, reviewer, commentator: *Brooks Atkinson was the drama critic of* The New York Times *for many years.* **2.** faultfinder, censor, slanderer, defamer: *I may make a mistake once in a while, but who appointed you as my critic?*

critical *adj.* **1.** faultfinding, carping, condemning, reproachful, disapproving: *Please stop nagging me: you have no reason to be so critical of everything I do or say.* **2.** dangerous, risky, hazardous, perilous: *His health was in critical condition and the doctor ordered him to rest.* **3.** crucial, important, decisive: *The timing in putting a new product on the market can be critical.* **ant. 3.** unimportant, trivial.

crooked *adj.* **1.** bent, twisted, curved, hooked, zigzag: *A crooked path wove among the boulders to the pond.* **2.** dishonest, criminal, corrupt: *The directors were embarrassed when they discovered that the treasurer was crooked and had stolen money.* **ant. 1.** straight. **2.** honest, upright.

crop *n.* harvest, produce, yield: *Because of lack of rainfall* *the crop will be poor this year.* vb. cut, lop, mow, clip: *I think you look better with your hair cropped short.*

cross vb. **1.** traverse: *Don't cross the street against the lights.* **2.** mingle, mix, interbreed: *If you cross a scottie with a poodle you get a "scoodle."* **3.** thwart, frustrate, oppose: *Once Reginald has his mind made up, it's not a good idea to cross him.* adj. irritable, annoyed, testy, cranky, ill-natured, bad-tempered, snappish; mean, angry: *Our teacher was very cross with those children who hadn't done their homework.* **ant.** adj. good-natured, cheerful.

crouch vb. stoop, duck: *We crouched low behind the bushes so we wouldn't be seen.* **ant.** stand.

crowd n. throng, swarm, host, flock, mob, pack: *There was a crowd of people waiting in front of the White House to see the President.* vb. **1.** throng, swarm, mob: *We crowded onto the football field after the game.* **2.** squeeze, cramp, pack; shove, push: *We were crowded in the tiny cabin.*

crown n. **1.** circlet, coronet, tiara: *The princess wore a gold crown studded with precious stones.* **2.** head, skull: *Jack fell down and broke his crown.* vb. coronate: *She was crowned queen in a ceremony that lasted for seven hours.*

crude adj. **1.** unfinished, rude, raw, coarse: *On the workbench stood a crude sculpture of a figure that I couldn't recognize until I was told it was of my sister.* **2.** unpolished, unrefined, coarse, graceless, boorish: *Rennie's manners are very crude.* **ant. 1.** finished, polished. **2.** refined, genteel, cultured.

cruel adj. heartless, mean, merciless, unmerciful, pitiless, ruthless, brutal, inhuman: *I think it's cruel to forbid your little brother to go to the movies with us.* **ant.** kindhearted, compassionate, merciful.

cruelty n. meanness, harshness, brutality, savagery: *Cruelty to animals is against the law.* **ant.** kindness, compassion.

crush vb. break, smash, crash: *The machine quickly crushed all of the stones into smaller sizes suitable for driveways and other uses.*

cry vb. **1.** shout, yell, yowl, scream, roar, bellow: *When I saw the rock falling I cried out as loudly as I could.* **2.** weep, wail, sob, bawl: *When the baby cries, either feed her, change her, or make sure nothing is hurting her.* **ant. 2.** laugh.

cultivate *vb.* **1.** farm, till, plant, seed, harvest: *Although he owns about 1,000 acres of farmland, Mr. Snyder cultivates only half of that.* **2.** educate, refine, teach, nurture: *Our parents cultivated in all their children a desire to learn and the habit of reading.*

cultural *adj.* educational, civilizing, instructive, elevating: *Living in a town with a university means that there are many cultural activities available—theater, courses in many subjects, community projects in health, and so on.*

culture *n.* **1.** education, learning, humanism, civilization: *Western and eastern cultures differ widely.* **2.** refinement, breeding, cultivation, upbringing: *From her bad manners and rude behavior you could tell at once that she was totally lacking in culture.*

cunning *adj.* **1.** clever, tricky, wily, foxy, crafty: *Even at the age of three, Betsy was cunning enough to get what she wanted from anyone.* **2.** skillful, clever, ingenious: *That box was carved by a cunning hand from a solid piece of wood.* *n.* **1.** skill, ability: *Her cunning was matched only by her beauty.* **2.** craft, wiliness, foxiness, shrewdness, cleverness, slyness, deceit: *Another example of his cunning was the way he was able to persuade people to give him their money for his fake schemes.* **ant.** *adj.* **1.** simple, naive, gullible. *n.* **2.** simplicity, openness.

curb *n.* check, restraint, control: *The new tax law was an effective curb on expense accounts for executives.* *vb.* check, restrain, control: *It required stern measures to curb waste of the state's natural resources.* **ant.** *vb.* encourage, foster.

cure *n.* remedy, treatment, medicine: *People used to think that sulfur and molasses were a cure for almost anything.* *vb.* heal, remedy: *The salesman told us that snake oil would cure my broken leg.*

curious *adj.* **1.** inquiring, inquisitive, interested; nosy, prying: *If you weren't so curious about things that don't concern you, you wouldn't get into so much trouble.* **2.** peculiar, odd, strange, unusual, queer: *There was a curious animal with a red plume and a white tail and blue fur sitting on the fence.* **ant.** **1.** incurious, indifferent, uninterested.

current *adj.* present, up-to-date, modern: *The current craze for horror movies is bad for children.* *n.* stream, tide: *The current carried the sailboat down the river and out* *into the sea.* **ant.** *adj.* out-of-date, outmoded, old-fashioned.

curse *n.* **1.** oath, ban: *The witch's curse caused the children to shout and dance wildly.* **2.** trouble, misfortune, evil: *The rain, originally a blessing, turned into a curse after two weeks without letup.* *vb.* swear, denounce, condemn: *When the police finally caught the thief, he cursed them for finding him.* **ant.** *n.* **1.** benediction. **2.** blessing, boon, advantage.

curtain *n.* drape, drapery, shade, blind: *A dark curtain over the window prevented any light from entering the room.*

cushion *n.* pad, pillow: *There was a comfortable red cushion at each end of the couch.* *vb.* absorb, check: *This foam rubber is packed into the box to cushion the shock during shipping.*

custom *n.* habit, practice, rule: *By custom, the entire family would have dinner together at Thanksgiving.*

customary *adj.* usual, common, habitual, regular: *The customary procedure is to ring the bell and wait for someone to open the door.* **ant.** unusual, rare, unaccustomed.

customer *n.* client, patron, buyer: *The shop closed at six o'clock and no customers were allowed in after five-thirty.*

cut *vb.* **1.** gash, slash, prick, nick: *I cut my finger on the point of the blade.* **2.** sever, slice, carve, cleave, slit: *That knife isn't sharp enough to cut the bread.* **3.** mow, lop, chop, crop: *The grass was cut once already this week.* **4.** reduce, lower, lessen: *The government may cut spending in order to curb inflation.* *vb. phr.* **cut back** reduce, decrease: *The budget for school supplies was cut back by 20 percent.* **cut in** interrupt, interfere, butt in: *When the teacher was talking, Phil cut in to ask if he could leave the room.* **cut off** stop, cease, end, terminate: *The moderator cut off debate after 20 minutes.* **cut short** finish, stop, quit, end: *The performance was cut short by the power failure.* *n.* incision, slash, gash, slit: *The nurse bandaged the cut on Janet's finger.*

dagger   *n.* blade, stiletto, knife: *The assassin plunged the dagger into the back of his victim.*

dainty   *adj.* delicate, petite, pretty, beautiful, graceful, fine, elegant: *Only Cinderella's dainty foot would fit into the glass slipper.* **ant.** clumsy, oafish, lumpish.

dam   *n.* levee, dike, barrier: *The beavers built a dam across our stream and flooded part of our land.* *vb.* obstruct, block, stop; check, slow: *A huge tree fell down in the storm and dammed up the drain.*

damage   *n.* impairment, injury, harm; destruction: *The hurricane caused millions of dollars worth of damage along the coast.* *vb.* impair, injure, harm, mar: *The telephone lines were damaged when the truck hit the utility pole. Gossiping about a person can damage his reputation.* **ant.** *vb.* repair, rebuild, improve, fix.

damn   *vb.* condemn: *Because of his poor performance in the movie, he was damned to unemployment.*

damp   *adj.* moist, dank, humid: *When the weather is damp, I can't open this closet door because it sticks.* *n.* moisture, dampness, dankness, humidity, wetness: *The damp in the walls makes the plaster mildew.* **ant.** *adj.* dry, arid.

dampen   *vb.* **1.** moisten, wet: *It is better to dampen clothes before ironing them.* **2.** slow, retard, inhibit, moderate: *The noise of the traffic outside was dampened by the thick stone walls.*

danger   *n.* peril, risk, hazard, uncertainty, threat: *Weakened by the long swim from the boat, the boys were in danger of drowning in the swift current.* **ant.** safety, security.

dangerous   *adj.* perilous, hazardous, risky, uncertain, unsafe: *It's very dangerous to play close to the road.* **ant.** safe, secure.

dare   *vb.* **1.** brave, risk: *The acrobat dared to walk the tightrope over the river, 200 feet below.* **2.** challenge: *Rosemarie dared George to swim across the lake.*

daring   *adj.* brave, fearless, intrepid, courageous, bold, valiant: *Entering the lion's cage carrying only a chair and whip is very daring.* *n.* bravery, courage, valor: *Vincent's* *reputation for daring began when he saved three children from a burning house.* **ant.** *n.* cowardice, timidity.

dark *adj.* **1.** shadowy, unlit, murky, gloomy, dim, dusky, shaded, sunless, black: *The half of the earth facing away from the sun is always dark.* **2.** dismal, sad, gloomy, unhappy: *The period before the war was a dark time for many people.* **ant. 1.** light, illuminated, bright. **2.** cheerful, happy.

darling *n.* beloved, dear, sweetheart, favorite: *Anthony was the darling of all the teachers. adj.* dear, beloved: *Richard's mother called him "Darling baby" until he was 25 years old.*

dart *n.* barb, arrow, missile: *The dart hit the target but missed the bull's-eye. vb.* run, scurry, scamper, hasten, dash: *From the top of the tall building, the people on the street below looked like ants darting to and fro.*

dash *vb.* **1.** strike, smash, beat, break: *In the darkness, we could hear the surf dashing on the rocks ahead of the ship.* **2.** run, scurry, scamper, rush, dart: *At rush hour, thousands of people dashed down the stairs into the subway. n.* bit, sprinkling, scattering, pinch, hint: *Add just a dash of pepper before serving.*

data *n.* information, facts, evidence, statistics: *We still have too little data about the habits of the whale to draw any conclusions.*

daunt *vb.* frighten, discourage, intimidate: *Whenever I went to see the president of the company about a raise, I felt his manner so daunting that I forgot to ask him.* **ant.** encourage, enspirit.

dauntless *adj.* brave, fearless, undaunted, bold, intrepid, courageous, valiant: *Our dauntless navy won more battles with fighter planes than with the ships' guns.* **ant.** cowardly, timid, fearful.

dawn *n.* **1.** sunrise, daybreak: *The duel was arranged: it would be pistols at dawn in the park.* **2.** beginning, origin, start: *At the dawn of civilization, man already used a highly developed language.* **ant. 1.** sunset, dusk, nightfall. **2.** end, finish, conclusion.

daydream *vb.* muse, woolgather: *You'll never amount to anything if all you do is daydream.*

daze *vb.* stun, confuse, perplex, puzzle: *The author was dazed by the publicity and fame his first novel had brought him. Roger was dazed by the blow he received on the head. n.* stupor, confusion, bewilderment: *I just* *walked around in a daze after learning about winning the scholarship.*

dazzle *vb.* astonish, bewilder, surprise, stupefy, stun, impress: *Victor, who had never met a movie star before, was dazzled by Dorothea's charm and beauty.*

dead *adj.* **1.** deceased, lifeless, defunct; gone, departed: *Janet forgot to water her violets for a week, and when she looked at them, they were dead. Donald's great grandfather has been dead for 20 years.* **2.** inert, motionless, still, inoperative, inoperable, inactive: *The engine went dead right in the middle of a highway traffic jam.* **ant. 1.** alive, animate. **2.** active, functioning.

deaden *vb.* numb, paralyze, anesthetize: *The ointment helped to deaden the pain of my sunburn.*

deadlock *n.* stalemate, standstill, impasse: *When neither management nor labor would yield in its demands or concessions, the situation reached a deadlock.*

deadly *adj.* **1.** fatal, lethal, deathly, mortal: *After the train wreck, deadly gas escaped from one of the tank cars and the nearby town was evacuated.* **2.** deathly, baleful: *Margaret's face turned deadly pale when she learned of the accident.*

deaf *adj.* **1.** unhearing, stone-deaf: *After the explosion, Tim was deaf in one ear for almost a week.* **2.** unheeding, unheedful, unaware, stubborn, inattentive, oblivious: *My father was deaf to my pleas for an increased allowance.* **ant. 2.** conscious, aware.

deal *vb.* **1.** treat, cope, act, attend: *Our former principal had methods for dealing with mischievous boys.* **2.** trade, barter, do business, buy and/or sell, bargain: *My company refuses to deal with anyone who isn't completely honest.* **3.** distribute, apportion, deliver, give: *I was dealt three aces and two kings.*

dear *adj.* **1.** loved, beloved, darling: *His dear wife would meet his train every evening.* **2.** expensive, costly, high-priced: *That new hat was much too dear for someone on my salary.* **ant. 1.** hateful. **2.** cheap, inexpensive, reasonable.

death *n.* demise, decease, passing, extinction: *The death of our dog was a sad occasion in the family.* **ant.** life.

debate *vb.* argue, dispute, contend, discuss: *We debated the merits of French and domestic wines until midnight.* *n.* discussion, dispute, argument, controversy: *The debate* *in the Senate over the new welfare bill went on for a week.* **ant.** *n.* agreement, accord.

debt   *n.* obligation, liability: *We owe a debt to our teachers, who are dedicated to improving us in every way.*

decay   *vb.* **1.** rot, spoil, decompose, molder: *If you don't keep fresh food under refrigeration, it will decay rapidly.* **2.** deteriorate, decline, wither, perish, die: *In the Dark Ages, western culture decayed so badly that there was little literature for several hundred years. n.* **1.** decline, downfall, collapse: *The decay of the Roman Empire was caused by internal corruption.* **2.** rot, decomposition, mold, rottenness: *Some bakeries add chemicals to their breads and rolls to retard decay.* **ant.** *vb.* grow, progress, flourish.

deceit   *n.* deceitfulness, deception, fraud, dishonesty, guile: *Because of the manager's reputation for deceit, nobody would patronize his restaurant.* **ant.** honesty, forthrightness, openness.

deceitful   *adj.* insincere, false, dishonest, fraudulent, deceptive: *It was deceitful of him to pretend to be so friendly and then tell everyone in town that I was nasty.* **ant.** honest, sincere.

deceive   *vb.* mislead, cheat, swindle, defraud, hoax, hoodwink, fool: *I was deceived by the girl's friendly manner and couldn't imagine she would do anything so underhanded.*

decent   *adj.* proper, becoming, fitting, appropriate, *Hortense's behavior has always been very decent.* **ant.** indecent, improper, indecorous, unsuitable.

deception   *n.* trickery, treachery, craftiness, deceit: *If he continues to practice every deception, he won't have any friends left at all.* **ant.** honesty, openness, frankness, probity.

deceptive   *adj.* deceiving, false, misleading, unreliable, tricky; deceitful, dishonest: *That pink lens gives a deceptive image of the true colors in the painting. Because of his deceptive dealings, the merchants asked my uncle to leave town.* **ant.** real, true, authentic.

decide   *vb.* determine, settle, choose, resolve: *We decided to leave at four o'clock to miss the weekend traffic.* **ant.** hesitate, waver.

decision   *n.* determination, resolution, settlement: *The judge's decision was final.*

declaration *n.* announcement, pronouncement, statement, assertion, affirmation, notice: *The company issued a declaration that it would seek greater profits from its real-estate holdings in the coming year.*

declare *vb.* say, state, proclaim, announce, pronounce, affirm, assert: *When he reached the age of 21, Edward declared that he would move to Chicago.* **ant.** deny, suppress.

decline *vb.* **1.** refuse, deny, reject: *Vernon's mother offered me some candy, but I declined.* **2.** lessen, deteriorate, weaken, fail, diminish: *Profits continued to decline after the company stopped advertising.* *n.* **1.** lessening, weakening, diminution: *After the accident, my brother's health went into a decline, but then he recovered completely.* **2.** descent, slope, incline, hill: *Soapbox cars, which have no motors, are always raced down a gentle decline.* **ant.** *vb.* **1.** agree, accept. **2.** improve, increase, grow. *n.* **1.** improvement.

decompose *vb.* rot, decay, molder: *By springtime, the autumn leaves were completely decomposed.*

decorate *vb.* **1.** ornament, paint, color, enhance: *The bedroom was decorated in different shades of blue.* **2.** furnish, furbish: *The old farmhouse was decorated with early American furniture.* **ant.** **1.** deface, mar.

decoration *n.* **1.** ornamentation, adornment, furnishing: *The decorations for our Christmas tree are stored in the attic.* **2.** medal, citation, award: *My father won seven decorations for bravery during the war.*

decrease *vb.* lessen, diminish, decline, dwindle: *The number of complaints about the new cars decreased after the manufacturer recalled them for repairs.* *n.* lessening, diminution, decline: *It will be a long time before we see any decrease in the cost of living.* **ant.** *vb.* increase, expand. *n.* increase, expansion.

decree *n.* edict, order, declaration: *The new government issued a decree that filling stations would be open only 12 hours a day.* *vb.* order, declare, announce: *The king decreed that all prisoners would have their sentences reduced.*

dedicate *vb.* **1.** consecrate, sanctify, hallow: *The grounds were dedicated as a cemetery for those who had died in the war.* **2.** set apart *or* aside, devote, assign: *He dedicated all of his free time to helping the elderly.*

deduct *vb.* subtract, eliminate, take away: *Taxpayers in the*

U.S. are allowed to deduct all interest payments from their gross incomes. **ant.** add.

deed *n.* **1.** act, action, achievement, feat: *For his deed of heroism in rescuing the little girl, the Boy Scout received a scholarship from the girl's father.* **2.** title, document, certificate: *After we met with the lawyers at the bank, we were given the deed to the house.*

deem *vb.* judge, determine, regard, consider, hold: *The boy's aunt was deemed unfit to care for him.*

deep *adj.* **1.** low; bottomless, unplumbed: *They say that this pool is so deep that it has no bottom.* **2.** serious, acute, bad, grave: *That boy will find himself in deep trouble one of these days.* **3.** profound, obscure: *I can see from your expression that you are thinking deep thoughts.* **4.** absorbed, involved: *The two men were deep in conversation, and I didn't want to interrupt.* *n.* ocean, sea: *Many brave men are asleep in the deep.* **ant.** *adj.* **1.** shallow.

deface *vb.* mar, scratch, disfigure, mutilate: *There is a large fine against anyone caught defacing public property.* **ant.** beautify, decorate.

defeat *vb.* **1.** overcome, conquer, vanquish, overthrow, suppress: *The small scouting patrol was completely defeated by the enemy's superior forces.* **2.** thwart, foil, spoil, frustrate: *The thundershower defeated our plans for a picnic.* *n.* conquest, overthrow: *Loss of the fighter plane spelled defeat for us.* **ant.** *vb.* **1.** surrender, submit, yield.

defect *n.* flaw, weakness, imperfection, blemish: *There was a defect in the new toaster, so we returned it and got our money back.* *vb.* desert, abandon, leave, forsake: *The men who defected from the work squad were all rounded up and punished.* **ant.** *n.* perfection, flawlessness. *vb.* join, support.

defective *adj.* flawed, faulty, inoperable, inoperative, imperfect: *That garage sold me a defective tire for my bicycle and it went flat in a week.* **ant.** perfect, flawless, faultless.

defend *vb.* **1.** protect, guard, safeguard, shield: *The main army went out into the battle and left only 50 men to defend the women and children in the fort.* **2.** uphold, maintain: *She tried to defend her son's behavior, but everyone knew he had been wrong.* **ant.** attack.

defense *n.* **1.** protection, resistance: *Until only recently,*

*man was unable to provide defense against certain dis-
eases.* **2.** trench, bulwark, fortification, fort, barricade,
rampart, fortress: *The orange crates were no defense
against the oncoming tanks.*

defer *vb.* delay, put off, postpone: *If you have to leave tomorrow afternoon, how can we defer the decision until
tomorrow night?* **ant.** hurry, expedite, speed.

defiant *adj.* antagonistic, obstinate, rebellious: *The students
were defiant when told that the sports program would be
eliminated.* **ant.** submissive, yielding.

defile *vb.* corrupt, pollute, debase: *Our drinking water has
been defiled by the sewage from the town up the river.*
ant. purify.

define *vb.* **1.** explain; designate, name, label: *This dictionary defines words very thoroughly.* **2.** limit, fix, mark off,
set off, distinguish: *I could see his outline defined against
the windowshade.*

definite *adj.* **1.** certain, sure, positive, determined: *Our
plans for Christmas are definite—we're having dinner
at your house.* **2.** clear, sharp, distinct, obvious, plain:
*There, in the stone, was the definite outline of a dino-
saur's foot.* **ant.** indefinite, undetermined.

definition *n.* meaning, sense, explanation, interpretation:
*That old dictionary doesn't contain a definition for "jet"
engine because it hadn't been invented when it was
published.*

defy *vb.* challenge, oppose, dare, flout: *It is very rude of you
to defy your parents' orders about staying out late.* **ant.**
yield, submit, surrender.

dejected *adj.* depressed, unhappy, disheartened, discouraged,
downhearted, sad: *You shouldn't be dejected about missing the movie—it will come around again.* **ant.** happy,
cheerful, optimistic.

delay *vb.* **1.** postpone, put off, defer: *Mail delivery was
delayed for three days over the Christmas holidays.* **2.**
slow, hinder, retard; pause, hesitate: *Let's delay our decision about swimming until we hear the weather report.
When you hear the fire alarm, line up in the corridors
and don't delay.* *n.* slowdown, postponement: *During the
strike, there was a three-week delay in the delivery of
fresh produce.* **ant.** *vb.* hasten, forward, advance.

delegate *n.* ambassador, emissary, representative, envoy:
Three universities sent delegates to the convention. *vb.*

appoint, deputize, commission, authorize: *I was delegated to ask the teacher whether the class could have a party.*

delete *vb.* cancel, erase, remove, cross out: *The military censors deleted so much from my brother's letter that I could no longer understand what he had written.* **ant.** add.

deliberate *adj.* **1.** purposeful, intentional, studied, considered, planned, calculated, premeditated: *I believe that there was a deliberate effort to set fire to the house.* **2.** slow, methodical, careful: *The old man's deliberate walk was recognized by all who knew him.* *vb.* weigh, judge, consider, reflect: *We deliberated for a long time before deciding what we would give to our teacher for a wedding present.* **ant.** *adj.* **1.** accidental, unintentional, unplanned.

delicate *adj.* **1.** dainty, fine, fragile, frail: *The delicate cobwebs sparkled in the morning dew.* **2.** frail, weak, precarious: *For a month after his operation, my uncle was in delicate health, but he's fine now.* **3.** sensitive, critical, demanding: *The situation between Greece and Turkey has always been delicate.* **ant.** **1.** clumsy, heavy-handed, coarse. **2.** hale, hearty, strong.

delicious *adj.* savory, delectable, appetizing, luscious: *This clam chowder is the most delicious I've ever eaten.* **ant.** unpleasant, unpalatable.

delight *n.* pleasure, joy, enjoyment: *He is a loving father and takes great delight in his children. Why do you take delight in teasing me all the time?* *vb.* please, entertain, satisfy: *Nothing delights me more than your telling me that you are happy.* **ant.** *n.* revulsion, disgust, displeasure. *vb.* displease, revolt, disgust.

delightful *adj.* charming, pleasing, refreshing, pleasant, pleasurable: *Having a picnic on the beach can be a delightful experience.* **ant.** disagreeable, unpleasant, nasty.

deliver *vb.* **1.** transport, carry, convey: *Each year, on my friends' birthdays, I deliver gifts to them.* **2.** present, give, offer, address: *Yesterday my father was to have delivered a speech to 400 people.* **3.** liberate, set free, release, save: *The Emancipation Proclamation delivered the blacks from slavery in America.* **ant.** **3.** confine, imprison, enslave.

deluge *n.* flood, overflow: *There was a deluge of fan mail* *for the new rock star. vb.* flood, overflow: *The singer was so bad that the audience deluged him with tomatoes and eggs.*

delusion *n.* fantasy, illusion, phantasm: *Philip has delusions of grandeur thinking he's Napoleon!*

demand *vb.* **1.** request, call for, ask for, claim: *I demanded my rights.* **2.** challenge, command, charge, direct: *The teacher demanded that the noisy children leave the room.* **3.** require, need: *This night job demands more than I expected. n.* **1.** request, claim: *Women's demands for voting rights equal to men's were a long time being met.* **2.** requirement, obligation: *This job puts too many demands on my free time.* **3.** market, interest, call: *There isn't very much demand for buggy whips any more.* **ant.** *vb.* **1.** relinquish, waive.

demolish *vb.* destroy, ruin, raze, devastate: *The wrecking crew demolished the building in two hours—only a heap of stones remained.* **ant.** build, construct, erect.

demolition *n.* destruction, wrecking: *The demolition of the old railway station was accomplished by a charge of dynamite.* **ant.** construction, erection.

demonstrate *vb.* **1.** show, exhibit, prove: *The science teacher demonstrated how water could be made to run uphill.* **2.** explain, describe, illustrate, *The simple screw demonstrates an application of the principle of the inclined plane.* **3.** display, exhibit: *We demonstrated in front of Town Hall.*

demonstration *n.* **1.** show, exhibition, exhibit, presentation, display: *There was a demonstration at the planetarium that showed how the planets revolve around the sun.* **2.** protest, march, rally: *The police scattered the demonstration in front of the White House.*

den *n.* lair, cave, cavern: *Bears spend the winter hibernating in their dens.*

dense *adj.* thick, solid, packed, compact, crowded: *On New Year's Eve, dense hordes of people pack into Times Square to wait for the midnight signal.* **ant.** sparse, scanty.

deny *vb.* **1.** contradict, confute, repudiate, gainsay, dispute: *The suspect denied that he had taken the necklace from the case.* **2.** refuse, reject, disallow: *You can't deny me the right to answer your charge.* **ant.** **1.** admit, concede, confess. **2.** allow, permit.

depart *vb.* leave, go, withdraw: *The train doesn't depart* *until ten o'clock, so we have time for dinner.* **ant.** arrive, come.

depend *vb.* **1.** rely on, confide in, trust: *We are all depending on Samantha to win the swimming race.* **2.** be dependent on, be contingent on, rest on *or* upon: *Whether we win or not will depend on the total score.*

deposit *vb.* **1.** put, place, put down: *Our mail is deposited in the box in front of our house every day.* **2.** save, bank, store: *No matter how little money you have, you should get into the habit of depositing some in the bank regularly.* *n.* **1.** sediment, lees, dregs: *This wine throws a deposit, so you must decant it before serving.* **2.** addition, entry: *Please make this bank deposit for me when you go downtown.* **ant.** *vb.* withdraw. *n.* **2.** withdrawal.

depress *vb.* **1.** dispirit, dishearten, discourage; dampen: *Paul was depressed for three days after losing the championship match.* **2.** devalue, devaluate, cheapen: *The dollar was depressed yesterday on the international money market.* **ant.** **1.** cheer, exhilarate, exalt.

depression *n.* **1.** cavity, dip, hole, pothole, dent: *All that remained of the flying saucer was a smoking depression in the ground where it had stood.* **2.** despair, gloom, melancholy, sorrow, sadness, hopelessness: *My mother went into a period of depression after my brother broke his arm.* **3.** decline, recession, hard times: *Some people thought that the business depression of the 1970s would be worse than that of 1929.* **ant.** **1.** elevation, eminence. **2.** elation, happiness. **3.** boom.

deprive *vb.* deny, strip; bereave: *When a person is sent to prison, he is deprived of his rights as a citizen.* **ant.** supply, provide, provision.

depth *n.* deepness, profundity: *The depth of that oil well is more than three miles. That last book I read was lacking in depth.* **ant.** height, tallness, loftiness.

deputy *n.* assistant, lieutenant, aide, delegate: *The manager turned over all the responsibility to his deputy.*

derive *vb.* receive, obtain, get, acquire: *Mr. Thomas derives an income from the sale of petrified prickly pears.*

descend *vb.* move lower, climb down: *We descended from the rock with the aid of ropes.* **ant.** ascend, climb.

describe *vb.* portray, characterize, picture, narrate, relate, recount, represent: *I wish you would describe what happened at the campground that day.*

description *n.* account, narration, report, record: *A descrip-*

tion of the suspect omitted the fact that he was only three feet tall.

desert[1] *n.* waste, wasteland, wilderness: *It may some day be necessary to irrigate the deserts to provide more farmland. adj.* wild, barren, uninhabited: *Robinson Crusoe was cast ashore on a desert island.*

desert[2] *vb.* abandon, leave, forsake, quit: *When the cat deserted her kittens, our dog adopted them and took care of them.* **ant.** join, accompany.

deserter *n.* fugitive, runaway, defector, renegade: *In time of war, deserters from the armed forces were shot by a firing squad.* **ant.** loyalist.

deserve *vb.* earn, merit, be worthy of, warrant: *Some people believe that no matter what you do, good or bad, you get what you deserve in the long run.*

design *vb.* **1.** plan, intend, scheme, plot: *The trapdoor was designed to open if anyone tried to open the jewel case.* **2.** create, originate: *My sister designs clothes for a large manufacturer in Paris. n.* **1.** pattern, plan, blueprint, sketch: *These designs for the new monument were copied from old books.* **2.** meaning, intention, purpose, end, aim: *Veronica's design for the future did not include Harry as her husband.*

desirable *adj.* wanted, sought-after, wished-for, coveted: *Honesty is a desirable characteristic of anyone.* **ant.** unattractive, repellent.

desire *vb.* **1.** crave, long for, want, covet: *What I desire most of all right now is a delicious, nutty, caramel-flavored candy bar.* **2.** ask, request: *If you pick up the phone, just tell the maid who answers what you desire. n.* need, longing, want, craving, wish: *The magician said he could satisfy every one of Harvey's desires.* **ant.** *vb.* **1.** loathe, abhor, detest.

desolate *adj.* **1.** deserted, empty, lonely: *During the winter, the beach was desolate.* **2.** miserable, sad, unhappy, wretched: *When you're away from me I am just desolate.* **ant.** **1.** crowded, populous, teeming. **2.** cheerful, happy.

despair *n.* hopelessness, desperation, discouragement: *When the hundredth experiment resulted in failure, the research staff was in deep despair. vb.* lose heart, lose hope: *When I lost my watch while boating on the lake, I despaired of ever seeing it again.* **ant.** *n.* joy, hope, optimism.

desperate *adj.* despairing, hopeless, reckless: *The escaped murderers were desperate men who would stop at nothing to avoid capture.* **ant.** calm, collected.

despicable *adj.* mean, base, low, contemptible, worthless: *Beating any animal is a despicable thing to do.* **ant.** admirable, honorable, worthy.

despise *vb.* scorn, dislike, disdain, condemn: *All those who knew he had betrayed his country despised him.* **ant.** admire, like, honor.

despite *prep.* notwithstanding, regardless of, in spite of, even with: *Despite his poverty, Abraham Lincoln became an educated man.*

destiny *n.* fate, fortune, lot: *I guess it was not my destiny to become a famous writer.*

destroy *vb.* **1.** ruin, demolish, raze, waste: *These trees were destroyed by disease.* **2.** kill, slay, end, extinguish: *When I saw the train pulling out of the station, my vacation plans were destroyed.* **ant. 1.** create, start, undertake.

destruction *n.* devastation, demolition, ruin, extinction: *With the destruction of the old theater went memories of happy times spent there.* **ant.** creation, beginning.

detach *vb.* separate, disengage, divide: *The engine was detached from the rest of the train, which hurtled down the steep track at 100 miles per hour.* **ant.** attach, connect, hitch.

detain *vb.* delay, restrain, hold back, stay, retard: *The customs inspectors detained the young man for three hours because they suspected he was smuggling.* **ant.** forward, hurry, rush.

detect *vb.* determine, discover, ascertain, learn, find out: *I detected something suspicious about Carolyn's behavior yesterday.*

determine *vb.* **1.** decide, settle, resolve: *It was only a few minutes to determine who had eaten the candy—he had chocolate all over his chin.* **2.** fix, establish, define: *I wasn't able to determine exactly where my property ended and my neighbor's began.*

detest *vb.* despise, hate, loathe: *I detest fried squash.* **ant.** like, love, appreciate, savor.

develop *vb.* **1.** grow, expand, enlarge, advance, mature: *Anne has developed from a child into a beautiful, charm-*

ing young lady. **2.** reveal, become known, unfold: *It developed that Chris hadn't gone to the dance at all.* **ant. 1.** deteriorate, degenerate.

device *n.* **1.** machine, tool, utensil, instrument: *What kind of device could have been used to pick the lock to this door?* **2.** gadget, contrivance, *(slang)* whatsis: *That thing with seven wheels, a sail, two steam engines, and a horse is a strange device!*

devise *vb.* invent, create, originate, concoct: *After much thought, the boys devised a clever plan for escape from the cave where they had been trapped.*

devote *vb.* apply, dedicate, give: *With eleven children, how could my mother devote a lot of time to each one?* **ant.** relinquish, withdraw, withhold, ignore.

devour *vb.* gorge, gulp: *After working all day, Jim would come home and devour a huge dinner.*

devout *adj.* religious, pious, devoted: *I am a devout believer in treating others the way I'd want them to treat me.* **ant.** indifferent, scornful.

dictate *vb.* **1.** speak, deliver, record: *If he dictates too fast, I cannot take it down in shorthand.* **2.** order, command, direct: *The general dictated the conditions under which he would accept a surrender.*

dictator *n.* tyrant, despot, overlord: *A dictator decides what he wants the people to have and to do, and they can say nothing about it.*

die *vb.* **1.** decease, perish, expire, go, pass away: *Because of the advances in medicine, people aren't dying until they are much older.* **2.** decrease, diminish, fade, sink, decline, wither, wane, fail: *The candle, like the roses in the vase, is dying.* **ant. 2.** flourish, grow.

difference *n.* disagreement, inequality, contrast: *There is a difference between the way men and women regard the same things.* **ant.** similarity, likeness, kinship, compatibility.

different *adj.* **1.** unalike, unlike, differing, changed: *You and your sister are as different as can be.* **2.** various, miscellaneous: *There are fifteen different flavors of ice cream to choose from.* **ant. 1.** similar, alike, identical.

differentiate *vb.* distinguish, separate: *I know so little about plants that I can't differentiate one flower from another.*

difficult *adj.* **1.** hard: *Handling a horse-drawn plow is difficult.* **2.** intricate, complicated, obscure: *That college* *textbook is much too difficult for a child to understand.* **ant. 1.** easy. **2.** simple.

difficulty *n.* **1.** hardship, trouble: *Getting a good job after school can be a difficulty these days.* **2.** predicament, fix, trouble: *Barbie got herself into some difficulty at school last week.* **ant. 1.** ease.

dig *vb.* **1.** excavate, burrow, scoop out: *The men dug a hole in which to bury the treasure.* **2.** (*Slang*) understand; appreciate: *All the kids I know really dig cool rock music.*

digest *vb.* **1.** eat, consume: *After a huge meal, some snakes spend days digesting their food.* **2.** study, consider, reflect on: *Give me a few minutes to digest the teacher's remarks before replying.* **3.** summarize, shorten, abridge: *How can you digest the Bible into such a small book?* *n.* summary, abridgment, abstract, synopsis, précis: *Why should anyone want to read digests of great authors' books when the real pleasure comes from reading the originals?*

dignified *adj.* noble, serious, stately, solemn, elegant: *The dignified procession to the throne was led by the queen.*

dignify *vb.* elevate, honor: *My uncle was dignified by the grand reception given for him in London.* **ant.** humiliate, degrade, shame.

dignity *n.* distinction, stateliness, bearing: *The dignity with which the old man conducted himself won everybody's respect.*

dim *adj.* unclear, faint, shadowy, vague: *I could hardly make out the dim outline of the house in the fog.* **ant.** bright, brilliant. *vb.* obscure, dull, darken: *The houselights were dimmed as the curtain went up for the last act of the play.* **ant.** brighten, illuminate.

dimension *n.* measure, size, extent; importance: *The dimensions of the room did not leave much space for a large chest of drawers. After winning the scholarship, Patrick assumed a new dimension in his friends' eyes.*

diminish *vb.* lessen, shrink, reduce, wane: *Without water, the plant diminished to the size of a toothpick. When the new government came into power, the senator's importance diminished to practically nothing.* **ant.** enlarge, increase, wax.

diminutive *adj.* little, small, tiny, wee, minute: *At the side of the road, sitting on a fallen tree, was a diminutive* *green man playing a golden harp.* **ant.** big, large, great, huge, gigantic.

dine *vb.* eat, feast, lunch, sup: *We dined on steak and kidney pie.*

dip *vb.* plunge, immerse, submerge, wet: *Dip the burning stick into the water to make sure it's out.* *n.* plunge, swim: *I like to take a dip in the pool before breakfast.*

diplomatic *adj.* polite, tactful, gracious, discreet. *It was very diplomatic of him not to mention the huge spot on her skirt.* **ant.** impolite, rude, thoughtless, ungracious.

direct *vb.* **1.** command, manage, control, regulate: *The new president directed the company through one of its most profitable periods.* **2.** aim, sight, point, level: *completely frustrated, Betty directed her gaze skyward as if in appeal to a higher power.* **3.** indicate, guide, conduct, show: *Please direct me to the nearest police station.* *adj.* **1.** straight, unswerving: *When my son comes home after school, he makes a direct beeline to the kitchen for cookies and milk.* **2.** plain, straightforward, frank, sincere, earnest: *Please stop delaying and give me a direct, honest answer to my question.* **ant.** *adj.* **1.** crooked, indirect, swerving. **2.** dishonest, untruthful.

direction *n.* **1.** way, route: *After all I had told her, she drove off in the wrong direction.* **2.** management, guidance, supervision: *Under her direction, the school became one of the best in the country.*

directly *adv.* straight, immediately, at once: *Go Directly to Jail. Do Not Pass Go. Do Not Collect $200.*

dirt *n.* soil, filth, pollution, filthiness: *No matter how you try to keep them apart, kids and dirt seem always to go together.* **ant.** cleanness, cleanliness.

dirty *adj.* soiled, unclean, filthy, polluted: *I wouldn't drink that dirty water if I were you. Have you heard the story of the dirty shirt? Ha! That's one on you!* **ant.** clean, spotless, pure. *vb.* soil, foul, befoul, spot, pollute: *The town's drinking water was dirtied by the drains from the chemical-company plant.* **ant.** clean, cleanse, purify.

disability *n.* incapacity, unfitness, injury: *His disability kept him from going to work for a whole year.*

disable *vb.* cripple, incapacitate, weaken: *My grandfather was disabled in the First World War.* **ant.** strengthen.

disadvantage *n.* **1.** inconvenience, drawback: *The only disadvantage of my new job is that I have to get up at 5 o'clock.* **2.** handicap, hindrance, obstacle: *Her disad-*

vantage is that she cannot type. **ant.** benefit, advantage, convenience.

disappear *vb.* vanish; end: *In the twinkling of an eye the fairy disappeared and was never seen again. Horsecars have disappeared from the streets of American cities.* **ant.** appear, emerge.

disappoint *vb.* fail, dissatisfy; mislead: *I always seemed to disappoint my mother when she saw my report card.* **ant.** satisfy, please, gratify.

disappointment *n.* defeat, dissatisfaction, failure, discouragement: *I can't tell you the disappointment I felt when I arrived after a week's journey to find my father away on a holiday.* **ant.** satisfaction, pleasure, gratification.

disaster *n.* calamity, misfortune, accident, catastrophe: *Three hundred people were killed in the train disaster last week. It was a disaster when mother burned the turkey last Thanksgiving.*

discern *vb.* see, distinguish, recognize, differentiate, perceive: *Coming up the road in the snowstorm we could discern the men who were to rescue us. I discern your meaning now that you have explained more fully.*

discharge *vb.* **1.** relieve, unload, unburden: *Marie's responsibilities were not discharged until she finished washing the dishes.* **2.** fire, shoot: *The rabbit ran off into the woods when the gun discharged.* **3.** let go, dismiss: *When business got bad, three of us were discharged from our jobs.* **ant. 3.** employ, hire, enlist. *n.* **1.** explosion, firing, detonation: *The sudden discharge of the gun made me jump.* **2.** release, liberation; dismissal: *My father's discharge from the navy became final this week.* **ant. 2.** enlistment.

disciple *n.* follower, supporter; student, pupil: *Plato was a disciple of Socrates.* **ant.** leader, guide.

discipline *n.* **1.** training, practice, exercise, drill: *If you want to do well in sports, you must follow a strict discipline. Discipline in the armed services is not as severe as it once was.* **2.** order, control, regulation: *A neatly written paper shows good discipline. vb.* **1.** train, control, drill, teach: *Your puppy will make a better pet if you discipline him properly.* **2.** punish, correct, chastise: *In the old days, parents disciplined their children much more strictly than they do now.* **ant.** *n.* **2.** carelessness, negligence, sloppiness, messiness.

disclose *vb.* reveal, show, expose, uncover: *When the curtain* *was drawn back, a white mouse on a golden chain was disclosed, dancing on the tiny stage.* **ant.** hide, disguise, mask, conceal.

disconnect *vb.* separate, divide, unhook, detach, disengage: *The engineer disconnected the engine from the freight cars.* **ant.** connect, engage, attach, bind, unify.

discontinue *vb.* cease, end, stop; interrupt: *I have discontinued my subscriptions to all magazines for the time being.* **ant.** begin, start, launch, initiate.

discord *n.* conflict, disagreement: *Let us hope that with the new Congress, there will be less discord among the branches of the government.* **ant.** agreement, accord, concord.

discourage *vb.* dispirit, dishearten, depress: *Poor grades in school can be discouraging, especially when you've worked so hard.* **ant.** encourage, inspire, inspirit.

discover *vb.* find; learn, find out, ascertain, determine: *It wasn't until I went to work that I discovered how important school is. I can't remember the name of the explorer who discovered the Mississippi.* **ant.** conceal, hide.

discreet *adj.* tactful, judicious, prudent, wise; cautious, careful: *You should be discreet and not talk about family arguments to others.* **ant.** careless, incautious, tactless, indiscreet, imprudent.

discuss *vb.* talk about, deliberate, consider: *My father and I discussed what kind of job I might get for the summer.*

discussion *n.* talk, conversation, dialogue, conference: *The principal phoned my mother to arrange for a discussion of my behavior.*

disdain *vb.* scorn, reject: *She disdains the way her sister dresses.* **ant.** admire, respect, esteem, prize. *n.* scorn, contempt, haughtiness: *He treats everyone who has less money than he with disdain.* **ant.** admiration, respect, honor.

disdainful *adj.* scornful, contemptuous, haughty, arrogant: *You shouldn't be disdainful of those who are less well off than you.* **ant.** admiring, awed, regardful.

disease *n.* illness, sickness, affliction, ailment, complaint, disorder, malady, infirmity: *It wasn't until the 19th century that scientists understood that disease could come from germs.*

disgrace *n.* shame, dishonor, embarrassment: *Tim had to live with the disgrace of having been caught cheating.*

ant. honor, esteem. *vb.* shame, dishonor, embarrass, humiliate: *The army deserter was told that he had disgraced his uniform and his country.* **ant.** honor, respect.

disguise *vb.* mask, hide, screen, conceal, camouflage: *The detective disguised himself as a woman and waited in the street for the robber to attack.* **ant.** reveal, display, show. *n.* mask, coverup, makeup: *In her disguise as a flower girl, no one could recognize the bank president at the party.*

disgust *vb.* nauseate, sicken; offend, revolt, repulse: *The sight of an operation disgusts me.* *n.* distaste, nausea; aversion, revulsion: *The dead horse filled him with disgust.* **ant.** *n.* liking, admiration.

disgusting *adj.* revolting, repulsive, nauseous, nauseating, repugnant: *I thought that the horror show was too disgusting for children to see.* **ant.** attractive, appealing.

dishonest *adj.* corrupt, false, thievish: *The politicians in America are often tempted to be dishonest, but very few really are.* **ant.** honest, straightforward, upright.

dismal *adj.* gloomy, sorrowful, depressing, melancholy, dreary, somber: *The dismal winter weather made us yearn for a holiday in the Caribbean.* **ant.** cheerful, happy, charming, lighthearted.

dismay *vb.* scare, frighten, alarm; discourage, dishearten: *We were dismayed to learn that the only roads to town were buried by the avalanche.* **ant.** hearten, encourage. *n.* fear, terror, horror, dread: *You can imagine the neighbors' dismay when the poisonous snake escaped.*

dismiss *vb.* discharge, release, let go, liberate: *The teacher dismissed the class early before the holidays.* **ant.** engage, employ, hire.

disorder *n.* confusion, turmoil, tumult, chaos: *My older sister always leaves her room in terrible disorder.* **ant.** order, neatness, organization.

dispatch *vb.* **1.** send off *or* away: *I dispatched the letter the very same day the request came.* **2.** conclude, achieve, finish: *I had only one more thing to do and dispatched that as quickly as I could.* *n.* **1.** message, report, communication, communiqué: *The dispatch from the front lines said that our troops were advancing.* **2.** speed, promptness, quickness, swiftness: *My next visitor is a bore, and I shall get rid of him with dispatch.* **ant.** *n.* **2.** slowness, reluctance, hesitancy.

dispense *vb.* distribute, apportion, give out: *There is now a vending machine that dispenses hot soup. At Christmas, the president dispenses the bonus checks himself.*

disperse *vb.* scatter, spread (out), separate: *The seeds of many plants are dispersed by the wind.* **ant.** gather, collect, assemble.

display *vb.* **1.** exhibit, show, demonstrate: *There are strict rules about how the American flag should be displayed.* **2.** reveal, uncover, show: *Many people display their lack of knowledge as soon as they start talking.* *n.* showing, exhibit, exhibition, demonstration: *I have never seen such a display of patriotism as during the parade.* **ant.** *vb.* **2.** disguise, hide, conceal, cover.

dispose *vb.* arrange, settle; adjust: *The town council disposed of the question of which Christmas decorations to buy by agreeing to have none at all.*

disposition *n.* nature, character, temperament, personality: *Suzie has such a sweet disposition that you can't help liking her.*

dispute *vb.* **1.** argue, debate, quarrel, contest: *How can you dispute my statement that my birthday is March 21st?* **2.** oppose, deny, contradict: *Disputing the wisdom of the new law, the President vetoed the bill.* *n.* argument, quarrel, debate, controversy: *There was a dispute at the door about whether the tickets were valid or not.* **ant.** *vb.* agree, concur. *n.* agreement, accord, concurrence.

disregard *vb.* ignore, overlook, neglect: *In hiring people, employers must learn to disregard race, color, creed, and sex and to consider only character and qualifications.* *n.* inattention, neglect, oversight: *The policeman jumped into the icy stream with total disregard for his own safety.*

disrespectful *adj.* rude, impudent, fresh, impolite, impertinent; cheeky: *You must learn not to be disrespectful to adults.* **ant.** respectful, polite, courteous.

distant *adj.* remote, far, afar, away, separated: *A star that looks larger in the sky may, in fact, be more distant than one that looks smaller. Man developed from lower animals at some distant point in time.* **ant.** near, close.

distinct *adj.* **1.** individual, separate, different: *In nature, each species is distinct from every other, even though some may seem alike.* **2.** clear, definite, obvious, plain: *I have a distinct recollection that you promised to take me to the movies.* **ant.** **2.** indistinct, vague, uncertain, obscure.

distinction   *n.*   **1.** honor, renown, fame, repute, prominence, importance: *It is a great distinction to be selected a winner of the Nobel prize.* **2.** difference; characteristic: *Until a child is taught what they mean, he is unable to make a distinction between right and wrong.*

distinguish   *vb.*   **1.** separate, divide, differentiate, classify: *It is hard for anyone but the specialist to distinguish one seashell from another.* **2.** perceive, discern, recognize: *Even at that great distance I was able to distinguish George in the crowd.* **ant. 1.** blend, join, confuse.

distinguished   *adj.* renowned, famous, honored, eminent, illustrious, noted, important, celebrated: *Suzanne's father is a distinguished scientist who has won many prizes.* **ant.** obscure, unknown, undistinguished.

distract   *vb.*   **1.** divert, occupy: *I always found the radio too distracting when I was trying to do my homework.* **2.** confuse, bewilder: *Penny seemed distracted and unable to concentrate on what I was saying.* **ant. 2.** concentrate, focus.

distraction   *n.* amusement, entertainment, diversion; confusion: *After studying for days for examinations, Jonathan felt he needed some distraction and went to the movies.*

distress   *n.*   **1.** anguish, trouble, anxiety, worry, wretchedness; pain: *Maggie caused her mother great distress whenever she stayed out late at night.* **2.** danger, peril; disaster: *The small boat was in distress because of the storm.* *vb.* worry, trouble, grieve, make wretched: *Bill was distressed to learn that the school principal had written to his father.* **ant.** *n.* **1.** happiness, tranquillity, peacefulness. *vb.* please, charm, satisfy.

distribute   *vb.* share, deal, dispense, issue, dole, mete out, allocate, apportion: *The Salvation Army distributes food and clothing among the poor.* **ant.** collect, gather, assemble.

district   *n.* region, area, neighborhood, section: *These days, many children are taken by bus from the neighborhoods where they live to schools in distant districts.*

distrust   *vb.* suspect, doubt, mistrust: *The bank manager distrusted the new teller.* *n.* suspicion, doubt, mistrust: *A good relationship between people must be founded on confidence, without distrust.* **ant.** *vb.* trust. *n.* trust, confidence.

disturb   *vb.*   **1.** annoy, bother, vex: *Please don't disturb me when I am practicing on the piano.* **2.** worry, trouble:

Even though the doctor said you were fine, the condition of your cold disturbs me. **ant.** calm, pacify.

disturbance *n.* **1.** commotion, disorder, confusion: *The marchers in the street caused quite a disturbance in the traffic.* **2.** disorder, riot, brawl, fight: *The police were called to control a disturbance between the political clubs.* **ant.** calm, serenity, tranquillity.

diverge *vb.* branch off, separate, fork: *The road diverges when it comes to the river.* **ant.** join, converge, merge.

diversion *n.* distraction, entertainment, amusement, sport, recreation: *What do you do for diversion if you live in such a small town?* **ant.** routine.

divert *vb.* **1.** turn aside *or* away, deflect: *The bullet was diverted when it struck the sheriff's badge, and he was unhurt.* **2.** amuse, entertain, distract: *After a hard day's work, my father likes to be diverted by TV.* **ant. 2.** bore, tire, weary.

divide *vb.* **1.** separate, split, part, detach, sever, cleave: *Divide that apple into six pieces so we can share it.* **2.** apportion, share, allot, allocate, distribute, deal *or* parcel *or* dole out: *After the apple is cut up, we can divide it among the six of us.* **3.** disunite, split up, estrange: *Disagreements about the rights of women divided the political party from the start.* **ant. 1.** join, merge, combine. **2.** gather, collect. **3.** unite, unify.

division *n.* **1.** separation, partition, sharing: *In olden times, conquering soldiers were entitled to a division of the valuables in the cities and towns they captured.* **2.** section, part, segment, portion: *My father fought in the 83rd Division during the war.* **ant. 1.** agreement, union.

divulge *vb.* reveal, release, disclose, expose; admit: *After careful questioning by his mother, George divulged that he had gone to the movies instead of to school.* **ant.** conceal, hide.

dizzy *adj.* giddy, unsteady, light-headed: *After the blow on the head, the detective was dizzy for more than two hours.* **ant.** clearheaded, rational, unconfused.

do *vb.* **1.** execute, enact, carry out, finish, conclude, effect: *Success depends on everyone's doing his job the best he can.* **2.** accomplish, achieve, attain: *Don't just talk about it, do it!* *vb. phr.* **do away with** kill, murder, execute: *The pirates did away with all those who refused to join them.* **do over 1.** redo, rework, repeat: *I think you ought to do your homework over again because of the ink blots.*

2. redecorate, remodel: *The Robinsons have done over their entire house.* **do up** wrap (up), enclose, tie (up): *This is a beautiful gift—all done up with a red ribbon!*

doctrine *n.* teaching, teachings; dogma, belief, principle: *The philosophy that developed during the 18th century was based on the doctrine that all men are created equal.*

dodge *vb.* evade, elude, avoid; equivocate: *The policeman ran, zigzag, down the street, trying to dodge the robber's bullets. Don't try to dodge the question—you know there's a lot of prejudice in the world.*

dole *n.* alms, relief, welfare: *Don's father has been on the dole ever since he lost his job at the factory.* *vb.* deal, distribute, mete out: *The Red Cross doled out the food to the flood victims.*

domestic *adj.* **1.** home-loving: *I am really very domestic and like nothing better than a good book and comfortable chair by my own fireside.* **2.** native, home-grown, homemade: *If you buy domestic products, you stimulate the economy of your own country.* **ant. 2.** foreign, alien, outside.

domesticate *vb.* tame, train, teach; housebreak: *Man didn't learn to domesticate wild animals until less than 10,000 years ago.*

dominate *vb.* control, rule, govern, influence, manage, subjugate, tyrannize: *Some women are completely dominated by their husbands.*

donation *n.* gift, contribution, present, offering: *Any time of the year is the right time to make a donation to charity.*

doom *n.* **1.** fate, destiny, fortune: *The criminal had to wait till the judge passed sentence before learning his doom.* **2.** death, ruin, destruction: *The entire regiment rode into the valley and to its doom.* *vb.* **1.** destine, predestine, ordain, foreordain; decree: *The entire project is doomed to failure if you take that attitude.* **2.** sentence, condemn: *The judge doomed the murderer to death by hanging.*

doubt *vb.* distrust, mistrust, question, suspect: *The detective doubted that Professor Twinkle had been home all evening after he noticed the mud on his shoes.* *n.* **1.** uncertainty, indecision, misgiving, skepticism, disbelief: *I have my doubts about the truth of your story of being brought up by wolves.* **2.** indecision, hesitancy: *When we saw the fox running away with the chicken between his jaws, we no longer had a doubt about the identity of the culprit.* **ant.** *vb.* trust, believe. *n.* belief, trust, confidence, reliance.

doubtful *adj*. dubious, uncertain, questionable, unsettled, undetermined, unsure: *The result of the race is doubtful until it's over. I am doubtful that I'll be able to go to the party.* **ant.** certain, definite, sure, settled.

downcast *adj*. dejected, sad, depressed, downhearted, discouraged, unhappy, dispirited, despondent, crestfallen: *Janet has been so downcast since her puppy got lost, we ought to cheer her up.* **ant.** cheerful, happy, lighthearted, encouraged.

downfall *n*. comedown, destruction: *Dishonesty among his own staff contributed to the downfall of the crooked politician.*

downgrade *vb*. lower, reduce, decrease, diminish; depreciate: *Many more students have been admitted to colleges since the requirements were downgraded.* **ant.** upgrade, improve, appreciate.

downhearted *adj*. sad, gloomy, depressed, downcast: *You shouldn't be so downhearted about losing the game; you'll have another chance to win next week.* **ant.** cheerful, happy, enthusiastic.

drag *vb*. pull, draw, tow: *Stop dragging that poor kitten about on a leash.*

drain *vb*. **1.** draw off, empty, tap: *The man drained his glass in one gulp. The conservationists fight the draining of swamps and wetlands where birds, fishes, and other wildlife breed.* **2.** exhaust, empty, sap, waste; milk: *Your annoying manner drains me of all patience.* *n*. tap, duct, channel, pipe: *I pulled the stopper out of the sink and watched the water go down the drain.* **ant.** *vb*. fill, fulfill.

drama *n*. play, piece, show, production: *I am going to take courses in drama because I like the theater.*

dramatist *n*. playwright: *George Bernard Shaw was one of the most famous Irish dramatists.*

draw *vb*. **1.** sketch, trace, depict, picture: *The artist drew an excellent likeness of Anne in only a few minutes.* **2.** drag, haul, tow, pull, tug: *The oxen drew the heavy wagon up the muddy hill.* **3.** attract: *The parade drew a large crowd to the arena where the circus was to take place.* *vb. phr.* **draw back** withdraw, recoil, retreat: *She drew back when she saw the box was full of snakes.* **draw on** or **upon** employ, use: *When you want to get something done properly, you must draw on all of your resources.* **draw up** draft, prepare: *Our lawyer drew up the documents for us to sign.* **ant.** *vb*. **2.** push, propel.

dread *vb.* fear: *I used to dread being in that teacher's class.* *n.* fear, terror,. horror: *Moriarty never overcame his dread of high places.* **ant.** *n.* confidence, security.

dream *n.* **1.** reverie, daydream: *I had a dream about you yesterday.* **2.** fantasy, hope, wish, fancy: *His dreams of glory included landing on Mars and becoming a billionaire.* *vb.* imagine, fantasize, invent, fancy: *She dreams of becoming a* Vogue *model.*

dreary *adj.* dismal, gloomy, cheerless, chilling, depressing: *With unemployment at its height, my job prospects are pretty dreary right now. When it rains day after day in the country, life can seem dreary.* **ant.** cheerful, hopeful, bright, encouraging.

dress *n.* **1.** gown, frock, costume: *I like that low-cut dress on you.* **2.** attire, garb, wardrobe, clothing, garments, clothes, apparel; habit; livery: *Will Nancy's party require everyone to wear evening dress?* *vb.* **1.** clothe, garb, don, wear, attire; robe: *How are you going to dress for the masked ball?* **2.** prepare, treat, attend: *The doctor dressed my cuts and bruises and I was almost as good as new.* **ant.** *vb.* **1.** undress, disrobe, strip.

drift *vb.* float, sail, wander: *The empty boat drifted about in the current until it finally came to rest on the beach.* *n.* tendency, intention, direction: *In women's fashions there seems to be a drift toward repeating the styles of the 1930s and 1940s.*

drink *vb.* swallow, sip, gulp, imbibe: *You shouldn't drink a lot of cold water when overheated from exercise.* *n.* swallow, sip, gulp, beverage, potion, refreshment: *There's nothing like a long, cool drink of plain, fresh water when you're thirsty.*

drip *vb.* drop, dribble, trickle: *Can't you make that faucet stop dripping?*

drive *vb.* **1.** control, direct, run, handle: *Do you know how to drive a car?* **2.** impel, propel, push, urge: *I tried to reach the canoe but was driven back by the wind and the waves.* *n.* **1.** ride, journey, trip, outing, tour, run: *On Sundays, we used to go for a drive in the wagon.* **2.** pressure, energy, urge, vigor, effort, force: *Some people just have more drive than others.*

droop *vb.* sag, sink, settle: *The flag drooped without any wind to make it flutter.* **ant.** straighten, rise.

drop *vb.* **1.** drip, dribble, trickle: *The rain ran down the roof and dropped, into the barrel.* **2.** fall, tumble: *At the* *sound of the first shot, the soldiers dropped to the ground. n.* **1.** droplet, gob, drip; trickle: *There's a drop of rain right at the end of your nose.* **2.** reduction, fall, slump, slip, decline: *I haven't noticed a drop in the price of gum.* **3.** speck, dab, scintilla: *There's not one drop of evidence against her.*

drove *n.* herd, flock: *The drove of cattle was resting for the night.*

drug *n.* medicine, remedy: *There's a drug for almost everything today; whether it cures or not is another matter. vb.* anesthetize, stupefy, numb, benumb: *The doctor drugged me so I wouldn't feel the pain when he set my broken arm.*

drunk, drunkard *n.* drinker, sot, alcoholic, dipsomaniac: *In most countries, drunks are forbidden to drive cars.*

dry *adj.* **1.** arid, dehydrated, waterless, parched: *If you don't believe that the desert is dry, you've never been there.* **2.** dull, boring, tedious, tiresome: *I found that educational program on lampshade making too dry to hold my interest. vb.* dehydrate, desiccate: *Partly dried plums are called prunes.* **ant.** *adj.* **1.** wet, soaked, moist. **2.** interesting, attractive, fascinating.

due *adj.* **1.** owing, payable, owed, unpaid: *My rent is due at the end of the month.* **2.** expected, imminent: *The ship was due yesterday.*

dull *adj.* **1.** boring, tiring, tiresome, uninteresting: *Instead of seeing a movie on the history of piracy, we saw a dull one on how to grow rutabagas.* **2.** blunt, dulled: *That knife is so dull it couldn't cut a banana.* **3.** slow, dumb, stupid, unimaginative: *That fellow is the dullest one in our class.* **4.** unfeeling, insensible, lifeless, dead: *She's so dull that nothing interests her except eating and sleeping.* **ant.** **1.** fascinating, interesting, engaging. **2.** sharp, keen. **3.** bright, intelligent, quick. **4.** alert, animated, spirited.

dumb *adj.* **1.** dull, stupid, ignorant: *Sadie is so dumb she failed every course in school.* **2.** speechless, mute: *Some people who seem to be dumb are really only deaf.* **ant. 1.** intelligent, bright, lucid, quick.

dungeon *n.* prison, cell, jail, keep: *The Count of Monte Cristo was kept in a dungeon for twenty years, after which he escaped.*

durable *adj.* lasting, firm, enduring: *You must use a durable paint on the outside of a boat.* **ant.** perishable, unenduring, short-lived.

dutiful *adj.* faithful, obedient, docile: *The big dog obeyed his young master like a dutiful pet.* **ant.** willful, disobedient, headstrong, unruly.

duty *n.* **1.** obligation, responsibility, conscience, faithfulness: *It is every citizen's duty to report a crime when he sees one.* **2.** function, responsibility, part, assignment: *Every person in this naval unit is expected to perform his duty no matter what the cost may be.*

dwarf *n.* runt, midget: *Only a dwarf could have crawled through that opening.* *vb.* stunt, reduce, minimize: *I'm more than six feet tall, but that basketball player dwarfed me easily.* *adj.* dwarfish, tiny, minuscule: *A dwarf apple tree gives large apples.* **ant.** *n.* giant.

dwell *vb.* reside, live, abide: *Most people in cities dwell in apartment houses and not private homes.*

dwindle *vb.* diminish, wane, lessen, decrease: *Because their nesting sites were destroyed, the number of ospreys has dwindled almost to extinction.* **ant.** increase, wax, gain, grow.

✖ E ✖

eager *adj.* keen, fervent, enthusiastic: *I am very eager to go to the rodeo, but my mother won't let me go alone.* **ant.** indifferent, uninterested, uninvolved.

earn *vb.* deserve, merit, win; realize, clear, net, collect: *Virginia really earned her position as class president. How much do you earn per hour in your new job?*

earnest *adj.* sincere, serious, determined, eager: *Alan is so earnest about his studies that I know he will do well in school.* **ant.** insincere, frivolous, indifferent.

earth *n.* **1.** world, globe: *The earth is about 93 million miles from the sun.* **2.** sod, turf, dirt, soil, ground: *When planting tomatoes, make sure the earth is pressed firmly around the roots.*

earthly *adj.* worldly, everyday, mundane: *Earthly necessities cannot compare with the spiritual.* **ant.** heavenly.

earthy *adj.* **1.** earthen, earthlike: *The earthy pots lay about the Indian campfire.* **2.** coarse, unrefined, crude, vulgar: *The audience was shocked by the comedian's earthy humor.* **ant. 2.** refined, elegant, tasteful.

ease *n.* **1.** comfort, rest, relaxation, repose, contentment, contentedness: *My father takes his ease on Sundays by watching football or baseball on TV.* **2.** naturalness, facility, skillfulness, cleverness: *It is such a pleasure to watch the ease with which a master craftsman works.* *vb.* comfort, relieve, alleviate, soothe; lighten, lessen, reduce: *That liniment certainly helped ease the pains in my legs. If you'll ease up on the brake, we can let the car roll ahead a little.* **ant.** *n.* **2.** difficulty, trouble, effort. *vb.* aggravate, worsen, heighten, intensify.

easy *adj.* **1.** simple, effortless: *Preparing a dictionary is not as easy as it may seem.* **2.** comfortable, unhurried, leisurely: *Because he was stationed in Washington during the war, my uncle had it pretty easy in the navy.* **ant.** difficult, awkward, strenuous.

eat *vb.* **1.** consume, chew, devour, swallow: *Eat your spinach and you'll be as strong as Popeye.* **2.** dine, lunch, breakfast; feast: *We eat at about seven o'clock in the evening, after my father returns from work.*

economical *adj.* thrifty, provident, sparing, careful, frugal: *It is often more economical to buy larger sizes of food products because they cost less per serving.* **ant.** wasteful, lavish, unsparing.

ecstasy *n.* rapture, delight, pleasure: *What ecstasy it is to see a beautiful painting or hear beautiful music.* **ant.** misery, unhappiness, agony.

edge *n.* border, rim, brink, threshold, boundary, margin: *The northern edge of the lake is where we swim. Don't cut yourself on the sharp edge of that piece of paper.* *vb.* **1.** border, trim: *She edged the neck and sleeves of the dress with lace.* **2.** inch, move little by little, sidle: *Roger edged over to Michele and grasped her hand.* **ant.** *n.* middle, center.

edgy *adj.* nervous, tense, irritable, touchy: *Miles gets a little edgy when he hasn't had enough sleep.* **ant.** tranquil, undisturbed, peaceful, bland.

educate *vb.* teach, train, instruct, school: *The people who are trying to educate others are specially skilled at their work.*

education *n.* **1.** instruction, training, schooling: *There are many excellent schools and colleges where you can get a good education.* **2.** culture, learning, knowledge: *It is almost impossible to do the things you want to do without the proper education.* **ant.** illiteracy.

eerie *adj.* weird, strange, fearful, spooky: *The old deserted mansion had an eerie feeling about it.*

effect *n.* **1.** result, outcome, consequence, end: *There was a time when the effect of being naughty was a sound spanking.* **2.** significance, importance, meaning: *Some kinds of punishment have almost no effect at all.* *vb.* **1.** accomplish, achieve: *A compromise between the union and the management was effected at three o'clock.* **2.** cause, make; bring about: *Conservation of our natural resources has effected many changes in the spread of large cities.* **ant.** *n.* **1.** cause.

effective *adj.* productive, efficient, practical: *Advertising has been shown to be a most effective aid in selling merchandise and services of all kinds.* **ant.** ineffective, wasteful, useless.

efficient *adj.* **1.** effective, useful, serviceable: *The lever is a very efficient machine.* **2.** competent, apt, adept, able, capable, talented, skilled, clever: *Phil has proved himself* *to be one of the most efficient workmen in the plant.* **ant. 1.** useless, unworkable. **2.** inefficient, ineffective, clumsy, awkward.

effort *n.* endeavor, attempt, try; struggle: *With a huge effort, the fat boy was able to jump over the three-foot-high bar.*

elaborate *adj.* ornate, ornamented, decorated, decorative; complicated, complex: *The Victorian style of architecture is one of the most elaborate that was ever developed.* *vb.* decorate, embellish; develop, detail: *The director of the department elaborated on his plan for reorganizing the division.* **ant.** *adj.* simple, unadorned, stark. *vb.* simplify, streamline.

elastic *adj.* flexible; resilient, pliable: *Rubber is one of the most elastic materials known.* **ant.** rigid, inflexible, stiff.

elect *vb.* choose, select, vote for: *The people elected Victor as their representative.*

elegant *adj.* fine, refined, cultivated; tasteful, choice: *My grandmother and grandfather were an elegant couple who were invited to many important affairs in London.* **ant.** crude, unpolished, coarse, tasteless.

elementary *adj.* **1.** basic, primary, fundamental: *An elementary rule of competition is good sportsmanship.* **2.** simple, uncomplicated: *The explanation of how the prisoner escaped from the locked cell is elementary.* **ant. 2.** complex, complicated, involved, sophisticated.

elevate *vb.* raise, lift: *With one hand the giant elevated one end of the car while I changed the tire.* **ant.** lower, drop.

eliminate *vb.* remove, get rid of, leave out, omit: *Although he played a good game of tennis, Wilbur was eliminated from the finals when he lost to Maurice.*

elude *vb.* evade, avoid, dodge: *The fox eluded the hunting party and ended up safe in his burrow.* **ant.** include, add.

embarrass *vb.* shame, abash, confuse: *My teacher always embarrasses me by asking me questions I can't answer.*

emblem *n.* sign, token, symbol, badge, mark: *That emblem on the car means it is a Rolls Royce.*

embrace *vb.* **1.** hug, clasp: *When I found her in the crowd, I embraced my mother.* **2.** include, contain, cover: *The categories of animal, vegetable, and mineral embrace all things on earth except water, the atmosphere, and many other familiar things.* **ant. 2.** exclude, bar.

emerge *vb.* come forth, appear; surface: *We all waited for the star to emerge from the stage door.* **ant.** recede, retreat, disappear.

emergency   *n.* crisis, predicament: *I seldom visit my sister, but she knows she can count on me in an emergency.*

eminent   *adj.* distinguished, famous, celebrated, renowned, important, prominent: *Martin's father is an eminent doctor who has been invited to join the President's committee.* **ant.** unknown, undistinguished, ordinary, commonplace.

emit   *vb.* discharge, expel, eject: *The volcano emits poisonous fumes for two days after each eruption.*

emotion   *n.* feeling, sentiment: *I have mixed emotions when I see that play: I don't know whether to laugh or cry.*

emotional   *adj.* **1.** passionate, ardent, stirring: *That display was one of the most emotional scenes I've ever seen.* **2.** hysterical, overwrought, zealous, enthusiastic, impetuous: *I can't understand why my mother gets so emotional just because I keep breaking my arm playing football.* **ant.** calm, tranquil, placid.

emphasis   *n.* stress, accent: *I think that our history teacher puts too much emphasis on the history of Brazil. The first syllable of "funny" receives much more emphasis than the second.*

emphatic   *adj.* definite, positive, energetic, forceful, strong: *The speaker made an emphatic point that turned out to be completely wrong.* **ant.** quiet, lax, unforceful.

employ   *vb.* **1.** use, utilize, apply: *It isn't necessary to employ foul language just because you're angry.* **2.** hire, engage, retain: *The company employs people according to their skill.* *n.* employment, service: *My sister left the employ of that restaurant last week.* **ant.** *vb.* **1.** waste, ignore, disregard.

employee, employe   *n.* worker, laborer, wage-earner, servant: *The largest company in our town has more than 5,000 employees.* **ant.** employer, boss.

employer   *n.* boss, proprietor, owner, management, manager, supervisor, superintendent: *Our employer gives us ten paid holidays a year.* **ant.** worker, employee.

employment   *n.* work; job, position: *I was looking for employment after school and on Saturdays.*

empty   *adj.* vacant, unoccupied, void, blank: *Except for the gold coin, the box was empty. I sat staring at the empty sheet of paper, wondering what to write about.* *vb.* void, unload, evacuate: *Empty that bucket of water outside.* **ant.** *adj.* full, filled. *vb.* fill.

enchant   *vb.* charm, fascinate, delight, bewitch: *My mother's* *friend enchanted us with her stories about India and China. The figures in the enchanted picture kept moving about.* **ant.** bore, tire.

enclose *vb.* surround, encircle: *We built a fence that enclosed the entire ranch.* **ant.** exclude.

encounter *vb.* meet, come across, face: *We encountered our old neighbors while shopping at the supermarket.* *n.* meeting; appointment, rendezvous: *Let me tell you about an encounter I once had with a poisonous snake.*

encourage *vb.* inspirit, support, inspire: *After meeting with the basketball coach, I was encouraged to try out for the team.* **ant.** discourage, dissuade, deter.

end *n.* **1.** extremity, tail-end, termination: *After winding it for three hours, I finally came to the end of the string.* **2.** limit, termination, bound: *Before Einstein, scientists used to think that space had no end.* **3.** finish, conclusion, termination, close: *The symphony came to an end and we all applauded.* **4.** aim, purpose, object, intent: *What end have you in view when you behave so badly?* *vb.* stop, finish, terminate, close, halt: *I wish that nations could end all their wrangling so we could have peace.* **ant.** *n.* beginning, start, opening, launch. *vb.* begin, start, launch, initiate.

endeavor *vb.* try, attempt, strive, struggle: *If you promise to be good, I'll endeavor to forgive you.* *n.* try, attempt, exertion, struggle: *Phoebe has made a serious endeavor to memorize her part in the school play.*

endow *vb.* give, bestow: *Cynthia is endowed with the most beautiful hair I've ever seen.* **ant.** divest.

endure *vb.* **1.** last, continue, persist: *The kinds of governments that limit the power of the people cannot endure for long.* **2.** suffer, bear, undergo, experience: *I don't think I could endure the pain and discomfort of another broken arm.* **ant.** **1.** fail, perish, die.

enemy *n.* foe, adversary, opponent, antagonist, rival: *By his continual unpleasant reviews, the critic made many enemies.* **ant.** friend, colleague, cohort, ally.

energetic *adj.* vigorous, active, forceful, potent: *Only the energetic pursuit of justice can achieve liberty for all.* **ant.** lazy, indolent, sluggish, lax.

energy *n.* power, force, strength, vigor: *If you put as much energy into your schoolwork as you do into football, you'd be at the top of your class.* **ant.** lethargy, feebleness.

engage *vb.* **1.** employ, occupy: *I am engaged in research* *for a new project.* **2.** employ, hire, retain: *She was engaged as a secretary, but she has now been made president of the company.* **ant. 1.** disengage. **2.** fire, dismiss, discharge.

engaged *adj.* **1.** betrothed, affianced, spoken for: *Vera and Ed were engaged for only a few months before their marriage.* **2.** occupied, busy: *I can't connect you now, the line is engaged.*

engaging *adj.* beguiling, enchanting, charming: *My sister's boyfriend has such an engaging manner that we can't help liking him.* **ant.** boring, ordinary.

enjoyment *n.* delight, pleasure, gratification: *Some people derive enjoyment from helping others.* **ant.** displeasure, abhorrence.

enlarge *vb.* increase, amplify, extend, expand, magnify. *The balloon became greatly enlarged as gas was pumped into it.* **ant.** decrease, diminish, wane, shrink.

enlighten *vb.* inform, teach, educate: *The most politically advanced nations have the most enlightened citizens.* **ant.** confuse.

enlist *vb.* enroll, enter, sign up, register: *Instead of waiting to be drafted, my father enlisted in the navy.* **ant.** leave, abandon, quit.

enormous *adj.* huge, immense, gigantic, vast, colossal, stupendous, gargantuan: *From the ground sprang up an enormous beanstalk, which reached right up to the sky.* **ant.** small, diminutive, tiny, slight, infinitesimal.

enrage *vb.* infuriate, anger, madden: *The enraged mob crowded against the prison gates.* **ant.** soothe, appease, calm.

enroll *vb.* enlist, register, sign up: *Jim's father enrolled in some adult-education classes at the university.* **ant.** leave, quit, abandon.

ensue *vb.* follow, succeed; arise, result: *An argument started and, in the ensuing fight, three men were hurt.*

enterprise *n.* **1.** project, venture, undertaking: *America is one of the few countries where a new enterprise can succeed.* **2.** courage, boldness, drive, energy: *Bob has the enterprise necessary to do well in anything he gets involved in.*

enterprising *adj.* resourceful, energetic: *It's very enterprising of Bill to establish his own repair shop.* **ant.** indolent, lazy, unresourceful, sluggish.

entertain *vb.* amuse, divert; interest: *We were all entertained by the clowns.* **ant.** bore, tire.

enthusiasm *n.* eagerness, zeal, earnestness: *Jean's enthusiasm for scuba diving led to her interest in marine biology.* **ant.** indifference, unconcern.

enthusiastic *adj.* eager, zealous, earnest: *We were so enthusiastic about the new football team that we bought a season ticket to see their games.* **ant.** indifferent, aloof, unconcerned.

entire *adj.* whole, complete; intact, undivided: *The entire car was being supported by only one nail. The magician seemed to slice through the orange with the sword yet leave it entire.* **ant.** partial, incomplete, separated, divided.

entitle *vb.* authorize, allow, empower: *Knowing the President doesn't entitle you to address him by his first name.*

entrance *n.* entry, door, access, gate, opening: *The entrance to the enchanted cottage was through a door made of gingerbread.* **ant.** exit.

entreat *vb.* beg, plead, implore: *Nellie entreated her husband to stop watching TV and pay some attention to her.*

entreaty *n.* appeal, plea: *The math teacher ignored every entreaty to give the class another day to study before the test.*

environment *n.* surroundings, habitat, conditions: *Growing up in a bad environment can determine whether or not a youngster becomes a criminal.*

envy *n.* jealousy, covetousness: *Millie regarded her sister's new coat with envy.* *vb.* covet: *You shouldn't envy your friends' property.* **ant.** *n.* generosity.

episode *n.* event, occurrence, incident: *I considered living in the city as just another episode in my life.*

equal *adj.* **1.** equivalent; same, identical: *All men and women are supposed to be equal in the eyes of the law. Four is equal to two plus two.* **2.** even, regular, uniform: *Equal rights are provided for under the Constitution.* *vb.* match: *The wealthy man said that he would equal any contribution to the library fund.* **ant.** *adj.* **1.** unequal, different. **2.** uneven, irregular.

equip *vb.* furnish, outfit, provide: *Before we left, we made sure that we were fully equipped with all the camping gear we might need.*

equipment *n.* material, materials, utensils, apparatus: *What kind of equipment would I need to become a stamp collector?*

era *n.* period, time, age: *The electronic era began with the invention of the transistor.*

erase *vb.* remove, obliterate, expunge; cancel: *The police made the boys erase all of the writing on the wall.* **ant.** include, add.

erect *adj.* upright, vertical, straight: *Sometimes I get a little dizzy when I stand erect after bending over.* *vb.* build, construct, raise; set up: *The men erected the temporary building in less than two days.* **ant.** *adj.* horizontal, flat. *vb.* demolish, raze, flatten.

erroneous *adj.* mistaken, wrong, inaccurate, incorrect, false, untrue: *The teacher gave a failing grade to all those who had more than three erroneous answers on the examination.* **ant.** correct, right, accurate, true.

error *n.* mistake, oversight, inaccuracy, slip, blunder: *There are too many spelling errors in this report.*

escape *vb.* **1.** run away, steal away, flee: *Three prisoners have escaped from the county jail.* **2.** avoid, elude, evade: *Running away through the swamp, the men escaped their pursuers.* *n.* flight, departure; release: *The criminal's escape was reported on the radio.*

escort *n.* guard, protection, convoy; guide: *The murderer was brought to the jail by an armed escort.* *vb.* accompany, attend, usher; guard, protect: *The shipment of gold was escorted by ten men with shotguns.*

especially *adv.* particularly, unusually, chiefly, specially: *An especially heavy guard was set up around the palace after the threatening phone call.*

essence *n.* character, principle, nature, basis: *The essence of the problem lay in the fact that Reggie didn't want to go to school.*

essential *adj.* important, necessary, vital, critical, indispensable: *In addition to knowing the subjects he is teaching, it is essential that a teacher be kind and understanding.* *n.* necessity, requirement: *Oxygen is an essential for all mammals.* **ant.** *adj.* unimportant, dispensable, inessential, unnecessary.

establish *vb.* found, form, set up, begin: *The colonists established a new village at the mouth of the river.* **ant.** discontinue, disperse, scatter.

esteem *vb.* prize, value, regard highly, revere, respect: *The students as well as the teachers esteemed the headmaster of the school as a great educator.* *n.* respect, reverence, regard, honor, admiration: *The captain was held in* *esteem by his crew.* **ant.** *vb.* disdain, disregard, scorn. *n.* scorn, contempt.

estimate *vb.* value, gauge, evaluate, judge, compute: *The expert estimated that our paintings were worth almost one million dollars.* *n.* value, evaluation, computation: *The insurance company considered the estimate too high for repairing the old car.*

eternal *adj.* everlasting, endless, perpetual: *Most religions believe that their god or gods are eternal.* **ant.** brief, passing, temporary, transient.

etiquette *n.* decorum, (good) manners: *This book on etiquette has a chapter about how to invite people to a party.*

evade *vb.* elude, avoid, escape, dodge: *The fox evaded the hunters by doubling back on the trail.* **ant.** meet, confront, face.

evaporate *vb.* vaporize; disappear, vanish: *The water evaporated into the air. Our picnic plans evaporated when we saw the storm coming.* **ant.** appear, condense.

even *adj.* **1.** level, smooth, flat: *It was easier to walk where the ground was even.* **2.** equal, balanced, square: *If I give you the dollar I owe you we'll be even.* **3.** parallel: *The police car drew up even with us.* *adv.* just, exactly: *Even as I was watching, the sun disappeared and it started to rain.* **ant.** *adj.* **1.** bumpy, irregular. **2.** unequal, unbalanced. **3.** divergent.

evening *n.* dusk, twilight, nightfall, sundown: *Toward evening the stars came out.* **ant.** dawn, sunrise.

event *n.* occurrence, incident, episode: *I ought to explain the events that led up to my decision to write this book. The study of history is essential to the understanding of current events.*

eventual *adj.* ultimate, consequent: *The eventual result of crime is usually punishment.* **ant.** current, present.

ever *adv.* **1.** always, continuously, constantly: *The sea, like the clouds in the sky, is ever changing.* **2.** at all, at any time: *Haven't you ever told a lie?* **ant.** never.

evidence *n.* **1.** proof, testimony, grounds: *I know you think he took your umbrella, but have you any real evidence?* **2.** indication, sign: *The best evidence I have is that I saw him using it when it was raining.*

evident *adj.* clear, plain, obvious, apparent: *It was evident from the chocolate around his mouth that Ronnie had eaten the candy.* **ant.** unclear, obscure, doubtful, uncertain.

evil *adj.* **1.** sinful, immoral, wicked, bad: *Some people used to think that any kind of entertainment on Sunday was evil.* **2.** harmful, injurious: *Drinking alcoholic beverages is an evil practice.* *n.* harm, woe; badness, wickedness, sin: *Evil to him who does evil.* **ant.** *adj.* **1.** virtuous, moral, upright, good. **2.** beneficial, advantageous, useful. *n.* goodness, virtue, uprightness.

evolve *vb.* develop, grow, emerge, result: *The way society evolved in that country, there was neither need nor opportunity for education.*

exact *adj.* correct, accurate, errorless, faultless: *Yours is an exact copy of that painting in the museum.* **ant.** inexact, inaccurate, faulty.

exaggerate *vb.* overstate, magnify: *I knew Tommy was exaggerating when he said that the elephant was as big as a house.* **ant.** minimize, understate, diminish.

examination *n.* **1.** inspection, scrutiny, investigation: *The jury was cautioned to rely only on a careful examination of the testimony and the evidence.* **2.** test: *I haven't yet studied for my math examination.*

examine *vb.* inspect, investigate, scrutinize: *After examining me carefully, the doctor said I was fit as a fiddle.*

example *n.* sample, specimen, model: *This is a fine example of the sand paintings done by the Indians.*

exceed *vb.* beat, surpass, outdo, excel: *The workmanship on this box exceeds any I have ever seen.*

excel *vb.* outdo, surpass, exceed: *Matilda excels at sports.*

excellence *n.* superiority, distinction: *Frank was given an award for excellence in seamanship.* **ant.** inferiority, poorness, badness.

excellent *adj.* fine, superior, wonderful, marvelous: *Dave is an excellent swimmer.* **ant.** inferior, poor, bad, terrible, substandard.

except *prep.* save, but, excepting, barring, excluding: *Everyone wanted to go skiing except Donald.*

exceptional *adj.* unusual, different, strange, irregular, abnormal: *You must admit that a house made out of gingerbread and candy icing is very exceptional, indeed.* **ant.** unexceptional, ordinary, commonplace.

excess *adj.* profuse, abundant, immoderate: *The government checked up on all companies they thought might be earning excess profits.* *n.* profusion, lavishness: *Baggage weighing in excess of 44 pounds is charged for at a high rate.* **ant.** *adj.* sparse, inconsequential, meager.

exchange   vb. trade, swap; barter: *I exchanged a dollar for four quarters.* n. **1.** trade, interchange: *In exchange for the three neckties, Suzie took a pair of warm gloves.* **2.** market: *Don't invest all your money in the stock exchange.*

excite   vb. stir up, arouse, stimulate; move: *The thought of going canoeing on the river excited us.* ant. lull, bore.

exclamation   n. outcry, shout, clamor: *With an exclamation of disgust, he turned and left the restaurant.*

exclude   vb. keep out, shut out, bar, except: *I cannot understand why we were excluded from membership in the club.* ant. include, embrace, involve.

exclusion   n. bar, exception, rejection: *The boys' exclusion from the theater came about because of their rowdy behavior.* ant. inclusion.

exclusive   adj. **1.** limited, restricted, restrictive, selective: *Do I have your exclusive permission to represent you?* **2.** select, fashionable, choice: *We can't afford to stay at an exclusive hotel, so we go to a boarding house.* ant. **1.** general, unrestricted. **2.** ordinary, unfashionable, common.

excuse   vb. forgive, pardon: *Please excuse Phil for speaking rudely; he didn't mean it.* n. explanation, reason, plea, apology: *The teacher accepted Sam's excuse for lateness.* ant. vb. condemn.

execute   vb. **1.** carry out, do, complete, achieve: *Every soldier is expected to execute the orders given him.* **2.** kill, put to death, hang: *Three men convicted of murder were executed last week.*

exercise   n. **1.** practice, drill, training; gymnastics, calisthenics: *Exercise is good for you. The old man said he did exercises every morning.* **2.** use, application, employment. *The exercise of a citizen's rights is a duty.* vb. train, drill, practice: *Don't exercise after a large meal.*

exertion   n. effort, attempt, endeavor, strain: *The exertion of carrying the couch upstairs made us all out of breath.*

exhaust   vb. **1.** tire, fatigue, wear out: *I was exhausted from chopping wood for three hours.* **2.** use, use up, consume; spend: *If man isn't careful, he may exhaust many of the natural resources of the earth.* ant. **1.** refresh, renew. **2.** replenish, replace.

exhibit   vb. **1.** show, display, demonstrate: *At the World's Fair some manufacturers exhibited their future product designs.* **2.** show, display, betray, reveal: *With a sneer Sophie exhibited her hatred for fried spinach.* n. show, display, demonstration, exhibition: *We saw an interesting exhibit of weaving at the county fair.* **ant.** *vb.* conceal, hide, disguise.

exile *vb.* banish, cast out, expel, deport: *The government once exiled criminals to distant colonies.* *n.* banishment, deportation, expulsion: *The exile of the king was forced by the revolutionaries.*

expand *vb.* enlarge, swell, inflate; bloat: *As the gas tank emptied, the balloon expanded and began to rise.* **ant.** shrink, shrivel, contract.

expect *vb.* anticipate, await, look forward to: *I was expecting you to say that. Your father was expected on the noon train.*

expedition *n.* journey, voyage, trip, excursion: *Tom's grandfather went on an expedition to South America early in this century.*

expel *vb.* drive out *or* away, discharge; banish, deport, exile: *The unpleasant man was expelled from the restaurant. They expelled the aliens from the country.* **ant.** invite, accept.

expend *vb.* use, consume, exhaust: *Too much energy was expended in shoveling the snow when a machine could have been used.* **ant.** conserve, reserve, ration.

expense *n.* cost, price, charge, payment: *The expense of the trip would be covered by the sponsors of the contest.*

expensive *adj.* dear, costly, high-priced: *We bought a small car last year because gasoline was so expensive.* **ant.** inexpensive, modest, low-priced, low-cost, cheap.

experience *n.* **1.** encountering, living, existence: *I have had a little experience in dealing with naughty children.* **2.** knowledge, background, skill: *You don't have enough experience to be an executive in this company.* *vb.* feel, live through, undergo: *No one can know what war is like until he has experienced it.* **ant.** *n.* inexperience, naiveté.

experienced *adj.* skilled, accomplished, expert, practiced, able, qualified: *My mother is an experienced teacher of foreign languages.* **ant.** inexperienced, untutored, naive, unpracticed.

experiment *n.* test, trial; research: *Some people don't approve of doing experiments on animals.* *vb.* test, prove, try, examine: *The scientists are going to experiment on human beings for the next space launch.*

expert *n.* authority, specialist: *It takes many years of train-*

ing to become an expert in Chinese art. adj. skillful, experienced, knowledgeable, skilled: *The factory has three job openings for expert tool makers.* **ant.** *adj.* unskilled, untrained, inexperienced.

expire *vb.* terminate, end, cease; die: *My subscription expires with the next issue of the magazine. The old man expired on the steps of the church.*

explain *vb.* **1.** clarify, define, interpret: *Scientists cannot explain how the earth began.* **2.** justify, account for: *How do you explain what you were doing at the movies when you were supposed to be at school?*

explanation *n.* **1.** description, definition, interpretation: *Please give me an explanation of how the Constitution is applied to defend citizens' rights.* **2.** account, justification; reason; excuse: *The teacher refused to accept Beth's explanation for why she was late.*

exploit *n.* feat, accomplishment, achievement: *Riding a bicycle on a tightrope across Niagara Falls is a fantastic exploit.*

explore *vb.* investigate, examine: *Can you imagine how brave the men must have been who first explored central Africa?*

expose *vb.* reveal, bare, uncover, display, disclose: *The theater curtain was pulled back to expose a man in chains submerged in a glass tank filled with water.* **ant.** conceal, hide, cover, mask.

express *vb.* state, declare: *A civilized person learns to express himself clearly.* *adj.* **1.** specific, precise, exact, special: *I went to the grocery for the express purpose of buying celery and then forgot it.* **2.** nonstop, quick, direct, rapid, fast: *The express train doesn't stop at those small stations.* **ant.** *adj.* **2.** local.

expression *n.* **1.** statement, declaration: *The teacher asked for an expression of interest from all those who wanted to go to the museum.* **2.** look; air: *Michele had a horrified expression on her face when we showed her the snake.*

exquisite *adj.* **1.** delicate, dainty, elegant, beautiful: *Have you ever noticed the exquisite workmanship of the crown jewels?* **2.** fine, excellent, superb, matchless, perfect: *The exquisite furnishings of the palace were known throughout the world.*

extend *vb.* **1.** stretch, stretch out: *The forest extended as far as the eye could see.* **2.** lengthen: *The ladder can be extended another six feet.* **3.** give, offer, grant; yield: *We* *all extend you our best wishes on your birthday.* **ant. 2.** shorten, abbreviate, curtail.

extension *n.* stretching, expansion, enlargement, increase: *The teacher gave us an extension of the time in which to prepare our papers.*

extensive *adj.* wide, broad, spacious, vast: *In the central part of the United States is an extensive region of farmland.* **ant.** confined, restricted, narrow.

extent *n.* degree, measure, amount, range: *My French improved after my visit to Paris to the extent where I could understand everything said to me.*

exterior *n.* outside, face, surface, covering: *The exterior of our school is painted white. adj.* outside, outer, external: *Exterior paints are made with materials that resist weathering.* **ant.** *n.* interior, inside, lining. *adj.* inner, internal, interior.

external *adj.* exterior, outer, outside: *The external features of the books seem similar, but their content is very different.* **ant.** internal, interior, inner, inside.

extinct *adj.* dead, lost, gone, vanished: *We must preserve our wildlife lest it become extinct.* **ant.** alive, present, extant, flourishing.

extract *vb.* draw out, withdraw, pull out, remove: *The knight extracted the sword from the stone where it had been embedded. n.* essence, distillate: *The doctor prescribed an extract of cascara for my stomach ache.* **ant.** *vb.* insert, introduce, penetrate.

extraordinary *adj.* unusual, exceptional, rare, uncommon, remarkable: *The reason I learned so much at school is that I had an extraordinary teacher.* **ant.** ordinary, commonplace, usual.

extravagant *adj.* wasteful, lavish, excessive: *Philip and Peter were so extravagant that they spent their money in a day.* **ant.** frugal, economical, prudent, thrifty, provident.

extreme *adj.* **1.** utmost, greatest: *Tim's extreme nervousness made his hands shake.* **2.** furthest, outermost, endmost, ultimate: *In the picture at the extreme right the monkey is washing his hands.* **3.** excessive, immoderate: *This morning I am suffering from an extreme pain in the neck. n.* end, limit, extremity: *I can understand being angry, but jumping up and down is going to extremes.* **ant.** *adj.* **3.** modest, moderate, reasonable.

⊰ F ⊱

fable *n.* **1.** parable, tale, legend, myth, story: *Aesop's Fables are among the most popular in the world.* **2.** falsehood, fib, fiction, tale; lie: *That story about his getting a medal for swimming was a complete fable.*

fabric *n.* cloth, material, textile: *This is too lightweight a fabric for a winter coat.*

fabricate *vb.* make, manufacture, assemble, construct, form: *It is now possible to fabricate many parts of a new house in a factory and then put it together at the site.* **ant.** destroy, demolish, raze.

fabulous *adj.* fantastic, unbelievable, amazing, astonishing, astounding: *The returning explorer told a fabulous story about finding a golden mountain.* **ant.** commonplace, ordinary.

face *n.* **1.** look, expression; features, visage, countenance: *Roger made a funny face when the teacher wasn't looking. She has a friendly face.* **2.** front, façade: *The face of the cliff was too steep for us to climb.* *vb.* meet, encounter, confront: *I'll never be able to face Louis now that I know he tried to kiss my sister.* **ant.** *vb.* avoid, evade, shun.

facility *n.* **1.** ease, skill, skillfulness, ability: *The instructor skis down that steep slope with such great facility.* **2.** equipment, material: *This laboratory is equipped with every modern facility for research.* **ant.** **1.** difficulty, effort, labor.

fact *n.* truth, certainty, actuality, reality: *It is now known to be a fact that the earth is shaped like a ball.*

factual *adj.* correct, accurate, true: *The newspaper reporter gave a factual account of the disaster.* **ant.** erroneous, invented, fabricated, incorrect.

faculty *n.* ability, capacity, talent: *Spencer has the faculty of making everyone like him.*

fade *vb.* **1.** pale, bleach, discolor: *These curtains have faded from being in the bright sunlight.* **2.** diminish, weaken, fail: *My strength began to fade and I was afraid I couldn't hold on any longer.* **ant.** **2.** increase, grow, wax.

fail *vb.* **1.** fall short, miss, founder: *The explorer failed* *in his attempt to find the source of the Nile.* **2.** disappoint: *Don't fail me now that I've invested so much in your success.* **3.** fade, weaken; dwindle: *Her strength failed when she reached the top.* **ant. 1.** succeed.

failure   *n.*   **1.** failing, unsuccessfulness: *The team's failure to win the game was due to lack of training.* **2.** deficiency, insufficiency: *The president's failure as a good supervisor brought about the closing of the business.* **ant.** success, achievement, accomplishment.

faint   *adj.*   **1.** dim, faded, indistinct: *The writing on the wall of the tomb was too faint to read.* **2.** feeble, weak, half-hearted: *We heard faint cries coming from inside the box.* *vb.* swoon, lose consciousness, collapse: *Ted's mother fainted when the hospital phoned about his accident.* **ant.** *adj.* **1.** clear, sharp, distinct. **2.** strong, forceful, loud.

fainthearted   *adj.* timid, shy, bashful; cowardly: *Watching a surgical operation is not for fainthearted people.* **ant.** brave, courageous, stouthearted, fearless.

fair[1]   *adj.*   **1.** just, impartial, unbiased, objective, unprejudiced; honest: *The umpire made a fair decision when he called the runner safe.* **2.** ordinary, average, not bad: *My marks for the semester were fair.* **3.** light, white, milky, blond: *She had fair hair but a swarthy skin.* **4.** beautiful: *Every knight yearned to save a fair damsel in distress.* **5.** sunny, pleasant, bright, unclouded: *The weather forecaster predicted it would be fair for our picnic tomorrow.* **ant. 1.** unfair, unjust, biased. **3.** dark, dusky, swarthy. **4.** stormy, cloudy, threatening.

fair[2]   *n.* exhibit, exhibition, festival, bazaar, carnival: *I know some people who visited the New York World's Fair in 1939.*

fairy   *n.* pixie, sprite, elf, brownie: *Don't you believe in fairies?*

faith   *n.*   **1.** trust, reliance, belief: *I have faith in everything you say.* **2.** belief, religion, creed: *The rights of Americans are equal regardless of their faith.* **ant. 1.** mistrust, distrust, disbelief.

faithful   *adj.*   **1.** loyal, devoted, trustworthy, trusty, true: *My dog is the only faithful friend I have, and I don't have a dog.* **2.** credible, accurate, strict: *The artist had painted a faithful copy of the museum picture.* **ant. 1.** disloyal, faithless, treacherous. **2.** inaccurate, erroneous, wrong.

fake *adj.* false, pretended, phony: *The counterfeiters were printing fake dollar bills until they were arrested. n.* fraud, cheat; counterfeit, forgery, imitation: *The man who promised to cure your cold is a fake. This diploma is a fake.* **ant.** *adj.* genuine, real, authentic.

fall *vb.* **1.** drop, descend; plunge, topple: *After the lumberjack had made a deep cut in the trunk, the tree began to fall.* **2.** die: *Two thousand brave soldiers fell in the last battle of the war.* **3.** lower, decrease, diminish: *The price of sugar has fallen during the last month. n.* **1.** autumn: *I have to go back to school next fall.* **2.** drop, decline, collapse, spill: *Prices haven't taken a fall like that for many years.* **ant.** *vb.* **1.** rise, soar, ascend. **3.** rise, increase, climb. *n.* **2.** rise, ascent, increase.

falsehood *n.* fib, story, untruth, lie: *Ben has told so many falsehoods that no one believes him even when he tells the truth.* **ant.** truth.

falter *vb.* stumble, hesitate, tremble: *Once your mind is made up, you should go ahead and not falter.*

fame *n.* name, reputation, renown, honor, glory: *The person who cures the common cold will be assured of great fame.* **ant.** anonymity.

famed *adj.* renowned, known; famous: *My grandfather was famed far and wide as the best shot in the county.* **ant.** unknown, anonymous, obscure.

familiar *adj.* **1.** known, common, frequent, well-known: *That song sounds familiar—I think it's "America, the Beautiful."* **2.** well-acquainted, friendly, close, intimate: *Jennie was a familiar friend at our house.* **3.** well-acquainted, well-versed: *I am quite familiar with the rules of the club.* **ant.** **1.** unfamiliar, unknown, foreign, alien. **2.** rare, distant. **3.** ignorant, unaware.

familiarity *n.* knowledge, understanding, awareness, comprehension: *After studying it for so many years, Don should have some familiarity with the subject.* **ant.** ignorance.

family *n.* relatives, tribe, relations, house: *During their first years of marriage, Connie and Fred's families helped the young couple financially.*

famine *n.* want, hunger, starvation: *When the crops failed, there was a famine in which thousands died.* **ant.** plenty.

famous *adj.* well-known, renowned, celebrated, famed, eminent, illustrious: *The mayor told my father that the town was proud to have such a famous resident.* **ant.** unknown, obscure, anonymous.

fancy   *n.* imagination, fantasy; taste: *My mother said that the pink tile in the kitchen didn't suit her fancy. adj.* **1.** ornate, ornamented, elaborate: *The decorations on that dress are too fancy for my taste.* **2.** special, deluxe: *We received a basket of fancy fruit for Christmas.* **ant.** *adj.* plain, unadorned, simple, undecorated.

fantastic   *adj.* unbelievable, incredible, unreal, unimaginable: *My sister looks just fantastic in her new dress. We heard a fantastic story about witches and goblins.*

fascinate   *vb.* attract, charm, bewitch, enchant: *We were fascinated by the wild animal exhibits at the museum of natural history.* **ant.** bore.

fashion   *n.* **1.** manner, way, method, mode: *The teacher spoke to the children in a friendly fashion.* **2.** style, mode, custom, vogue: *Alexandra's mother dresses in the fashion of the 1930s. vb.* make, shape, mold, form: *The potter fashioned the vase in a few minutes.*

fashionable   *adj.* stylish, chic, modish, smart: *Nicole's mother is always dressed in the most fashionable clothes.* **ant.** unfashionable, dowdy.

fast   *adj.* **1.** quick, rapid, swift, speedy: *A fast horse could get me back to the ranch in less than an hour.* **2.** secure, solid, staunch, firm: *Before leaving the house, we made sure that there was a fast lock on the door. adv.* **1.** quickly, rapidly, swiftly, speedily: *How did you get back here so fast?* **2.** tightly, securely, firmly: *The fishermen held fast to the overturned boat.* **ant.** *adj.* **1.** slow, sluggish. **2.** loose, insecure.

fasten   *vb.* attach, fix, join, secure, pin: *You don't even know how to fasten a button to a shirt!* **ant.** loosen, loose, free, release, unclasp.

fat   *adj.* **1.** fatty, oily, greasy: *The doctor told me not to eat so many fat foods.* **2.** obese, plump, fleshy, stout, chubby: *Betty used to be fat, but since her diet has lost a lot of weight.* **3.** thick, wide: *The lawyer carried a fat briefcase into court.* **ant.** **2.** thin, lean, emaciated, slim, scrawny.

fatal   *adj.* **1.** deadly, lethal, mortal: *The wound from the sword proved to be fatal, and the soldier died that night.* **2.** fateful, doomed, inevitable: *Any mistake in timing dur-*

*ing a rocket launching could be fatal for the entire proj-
ect.* **ant. 1.** nonfatal.

fate *n.* fortune, luck, chance, destiny: *It was fate that we
should meet here, at the edge of the cliff.*

fatherly *adj.* paternal, paternalistic, protective, kind: *My
cousin gave me some fatherly advice before I was sent
away to school.*

fatigue *n.* weariness, exhaustion, tiredness: *After three days
in the wilderness, the child was found suffering from
fatigue and exposure.* **ant.** energy

fault *n.* **1.** defect, imperfection, flaw, blemish, weakness:
*The mechanic could find no fault with the engine in my
car.* **2.** blame, responsibility: *It's your own fault you have
a cold if you won't wear your scarf.*

faulty *adj.* defective, imperfect, damaged, broken: *There
was a faulty lock on the door and the thieves broke in
there.* **ant.** perfect, flawless, whole.

favor *n.* approval, liking, benefit: *In Ken's favor, I must admit that he works very hard.* *vb.* **1.** approve, like, prefer:
I favor support for local libraries. **2.** prefer, patronize,
support: *The girls favor having a swimming team.* **ant.**
vb. disapprove, deplore.

favorite *n.* pet, darling: *Irena is the teacher's favorite. adj.*
favored, preferred, liked: *My favorite ice cream is chocolate.*

fear *n.* fright, dread, terror, alarm, dismay, anxiety: *As the
killer approached him with knife drawn, Ron felt his
fear overcome him.* *vb.* dread, be afraid of: *This snake is
completely harmless, and you have nothing to fear.*

fearless *adj.* brave, courageous, bold: *The leader of the band
of pirates was fearless and would fight with anyone.* **ant.**
fearful, timid, cowardly.

feast *n.* banquet; dinner, barbecue: *After the wedding ceremony, we were all treated to a feast at the bride's father's
home.* *vb.* dine, gluttonize: *We feasted on venison and
roasted ox.*

feat *n.* achievement, act, deed: *Leaping across the canyon
was a feat for the motorcycle rider.*

feature *n.* quality, characteristic, trait: *One of the features
of life in America is political independence.* *vb.* star, promote: *Last week the shop featured blue jeans at half
price.*

fee *n.* pay, payment, remuneration: *The lawyer charged a lot
as a fee for his services.*

feeble *adj.* weak; frail, sickly, infirm: *The old man made a feeble attempt to fight off the robbers.* **ant.** strong, powerful, potent.

feed *vb.* nourish, satisfy: *My father had six mouths to feed and always worked very hard.* *n.* fodder, forage, food: *The farmer stocked up on feed for his cattle for the winter.*

feel *vb.* experience, sense; perceive: *I tried to feel pity for the doomed criminal. John felt his way along in the dark.*

feeling *n.* **1.** emotion, sentiment, sympathy: *Finding her lost kitten gave Susan a feeling of joy.* **2.** attitude, belief, thought, opinion: *My mother had a feeling that I would do well in school.*

ferocious *adj.* fierce, savage, bloodthirsty, wild: *The old house was guarded by two ferocious dogs.* **ant.** gentle, playful, calm, harmless.

fertile *adj.* productive, rich, fruitful: *The bottom land on our farm is the most fertile. Judy has a fertile mind and is always coming up with new ideas.* **ant.** barren, sterile, unproductive.

festive *adj.* merry, gay, joyful, joyous: *All of his friends had a festive time at Miles's birthday party.* **ant.** sad, mournful, morose, gloomy.

fetching *adj.* attractive, charming, pleasing: *The movie star was wearing a fetching gown of red silk.*

feud *n.* quarrel, argument, dispute, strife: *Because of the feud between them, the two families hadn't spoken to one another for years.*

fierce *adj.* savage, ferocious, furious, violent, wild: *The circus specialized in exhibiting fierce lions and tigers trained to perform for the crowds.* **ant.** gentle, peaceful, harmless.

fight *n.* battle, war, conflict, combat: *When the enemy gunboat fired a shot across our bows, we knew we had a fight on our hands.* *vb.* combat, battle, struggle: *Brothers shouldn't fight against each other.*

figure *n.* **1.** pattern, design: *This necktie has figures of sailboats on it.* **2.** form, outline, shape, mold, frame: *My girl friend has a nice figure. We could see the figure of a man against the sky at the top of the hill.* *vb.* calculate, reckon, determine, compute: *I've already figured my income tax for this year.*

filth *n.* dirt, foulness, pollution, sewage: *The town on the river was responsible for the filth we saw floating by.*

filthy *adj.* dirty, foul; polluted, contaminated: *Those socks of yours are filthy because you never wash them. The lake where we used to swim became filthy after the factory dumped its wastes into it.* **ant.** clean, pure, unspoiled.

final *adj.* last, ultimate, terminal, concluding: *This will be the final call for dinner.* **ant.** first, initial, beginning, starting.

fine *adj.* **1.** excellent, superior, superb, choice, exquisite, perfect: *After living in France, we developed a taste for fine foods and wines.* **2.** thin, minute; powdered: *The holes in the strainer are too fine to allow the noodles to pass through. The stone was ground down to a fine consistency.* **ant. 1.** inferior, poor, squalid. **2.** coarse, broad.

finish *vb.* **1.** end, terminate, close, conclude: *The opera finished on a note of triumph. Please finish whatever you are doing so that you can help me wash the dishes.* **2.** consume, use up, complete: *Finish your lima beans and then we'll see if you deserve ice cream for dessert.* *n.* **1.** conclusion, end, close, termination: *I've written a new finish for my play; do you want to read it?* **2.** surface, patina, polish: *We had to have a new finish put on the table because you spilled paint on it.* **ant.** *vb.* **1.** begin, start, open. *n.* **1.** opening, start, beginning.

firm *adj.* **1.** rigid, stiff, solid; unchanging, inflexible, steadfast, unshakable: *Quentin was firm in his conviction that his father was innocent of the theft. The house was on a firm foundation.* **2.** compact, dense, hard: *For a really sound sleep, I prefer a firm mattress.* *n.* company, business, concern; partnership, corporation: *My uncle works for a firm that manufactures striped paint.* **ant.** *adj.* **1.** limp, drooping, soft, weak. **2.** soft, squashy.

fit *adj.* **1.** suited, suitable, appropriate, proper, fitting: *It wasn't a fit night out for man or beast.* **2.** ready, prepared, suited, fitted: *We had all our equipment and were fit to go camping.* **3.** healthy, robust: *The doctor said I could keep fit if I continued to get exercise.* *vb.* **1.** conform: *That dress doesn't fit you at all.* **2.** agree, suit, belong, harmonize: *They made the punishment fit the crime.* **3.** equip, fit out, outfit, provide: *We were fitted out for the safari by the biggest store in New York. After the robbery, we had to fit the window with new panes of glass.* *n.* **1.** conformation: *The shoes were a good fit.* **2.**

spasm, convulsion, seizure, attack: *Dinah was doubled over in a fit of laughing.*

fitting *adj.* suitable, apt, proper, due: *It isn't fitting for a young person to be impolite to adults.* **ant.** unsuitable, inappropriate, improper.

fix *vb.* **1.** attach, rivet, cement, fasten, pin, tie, secure, affix: *The teacher fixed the sign to the bulletin board.* **2.** repair, mend: *The man at the shop on the corner can fix radios.* **3.** determine, establish, pinpoint: *We fixed a time for my next appointment.*

flame *n.* fire, blaze: *It was the flame from one match that caused the huge forest fire.*

flash *n.* **1.** flame, flare: *The people's faces were lit up by the flash from the camera.* **2.** instant, wink, second, twinkling: *In a flash, Santa Claus was back up the chimney.* *vb.* gleam, sparkle, twinkle, glitter: *Maureen's eyes flashed with anger.*

flat *adj.* **1.** level, even, smooth: *The land was as flat as a pancake as far as the eye could see.* **2.** dull, uninteresting, boring, lifeless: *We all found the play a little flat.* *adv.* evenly, smoothly: *That rug should lie flat on the floor. The poster was pasted down flat against the wall.* **ant.** *adj.* **1.** uneven, rough, bumpy. **2.** interesting, stimulating.

flavor *n.* **1.** taste, savor, tang: *This soup has the flavor of lemon.* **2.** quality, characteristic, essence, character: *That painting really gives you the flavor of the sea.* *vb.* season, spice: *Vickie flavored the salad dressing with cheese.*

flaw *n.* imperfection, spot, fault, blemish, defect: *The manufacturer called back all of the new model cars because there was a flaw in the brake system.*

flee *vb.* run away, desert, escape: *When we saw the watchdog coming towards us, we all fled.*

fleet *adj.* swift, fast, rapid, quick: *In ancient times, the news was carried by fleet runners between towns.* **ant.** slow, sluggish.

fleeting *adj.* temporary, brief, passing, swift: *I caught only a fleeting glance at the sign as we sped by and couldn't read it.* **ant.** permanent, fixed, stable, lasting.

flexible *adj.* **1.** elastic, supple, pliant, pliable: *You'll need a flexible wire to reach into that clogged drain.* **2.** yielding, easy, agreeable, adaptable: *My plans for this evening are flexible, so I can meet you at any time.* **ant.** inflexible, rigid, firm, unyielding, fixed.

flimsy *adj.* weak, wobbly, frail, fragile: *I wouldn't put that heavy sculpture on such a flimsy table. Saying that he had a pain in his toe was giving a pretty flimsy excuse for staying home.* **ant.** strong, firm, stable.

fling *vb.* toss, throw, pitch: *Walter flung the curtain aside and stepped into the room.* *n.* party, celebration, fun: *Roberta has had her fling and can now get back to more serious things.*

flit *vb.* fly, skim, dart: *The hummingbird flits from flower to flower drinking up the nectar.*

flock *n.* group, gathering; herd, flight, swarm, school: *A flock of birds flew about in the sky over the meadow.*

flood *n.* deluge, overflow: *After two weeks of rain, we knew that the river would rise over its banks and cause a flood.* *vb.* deluge, overflow, inundate: *When the sink drain clogged up, the water flooded the bathroom floor.*

flourish *vb.* **1.** grow, succeed, prosper: *Because of his hard work, Dick's business flourished, and he was soon employing twenty people.* **2.** wave, brandish: *The Samurai flourished his great sword.* **ant.** **1.** decline, die.

flow *vb.* **1.** stream, pour, run: *The mill stream flowed right under the middle of the building.* **2.** spurt, squirt, gush, spout: *We couldn't stop the oil from flowing out of the broken pipe.* *n.* outpouring, discharge, stream: *The doctor first tried to stop the flow of blood from the wound.*

fluent *adj.* flowing, glib: *I am not yet fluent in Spanish.*

fluid *n.* liquid; gas: *Water is one of the most common fluids on earth.* *adj.* liquid, liquefied, running; gaseous: *You have to heat the butter or lard until it is fluid for this recipe.*

flush *adj.* even, level, flat: *Then we sanded down the door of the cabinet till it was flush with the top.*

fly *vb.* **1.** soar, wing, hover, flit: *At the sound of our footsteps, the scarlet bird flew away.* **2.** flee, escape, withdraw: *The minute the door was left open unguarded, the prisoners flew out.*

foam *n.* lather, froth: *Ed's father explained that one isn't supposed to use shaving foam with an electric razor.*

foe *n.* enemy, adversary, antagonist, opponent: *We met the foe on the battlefield and finally conquered them all.* **ant.** friend, ally.

fog *n.* **1.** mist, cloud, haze: *We couldn't see our way in the dense fog.* **2.** confusion, daze, stupor: *Millie is in* *such a fog that she hardly recognizes her friends. vb.* befog, steam, obscure, blur: *The windshield was fogged by our breath.*

fold *vb.* **1.** double, lap, overlap: *After folding your paper in half, write your name at the top on the left.* **2.** clasp: *Ricky folded his arms across his chest and waited for Vincent to do something. n.* lap, pleat, tuck, overlap: *Put two folds into the napkin when you set the table.*

follow *vb.* **1.** succeed, ensue: *Let's play "follow the leader." The mother duck swims along first, and the baby ducklings follow.* **2.** obey, heed, observe: *If you want to play any game at all, you must follow the rules.* **3.** chase, pursue, track; trace: *Bloodhounds can follow even the faintest scent.* **ant. 1.** lead.

follower *n.* pupil, disciple: *The followers of the founder of the new religion gave him enormous amounts of money.* **ant.** leader.

following *n.* supporters, disciples, public: *For a young man, he has quite a large following.*

folly *n.* silliness, stupidity: *People once thought that steam engines wouldn't work, so they called the first steamboat "Fulton's Folly."*

fond *adj.* **1.** attached, affectionate: *I am very fond of chocolate ice cream.* **2.** affectionate, loving, tender: *Carolyn was aware of the fond looks being given her by Patrick.*

fondness *n.* liking, affection, partiality: *We have all developed a fondness for Valerie.* **ant.** unfriendliness, hostility.

food *n.* sustenance, bread, victuals, provisions: *The price of food has increased by more than 10 percent during the period.*

fool *n.* **1.** clown, jester: *The king always insisted on having the fool at his side.* **2.** idiot, dolt, dope, dunce, simpleton, blockhead, ninny, nincompoop, nitwit, oaf, jackass, buffoon, goose: *If you think you can commit a crime without getting caught you are a fool.* *vb.* **1.** jest, joke, play: *I didn't mean anything cruel—I was just fooling.* **2.** deceive, trick, hoax, hoodwink: *The magician had us all fooled—we were sure the hat was empty, but he pulled two rabbits from it!*

foolish *adj.* silly, senseless, stupid, simple: *Playing with matches is one of the most foolish things you could do.* **ant.** sensible, sound, reasonable, rational.

forbid *vb.* ban, disallow, prohibit, prevent: *I think they* *ought to forbid parking in front of the school. My mother forbade me to see that movie.* **ant.** allow, permit, let.

force *n.* strength, power, energy, might: *The force of the wind is strong enough to knock down that building. vb.* **1.** compel, oblige, coerce, make: *I was forced to accept a purple car because it was the only one available.* **2.** drive, impel, push: *We forced our way through the crowd.*

foreign *adj.* strange, unfamiliar, alien, different, exotic: *Our neighbors come from many foreign countries.* **ant.** familiar, ordinary, commonplace.

foreigner *n.* alien, stranger, outsider, newcomer: *I'm a foreigner in these parts myself, so I can't tell you where the bus stops.* **ant.** native, resident.

foreman *n.* supervisor, superintendent, super, overseer, boss: *The foreman of that department has thirty men working for him.*

forest *n.* wood, woods, woodland, grove, copse: *The children entered the forest and soon found a tiny house made of gingerbread.*

forever *adv.* always, hereafter, evermore, everlastingly: *Nobody lives forever.* **ant.** temporarily, fleetingly.

forgive *vb.* pardon, excuse: *If you apologize, the teacher might forgive you.* **ant.** censure, blame.

forgo *vb.* release, relinquish: *If you buy that model, you'll have to forgo the price reduction.*

form *n.* **1.** shape, figure, outline: *The prince disappeared, then reappeared in the form of a frog.* **2.** mold, pattern: *My father made this form so that I could cast my own lead soldiers.* **3.** kind, sort, type, style: *Vinyl is one of the many forms of plastic.* **4.** blank, paper, document: *Please fill in this form on both sides. vb.* **1.** mold, fashion, make, model, construct: *As we watched, the glassblower formed a goblet from a blob of molten glass.* **2.** instruct, teach, develop, educate: *Many believe that parents have more influence in forming a child's mind than do teachers.* **3.** take shape, grow, develop, appear: *I have watched clouds form in the sky directly over that mountain.*

formal *adj.* **1.** conventional, conformist: *The formal way to do it is to send an application in by mail.* **2.** ceremonial, ritual: *There will be a formal marriage ceremony at the church, and you are expected to wear formal clothes.* **ant.** informal, unceremonious.

former *adj.* previous, earlier, erstwhile, one-time: *There's* *my former English teacher, Miss Crumtooth.* **ant.** present, current.

formidable *adj.* imposing, alarming, terrifying, frightful, terrible, horrifying: *The knight was swinging a huge, formidable sword round and round his head. Ed is a formidable chess player.*

forsake *vb.* desert, give up, abandon, forgo: *We have forsaken life in the city for a healthier, happier life in the country.*

forth *adv.* forward, onward, out: *The young king rode forth to conquer the enemy.*

forthright *adj.* direct, honest, candid, frank, outspoken: *I wish you would be more forthright and tell me what you think.* **ant.** devious, tricky, roundabout.

forthwith *adv.* immediately, at once, without delay: *I was told to pack my belongings forthwith and to leave as soon as possible.*

fortify *vb.* strengthen, bolster, buttress: *The general fortified the town with a great wall and then fortified himself with a large whiskey.*

fortunate *adj.* lucky, blessed, charmed: *You are fortunate to have been brought up in a happy home.* **ant.** unfortunate, unlucky, cursed.

fortune *n.* **1.** luck, chance, lot, fate: *By good fortune, the gypsies were very kind to the lost boy.* **2.** wealth, riches: *Nellie will inherit a fortune when her grandfather dies.*

forward *adv.* onward, ahead: *We marched forward till given the order to halt. adj.* **1.** front, first, leading, foremost: *The forward wagons sank into the marsh before they could stop.* **2.** rude, bold, arrogant, fresh, impertinent, impudent: *Manuel's forward attitude made him few friends.* **ant.** *adv.* backward, rearward. *adj.* **1.** rearmost, last. **2.** shy, demure, retiring.

foul *adj.* **1.** dirty, filthy, unclean, impure, polluted: *The people who live in that factory town are always breathing foul air.* **2.** evil, wicked, vile, sinful: *What a foul deed! stabbing someone in the back!* **3.** stormy, bad, rainy: *We sailed through some foul weather as we rounded Cape Horn.* **ant.** **1.** clean, pure, immaculate. **2.** saintly, good. **3.** clear, sunny, calm.

found *vb.* establish, organize: *Our forefathers founded a great country.*

foundation *n.* basis, establishment, ground: *The foundations of liberty were the guiding principles of those men.*

fracture *n.* break, crack; rupture: *There was a slight fracture in the dam, but it increased to a dangerous size overnight. vb.* break, crack; rupture: *When I fell, my arm was fractured in two places.*

fragile *adj.* delicate, breakable, frail, weak: *That package is fragile, and if you drop it, it will break.* **ant.** sturdy, hardy, stout, strong.

fragment *n.* bit, part, piece, scrap, remnant: *After the tank exploded, a fragment of it was found two miles away.* **ant.** whole.

fragrance *n.* smell, odor, aroma, perfume, scent: *The fragrance of the orange blossoms in the grove is very sweet.*

fragrant *adj.* sweet-smelling, aromatic, perfumed, scented: *The air in the florist's shop was fragrant from the flowers.* **ant.** malodorous, noxious, smelly.

frail *adj.* weak, fragile, breakable, feeble, delicate: *In the wheelchair sat a frail old lady. A stubbed toe is a frail excuse for being absent from school.* **ant.** strong, sturdy, hardy, powerful.

frame *n.* **1.** skeleton, framework, support: *The frame of this house is too weak to support a slate roof.* **2.** border, molding: *The paintings in the museum have gold frames around them. vb.* **1.** mount, enclose, border: *I have sent the painting of my father out to be framed.* **2.** plan, imagine, construct, structure, compose, outline: *Let us try to frame our activities for the next few months.*

frank *adj.* candid, open, forthright, honest, unreserved, sincere, direct: *It isn't always a good idea to give others your frank opinion of them.* **ant.** devious, dishonest, tricky.

frantic *adj.* wild, frenzied, delirious, excited; hysterical, mad, crazy: *My mother was frantic with worry when I stayed out all night.* **ant.** calm, tranquil, composed.

fraud *n.* deceit, trickery, treachery: *The officers of the company that was selling the fake jewelry were arrested for fraud.*

fraudulent *adj.* fake, deceitful, tricky, dishonest: *These ten-dollar bills are fraudulent—they have Cary Grant's picture on them!*

freak *n.* monster, abnormality, oddity, curiosity: *I was always scared to visit the freak show at the carnival.*

free *adj.* **1.** independent, unrestrained, unrestricted, liberated: *America is a free country, but that doesn't mean it costs nothing to live there.* **2.** gratuitous, without charge: *The shop was giving away one free candy bar for every five you bought.* **3.** loose, unfastened, unattached: *We tied one end of the string to a tree and fixed the balloon to the free end. vb.* release, liberate, set free, emancipate: *Lincoln freed the slaves. The hunter freed the animals caught in the traps.* **ant.** *vb.* enslave, entrap, snare.

freedom   *n.* liberty, independence: *People everywhere are struggling for freedom from want.* **ant.** slavery, servitude, bondage.

freight   *n.* cargo, load, shipping, shipment: *This ship carries freight and has room for only twelve passengers besides the crew.*

frenzy   *n.* excitement, agitation; craze: *Every time I mention your name, she goes into a frenzy of anger.*

frequent   *adj.* common, customary, habitual: *The wren was a frequent visitor to the birdhouse near our garage. vb.* habituate, visit often: *The teacher noticed that you have been frequenting the library lately.* **ant.** *adj.* infrequent, uncommon.

fresh   *adj.* **1.** recent, new, current, late: *The farmer had already planted a fresh crop of wheat. These eggs are very fresh.* **2.** pure, sweet, drinkable, safe: *This water from your own well is very fresh and doesn't taste of chemicals.* **3.** rested, healthy, energetic, vigorous: *The Pony Express rider exchanged his tired horse for a fresh one.* **4.** different, original: *We need some fresh ideas for the project.* **5.** inexperienced, unskilled, untrained: *Let's give that young fellow a chance—he's fresh out of school.* **ant. 1.** old, out-of-date. **2.** impure, polluted, foul. **3.** exhausted, tired. **4.** stale, unoriginal. **5.** mature, seasoned, experienced.

fret   *vb.* worry, anguish, grieve; torment: *I wish you wouldn't fret about me so much—I feel fine.*

fretful   *adj.* irritable, peevish, testy, touchy, short-tempered: *The train was already an hour late, and we were getting fretful waiting.* **ant.** calm, easygoing.

friend   *n.* companion, acquaintance, crony, chum, mate: *Anyone who isn't completely honest can't be a friend of mine. Nicole arrived with a few friends for the weekend.* **ant.** enemy, foe.

fright   *n.* fear, terror, alarm, panic: *In his fright at seeing the lion right in his path, Steve's hair stood on end.*

frighten *vb.* alarm, scare, terrify, panic: *That dog's bark doesn't frighten me at all.*

fringe *n.* border, edge; hem, edging, trimming: *The bedspread has a blue fringe with gold tassels at the corners.*

front *n.* **1.** face, façade: *The front of the house is painted green.* **2.** beginning, start, head: *Paul always tries to sneak in at the front of the line for ice cream.* *vb.* face, border, look out on: *Our house fronts on the main street.* **ant.** *n.* **1.**, **2.** back, rear.

frontier *n.* boundary, border: *The small group crossed the frontier into Switzerland at midnight.*

frugal *adj.* thrifty, economical, provident: *Even a frugal housekeeper has trouble making ends meet during inflation.* **ant.** improvident, spendthrift, prodigal.

fruitful *adj.* fertile, productive, rich, abundant: *The farmers have had a fruitful harvest this year.* **ant.** barren, lean, unproductive, fruitless.

fruitless *adj.* sterile, unproductive, barren; vain, futile: *All efforts to convince Manny that he ought to get a job were fruitless.* **ant.** fruitful, productive, fertile.

frustrate *vb.* defeat, discourage, prevent: *My attempts to convince my mother to let me go on the picnic were frustrated by my father's arguments.* **ant.** satisfy.

fugitive *n.* runaway, deserter, refugee: *The fugitive from the jail break was found hiding in our garage.*

fulfill *vb.* complete, do, accomplish, realize, effect, carry out: *Fred has at last been able to fulfill his lifelong ambition to become a musician.*

full *adj.* **1.** filled, complete; replete: *Don't talk with your mouth full. Since the heavy rains, the reservoir has been full.* **2.** taken, occupied, in use. *Get to the movies early because later on, every seat will be full.* **ant.** empty, vacant.

fume *n.* smoke, vapor, steam, gas: *The fumes from the back of the car were very strong.* *vb.* **1.** smoke: *The smokestack fumed with a yellow fog.* **2.** rage, rave, storm: *The customer was fuming because the waiter spilled the soup down his neck.*

fun *n.* pleasure, amusement, entertainment, merriment, enjoyment, sport, gaiety: *We all had lots of fun at Irene's party.*

function *n.* **1.** use; activity, operation: *The function of a teacher is to teach; that of a student, to learn. The function of a watch is to keep accurate time.* **2.** ceremony, affair, celebration, party, gathering: *The ambassador attended the function at the embassy.* *vb.* operate, work, run: *My new car doesn't function properly.*

fundamental *adj.* basic, elementary, essential, principal, underlying, primary: *The conservation of matter is a fundamental law of physics.* *n.* basics, elements, essential, principle: *Before learning the details, you must learn the fundamentals.*

funny *adj.* humorous, amusing, droll, comic, comical, laughable: *The speaker told funny stories after dinner.* **ant.** unamusing, unfunny, humorless.

furious *adj.* enraged, angry: *My mother was furious when she found that someone had eaten the pie she had made for dinner.* **ant.** calm, serene.

furnish *vb.* **1.** supply, provide: *My uncle Harry is in business to furnish companies in the area with office equipment.* **2.** decorate, appoint, outfit: *We winterized our attic and furnished two bedrooms there in Early American style.*

furthermore *adv.* further, also, moreover: *Furthermore, I don't want to go because I have a headache.*

fury *n.* **1.** rage, anger, wrath, frenzy: *Imagine my father's fury when he found the scratch on his new car!* **2.** violence, ferocity, ferociousness, fierceness: *After a short period of calm, the hurricane struck again in its full fury.* **ant.** serenity, calmness.

fuss *n.* bother, ado, to-do, commotion: *Why make so much fuss about some water on the kitchen floor?* *vb.* bother, annoy, pester, irritate: *I'll get the work done faster if you stop fussing at me about it.*

futile *adj.* **1.** useless, pointless, vain, idle, worthless: *Trying to persuade Thomas to do his homework is futile during baseball season.* **2.** unimportant, minor, trivial: *Don't waste your time in futile activities.* **ant.** **1.** worthwhile, valuable. **2.** important, serious, weighty.

future *adj.* coming, to come, approaching, impending, imminent, destined: *The future plans for our company were approved at the last meeting.* **ant.** past, bygone, former.

⤶ G ⤷

gain *vb.* **1.** obtain, get, acquire, win, earn: *The home team gained a victory in the last few minutes of the game.* **2.** improve, better, advance: *The candidate was gaining in the farm districts.* **3.** increase in: *Eating cake will make you gain weight.* *n.* **1.** profit: *There was a 10 percent gain in earnings this year.* **2.** increase, improvement, advantage: *We have been making gains in our fight against poverty.* **ant.** *vb.* lose. *n.* loss.

gallant *adj.* **1.** brave, valiant, valorous, bold, courageous: *Many gallant soldiers died in that battle.* **2.** polite, courteous, noble: *Our grandfather had a reputation among the ladies for being gallant.*

gamble *vb.* **1.** bet, wager, game: *The countess gambled until she lost all of her money at the casino.* **2.** risk, hazard, venture: *Don't gamble with your health.* *n.* chance, risk: *It's a gamble whether my talk with Lester will do any good.*

game *n.* **1.** amusement, entertainment, play, sport, pastime: *The games will start as soon as all of the children arrive.* **2.** contest, competition: *The game between the two teams was canceled because of rain.*

gang *n.* band, troop, group, company, crew; horde: *The ship was captured by a gang of pirates.*

gangster *n.* hoodlum, crook, criminal, gunman, hit man; soldier: *There was a rumor that gangsters were in control of the racetrack.*

gap *n.* space, interval; break: *There's a gap between the floor and the wall.*

garbage *n.* refuse, waste, trash: *If you're going out, please leave the garbage in the can.*

gasp *vb.* puff, pant, wheeze: *Harold finally reached the surface of the pond, gasping for breath.*

gather *vb.* **1.** assemble, collect, accumulate, come *or* bring together: *At Christmas, we gather our friends around us for a party. The relatives of the slain man gathered at the grave.* **2.** understand, learn, assume: *I gathered from*

140

what the teacher said that the exam would be next week.
ant. 1. disperse, scatter, dispel.

gathering *n.* crowd, meeting, assembly, company, throng: *There was a huge gathering on the steps of the courthouse.*

gay *adj.* **1.** joyful, joyous, jovial, gleeful, merry, cheerful, happy: *What a gay time we had at Cecile's house last night!* **2.** bright, colorful, brilliant: *The ballroom was decorated in gay colors for the dance.* **ant.** sad, mournful, somber, sorrowful.

gaze *vb.* stare, gape, goggle at, look: *The magician gazed deep into my eyes, trying to hypnotize me.*

general *adj.* **1.** indefinite, miscellaneous, inexact, vague: *Our general plans call for leaving tomorrow, but we haven't worked out the details yet.* **2.** common, usual, regular, customary: *The general way to do it isn't good enough.* **ant. 1.** definite, specific, exact, precise.

generate *vb.* create, produce, make: *That small business doesn't generate enough income to keep the family alive. The atomic plant on the river generates electricity for the entire area.*

generous *adj.* **1.** charitable, liberal, unselfish: *Mr. Storm made a generous contribution to the museum.* **2.** noble, big, honorable: *The committee has been very generous with its efforts to help the poor.* **ant. 1.** stingy, mean, selfish, tightfisted.

genius *n.* **1.** ability, talent, intellect, gift, aptitude: *My brother has a genius for mathematics.* **2.** prodigy, brain: *My brother is a genius at mathematics.*

gentle *adj.* **1.** friendly, amiable, mild, kindly, kind: *Ken is so gentle he'd never say anything to hurt anyone's feelings.* **2.** tame, cultivated, civilized: *That tiger cub is as gentle as a lamb.* **ant. 1.** mean, nasty. **2.** rough, uncouth.

genuine *adj.* **1.** real, actual, true: *If that were a genuine diamond, you'd be able to scratch glass with it.* **2.** sincere, unaffected, definite: *When I told you that I loved you, my feelings were completely genuine.* **ant. 1.** fake, bogus, counterfeit, false. **2.** insincere, pretended, sham.

get *vb.* **1.** acquire, obtain, secure, procure, gain: *Where did you get that funny hat?* **2.** fetch: *Go and get your coat: we're leaving.* **3.** remove, carry, take: *Get that bicycle out of the street!* **4.** prepare, ready, make ready: *You'll have to get your own breakfast.* **5.** persuade, in-

duce, urge: *Sam can get anyone to do anything.* **6.** come,
approach, near: *Get over here to my house as soon as
you can.* **7.** arrive at, reach, come to: *When does the
circus get to town? vb. phr.* **1. get along** succeed, prosper:
Will he be able to get along without his mother? **2. get
by** manage, survive: *I'll get by all right on three dollars a
week.* **3. get in** enter; arrive: *Get in the car at once! My
train gets in at noon.* **4. get off** disembark, alight: *The
train stopped with a jerk and he got off.* **5. get over**
overcome, recover, survive: *My father got malaria during the war and he's never gotten over it.* **6. get up** arise,
rise: *I get up at seven o'clock to go to school.*

ghastly *adj.* **1.** horrifying, horrible, macabre, frightful,
frightening, dreadful, hideous, grisly: *Being in a war is a
ghastly experience.* **2.** pale, wan, white, deathly: *When
Clarissa hung up the phone she looked ghastly.*

ghost *n.* **1.** specter, phantom, spirit, spook: *Have you ever
seen a ghost?* **2.** trace, vestige, hint, suggestion: *Without
a lot of practice, our team hasn't the ghost of a chance
to win the game.*

giant *n.* colossus, Goliath, Cyclops, monster: *The giant
broke the telephone pole as if it were a matchstick. adj.*
gigantic, huge, colossal, monstrous, enormous: *I had a
giant ice-cream cone and now I can't eat my dinner.* **ant.**
n. dwarf, midget, runt. *adj.* small, tiny, minuscule, infinitesimal.

gift *n.* **1.** present, offering, donation: *Although I like to
receive gifts, I get much pleasure from giving them, too.*
2. talent, genius, ability, aptitude: *Martin's gift for playing the kazoo won him a scholarship.*

gigantic *adj.* huge, enormous, giant, large: *I never realized
how gigantic the moon rockets were until I saw one.*
ant. small, little, tiny, infinitesimal.

gingerly *adj.* cautiously gentle: *We made a gingerly progress
along the slope of the cliff. adv.* carefully, cautiously,
gently: *The police bomb squad handled the mysterious
package very gingerly.* **ant.** *adv.* roughly.

give *vb.* **1.** furnish, provide, donate, supply, contribute,
grant, present: *I never realized how much your father
has given to the town, both in time and money.* **2.** yield,
give in, give way: *I felt the floor begin to give a little
where we were standing.* **3.** produce, develop, yield: *This
orchard won't give fruit for seven years.* **4.** sacrifice, give
up, donate: *I have but one life to give for my country.*

vb. phr. **give away** betray, reveal, divulge: *Whenever Peter tells a lie, he gives himself away by stuttering.* **give in** yield, submit, surrender; admit: *The weather was so beautiful that the teacher finally gave in and let the children go home early. When they tortured him, he finally gave in and told them where the money was hidden.* **give off** emit, give off: *The chemicals give off a smell like burning rubber.* **give out a.** distribute, deal, dole: *The man at the corner is giving out free chewing gum.* **b.** weaken, tire: *My arm gave out and I couldn't play tennis any more.* **c.** publish, make known *or* public, publicize, advertise: *The office refused to give out any details of the crime till the police arrived.* **give up a.** stop, cease, discontinue, end: *I've tried to give up smoking, but I can't.* **b.** surrender, yield, submit, cede: *The robbers gave up when surrounded by the ploice.* **ant.** *vb.* **1.** take.

glad   *adj.* **1.** pleased, happy, satisfied, delighted: *I'm so glad that you're coming to my party!* **2.** cheerful, happy, joyous, joyful: *I heard the glad tidings: Marie is going to get married!* **ant. 1.** unhappy, sad, morose. **2.** gloomy, somber, dismal.

glamour   *n.* allure, charm, attraction: *We'll never again see the glamour of Hollywood in the 1930s.*

glance   *vb.* **1.** peek, glimpse, look: *She glanced in my direction, and I knew I had to meet her somehow.* **2.** reflect, rebound, ricochet: *The bullet glanced off the wall and buried itself in the mattress.* *n.* peek, glimpse, look: *I caught a glance of the car as it sped around the corner.*

glare   *n.* dazzle, flash, brilliance: *I couldn't make out who it was in the glare of the spotlight.* *vb.* scowl, start: *The speaker would glare in the direction of anyone who caused a disturbance.*

gleam   *n.* **1.** glimmer, glimmering, flash: *At that moment, I caught the gleam of a light in the depths of the cave.* **2.** shine, reflection, sparkle: *The gleam of candlelight on silver and crystal will always remind me of my father's home.* *vb.* shine, sparkle, glimmer: *The moon gleaming on the water looked like a silver path to the horizon.*

glide   *vb.* slide, slip, flow: *We went gliding along in the canoe, not making a sound on the still water of the lake.*

glimpse   *n.* peek, glance, impression: *We caught glimpses of the mountain ahead of us through the trees.*

glisten   *vb.* shine, glitter, shimmer, glimmer, sparkle, glister:

Mandy's eyes glistened with tears as she was told about her kitten's death.

glitter *vb.* sparkle, glisten, shimmer, glimmer, shine: *The calm sea glittered in the sunlight. n.* light, splendor: *The train dived with a roar into the tunnel beneath the glitter and swank of Park Avenue.*

global *adj.* worldwide, international, universal; round-the-world: *The United Nations is a global organization. We made a global flight in just 48 hours.*

globe *n.* sphere, orb, ball: *The astronauts could see the earth hanging in space like a blue globe.*

gloom *n.* **1.** darkness, shade, shadows, dimness: *I heard footsteps but could see nothing in the gloom.* **2.** sadness, melancholy: *A feeling of gloom came over us when we thought about the hungry people.* **ant. 1.** brightness. **2.** cheerfulness, happiness.

gloomy *adj.* **1.** sad, melancholy, morose, downcast, down-hearted, glum, unhappy: *The news that the movie theater was to close made us all gloomy.* **2.** dark, dim, shadowy, dismal: *The old, gloomy house had not been lived in for years—except by ghosts.* **ant. 1.** happy, cheerful, merry, highspirited. **2.** sunny, bright.

glorious *adj.* **1.** famous, renowned, noted, famed, distinguished, splendid, celebrated: *It is our glorious tradition that attracts members to the club.* **2.** delightful, admirable, wonderful: *I've had a glorious day here in New England.*

glory *n.* **1.** honor, eminence, renown: *His bravery in battle has won him much glory.* **2.** splendor, magnificence, grandeur: *Can we ever forget the glory that was Greece?*

glossary *n.* lexicon, dictionary: *If there are any words you don't understand, they are explained in the glossary.*

glow *n.* **1.** gleam, light: *I saw the glow of the city against the sky as we approached.* **2.** warmth, heat: *The fire cast a warm glow on the children's faces. vb.* **1.** gleam, glimmer, shine: *The hot embers glowed in the fireplace after the flames died down.* **2.** radiate, shine: *Their faces glowed with the expectation that Santa Claus would soon be there.*

gnaw *vb.* eat, chew, erode: *The dog gnawed hungrily at the bone. The feeling that I had forgotten something gnawed at me.*

go *vb.* **1.** leave, depart, withdraw: *All evening long, people* *kept coming and going in the large hall.* **2.** proceed, move, travel; progress: *Let's go to the movies. My parents went to California for a holiday.* **3.** become: *Stop teasing me or I'll go crazy.* **4.** agree, harmonize, fit, suit: *That tie doesn't go with that shirt.* **5.** operate, function, work, run: *The car won't go unless you have the key.* **6.** pass, elapse: *When you're busy, the day goes very quickly. vb. phr.* **1.** **go by** pass, proceed. *I go by your house every morning. Why do the days seem to go by so slowly?* **2.** **go off** explode, blow up: *Don't let that firecracker go off in your hand!* **3.** **go on a.** continue, persevere, persist: *I just can't go on without you.* **b.** happen, take place, occur: *At our house there's a lot going on all of the time.* **4.** **go over** examine, scan, study: *The doctor went over me with a fine-tooth comb.* **5.** **go through** experience, undergo, endure: *Please don't ask me any more questions: I've gone through enough for one day.* **6.** **go with** harmonize, match, suit, agree, complement. *This gray hat will go with almost anything in my wardrobe.* **7.** **go without** want, need, require, sacrifice: *When times are hard, we sometimes have to go without.* **ant.** *vb.* **1.** come.

goal *n.* aim, object, target, end, purpose: *Before thinking of anything else, your immediate goal should be to complete your education.*

good *adj.* **1.** qualified, suited, suitable, apt, proper, capable, fit: *We have had a great many good applicants for the opening.* **2.** generous, kindly, kind, friendly, gracious, obliging: *There's nothing more important in the country than having good neighbors.* **3.** pleasant, agreeable, pleasurable, satisfactory, fine: *Did you have a good time at the party?* **4.** well-behaved, obedient, proper: *If you're a good girl, you can have ice cream for dessert.* **5.** healthy, sound, normal: *You have good hearing to be able to hear a footstep at that distance!* **6.** honorable, reliable, trustworthy, safe: *Don't worry about lending John a quarter— he's good for the money.* **7.** favorable, excellent, profitable: *Business prospects are good for the future. n.* **1.** benefit, welfare, advantage, profit: *You'll do it now, if you understand it's for your own good.* **2.** virtue, righteousness: *Embrace the good and shun evil.* **ant.** bad. **3.** kindness, beneficence: *The good that men do is often buried with them when they die.* **ant.** evil.

good-by *interj.* so long, see you soon, adios, au revoir, auf

Wiedersehen, adieu, farewell: *I had to say good-by to my parents at the railway station.*

goodness *n.* honesty, virtue, good, integrity: *Even in the most evil human being there is some goodness.* **ant.** dishonesty, badness, evil, corruption, sin.

gorge *n.* pass, defile, ravine: *The outlaws lay in wait for the stagecoach at the edge of the gorge.* *vb.* stuff, cram, fill: *Of course you can't eat your dinner after gorging yourself on popcorn.*

gorgeous *adj.* splendid, magnificent, grand, dazzling: *The peacock has a truly gorgeous tail.* **ant.** ugly, homely, squalid.

gossip *n.* **1.** prattle, prate, hearsay, rumor: *Don't believe what you hear about Henry—it's just gossip.* **2.** blabbermouth, meddler, snoop, tattler: *That nosy Mrs. Parker is just a back-fence gossip.* *vb.* prattle, tattle, chatter, blab: *I knew they must have been gossiping about me because they stopped talking the minute they saw me.*

govern *vb.* rule, control, guide, run; command: *The new President governs as he sees fit. The laws governing the use of firearms are complicated.*

government *n.* **1.** rule, control, command, direction, authority, jurisdiction: *The U.S. has a democratic form of government.* **2.** administration, regime: *The government has the power to levy taxes.*

gown *n.* dress, frock; robe: *Hortense wore a blue silk floor-length gown to the party.*

grab *vb.* seize, clutch, grasp: *As we were leaving the party, Steve grabbed me and pulled me aside to whisper something in my ear.*

grace *n.* **1.** gracefulness, ease, elegance: *I admire the grace with which you got rid of that awful bore.* **2.** charm, attractiveness, beauty: *The princess is noted for her grace.*

gracious *adj.* **1.** kind, friendly; courteous, polite: *It was very gracious of you to allow me to invite my friend for dinner.* **2.** tender, merciful, mild, gentle: *How gracious your wife is to take care of me when I'm ill.* **ant.** **1.** rude, impolite, discourteous, thoughtless.

gradual *adj.* little by little, slow, moderate: *A gradual change came over the doctor until he turned into a beast before our very eyes.* **ant.** sudden, swift, abrupt.

graft *n.* cheating, fraud, dishonesty, theft, corruption: *The entire town council was being investigated for graft.*

grand *adj.* **1.** splendid, elaborate, great, royal, stately: *The*

Rockefellers have always lived in a grand style. **2.** fine, noble, dignified: *My grandfather was truly a grand old man.* **3.** chief, principal, main: *We had dinner in the grand ballroom.* **ant. 1.** humble, modest, unassuming.

grant *vb.* **1.** give, bestow, confer, award: *Larry was granted a leave of absence from the university.* **2.** agree, allow, concede, accept: *The detective granted that I couldn't have been at the scene of the crime.* *n.* award, bequest, gift: *My sister received a $1,000 grant for study abroad.* **ant.** *vb.* **1.** deny.

grasp *vb.* **1.** seize, hold, grab, clasp, grip, clutch: *Howard grasped the gun by the barrel and wrenched it from the robber's hand.* **2.** perceive, understand, comprehend: *I don't quite grasp what you're trying to tell me.* *n.* **1.** grip, clutches, clasp, hold: *The coin fell from my grasp and slipped down between the bars of the sewer grating.* **2.** reach, understanding, capacity: *That book is beyond the grasp of a seven-year-old.*

grateful *adj.* appreciative, thankful: *The president of the charity drive was very grateful for your contribution.* **ant.** ungrateful, thankless, grudging.

gratify *vb.* satisfy, please: *I was very gratified to see the results of the examination.* **ant.** frustrate.

grave *adj.* **1.** sober, thoughtful, solemn, serious: *When I saw the doctor's grave expression I knew something was wrong.* **2.** important, serious, weighty: *If we don't catch that poisonous snake, we shall have a grave problem.* **ant. 1.** happy, merry, frivolous, jolly. **2.** trivial, unimportant.

gravity *n.* seriousness, importance; concern: *It wasn't until fourteen people were hospitalized that we realized the gravity of the disease.* **ant.** triviality.

great *adj.* **1.** large, big, huge, enormous, immense, gigantic: *A great mountain loomed over us.* **2.** noteworthy, worthy, distinguished, remarkable: *Those who wrote the Constitution of the U.S. were great men.* **3.** chief, leading, main, principal: *Sheldon has always been a great friend of mine.* **ant. 1.** small, diminutive. **2.** insignificant, trivial. **3.** minor.

greed *n.* avarice, greediness, covetousness: *The mayor's greed led him to steal money from the city's treasury.* **ant.** generosity, selflessness, unselfishness.

greedy *adj.* selfish, covetous, grasping, avaricious: *The greedy old man ate all of the food and left nothing for his children.* **ant.** generous, giving, unselfish.

greet *vb.* meet, welcome: *The town sent a band down to the train to greet the returning hero.*

grief *n.* sorrow, sadness, distress, suffering, anguish, woe, misery: *The mother's grief over her son's dying was not hard to understand.* **ant.** joy.

grieve *vb.* **1.** lament, mourn, weep: *Peggy grieved over the loss of her puppy for weeks.* **2.** distress, sorrow, sadden, hurt: *It grieves me to realize that all people are not honest.* **ant.** rejoice, celebrate.

grievous *adj.* dreadful, awful, gross, shameful, outrageous, regrettable, lamentable: *Lending Bobby my car turned out to have been a grievous error.*

grim *adj.* **1.** stern, severe, harsh: *The principal gave the students a grim warning about writing on the walls.* **2.** ghastly, sinister, frightful, horrible, grisly: *The skull nailed to the tree was a grim reminder that we were far from being safe.*

grind *vb.* **1.** powder, pulverize, mill, crush: *The corn was ground to meal between the two stones.* **2.** sharpen; smooth, even: *Try to grind down the rough spots.*

grip *n.* **1.** hold, grasp, clutch, clasp: *My grip on the branch was weakening and I was about to plummet to the rocks below.* **2.** suitcase, valise, satchel, bag: *I want to check these grips and pick them up later.* *vb.* seize, grasp, hold, clutch: *Grip the handle tightly and don't let go until I tell you to.*

groan *vb.* moan; sob: *Did you have a bad dream? I heard you groaning in your sleep last night.*

groove *n.* slot, channel, scratch, furrow: *The carpenter cut a groove in each board to support the shelf.*

gross *adj.* **1.** improper, rude, coarse, indecent, crude, vulgar: *Please don't use gross language around me.* **2.** outrageous, extreme, grievous, shameful: *The innocent man's conviction was a gross miscarriage of justice.* **ant. 1.** refined, cultivated, polite.

ground *n.* **1.** land, earth, soil: *My great-grandfather built his log cabin on a small plot of ground.* **2. grounds** basis, foundation, base: *You have no grounds for saying such things about me.* *vb.* train, educate, instruct: *I was well grounded in history.*

groundless *adj.* unfounded, baseless: *Your assumption that I was the guilty one was groundless.*

group *n.* gathering, collection, set, assembly, assemblage: *A group of us went out for pizza. There is an interesting* *group of exhibits at this end of the hall. vb.* gather, collect; sort, classify: *Group all of the red flowers together.*

grow *vb.* **1.** enlarge, increase, swell, expand: *Watch that house grow.* **2.** develop, flower: *The rosebushes grow very well in this soil.* **3.** cultivate, raise, produce, nurture: *My father grows tomatoes every year.* **ant. 1.** shrink, decrease.

growth *n.* increase, development: *The growth of that sunflower has been incredible!*

grudge *n.* resentment, ill will, spite, bitterness: *He has a grudge against me because I took away his girlfriend.*

grumble *vb.* complain, protest, fuss: *Frances grumbled a bit when her mother wouldn't allow her to go to the dance.*

guarantee *n.* warranty, commitment, promise, pledge: *The manufacturer's guarantee says that he will replace any defective parts for nothing. vb.* warrant, promise, pledge, insure: *I can safely guarantee you'll be home before midnight.*

guard *vb.* protect, preserve, shield, defend: *Two armed men were guarding the bank. You must guard against catching a cold. n.* protector, sentry, watchman, sentinel: *There is a guard at every door during the king's visit.* **ant.** *vb.* neglect, ignore, disregard.

guess *vb.* suppose, think, imagine, believe: *Now that your work is finished, I guess you'll be leaving. n.* notion, opinion, hypothesis, theory: *I'll give you three guesses how I got here last night.* **ant.** *vb.* know.

guest *n.* visitor, caller, company: *I see from the extra table setting that you are expecting a guest for dinner.* **ant.** host.

guide *vb.* **1.** lead, direct, conduct, steer, pilot: *I wish I had someone who could guide me through the forest.* **2.** influence, affect: *Let good judgment guide you throughout your life. n.* director, pilot, steersman, leader: *We were able to hire a Sherpa guide for the climb.* **ant.** *vb.* **1.** follow. *n.* follower.

guilt *n.* blame, fault; sin, offense, misstep: *Why do people who do something wrong often try to pin the guilt on someone else?*

guilty *adj.* responsible, culpable, blameworthy: *The jury found the defendant guilty of murder in the first degree.* **ant.** innocent, blameless, guiltless.

gulf *n.* **1.** chasm, abyss, ravine, canyon: *The gulf that* *separated us from the lion was fortunately too wide for him to leap over.* **2.** inlet, sound, bay: *Have you ever been in the Gulf of Mexico?*

gush   *vb.* spurt, flow, pour, stream: *The water gushed from the drains during the storm.*

gutter   *n.* drain, trough, ditch, sewer: *As the car passed close by, it splashed water from the gutter all over my shoes and stockings.*

๏ H ๏

habit *n.* **1.** addiction, compulsion, disposition: *Reginald has a nasty habit of chewing his nails.* **2.** custom, practice: *You ought to get into the habit of brushing your teeth after every meal.*

habitation *n.* dwelling, abode, home: *Human habitations were cut into the cliffside.*

haggard *adj.* gaunt, drawn, worn, careworn: *After driving through the storm for six hours Noel's father looked very haggard.* **ant.** fresh, animated, bright, clear-eyed.

hail *vb.* greet, welcome, address: *The tax refund was hailed by many as the solution to the crisis.*

hale *adj.* hearty, healthy, robust, vigorous: *Despite three days and nights in the open boat, the boys were found to be quite hale.* **ant.** feeble, weak.

halfhearted *adj.* indifferent, uncaring, cool, unenthusiastic: *Wilbur made a halfhearted attempt at water-skiing, but fell in each time.* **ant.** enthusiastic, eager, earnest.

halfwit *n.* dunce, idiot, dope, fool, simpleton: *Anybody who would spend three hours trying to find a bucket of steam must be a real halfwit.*

hall *n.* passage, corridor, hallway; vestibule, lobby, foyer: *I was standing in the hall outside the classroom when you came along.*

halt *vb.* stop, cease, hold: *The train halted in the station to discharge and receive passengers.* *n.* stop, end: *The government has called a halt to sugar rationing.* **ant.** *vb.* start, begin. *n.* start, beginning.

hamper *vb.* hinder, prevent, obstruct, thwart: *I was hampered from swimming by my clothes and heavy shoes.* *n.* basket, creel: *We carried our sandwiches in a wicker hamper.*

hand *n.* **1.** helper, farmhand, assistant, laborer: *We have three hired hands at the farm.* **2.** aid, help, support: *Can someone please give me a hand with this piano?* *n. phr.* **1. at hand** near, nearby, close: *The boy's tenth birthday was at hand.* **2. by hand** manually: *This desk was made entirely by hand.* **3. on hand** available, ready, convenient, in stock: *We always keep spare parts for the engine on hand.* *vb.* give, pass, deliver: *Please hand me that wrench.* *vb. phr.* **1. hand down** pass on, bequeath, give: *That hunting rifle has been handed down for more than seventy years.* **2. hand in** deliver, submit, give: *We handed in our compositions yesterday.* **3. hand out** distribute, pass out: *A man in the street was handing out these leaflets.*

handicap *n.* disadvantage, hindrance: *In spite of great improvement, the color of a person's skin can still be a handicap.*

handily *adv.* easily, readily, smoothly: *The other horses couldn't run well on a wet track, so Dissipation won handily.* **ant.** awkwardly, clumsily, ineptly.

handsome *adj.* **1.** good-looking, fine, comely: *Don is as handsome as a movie star.* **2.** generous, large, big, liberal, ample: *My employer gave me a handsome bonus at Christmas.* **ant. 1.** ugly, homely, unattractive. **2.** mean, petty, stingy, niggardly.

handy *adj.* **1.** ready, at hand, near, nearby, close: *When the Indians were on the warpath, the pioneers always kept their guns handy.* **2.** helpful, clever, useful: *A can opener is a very handy gadget.* **ant.** inconvenient.

hang *vb.* **1.** suspend, dangle, drape: *The flag was hung from the railing of the balcony.* **2.** execute, kill, lynch: *The murderer was hanged the next morning.*

happen *vb.* occur, take place, come to pass: *We'll probably never know the truth of what happened when they were marooned on the desert island.*

happiness *n.* joy, delight, joyfulness, joyousness, elation, ecstasy: *Children can bring so much happiness into a home.* **ant.** sadness, gloom, melancholy.

happy *adj.* **1.** pleased, contented; satisfied: *I'm so happy to see you I could hug you! Jimmy was happy to be home again.* **2.** lucky, fortunate: *By a happy coincidence, the policeman came along just then and the thief ran off.* **ant. 1.** sad, gloomy, sorrowful. **2.** unlucky, inconvenient, unfortunate.

harbor *n.* port, haven, anchorage: *New York is one of the busiest harbors in the world.* *vb.* shelter, protect: *Harboring a fugitive from justice is against the law.*

hard *adj.* **1.** firm, solid, rigid, unyielding, compact, dense: *I could not dig the shovel into the hard ground. This stale bun is as hard as a rock.* **2.** difficult, laborious, exhausting: *Hard work never hurt anybody.* **3.** difficult, complicated, puzzling, tough, intricate: *We won't get any of the really hard problems to solve till we get to college.* **4.** severe, stern, harsh, strict, demanding: *Things will go hard for anyone who disobeys.* **5.** shrewd, hard-headed, unsympathetic, cool, cold: *Shirley really drives a hard bargain.* *adj. phr.* **hard up** up against it, poor, poverty-stricken; broke: *During the Depression, many once-wealthy families were really hard up.* *adv.* energetically, vigorously, forcefully, earnestly: *My father has worked hard all his life.* **ant.** *adj.* **1.** soft, pliable, yielding. **2.** easy, undemanding, comfortable. **3.** simple, uncomplicated, direct. **4.** lenient, easygoing.

harden *vb.* solidify, petrify: *Once that glue hardens, you won't be able to separate the pieces of the plate.* **ant.** soften, loosen.

hardly *adv.* scarcely, barely: *I had hardly been home for a minute when Phil gave me the bad news.*

hardship *n.* difficulty, trouble, affliction: *Although it was a terrible hardship after my uncle died, my aunt put all of her children through school.*

hardy *adj.* vigorous, sturdy, tough, strong: *You have to have a hardy constitution to live through a winter in northern Canada.* **ant.** weak, feeble, frail, fragile, decrepit.

harm *n.* **1.** damage, hurt, injury: *Your father wouldn't let any harm come to you.* **2.** evil, wickedness, wrong: *Although they don't want to admit it, gossips really wish to do harm.* *vb.* hurt, damage, injure, cripple: *Alan is so gentle, he wouldn't harm a fly.*

harmful *adj.* mischievous, hurtful, injurious: *Using medicine all the time can be harmful.* **ant.** beneficial, advantageous.

harmless *adj.* innocent, painless: *The coloring matter used in foods is supposed to be harmless.* **ant.** harmful, injurious, dangerous.

harmonious *adj.* **1.** melodious, tuneful: *Those boys certainly make a harmonious trio.* **2.** amicable, congenial: *The two companies reached a harmonious settlement of the lawsuit.* **ant.** **1.** discordant, dissonant. **2.** quarrelsome, discordant, disagreeable.

harmony *n.* agreement, accord, unity: *Everyone in our family got along very well in a spirit of harmony and friendship.* **ant.** discordance, disagreement, conflict.

harness *vb.* yoke, control: *For many years scientists have* *been developing means for harnessing tides for electric power.*

harsh *adj.* **1.** rough, severe, tough, unpleasant, unkind, stern, cruel: *The police may have to take harsh measures to control the drug traffic.* **2.** rough, coarse, jarring: *The harsh cry of the raven was heard in the woods.* **ant. 1.** easy, soothing, gentle. **2.** melodious, pleasing.

harvest *n.* crop, yield: *America can expect another successful wheat harvest next year.* *vb.* gather, collect, pick, glean, reap: *What is not sown cannot be harvested.*

haste *n.* **1.** rush, hurry, rapidity, speed: *Those who were not fighting the flames left the dangerous area with haste.* **2.** scramble, hurry, flurry, rush, heedlessness: *If you marry in haste, you may repent at leisure.* **ant. 1.** sluggishness, sloth.

hasten *vb.* **1.** hurry, rush, run, scurry, scamper, dash, sprint: *Timothy hastened to be first in line for ice cream.* **2.** hurry, rush, dispatch, quicken, urge, press, speed: *Mother hastened us on to school in the mornings.* **ant. 1.** dawdle, linger, tarry.

hat *n.* bonnet, headgear, headpiece; helmet: *In this weather you must wear a hat.*

hatch *vb.* brood, breed, bring forth, incubate: *Three tiny blue eggs hatched and the baby birds started peeping at once.*

hate *vb.* detest, abhor, loathe, despise; disfavor, dislike: *I have never understood why Cinderella's stepmother and half-sisters hated her so.* *n.* hatred, loathing, abhorrence; dislike: *The Chief Justice has a hate of injustice.* **ant.** *vb.* like, love, admire. *n.* liking, love, esteem.

hateful *adj.* detestable, loathsome, offensive: *Nobody gets along with him because he's such a hateful little boy.* **ant.** lovable, likable, admirable.

hatred *n.* hate, loathing, aversion: *Nothing could compare with Tessa's hatred for toasted cheese sandwiches.* **ant.** liking, appreciation.

haughty *adj.* aloof, proud, prideful, arrogant: *Just because her family has more money than mine she acts in such a haughty way.* **ant.** humble, simple, down-to-earth, unaffected.

haul *vb.* drag, draw, pull, tow: *It took three of us to haul the fallen tree off the road.*

have *vb.* **1.** hold, possess, own: *Dick has a pony that he got for his birthday.* **2.** contain, include: *The truck has* *room for all our furniture.* **3.** get, receive, obtain, take, gain, acquire: *Have another cookie with your milk.* **4.** engage in, experience, undergo: *My father had 20 years of army service.* **5.** maintain, uphold, hold, believe, say, assert, testify: *As the officer would have it, we drove into the wall on purpose.* **6.** bear, give birth to, bring forth, beget: *Annemarie just had twins.*

hazard *n.* peril, risk, danger: *Driving too fast is a hazard not only to yourself but to other drivers. vb.* offer, tender, dare: *I'd hazard a guess that there will be more than 300 million people in America by the year 2000.*

hazardous *adj.* perilous, dangerous, risky: *The road through the mountains is too hazardous to take at night.* **ant.** safe, secure.

head *n.* **1.** supervisor, leader, commander, director, chief: *We went to talk to the head of the English department about our grades.* **2.** source, start, beginning, origin: *It took explorers many years to find the head of the Nile. vb.* lead, direct, command: *Isaac will head this project and tell the workers what they must do. adj.* chief, leading, principal, main: *The head man of the tribe signaled that we were to put down our weapons.*

headstrong *adj.* stubborn, obstinate, willful: *Charlie is so headstrong that you'll never convince him he ought to go.* **ant.** amenable, easygoing.

headway *n.* progress, movement, advance: *The jungle was so thick that the explorers could make no headway.*

heal *vb.* cure, restore: *The medicine healed the cut in a few days.*

healthy *adj.* hale, hearty, robust, vigorous, strong, sound; healthful: *Two weeks after his operation, Adam was healthy enough to go camping. Drinking liquor isn't healthy.* **ant.** unhealthy, ill, sick, unwholesome.

heap *n.* pile, stack, mound, collection, accumulation: *There was a heap of rubbish at the side of the road. vb.* pile, stack, mound, collect, accumulate: *We kept heaping the sand in one place till there was a hill 20 feet high.*

hear *vb.* listen, hearken; detect, perceive: *Hear what I have to say before you blame me. Can you hear the song of the nightingale?*

heart *n.* **1.** center, core: *The heart of the problem was that we didn't believe anything Jack said.* **2.** sympathy, feeling, sentiment: *Dave has so much heart he'd do anything for you.*

heat *n.* **1.** warmth, hotness, temperature: *The heat of the ice couldn't be more than 32° Fahrenheit. The heat from the fire singed the blanket.* **2.** passion, excitement: *They said that he struck her in the heat of anger.* **3.** warmth, zeal, ardor: *The heat of his enthusiasm for a swim was quickly chilled by the frigid water.* *vb.* warm, inflame, cook: *It takes a long time to heat water on a wood stove.* **ant.** *n.* **1.** coolness, cold, coldness, iciness, chilliness. *vb.* cool, freeze, chill.

heave *vb.* **1.** hoist, boost, raise: *With one final push they heaved up the box.* **2.** haul, pull, tug: *Three men heaving on the rope couldn't lift the safe.*

heaven *n.* paradise; empyrean: *We may never be able to prove that there is such a place as heaven.*

heavenly *adj.* **1.** blissful, divine, saintly, angelic, holy, blessed: *The minister had a heavenly expression on his face.* **2.** celestial: *Astronomers observe the motions of the heavenly bodies.*

heavy *adj.* **1.** weighty, ponderous: *That trunk is too heavy for you to lift by yourself.* **2.** intense, concentrated, severe: *There was a very heavy snowfall last week and the skiing is now excellent.* **3.** burdensome, oppressive, harsh, depressing: *The atmosphere was heavy when I walked into the courtroom.* **4.** sad, oppressed, serious, grave, gloomy, mournful, melancholy, dismal: *The heavy news he had to tell us was that the company had failed and we were all dismissed.* **5.** boring, dull, tiresome: *I found the play quite heavy going.* **ant. 1.** light, buoyant, airy. **2.** light, insignificant, minimal. **3.** cheerful, happy.

heed *vb.* obey, regard, observe: *You'd better heed the traffic lights when crossing the street.* *n.* attention, mind: *Pay Jean no heed—she's only teasing you.* **ant.** *vb.* ignore, disregard, overlook, disdain.

height *n.* **1.** altitude, elevation, tallness: *What is the height of that skyscraper?* **2.** mountain, peak, prominence: *We looked down on the valley from the height.* **3.** acme, pinnacle, maximum: *Crossing the street with your eyes closed is the height of stupidity.* **ant.** depth.

hello *interj.* hi!, hiya!, greetings, good morning, good afternoon, good evening: *I said hello to everyone when I first walked into the room.* **ant.** good-by, farewell, so long.

help *vb.* **1.** aid, assist, support; back, encourage: *Can* *someone please help me lift this piano? In these times, we help all the needy we can.* **2.** avoid, prevent: *I can't help hiccuping.* **3.** wait on, attend, serve: *Please, help yourself to some more corned beef and cabbage. n.* aid, assistance, support, relief: *We need all the help we can get—Whether it's people donating merchandise, their time and effort, or their money.*

helper *n.* assistant, aide; supporter: *The driver of each truck must have a helper for loading and unloading.*

helpful *adj.* advantageous, profitable, valuable: *Your advice about returning to school to complete my education was most helpful.* **ant.** useless, futile, worthless.

helpless *adj.* **1.** dependent, feeble, weak, disabled: *My brother has been helpless in a wheelchair since his operation.* **2.** unresourceful, incompetent, inept, incapable: *Sarah is completely helpless when faced with a machine that won't work.* **ant. 2.** competent, resourceful, enterprising.

herd *n.* flock, crowd, group, drove, pack: *A herd of elephants stampeded toward us, and we had no place to hide. vb.* group, gather, crowd: *The guide herded all of the tourists into the bus for the ride home.*

heritage *n.* legacy, birthright, inheritance, patrimony: *Americans have a heritage that they can be proud of.*

hermit *n.* anchorite, recluse, eremite: *Do you want to live all alone, never speaking to anyone, like a hermit?*

hero *n.* champion, paladin, idol: *Rock music stars were the teenagers' heroes during the 1960s. The hero of the battle was awarded a medal.*

heroic *adj.* valiant, brave, valorous, dauntless, gallant, courageous, bold, fearless: *The firemen made a heroic effort to save the family, and everyone was finally carried out.* **ant.** cowardly, fainthearted, timid.

heroism *n.* bravery, valor, gallantry, courage, boldness: *For his heroism, the knight was given huge estates by the king.* **ant.** cowardice, uncourageousness, timidity.

hesitate *vb.* pause, wait, delay: *He who hesitates is lost— except when crossing the street.* **ant.** proceed.

hide *vb.* conceal, cover, mask, screen, camouflage, cloak, shroud, veil: *You can't hide your true feelings from me. n.* skin, pelt, leather, fur: *The hides of buffaloes were once worth a lot of money.* **ant. vb.** show, display, reveal.

hideous *adj.* ugly, frightful, frightening, shocking, horrible, horrifying, terrible, terrifying, monstrous, gross, grisly: *The man was convicted of the hideous crime and sentenced to die.* **ant.** beautiful, lovely, ethereal, beauteous.

high   *adj.*   **1.** tall, lofty, towering: *That's a very high building.* **2.** raised, shrill, high-pitched, strident, sharp: *She speaks in a very high voice that gets on my nerves.* **3.** important, prominent, powerful: *A high officer in the government gave me the news.* **4.** dear, expensive, costly, high-priced: *The jeweler asks high prices for gold these days.* **5.** serious, grave, extreme: *The spy was arrested for high crimes against the state.* **ant. 1.** low, short, lowly. **2.** deep. **3.** lowly, unimportant, insignificant. **4.** reasonable, inexpensive. **5.** petty, trivial.

highly   *adv.* very, extremely: *The suspect gave a highly suspicious account of his whereabouts last night.*

highway   *n.* speedway, parkway, turnpike, freeway, superhighway, skyway: *The car was speeding down the highway at 90 miles per hour.*

hinder   *vb.* interrupt, hamper, slow, delay, obstruct, interfere with, block, thwart, prevent, stop: *The sled was speeding down the hillside with nothing to hinder it.* **ant.** advance, further, promote.

hindrance   *n.* delay, interruption, obstruction, interference, barrier, obstacle: *Approval of the committee removed the last hindrance from the plan for building the new civic center.*

hinge   *vb.* depend, rely, pivot: *Success of the project hinges on getting enough people to support it.*

hint   *n.* suggestion, tip, clue; whisper, taste, suspicion: *If you don't get the answer in ten seconds, I'll give you a hint. There was just a hint of curry in the soup.* *vb.* suggest, mention: *Are you hinting that Felix has been going out with my girl friend?*

hire   *vb.* **1.** employ, engage, retain, enlist: *The factory hired 200 people today.* **2.** rent, lease, charter: *We hired a car in Chicago and drove the rest of the way home.* *n.* rent, rental, lease, let, charter: *The marina advertised boats for hire for as little as $3 per hour.* **ant. 1.** dismiss, fire.

history   *n.* chronicle, annal, record, account, narrative, tale, memoir, story: *The old lady told me the entire history of her family, going back three generations.*

hit   *vb.* **1.** strike, smite: *The ball hit the wall and bounced off. Stop hitting kids smaller than you.* **2.** find, come upon, discover: *I hit upon a plan whereby we could eat* *our cake and have it, too. n.* blow, stroke: *She gave him a hit right in the face.*

hitch *vb.* tie, fasten, tether, harness: *Hitch the horses to the wagon and drive down to the sheriff to warn him. n.* hindrance, interruption, interference: *There's been a hitch in our plans and we can't go on the picnic.*

hoard *vb.* amass, save, store, secrete: *During the shortage, some people hoarded sugar and coffee. n.* store, stock, cache: *The police found a hoard of gold coins in a box in the chimney.* **ant.** *vb.* spend, use, squander.

hoarse *adj.* rough, raucous, deep, husky, grating, harsh: *We were hoarse from singing all last evening.* **ant.** clear.

hobby *n.* pastime, diversion, avocation: *My uncle collects seashells as a hobby.* **ant.** profession, vocation.

hoist *vb.* lift, raise, heave, elevate: *It will take four men to hoist that ladder up to the roof. n.* crane, derrick, elevator: *The hoist was too weak to lift the piano.*

hold *vb.* **1.** grasp, clasp, grip, clutch: *The woman disappeared into the crowd, leaving me there holding the baby.* **2.** have, keep, retain: *I am holding onto the prize money until the taxes have to be paid on it.* **3.** contain: *This bottle holds exactly one quart.* **4.** possess, have: *My uncle holds the rank of admiral in the Swiss navy.* **5.** conduct, observe, engage in: *The society is holding a meeting next month.* **6.** think, believe, maintain, consider, judge: *We hold these truths to be self-evident: life, liberty, and the pursuit of happiness.* **7.** remain, stick, adhere, cohere, cling: *Will that tiny drop of glue hold the entire car together? n.* **1.** grasp, grip: *Get a good hold on the fishing rod.* **2.** sway, influence, control: *The gangsters have some hold over the mayor, but we don't know what it is.*

hole *n.* **1.** opening, tear, rip, aperture: *I'm so embarrassed! I had a hole in my sock when I took off my shoe.* **2.** burrow, pit, cave, den, lair: *The bear crawled into his hole to hibernate for the winter.*

hollow *adj.* **1.** vacant, empty, unfilled: *The wall made a hollow sound where it was tapped, so we know it wasn't solid.* **2.** empty, false, flimsy, meaningless: *We lost so many men in the battle that ours was a hollow victory. n.* cavity, hole, depression, pit: *The dog crawled into the hollow in the rock and went to sleep. vb.* excavate, dig, shovel: *The pirates hollowed out a place in the hillside where they hid the treasure.* **ant.** *adj.* **1.** full, filled, solid.

holy *adj.* **1.** blessed, sacred, hallowed, consecrated: *We*

visited many holy places on our tour of Jerusalem. **2.**
saintly, sainted, divine, pious: *The people gave money to*
the blind beggar, for they considered him holy. **ant. 1.**
profane, unconsecrated, unsanctified.

homage *n.* respect, reverence, honor: *Do homage to those*
you love.

home *n.* **1.** family, hearth: *Wherever my wife and children*
are is home to me. **2.** residence, house, abode, dwelling,
habitation: *Several thousand homes have been built in*
the area already.

homely *adj.* plain, unattractive, ugly: *I don't understand*
why such a handsome man married such a homely
woman. **ant.** attractive, beautiful, handsome, comely,
pretty.

homesick *adj.* nostalgic; lonely: *Jennie was so homesick the*
first few days that she cried herself to sleep every night.

honest *adj.* **1.** truthful, trustworthy, moral, upright, honorable: *The bank tries to employ honest people.* **2.** open,
candid, forthright, frank, straightforward: *If you want*
my honest opinion, I think you treated her very badly,
and I don't blame her for biting you. **ant. 1.** dishonest,
fraudulent.

honesty *n.* **1.** integrity, uprightness, trustworthiness, fairness, honor: *Honesty is a virtue that we seek in all*
people. **2.** candor, frankness, sincerity: *In all honesty,*
you did steal the money, didn't you? **ant. 1.** dishonesty,
fraud.

honor *n.* **1.** respect, esteem, distinction: *It was an honor*
to be selected to head the refreshment committee. **2.**
principle, character, honesty, uprightness: *Although Jane*
didn't have to return the money, she did so as a matter
of honor. vb. **1.** respect, esteem: *We honored the mem-*
ory of the past president with a testimonial dinner. **2.**
admire, revere: *Honor the returning soldiers with more*
than a brass band at the train. **3.** accept, acknowledge,
clear: *The bank refused to honor my check.* **ant.** *n.* **1.**
dishonor, disgrace, shame. *vb.* **1.** dishonor, disgrace,
shame.

honorable *adj.* **1.** honest, noble, just, fair: *The hero fought*
well and went to an honorable death. **2.** illustrious,
famed, distinguished: *The honorable chairman of the*
council received a presidential award. **ant. 1.** dishonorable, shameful, humiliating.

honorary *adj.* complimentary, gratuitous: *My mother was given an honorary degree by the university.*

hop *vb., n.* leap, jump: *Why do you keep hopping about on one leg? Because with each hop I am giving the other leg a rest.*

hope *n.* **1.** expectation, anticipation; desire: *My parents have high hopes for me, which is why I am going all the way through school.* **2.** trust, faith, confidence: *There may not be food on the table, but there's hope in our hearts. vb.* desire, aspire, expect: *I hope Zeke will invite me to the dance.* **ant.** *n.* **2.** hopelessness, despair.

hopeful *adj.* confident, optimistic: *I am still hopeful that our team will win the championship.* **ant.** hopeless, despairing.

hopeless *adj.* **1.** despairing, desperate, forlorn: *With the score 10 to nothing, the situation looks hopeless.* **2.** incurable, fatal, disastrous: *His condition is hopeless: I don't think your pet turtle will live.* **ant.** hopeful, promising.

horizontal *adj.* **1.** level, even, plane, flat, straight: *Whichever way you look at it, the horizon is always horizontal.* **2.** sideways: *The surface of a dining table should always be horizontal so that the dishes won't slide off.* **ant.** vertical, upright.

horrible *adj.* horrifying, awful, terrible, horrid, dreadful, ghastly: *I felt and looked horrible after a sleepless night.* **ant.** wonderful, splendid.

horrid *adj.* shocking, horrifying, horrible, revolting, repulsive: *A horrid little man was standing at the entrance to the amusement park.*

horror *n.* **1.** terror, dread, alarm: *Horror movies frighten me.* **2.** loathing, hatred, aversion: *The soldiers had a horror of war.*

hospital *n.* clinic, infirmary, sanatorium, sanitarium; rest home, nursing home: *After the accident, I was taken to the emergency ward of the hospital.*

hospitality *n.* generosity, liberality, graciousness, warmth, welcome: *Because of George's hospitality, we stayed with him for a week after the fire in our house.*

hostile *adj.* unfriendly, antagonistic, warlike: *The Secretary of State considered the invasion a hostile act.* **ant.** friendly, hospitable.

hot *adj.* **1.** torrid, heated, burning, fiery, blazing, sizzling, roasting, frying, broiling, boiling, scorching, searing: *It can get very hot in the middle of the desert at noon.* **2.** spicy, sharp, biting: *If you didn't put so much pepper on it that pizza wouldn't be so hot.* **3.** excited, violent, passionate, ardent: *The question of how to save fuel and energy is a hot issue today.* **ant. 1.** cold, cool, chilly, freezing. **2.** bland, tasteless.

hotel *n.* inn, motel, hostelry, hostel: *The hotel in Aston Clinton has fine rooms and excellent food.*

hotheaded *adj.* reckless, rash, unruly; touchy, testy, short-tempered, irritable: *It isn't a good idea to give a person who is hotheaded too much responsibility.* **ant.** cool-headed, levelheaded, calm.

hound *vb.* pursue, harass, harry, pester: *Pete was constantly hounded by the people to whom he owed money.*

house *n.* abode, building, dwelling, residence: *I have to be back at my house by noon.* *vb.* shelter, lodge; harbor: *The new dormitory will house more than 500 students.*

howl *vb., n.* wail, yowl, cry; yell: *Crowded in the lonely cabin, we heard the wolf howling in the distance. With a howl, the dog leaped at the robber.*

hue *n.* color, shade, tone, tint: *The hues of the sunset reminded me of a rainbow.*

hug *vb., n.* embrace, clasp, press, grasp: *Monica hugged the frightened puppy close to her. Laura's father came home and gave her a big hug and a kiss.*

huge *adj.* enormous, gigantic, immense, colossal, tremendous; large, big: *A huge statue of a man once straddled the harbor entrance of Rhodes.* **ant.** small, tiny, diminutive, miniature.

humane *adj.* kind, thoughtful, kindly, merciful, kindhearted, tender, gentle, softhearted: *It would be humane to bring that dog home from the pound.* **ant.** cruel, mean, heartless.

humble *adj.* **1.** unassuming, modest, unpretending, unpretentious: *Abe Lincoln came from a humble home.* **2.** polite, courteous, respectful: *You should be more humble when talking to your elders.* *vb.* lower, reduce, degrade, downgrade, shame: *Visiting the Hall of Fame can be a humbling experience.* **ant.** *adj.* **1.** vain, proud, haughty.

humiliate *vb.* degrade, disgrace, shame, humble: *After having worked for the same company for 25 years, my father thought it humiliating to lose his job.*

humor   *n.*   **1.** amusement, joking, clowning, fun: *I really like the style of humor of the Marx Brothers.* **2.** mood, sentiment, disposition: *If you want to ask Dorothy for a favor, you'd better wait till she's in good humor.*

humorous   *adj.* funny, comical, comic, amusing: *The comedian told humorous stories all evening.* **ant.** serious, unfunny, sober, somber.

hungry   *adj.* famished, starved: *I certainly don't want to go swimming with a hungry shark.* **ant.** full, sated, glutted.

hunt   *vb.* **1.** chase, track, pursue, stalk: *I've been invited up to Canada to hunt moose.* **2.** seek, probe; scour: *She's been hunting for a new boyfriend.* *n.* chase, pursuit; search: *I went along on a fox hunt just for the ride.*

hurl   *vb.* fling, throw, pitch, cast: *The detective hurled the murderer's gun out of the window.*

hurry   *vb.* **1.** rush, run, speed, race, hasten: *Dinner is probably ready, so I'd better hurry home.* **2.** rush, hasten, urge, accelerate: *The police hurried the people along the passageway away from the fire.* *n.* rush, haste, bustle, ado: *Stop pushing! What's the hurry?* **ant.** *vb.* **1.** linger, tarry, dawdle.

hurt   *vb.* **1.** damage, harm, injure: *Did you hurt yourself when you fell down the stairs?* **2.** wound, distress, afflict, pain: *If you tell Alexa that she can't go because she's too young, you'll hurt her feelings.* *n.* injury, harm, pain. *I feel the hurt of knowing I'll never see him again.*

hush   *vb., n.* silence, quiet, still: *Please don't hush me when I want to say something. It is so peaceful in the hush of the evening.*

hustle   *vb.* hurry, hasten, race, run, speed: *Nora came hustling through the crowd to meet me.*

hut   *n.* cabin, cottage, shed, shanty: *We found a woodcutter's hut in the forest and spent the night there.*

hypnotize   *vb.* mesmerize, entrance, charm, fascinate: *Sonia was so beautiful that she didn't ask men to do things, she hypnotized them into it.*

ᦗ I ᦘ

idea *n.* **1.** thought, conception, concept: *I just had a great idea: let's have hot dogs for lunch!* **2.** notion, understanding: *I haven't the slightest idea of what you're talking about.* **3.** opinion, plan, belief, view: *The head of the company asked me what my ideas were for expansion.*

ideal *n.* **1.** model, example, sample, paragon, standard: *My ideal is a kitchen appliance that does the dishes by itself.* **2.** aim, objective, target, goal: *The ideals of the United Nations are peace and friendship throughout the world.* *adj.* perfect, complete, fitting, supreme: *This is an ideal spot for a picnic.*

identical *adj.* alike, indistinguishable, like; same: *Too bad; I bought the identical dress for $10 less.* **ant.** unalike, different.

identify *vb.* name, describe, classify: *At the police station, Jerry was able to identify the woman who had stolen his car.*

identity *n.* individuality, character, uniqueness, personality: *You must have some papers with you to establish your identity.*

idiot *n.* fool, nincompoop, dunce, moron: *Don't be an idiot: you can't hold your breath for five minutes.*

idiotic *adj.* stupid, senseless, foolish, inane, moronic, half-witted, thimble-witted, simpleminded, dimwitted: *It's idiotic to believe that you'll live forever.* **ant.** intelligent, bright, brilliant, smart.

idle *adj.* **1.** unemployed, inactive, unoccupied, unused: *Five hundred men were made idle by the layoffs at the factory.* **2.** lazy, sluggish: *An idle mind finds nothing interesting in the world.* **ant. 1.** active, busy, occupied, engaged.

idol *n.* **1.** image, symbol, graven image, god, statue: *The natives fell to their knees before an idol of their water god.* **2.** favorite, pet, darling: *The Three-headed Monster was the name of the new rock group that was the idol of the teenagers.*

ignorant *adj.* **1.** untrained, uneducated, illiterate, untaught: *Some of the applicants were too ignorant to qualify for* *the job.* **2.** unaware, unmindful, unwitting, uninformed: *Ignorant of the fact that she had just come in the back door, Bill went out to look for his sister.* **ant. 1.** educated, cultivated, cultured, schooled, lettered, learned. **2.** aware, informed.

ignore *vb.* disregard, overlook, omit, neglect: *Ignoring the danger to himself, Freddie dived into the river to save the puppy.* **ant.** notice.

ill *adj.* sick, unwell, unhealthy, diseased, ailing: *I felt ill after eating that turkey with chocolate sauce.* **ant.** well, healthy, fit.

illegal *adj.* unlawful, illicit: *Selling alcoholic beverages was illegal during Prohibition.* **ant.** legal, lawful, legitimate.

illuminate *vb.* **1.** light, light up, brighten, lighten: *A strange green glow illuminated the sky.* **2.** enlighten, explain, clarify, interpret: *The difficult lecture was illuminated by many illustrations and examples.* **ant. 1.** darken, shadow, becloud, obscure.

illusion *n.* mirage, delusion, hallucination, vision, fantasy: *The movie was so vivid that I had the illusion I was falling. The apple didn't turn into a scarf! That was a magician's illusion.* **ant.** reality, actuality.

illustrate *vb.* **1.** illuminate, decorate, adorn, embellish: *The book was illustrated with color photographs.* **2.** demonstrate, picture, show: *The salesman illustrated the use of the gadget by peeling potatoes with it.*

illustration *n.* **1.** picture, photograph: *This book contains hundreds of illustrations.* **2.** example, explanation: *At least one illustration has been provided for each entry in this dictionary.*

illustrator *n.* artist, painter: *The illustrator has been very careful to show details in his drawings.*

image *n.* **1.** likeness, representation, reflection: *Betsy stared at her own image in the mirror.* **2.** idea, picture, notion, conception: *In my mind there is an image of what I would want to become when I grow up.*

imaginary *adj.* unreal, fanciful, whimsical, fantastic: *The unicorn is an imaginary animal.* **ant.** real, actual.

imagine *vb.* **1.** conceive, picture, envisage, envision: *Imagine yourself floating down the Nile with Cleopatra.* **2.** suppose, believe, think: *I couldn't imagine what had happened to you.*

imitate *vb.* follow, copy, mimic, duplicate, reproduce: *Try to imitate my pronunciation of these French words.*

immediate *adj.* **1.** instant, instantaneous, present: *My immediate reaction to your request for a loan is "No."* **2.** near, next, close; prompt: *Let's take care of the immediate problems now and leave the others for later.* **3.** direct: *The immediate result of the plan was to give housing to the elderly.* **ant. 1.** long-range, distant. **2.** future.

immediately *adv.* at once, instantly, forthwith, directly, straightaway, promptly: *I want you to go now—your plane leaves immediately.*

immense *adj.* huge, enormous, vast, gigantic, great, large, big: *Before us stretched an immense crater, left there when the volcano had exploded.* **ant.** small, tiny, minuscule, petite.

immortal *adj.* undying, everlasting, eternal, timeless, endless: *Most cultures have developed religions whose gods are immortal.*

impact *n.* contact, striking, collision: *The bullet struck the wall with such impact that it went right through.*

impair *vb.* mar, damage, spoil, destroy: *The furnace was impaired by the leaking water pipe.*

impertinent *adj.* impudent, insolent, rude, disrespectful: *In the old days, when a student was impertinent to the teacher he was made to stand in the corner.* **ant.** polite, courteous, respectful.

impetuous *adj.* rash, hasty, impulsive: *Ken is so impetuous to have bought his wife a fur coat when he can't afford it.* **ant.** careful, cautious, thoughtful, prudent.

implement *n.* tool, utensil, instrument, device: *The diecutter uses precision implements in his trade.* *vb.* complete, fulfill, achieve, realize: *Audrey implemented her promise by showing up for work on Saturday.*

implore *vb.* beg, beseech, entreat: *I implored the judge to hear my side of the story.*

imply *vb.* hint, suggest, indicate, mention: *Without exactly saying so, Marty implied that he'd appreciate having another piece of chocolate cake.* **ant.** state, declare.

impolite *adj.* rude, unpleasant, discourteous, insolent, impertinent, uncivil: *Jennie's cousin was so impolite to my mother that I'll never invite him again.* **ant.** polite, courteous, respectful.

important *adj.* **1.** essential, significant, considerable, primary, principal: *The budget approval was an important step toward our getting the school buses.* **2.** famed, illustrious, well-known, famous, distinguished, notable: *We have had some very important people visiting us.* **ant. 1.** unimportant, trivial, trifling, secondary. **2.** inconsequential, anonymous.

impose *vb.* require, levy, demand: *The government has imposed high taxes on luxuries.*

impossible *adj.* unworkable, preposterous: *It will be impossible for us to go to the party tonight because we have to babysit. Many of the things we take for granted today were thought impossible less than 100 years ago.*

impress *vb.* **1.** influence, affect; awe: *All of the parents were well impressed by their children's achievements in the art class.* **2.** imprint, emboss, indent, mark, print: *The Roman general impressed his seal on the document.*

impression *n.* **1.** effect, mark, influence: *The President's speech made a deep impression on me.* **2.** mark, dent, indentation, depression: *The thief's shoe made an impression in the flower bed outside the window.* **3.** thought, belief, guess, opinion: *I have the impression that you'd rather not go.*

improper *adj.* **1.** unsuitable, unfit, inappropriate: *The manager told us that blue jeans and sweatshirts were improper attire for the restaurant.* **2.** indecent, naughty, unbecoming: *My father used to punish any of us whom he heard use improper language.* **ant.** proper, fitting, appropriate.

improve *vb.* better, refine, upgrade: *Maybe these new glasses will improve your vision.* **ant.** impair.

impudent *adj.* impertinent, fresh, insolent, insulting, rude: *Don't be impudent to the teacher, or you'll be kept after school.* **ant.** courteous, polite, respectful.

impulse *n.* **1.** whim, hunch, fancy, caprice, urge: *Fanny got an impulse to place a bet on a horse called "Bottoms Up."* **2.** force, surge, pulse: *The impulse of the waves keeps the pump going automatically.*

impulsive *adj.* hasty, rash; spontaneous, automatic: *Betsy is an impulsive shopper—she never makes a list and buys what she sees in the store.* **ant.** careful, cautious, prudent.

inaccurate *adj.* incorrect, wrong, mistaken, faulty: *To say that Gerald Ford is the 34th President of the U.S. is inaccurate.* **ant.** accurate, correct, right.

inactive *adj.* inert, motionless, still, idle: *That machine has been inactive for five years. The bank notified us that they wished to close inactive accounts.*

inanimate   *adj.* lifeless, mineral, vegetable: *A table, like a stone, is an inanimate object.*

incense   *vb.* enrage, infuriate, anger: *Terry's father was incensed to learn that she had taken the car without his permission.*

incentive   *n.* inducement, stimulus, impulse, encouragement: *As an incentive to buyers of new cars, the manufacturers were giving rebates of hundreds of dollars.* **ant.** discouragement.

incessant   *adj.* unending, eternal, continuous, perpetual, constant, relentless: *The woodpecker kept up his incessant hammering, preventing me from sleeping.* **ant.** intermittent, irregular, spasmodic.

incident   *n.* event, occurrence, happening: *The incident at the club last night may get many people into trouble.*

incidental   *adj.* secondary, unimportant, trivial: *Receiving a diploma is incidental to education; it's how much you learn that counts.* **ant.** fundamental, basic.

inclination   *n.* **1.** tendency, predisposition, preference, prejudice: *My inclination is to do nothing for a week and see what happens.* **2.** slope, slant, incline, lean: *The inclination of the Tower of Pisa continues to increase every year.* **ant. 1.** disinclination, reluctance. **2.** uprightness, straightness.

incline   *vb.* lean, slope, nod: *The bidder at the auction inclined his head slightly and the painting was sold.* **ant.** straighten.

include   *vb.* embrace, encompass, contain, involve: *Please don't include Sara in your plans to go skiing.* **ant.** exclude, omit.

income   *n.* salary, earnings, wages, pay; revenue, receipts, return: *At 5 percent per year, my income from each $100 in savings is at least $5.* **ant.** expense.

incompetent   *adj.* unfit, incapable, unqualified; clumsy, awkward: *The examiner found Hilda incompetent to drive a car.* **ant.** competent, able, skilled.

inconvenient   *adj.* inappropriate, awkward, troublesome, untimely: *You're not the only one! Everybody finds it inconvenient when the phone rings while he is in the bath.* **ant.** convenient, handy.

incorrect   *adj.* wrong, inaccurate, mistaken, erroneous: *32 is an incorrect total for the numbers 12, 15, 4.* **ant.** accurate, proper, suitable.

increase   *vb.* swell, enlarge, greaten, extend, grow, prolong, lengthen, broaden: *The river increased from the rains. My boss increased my salary this year.* *n.* enlargement, growth, expansion: *There has been a huge increase in the price of cheese during the past year.* **ant.** *vb.* decrease, shrink, lessen, diminish. *n.* decrease, lessening, shrinkage.

incredible *adj.* unbelievable, improbable: *Your excuse that an elephant fell on you and made you late is just incredible.* **ant.** credible, plausible, believable.

indeed *adv.* really, in fact, truthfully, surely, honestly: *This cabinet proves that Roger is indeed a fine craftsman.*

indefinite *adj.* uncertain, unsure, vague, unsettled, confused, confusing: *He was indefinite about when he would arrive, so we'll just have to wait.* **ant.** definite, decided, unequivocal.

independence *n.* liberty, freedom: *The early Americans fought hard for their political independence from England.* **ant.** dependence, reliance.

indicate *vb.* **1.** signify, symbolize, mean: *The hexagonal sign indicates that you are supposed to stop your vehicle.* **2.** point out, show, designate: *The state policeman indicated the best route to the park would be straight ahead.*

indifferent *adj.* unconcerned, uncaring, cool, insensitive, nonchalant: *My boss was indifferent whether I took my vacation in July or August.* **ant.** concerned, caring, earnest.

indignant *adj.* angry, irritated, aroused, exasperated, irate: *I was indignant that the other students had been dismissed while I had to remain.* **ant.** serene, calm, content.

individual *adj.* single, undivided, separate, apart, different, distinct; special: *Each student will be given his individual reading list for the summer.* *n.* person, human, human being: *Each individual will be given his own reading list for the summer.*

indolent *adj.* lazy, idle, slow, sluggish, inactive: *I wouldn't hire that indolent fellow—he just lies about all the time.* **ant.** vigorous, active, dynamic, zestful.

induce *vb.* persuade, influence, convince: *We induced Charles to go along to the movies with us.* **ant.** dissuade, discourage.

inducement *n.* lure, enticement, incentive, stimulus: *What sort of inducement will they offer to persuade us to try the new product?* **ant.** discouragement.

indulge *vb.* yield to, gratify, humor, satisfy: *Barbie is terri-bly spoiled because her parents indulge her every wish.*

industrious *adj.* hard-working, busy, diligent, persistent: *The ant is an industrious insect.* **ant.** lazy, indolent, shiftless.

inevitable *adj.* unavoidable, inescapable, sure, certain: *When the fugitive ran down the dead-end street, his capture was inevitable.*

inexpensive *adj.* low-priced, modest, economical; cheap: *This camera costs quite a bit, but, considering its quality, it's inexpensive.* **ant.** expensive, costly, dear.

inexperienced *adj.* untrained, green; uninformed, naive: *If one is inexperienced, he will earn less than if he is ex-perienced.* **ant.** skilled, experienced, seasoned, trained, sophisticated.

infamous *adj.* **1.** scandalous, shocking, shameful: *Because of his reputation for drinking and gambling, the prince became infamous.* **2.** wicked, evil, bad: *Everyone knows about the infamous Spanish Inquisition.*

infantile *adj.* childish, immature, babyish, naive: *Sucking your thumb is pretty infantile behavior.* **ant.** grownup, mature, adult.

infectious *adj.* catching, communicable, contagious, trans-ferable: *Keep away from Eustace: he has a highly infec-tious disease.*

inferior *adj.* lower, second-rate, mediocre: *The quality of frozen foods is not inferior compared with fresh.* **ant.** superior, higher.

infinite *adj.* vast, boundless, innumerable, numberless, end-less, unlimited, limitless: *I wouldn't say that there are an infinite number of ways to solve the problem. It seems as though the distance to the farthest star is infinite.* **ant.** finite, limited.

inflame *vb.* excite, arouse, incite, fire: *The speaker was trying to inflame the crowd enough to cause them to riot.* **ant.** calm, soothe.

inflammation *n.* irritation, soreness, infection: *The doctor told me that the red spot on my arm was inflammation caused by scratching a mosquito bite.*

inflate *vb.* swell, expand, blow up, distend: *Gradually, the huge balloon was inflated with gas. The price of fresh vegetables is inflated during the winter.* **ant.** deflate, collapse.

inflexible *adj.* rigid, unbending, firm, unyielding, immovable, steadfast: *The history teacher was inflexible that the papers be handed in by Tuesday.* **ant.** flexible, pliant, yielding, giving, elastic.

inflict *vb.* **1.** give, deliver, deal: *The gang that attacked us inflicted serious injuries to those who resisted.* **2.** impose, levy, apply: *The American colonists rebelled against the heavy taxes inflicted on them by the British.*

influence *n.* effect, sway, weight, control: *The political boss had great influence throughout the city.* *vb.* affect, control, sway, impress: *The scientist insists on keeping an open mind and will be influenced only by actual facts.*

inform *vb.* notify, advise, tell, relate: *Although I missed the meeting, the other members informed me about what had happened.*

information *n.* facts, data, knowledge, intelligence: *The information in all reference books is carefully checked for accuracy.*

informative *adj.* enlightening, instructive, educational: *The economic report was very informative.*

informer *n.* betrayer, traitor, tattler, rat: *Ezra was known as an informer because he told his mother all of the club's secrets.*

ingenious *adj.* clever, skillful, imaginative, inventive: *I had to admire the ingenious way you persuaded the teacher to let us leave early.*

ingredient *n.* element, component, constituent: *One of the most important ingredients in our food is salt.*

inhabit *vb.* occupy; live, dwell, *or* reside in: *A family of squirrels inhabits our attic.*

inheritance *n.* heritage, legacy, patrimony: *Barbie thought her uncle was rich, but her entire inheritance was only $100.*

initial *adj.* first, basic, primary, elementary: *When I heard the good news, my initial reaction was to tell everyone.* **ant.** last, final, terminal.

initiate *vb.* start, begin, commence, open: *I want to initiate the ceremony by welcoming you all to Boondock, Iowa.* **ant.** stop, finish, terminate.

initiative *n.* enterprise, enthusiasm, energy, vigor: *Nobody suggested that Bill clean up the yard: he did it on his own initiative.*

injure *vb.* harm, hurt, wound, damage: *My little toe was slightly injured in the accident, so I sued.*

injurious *adj.* harmful, hurtful, damaging, destructive: *Smoking can be injurious to your health.* **ant.** beneficial, useful, advantageous.

injury *n.* harm, damage, hurt: *The article in the newspaper had done injury to Mr. Scott's reputation, according to the jury.*

inmate *n.* prisoner; patient: *I was an inmate at that hospital for two weeks.*

inn *n.* hotel, lodge; motel: *We stayed at an inn in the country during our holiday.*

innocent *adj.* **1.** not guilty, blameless, faultless, virtuous: *The defendant was found to be innocent and was set free.* **2.** unknowing, naive, unsophisticated: *Innocent young people are not allowed to see that kind of movie.* **ant.** **1.** guilty, blameworthy. **2.** sophisticated, wise, worldly.

inquire *vb.* ask, question; investigate, examine: *We inquired whether Harvey was well enough to come out and play. The police inquired into the movements of the suspect the previous evening.*

inquiry *n.* examination, study, investigation: *The detective conducted an inquiry into the whereabouts of the victim.*

inquisitive *adj.* inquiring, questioning, prying, curious: *I wish that Sadie weren't so inquisitive and would mind her own business.* **ant.** uninterested, incurious.

insane *adj.* **1.** deranged, lunatic, demented, mentally unsound, mad, crazy: *The murderer was declared legally insane and did not stand trial.* **2.** senseless, foolish, stupid, idiotic: *You're insane to dive off that tower into a small tank of water.* **ant.** **1.** sane, coherent, rational.

insist *vb.* demand, require, command: *The lawyers insisted on seeing the president of the company.*

insolent *adj.* impertinent, rude, disrespectful, insulting: *That boy has to learn not to be insolent to his elders.* **ant.** polite, courteous, respectful.

inspect *vb.* examine, investigate: *All of our products are carefully inspected before being offered for sale.*

inspiration *n.* thought, impulse, idea, notion, hunch: *Ed's inspiration led to the invention of a new steering device.*

install *vb.* establish, set up, put in: *My father was installed as president of the club last night. The servicemen installed our new heater today.*

instance *n.* case, example, occasion, illustration, occurrence:

Last night's robbery is another instance of the rise in crime in that neighborhood.

instant   *n.* moment, flash, twinkling: *In an instant, the frog had turned into a handsome prince.*

instantly   *adv.* at once, immediately, right away, directly, instantaneously: *When the sergeant gives an order, he expects it to be obeyed instantly.*

instinct   *n.* feeling, intuition: *My instinct tells me that someone is watching us.*

institute   *vb.* establish, organize, found, launch, begin, initiate: *Last year we instituted the practice of having a coffee break in the afternoons. n.* establishment, organization; university: *Haven't you ever heard of the Illinois Institute of Technology?*

instruct   *vb.* **1.** teach, educate, train, tutor, school, drill: *The gym teacher instructed us in the manly art of self-defense.* **2.** order, command, direct: *We were instructed to be very quiet during the ceremony.*

instruction   *n.* **1.** teaching, training, education, schooling, guidance: *Miles plays the violin beautifully, and he's never had any instruction.* **2.** direction, order, command: *The instruction was to proceed to the end of the street and turn right.*

instrument   *n.* tool, implement, device; means: *The surgeon's instruments were neatly laid out in the cabinet.*

insult   *vb.* offend, outrage, humiliate: *I won't insult you by telling you what I think of that cake you baked. n.* offense, affront, outrage, scorn: *Even though you love your dog, telling me that I look like him is an insult.* **ant.** *vb.* flatter, praise. *n.* flattery, praise.

integrated   *adj.* combined, interspersed, mingled, mixed; desegregated, interracial, nonsectarian: *Our school system has been integrated since two years ago.* **ant.** segregated, separated, divided.

integrity   *n.* **1.** soundness, wholeness: *You can't remove a brick from that wall without threatening the integrity of the entire structure.* **2.** honesty, uprightness, honor, principle, virtue: *We need more men of integrity in our government.*

intellect   *n.* **1.** judgment, understanding: *The men who planned the lynching were of small intellect.* **2.** intelligence, mind, mentality, sense, reason, brains: *There can be no doubt that Albert Einstein was a man with enormous intellect.*

intellectual *adj.* intelligent, learned: *I don't think you will find this comic magazine too intellectual for you.* *n.* academic, scholar, academician: *The intellectuals are all in favor of a higher governmental appropriation for the arts.*

intelligence *n.* ability, skill, aptitude: *Herman is a student of high intelligence who gets good marks.*

intelligent *adj.* smart, bright, clever, quick, astute, alert, wise: *The more intelligent students learn all of the time, not only when they are studying.* **ant.** stupid, slow, unintelligent, dumb.

intend *vb.* mean; expect; plan, propose: *What do you intend to do about your dog when you take a holiday?*

intense *adj.* **1.** deep, profound, concentrated, serious, earnest: *Felicia was wrapped up in her own intense thoughts.* **2.** concentrated, great, heightened, intensified, exceptional: *The intense heat from the burning building scorched the trees nearby.*

intent *n.* aim, purpose, intention: *The man had been arrested for attacking the pedestrian with intent to kill him.* *adj.* concentrated, set; steadfast: *I was so intent on the book I was reading that I didn't hear you come in.*

intention *n.* plan, intent, purpose, expectation, design, aim, object: *Is it your intention to marry the banker's daughter?*

intentional *adj.* purposeful, deliberate, planned, intended: *I refuse to believe that his stepping on your toe was intentional.* **ant.** accidental, chance.

intentionally *adv.* purposefully, on purpose, deliberately, maliciously: *You sat on my hat intentionally!* **ant.** accidentally.

interest *n.* **1.** concern, care, attention: *The scientist examined the fossil with interest.* **2.** profit, advantage, benefit, gain: *It's in your own interest to do well in school.* **3.** share, ownership, credit: *Yes, I have a small interest in the ice-cream parlor down the street.* **4.** percentage, premium: *When Kathryn bought her house, she had to pay interest of 7 percent on her mortgage.* *vb.* **1.** attract, engage, absorb: *What you say about your uncle's jewel collection interests me.* **2.** entertain, amuse, engage: *I am interested by the theater.* **ant.** *n.* **1.** disinterest, apathy. *vb.* **1.** bore, weary.

interested *adj.* concerned, involved, affected: *You cannot be impartial: since you own a share in the property, you are* *an interested party.* **ant.** uninterested, unconcerned, indifferent.

interesting *adj.* attractive, fascinating, engaging, inviting: *That's one of the most interesting books I've ever read.* **ant.** uninteresting, boring, tedious, wearisome.

interfere *vb.* meddle, butt in, intervene: *I wish you wouldn't interfere when I'm trying to settle this matter with your brother alone.*

interference *n.* **1.** meddling, prying, intrusion: *Your interference in matters that don't concern you has gone far enough.* **2.** obstruction, obstacle, barrier: *Every time I have tried to settle the question the others have created some interference.*

interior *n.* inside, center: *She's not a landscape architect, she's an interior decorator. The interior of the house was painted yellow.* *adj.* inside, central, inner, internal: *The interior sections of the state were mostly swamplands.* **ant.** *n.* exterior, outside. *adj.* external, outer, outside.

internal *adj.* **1.** inner, interior, inside, private, intimate: *I don't think I want to reveal to you my internal feelings about her.* **2.** domestic, native: *Diplomatic relations are an international, not an internal matter.* **ant.** external, outer, surface.

interpret *vb.* **1.** explain, define; understand: *The way Lorenzo interpreted your remark, he thinks you don't like him.* **2.** translate, paraphrase: *Because the ambassador understood not one word of Russian, he hired Ivan to interpret what was being said.*

interrupt *vb.* **1.** intrude, break in, interfere, cut in (on): *Please don't interrupt me when I'm talking. If you always interrupt, how can you know what others think?* **2.** discontinue, stop, hinder, obstruct: *The trees on this side of the house interrupt the view of the seashore.*

interval *n.* gap, pause: *There should be a two-second interval between the strikings of the clock.*

intervene *vb.* come between, interfere, interrupt, intrude: *Two years intervened between the last two times I saw her.*

intimate *adj.* **1.** close, familiar, personal: *Shellie is one of my most intimate friends.* **2.** private, personal, confidential, secret: *We have always shared the most intimate details of our lives with each other.* **3.** thorough, complete, detailed: *I have an intimate understanding of the difficulty of building a bridge there.* *vb.* hint, suggest, imply: *Charlie intimated that if I were to offer to lend him a quarter, he wouldn't refuse it.*

intolerant *adj.* prejudiced, biased, bigoted: *You cannot expect fair treatment yourself if you are intolerant of the rights of others.* **ant.** tolerant, broadminded, fair.

intrigue *vb.* attract, charm, interest, captivate: *The dark-haired girl at the table in the corner intrigues me.* *n.* plot, scheme, conspiracy: *The cafés of Casablanca were famous as the scenes of many international intrigues.*

introduce *vb.* **1.** present; acquaint: *We were introduced to each other at Flora's house in Paris.* **2.** submit, propose, present, offer: *The committee has introduced a bill to the legislature to control the sale of guns.*

intrude *vb.* interrupt, infringe: *You have intruded on my privacy enough, and I must ask you to leave.*

intruder *n.* prowler, thief, trespasser, robber: *Although the jury didn't believe him, the accused man swore he had seen a bushy-haired intruder attack his wife.*

invade *vb.* penetrate: *The commandos invaded an unguarded part of the coast.*

invasion *n.* intrusion, attack: *The invasion of the continent began on D-Day, June 6, 1944.*

invent *vb.* create, make up, originate, devise, contrive: *I think that Felix invented that tale about his having been in the navy: he's only nine years old! Thomas Edison invented the electric light bulb.*

investigate *vb.* examine, inspect, explore, study: *The police investigated every possible suspect until they found one who could have been at the scene.*

investigation *n.* examination, exploration, inquiry, study, research, search: *A full-scale investigation revealed that the bank's president had been gambling away the depositors' money.*

invite *vb.* **1.** ask, bid: *They invited us for dinner and then gave us only toasted cheese sandwiches.* **2.** request, encourage, urge: *All furniture manufacturers were invited to bid on furnishing the governor's mansion.*

inviting *adj.* alluring, luring, appealing, tempting, attractive, encouraging: *That girl gave me an inviting smile, so I shall ask her to dance.* **ant.** uninviting, unattractive.

involuntary *adj.* automatic, reflex, uncontrolled; unintentional: *My wink was involuntary: I had an eyelash in my eye.* **ant.** voluntary, willed, willful.

involve *vb.* **1.** include, contain, embrace: *If your plans for*

*having dinner with the sheik involve me, I just want you
to know I don't eat sheep's eyes.* **2.** complicate, confuse,
entangle: *"This is one of the most involved cases I have
ever tried," said the judge.*

irregular *adj.* **1.** uneven, unequal, crooked: *The irregular
surface of this wall must accumulate a lot of dust.* **2.**
disorderly, random, unsettled, disorganized: *The hours
kept by the staff are irregular, and you can never be sure
when someone is in the office.* **ant. 1.** regular, even.

irritate *vb.* **1.** annoy, vex, pester, bother: *I find your constant whining about going to the movies very irritating.*
2. redden, chafe, inflame: *Stop scratching your eye or
you'll irritate it.* **ant. 1.** soothe, pacify, calm.

irritable *adj.* sensitive, touchy, testy, peevish, short-tempered,
fretful: *Irene is so irritable that you can't say anything
to her without getting her angry.* **ant.** cheerful, happy.

isolate *vb.* separate, disconnect, segregate, detach: *The doctor said that Ephraim should be isolated because the flu
is very contagious. The scientists were able to isolate the
valuable minerals from the ore.*

isolation *n.* separation, segregation, detachment; solitude,
loneliness: *After a few weeks, Robinson Crusoe began to
feel the effects of his isolation from other human beings.*

issue *n.* **1.** number, copy, edition: *Have you seen the Sunday issue of the newspaper?* **2.** problem, question, concern; matter, subject: *The TV quiz program dealt with
current events and with issues of importance to all of us.*
vb. **1.** appear, emerge, come out, come forth: *The smoke
issued from the chimney in great black clouds.* **2.** publish,
distribute, put out, send out, circulate, release: *A quar-
terly is issued four times a year.*

⋖⊱ J ⊰⋗

jail *n.* prison, penitentiary, reformatory; stockade, brig; dungeon, keep: *After spending 20 years in jail, the man was afraid to face the responsibilities of freedom.* *vb.* imprison, confine, detain, lock up, incarcerate: *She was jailed for shoplifting.*

jailer *n.* keeper, guard, warden, turnkey: *When he was sure the jailer was asleep, the prisoner unlocked his cell and escaped.*

jam *vb.* pack, crowd, force, ram, push, squeeze, wedge: *I don't see how they can jam eight tomatoes into that tiny can.* *n.* preserve, conserve: *Do you like jam with your peanut butter?*

jealous *adj.* envious; covetous: *Mother gave you two more pieces than me and I'm jealous. Oh, you're jealous of anyone who has more of anything than you—except maybe more punishment!*

jealousy *n.* envy; covetousness; greed: *His jealousy of his sister because she got better grades was unreasonable.*

jerk *vb.* twitch, quiver, shake: *When you jerked the tablecloth, you spilled the milk.* *n.* **1.** twitch, spasm, shake, quiver: *With a quick jerk, the horse threw the cowboy to the ground.* **2.** fool, dope: *I think you're a jerk for eating six candy bars.*

jet *n.* spurt, squirt: *When I turned on the tap, a jet of water hit me in the face.*

jewel *n.* gem, gemstone, stone; bauble: *The crown was made of gold set with diamonds and other jewels.*

job *n.* **1.** work, employment, trade, profession, position, calling, career, business: *With so many people unemployed, my father was lucky to have a job.* **2.** task, chore, duty: *Mother told me she had some jobs she wanted done around the house after school.*

join *vb.* unite, connèct, couple, assemble, link, fit, attach: *The pieces of the jigsaw puzzle joined together to form a picture of a sunset.* **ant.** split, separate, divide, sunder.

joint *n.* connection, link, coupling, union, junction: *I could see where the glue was oozing out of the joint between* *the parts. adj.* common, mutual, combined, connected: *If we make a joint effort, we can do it together.* **ant.** *adj.* separate, divided.

joke *n.* jest, prank, game, caper, antic; anecdote: *Tying a can to a dog's tail isn't a funny joke. vb.* jest, banter, laugh: *You go to your office on a camel every day? You must be joking!*

jolly *adj.* joyful, gleeful, gay, spirited, happy, cheerful, glad: *What a jolly fellow Santa Claus is!* **ant.** sad, somber, gloomy, melancholy.

jolt *vb., n.* jar, bump, bounce, shake, shock: *The electric wire touched my finger and jolted me. Everett got quite a jolt when he sat on that tack.*

journal *n.* **1.** diary, account, record: *Some people keep a journal every day of everything that happens to them.* **2.** newspaper, daily: *In our house we subscribe to* The Evening Journal.

journey *n.* trip, voyage, excursion, tour: *Our journey to Istanbul took three days on the train. vb.* travel: *The student journeyed two weeks to visit his old professor.*

joy *n.* delight, pleasure, happiness, gladness, satisfaction: *There is nothing to parallel the children's joy at visiting their grandmother at Christmas.* **ant.** unhappiness, misery, sadness, gloom.

judge *n.* arbiter, referee, umpire, arbitrator; justice, magistrate: *How can you be a judge of the matter when you don't know all of the facts? vb.* **1.** arbitrate, referee, umpire; decide, determine: *We judged that the home team had won because of the fouls.* **2.** estimate, guess, reckon, consider, regard: *I judged the distance as being about 90 feet.*

judgment *n.* **1.** decision, verdict, estimation, opinion: *In our judgment, the horse should not have been disqualified.* **2.** understanding, wisdom, discretion, sense, common sense, intelligence: *I think you showed good judgment when you reported the prowler to the police.*

jug *n.* jar, bottle, flagon, flask, pitcher: *There is a jug of cheap wine in the closet.*

jump *vb., n.* leap, spring, bound, vault, skip, hop: *Don't try jumping over that puddle or you'll fall into it. He's going to attempt a jump over the river next year while riding a horse.*

jumpy *adj.* nervous, touchy, sensitive, excitable: *Sally was so jumpy in the old house at night that she thought every* *sound was a ghost's footstep.* **ant.** calm, tranquil, un-ruffled.

junction   *n.*   **1.** joining, coupling, union: *The junction of the two families by marriage meant that the whole county was now under their control.* **2.** intersection, crossroads; connection, joint, weld, seam: *The rust started at the junction where the two sides of the box come together.*

junk   *n.* trash, scraps, rubbish, waste: *After the wreck, the car wasn't worth more than $10 as junk.* *vb.* scrap, discard, dump: *After 40 years of use and abuse, the broken-down bicycle was finally ready to be junked.*

just   *adj.*   **1.** fair, impartial: *I think that the referee's decision was just—the man was out at second.* **2.** rightful, lawful, legal, proper: *Since we had paid for the land, we had just title to it.*

justify   *vb.*   **1.** vindicate, clear, acquit, excuse: *I don't see how you can justify murder except in self-defense.* **2.** defend, explain, excuse: *Tom tried to justify his actions by claiming that he had been very tired.*

ເຊ K ຊ

keen *adj.* **1.** sharp, acute: *This hunting knife has such a keen edge I can split a hair with it.* **2.** quick, shrewd, bright, clever, intelligent: *Larry, you have a keen sense of humor.* **3.** enthusiastic, eager, interested: *I don't know if Ward is so keen to publish the book any more.* **ant. 1.** dull, blunted. **2.** dull, stupid, slow, obtuse.

keep *vb.* **1.** retain, hold, withhold, preserve, maintain: *When you borrow books from the library, you're supposed to return them, not keep them.* **2.** continue, persist in: *I wish you wouldn't keep saying the same thing over and over again.* **3.** save, store, hold: *You can't keep eggs for a month outside the refrigerator without their becoming rotten.* *vb. phr.* **keep back** delay, hinder, hold, check: *I couldn't keep back a sneeze.* **keep on** continue, persist in; endure: *The raven just kept on saying "Nevermore! Nevermore!" without stopping.* **keep up** maintain, sustain, support: *It must cost a lot of money to keep up such a large home.* *n.* **1.** room and board, maintenance, subsistence: *The farmhand worked just for his keep during hard times.* **2.** tower, dungeon: *The knight rescued the damsel from the keep of the king's castle.*

keeper *n.* jailer, warden, custodian, guard: *The lunatic escaped from his keeper at the asylum and hid in the forest. The lion attacked his keeper in the zoo.*

key *n.* clue; answer: *The key to the puzzle is to spell the words backward.*

kill *vb.* **1.** slay, execute, assassinate, murder: *The tiger killed two people and then ran into the jungle.* **2.** destroy, cancel, abolish: *Your attitude could kill any feeling of love I might have toward you.*

kind[1] *n.* sort, class, type, variety: *What kind of bird is that?*

kind[2] *adj.* friendly, gentle, kindly, mild, kindhearted, goodhearted, warm, tender, affectionate: *I'm kind to dumb animals and to intelligent people.* **ant.** cruel, brutal, mean, hardhearted.

kindle *vb.* **1.** ignite, fire, light: *You'll need some paper to kindle a fire.* **2.** excite, arouse, inflame, provoke: *The*

*new girl in class knew how to kindle a spark of dislike
into a flame of hatred.*

kingdom *n.* monarchy, realm, domain, empire: *At one time
the kingdom of Spain was one of the most powerful in
the world.*

kingly *adj.* regal, kinglike, royal, majestic, imperial: *The
kingly mansion was magnificent.* **ant.** lowly, squalid.

kit *n.* set; collection, outfit: *My cousin got a tool kit for
Christmas and built a table with it.*

knit *vb.* combine, join, mend, unite, heal: *The broken bone
in my hand knit in about six weeks.*

knob *n.* **1.** handle, doorknob: *You have to turn the knob
if you want to open the door.* **2.** bump, protuberance:
There's a knob on my head where the baseball hit me.

knock *vb., n.* rap, thump, whack, thwack, tap: *Please knock
on my door at seven tomorrow morning. I have a headache from that knock I got yesterday.*

knot *n.* **1.** group, cluster, collection, gathering, crowd: *A
small knot of people surrounded the injured man.* **2.**
tangle, twist, snarl: *My shoelaces were tied together in
a knot by some wiseguy.*

know *vb.* **1.** recognize: *I don't think I know you—have
we met?* **2.** understand, comprehend, see: *Do you know
what I'm talking about?* **3.** distinguish, discriminate: *I
wouldn't know him from Adam.*

knowledge *n.* **1.** information, learning, data: *Sidney's
knowledge of physics is rather limited.* **2.** understanding,
wisdom, judgment: *Man's knowledge of himself has increased enormously in the past century.*

❧ L ☙

label *n.* tag, marker, mark, sticker, stamp: *The label on this vase says it was made in Denmark. vb.* tag, mark, stamp: *All medicines should be labeled to show their ingredients.*

labor *n.* **1.** work, toil, drudgery: *Clearing out your attic would provide labor for five men for a week.* **2.** workingmen, workers, working class: *Management and labor reached an agreement last night, and the bus drivers returned to work today. vb.* work, toil, strive: *My father labored for many years for others before he could buy his own farm.*

laborious *adj.* **1.** difficult, tiring, burdensome, hard: *Shoveling coal is very laborious.* **2.** painstaking, industrious: *We had to admire the laborious detail of the ivory carvings.* **ant. 1.** easy, simple, restful, relaxing.

lack *n.* shortage, need, dearth, want, scarcity: *Driving over the speed limit shows a lack of good judgment. The lack of vitamins and protein in their diet made many of the people very weak and ill. vb.* want, need, require: *We are lacking three people to make up a baseball team.* **ant.** *n.* abundance, quantity, plentifulness, profusion.

lad *n.* boy, youth, fellow, chap, stripling: *Ted is a fine lad, but he may be too young to become the team captain.*

lag *vb.* fall behind, dawdle, linger, loiter, tarry, straggle: *Deliveries are lagging two weeks behind orders. n.* slack, slowdown, tardiness: *The lag in sales is due to the economic slump.*

lame *adj.* **1.** crippled, disabled, limping; deformed: *The horse could not be entered in the race because it was lame.* **2.** poor, unsatisfactory, weak, inadequate, faulty: *having to wash your hair is a pretty lame excuse for not arriving at work on time.* **ant. 2.** convincing, believable, plausible.

lament *vb.* mourn, weep, bemoan, grieve; regret: *The widows of the men killed in the explosion lamented their loss. n.* mourning, lamentation, moan, wail, moaning, wailing, weeping: *The widows' lament could be heard for many days after the accident.*

lamentable *adj.* deplorable, unfortunate: *The conditions under which some poor people live are lamentable.*

lane *n.* passage, alley, way: *The lane behind the houses is overgrown with rose bushes.*

language *n.* **1.** tongue, speech: *My uncle speaks three foreign languages.* **2.** dialect; jargon; patois: *Don't you dare use foul language in my presence! The technical language of mathematics is hard to understand.*

large *adj.* big, great, sizable, broad, massive, huge, vast, enormous, immense: *Elephants are large animals.* **ant.** small, little, tiny, diminutive.

largely *adv.* mainly, chiefly, mostly, principally: *The spring floods were caused largely by the heavy winter snows when they melted.*

lash *n.* whip, thong, cane, rod, knout: *The thief received five lashes in the public square.*

lass *n.* girl, maiden, damsel: *Kathy is a pretty lass.*

last *adj.* final, latest, ultimate, extreme, concluding: *The last time I saw her, she was wearing a green hat and coat.* *vb.* continue, remain, endure: *This pair of blue jeans has lasted for three years.* **ant.** *adj.* first, initial, starting, beginning.

latitude *n.* freedom, scope, range, extent: *If you give me only $10 to buy a pair of shoes, that doesn't give me much latitude of choice.*

laugh *vb., n.* chuckle, giggle, snicker, guffaw: *I wasn't laughing at you because you're not funny. Alexa gave a little embarrassed laugh when asked why she was late.*

laughable *adj.* amusing, funny, humorous, comical, ridiculous: *The way the otters play around the pond is laughable to watch.*

launch *vb.* **1.** fire, drive, propel: *The rocket was launched to the moon at dawn.* **2.** initiate, originate, start, begin: *The senator launched his campaign for president early in February.* **ant. 2.** stop, finish, terminate.

law *n.* rule, statute, order, decree, ruling: *The Congress passed a law for aid to the elderly.*

lawful *adj.* legal, legitimate: *Every American is entitled to his lawful rights.*

lawless *adj.* uncontrolled, uncivilized, wild, untamed, savage, violent: *The early days of the West were lawless until the pioneers started settling west of the Mississippi.* **ant.** law-abiding, obedient, tame.

lawyer *n.* attorney, counselor-at-law, counsel, counselor, advocate: *If you don't pay me the money you owe, I'll turn the matter over to my lawyer.*

lay[1] *vb.* **1.** put, place, set, deposit: *Please lay the book on the table.* **2.** wager, bet, risk, hazard, stake: *I'll lay you five to one that my horse wins.* *n.* **1.** position, site, location: *I've just started work, so give me a chance to get the lay of the land.* **2.** song, ballad, lyric, ode: *Sir Walter Scott wrote "The Lay of the Last Minstrel."*

lay[2] *adj.* **1.** laic, laical: *John's uncle is a lay member of the church, not a minister.* **2.** amateur, nonprofessional: *Since I wasn't a scientist, I could give only a lay opinion about the effects of the atomic power plant.*

lazy *adj.* indolent, slothful, idle, inactive, sluggish: *If you weren't so lazy, you might get more work done.* **ant.** ambitious, active, forceful, go-getting.

lead *vb.* **1.** guide, conduct, direct, steer: *The blind man's dog led him carefully across the street.* **2.** command, direct: *We need a strong man to lead us through the coming difficulties.* **ant.** follow.

leader *n.* director, chief, commander, head, manager, ruler: *The little green women stepped out of the space capsule and asked to be taken to our leader.* **ant.** follower, disciple.

league *n.* alliance, union, combination: *The National League won the pennant last year.*

leak *vb.* drip, flow: *This pipe is leaking and we'd better phone the plumber.*

lean[1] *vb.* **1.** slant, tilt, slope: *The Tower of Pisa leans over a little more each year.* **2.** rely, depend, trust: *When you go in to take the examination, you won't be able to lean on your notes.*

lean[2] *adj.* slender, slim, thin, lanky, gaunt, skinny: *The tall, lean cowboy sauntered into the saloon.* *n.* meat, sinew, muscle: *I've always wondered why Jack Sprat's wife "could eat no lean."* **ant.** *adj.* fat, portly, heavy, obese.

leap *vb. n.* jump, vault, spring, bound: *Jennie leaped up to kiss me when I entered the room. With a leap, the tiger was attacking the elephant.*

learn *vb.* acquire, gain, determine, find out; memorize: *How did you learn so many languages? I learned that you weren't planning to come from your note to Anne. Please learn this poem before class tomorrow.*

learned *adj.* scholarly, wise, educated, knowledgeable, well-informed: *The three learned men were asked to serve as* *advisors to the university.* **ant.** ignorant, uneducated, unlettered, illiterate.

learning *n.* knowledge, lore, scholarship, education: *Just because someone has a great deal of learning, that doesn't mean he has any understanding of people.*

lease *vb.* rent, charter, let: *If you want to lease an apartment, you'll have to see the landlord. The man who operates the marina will lease you a boat for the day.*

least *adj.* **1.** smallest, tiniest, minutest: *The least flycatcher is a very small bird.* **2.** slightest; trivial: *Don gets annoyed by the least little thing.* **ant. 1.** most.

leave *vb.* **1.** depart, go, quit; desert, abandon: *Evelyn left two days ago. The man in the witness box admitted to leaving his wife and two children.* **2.** bequeath, will: *Oscar's grandmother left him some money when she died.* *n.* **1.** permission, allowance, liberty, freedom, consent: *Do I have your leave to speak to the President?* **2.** furlough, vacation, holiday: *Andy will be on leave from the navy all next month.* **ant.** *vb.* **1.** arrive, come.

lecture *n.* speech, talk, address, lesson: *Last evening we attended an illustrated lecture on bird watching.* *vb.* speak *or* talk (to), address, teach, instruct: *The professor lectured the students about the plays of Shakespeare.*

legal *adj.* lawful, legitimate, honest: *There was a question about whether or not it was legal to show movies on Sunday.* **ant.** illegal.

legend *n.* story, tale, myth, folk tale, fable: *There is a legend that anyone who kisses the Blarney Stone acquires the gift of gab.*

legendary *adj.* **1.** traditional: *The strength of Hercules was legendary in Greek mythology.* **2.** mythical, fictitious, fanciful, imaginary: *Nobody is exactly sure whether King Arthur was real or legendary.*

legitimate *adj.* legal, lawful, right, proper, correct, valid: *My aunt is the legitimate heiress of the king of Transylvania.* **ant.** illegitimate.

leisure *n.* relaxation, ease, recreation, rest: *Nowadays, people have much more time for leisure than when they had to work 60 hours a week.*

leisurely *adj.* unhurried, casual, relaxed, comfortable: *We took a leisurely boat ride on the lake after dinner.* **ant.** hurried, pressed, forced, rushed.

lend   *vb.* loan, advance: *The most I could lend you is a dollar until the weekend.*

length   *n.* extent, measure, reach, stretch, longness: *The length of this string is three feet.*

lengthen   *vb.* extend, stretch, reach, prolong, grow, increase: *After Christmas, the days north of the equator lengthen until about June 22, the longest day of the year.* **ant.** shorten, contract, shrink.

lessen   *vb.* reduce, diminish, decrease, shrink, dwindle, decline: *If we add another hook, the strain in the one holding the picture now will be lessened.* **ant.** increase, swell, expand, multiply.

lesson   *n.* **1.** exercise, drill, assignment, homework: *I hope that all the students have completed the lesson for today.* **2.** instruction: *Your catching a cold ought to be a lesson to you to wear your coat.*

let   *vb.* **1.** permit, allow, grant: *Please let me go to the movies.* **2.** lease, rent: *There's an apartment to let on the next street.*

level   *adj.* **1.** even, smooth, flat, uniform: *The new board you put into the floor isn't level with the others.* **2.** horizontal, plane, flat: *On a level road, this car will get 36 miles per gallon of gas.* **3.** equivalent, equal: *My boat drew up level with the leader's, and then we started to pull ahead.* *vb.* **1.** even, equalize; smooth: *I have to level that picture so it hangs straight.* **2.** demolish, destroy, raze, flatten: *The entire center of the city was leveled by the bomb.*

levy   *n.* tax, charge, tool, free, duty: *There's a levy of 25 cents on every pack of cigarettes sold in the state.*

liable   *adj.* subject, accountable, answerable, responsible: *Parents are liable for damage done by their children.*

liar   *n.* falsifier, prevaricator, fibber, fabricator: *Anyone who says that Edward doesn't know how to play chess is a liar.*

liberal   *adj.* **1.** generous, openhanded, unselfish, kind: *Arnold has always been a very liberal tipper in this restaurant.* **2.** tolerant, unprejudiced, unbigoted, openminded: *I have always taken a liberal attitude toward women's rights.* **ant. 1.** stingy, cheap, tightfisted, selfish.

liberate   *vb.* free, release, loose, deliver: *Every year at Christmas the governor liberated prisoners who had served most of their sentences.* **ant.** imprison, confine, jail.

liberty *n.* freedom, independence: *Liberty means the freedom to do as one pleases within the law.* **ant.** bondage, servitude, slavery.

license *n.* **1.** permission, consent: *The trusty was given license to come and go as he pleased in the prison.* **2.** permit, authorization: *I have a driver's license that expires next month.* *vb.* permit, allow, sanction, authorize: *Frank is not licensed to practice medicine in this country.*

lid *n.* cover, top, cap: *I can't get the lid off this jar of mayonnaise.*

lie[1] *n.* falsehood, prevarication, fib, untruth, fiction, perjury: *It's a lie to say that I stole that cherry pie—my twin brother did it.* *vb.* fib, prevaricate, misinform: *Don't lie to me! I know you have no twin brother.*

lie[2] *vb.* **1.** recline, repose: *I lay in bed till noon today.* **2.** be situated *or* located: *The valley lies between the two mountains.* *n.* situation, location, site: *From the lie of that ball, I don't think you can hit it onto the green.*

life *n.* **1.** being, animation, existence, vitality: *There's still a breath of life in the injured man.* **2.** biography: *I've just finished reading a life of Lincoln.* **3.** vigor, vitality, energy, spirit, sparkle: *Irene is always the life of the party.*

lift *vb.* raise, elevate: *Don't try to lift that heavy box by yourself.*

light[1] *n.* **1.** illumination, radiance, brilliance, brightness: *There's not enough light here to read by.* **2.** lamp, fixture, chandelier, candle, bulb: *Please turn off the lights when leaving the room.* *vb.* **1.** illuminate, brighten: *That one candle isn't enough to light this room.* **2.** ignite, fire, burn, kindle: *I lit a fire in the sitting room.* *adj.* **1.** bright, clear, luminous, lit, illuminated: *This is a pleasant, light room to be in.* **2.** pale, whitish, bleached: *Your light yellow dress looks very well on you.* **ant.** *n.* **1.** dark. *vb.* **1.** darken. **2.** extinguish. *adj.* dark.

light[2] *adj.* **1.** unsubstantial, airy, buoyant, dainty: *If all the books are removed, this bookcase is very light.* **2.** giddy, frivolous: *Sometimes I think you're a bit light in the head.* **3.** trivial, shallow, slight: *I enjoy a little light reading before going to sleep.* **ant.** **3.** serious, heavy, weighty.

lightheaded *adj.* silly, frivolous, giddy, dizzy: *The remnants of the anesthetic made me feel lightheaded.* **ant.** clearheaded, sober, rational.

lighthearted *adj.* gay, carefree, cheerful, merry, happy, glad: *Phoebe's lighthearted manner gave no indication of the serious problems that faced her.* **ant.** sad, melancholy, somber, serious.

like *vb.* admire, esteem, fancy, care for, cherish, adore, love: *I like blueberry pie à la mode. Do you like me as much as I like you?* **ant.** dislike, disapprove, hate, loathe.

likely *adj.* probable, liable, possible, reasonable: *If I have a broken leg, it's not likely that I'll do much skiing this season. The governor is a likely candidate for U.S. senator.*

likeness *n.* **1.** resemblance, similarity: *Yes, there is a likeness between you and Napoleon.* **2.** image, representation, picture, portrait: *The king's likeness appears on all postage stamps, coins, and paper money.*

likewise *adv.* similarly; besides, also: *After you've watched how I peel this banana, I want you to do likewise. Likewise, Henry wanted to run for office.*

liking *n.* affection, partiality, fondness: *I've taken a liking to you, Donna, and would like to invite you out to dinner tonight.* **ant.** dislike, antipathy.

limit *n.* **1.** boundary, bound, extent, frontier, end: *The limits of our property are marked by those huge trees.* **2.** restraint, check, restriction: *There is no limit to your rudeness!* *vb.* check, hinder, restrain, restrict, confine: *You ought to limit the amount of candy you eat.*

limp[1] *adj.* flabby, soft, supple, limber, flexible: *After being left out in the rain, the pages of the book were all soggy and limp.* **ant.** stiff, rigid, hard.

limp[2] *vb.* hobble, falter, stagger: *The pirate came limping into the saloon on his pegleg.* *n.* hobble, lameness: *This limp comes from my sprained ankle.*

line *n.* **1.** row, array, file, sequence, series: *There was a line of medicine bottles on the shelf.* **2.** mark, stroke; outline: *After drawing a line at the top of your paper, write your name on it.* **3.** seam, crease, wrinkle: *The palm reader told my fortune from the lines in my hand.* **4.** division, limit, boundary: *I draw the line when it comes to three hot dogs in one day. Don't try to cross the state line near the river.* **5.** wire, cable; pipe; track: *When digging along the railway line, the men had to be careful to avoid cutting the telephone, power, and gas lines.* *vb.* line up, align, file, array: *I want all the children who are going to the zoo to line themselves outside at once.*

linger *vb.* loiter, stay, remain, tarry, dawdle: *Please don't linger near the front door after you leave the theater.*

link *n.* tie, bond, connection, connector, loop, coupling: *I cannot see any link between your wanting to see a movie and Bob's washing his car. vb.* connect, tie, couple: *The chains were linked to each other.*

lip *n.* brim, edge, rim: *The lip of the pitcher is cracked.*

list *n.* series, roll, record, register, slate: *Is Merrill's name on the list of candidates? vb.* record, register, post, file: *At the bottom of the application blank, please list all personal references.*

listen *vb.* hear, attend: *Listen to what your mother tells you, for Mother knows best.*

literal *adj.* word for word, verbatim, exact, precise: *This is a literal translation of the original.*

literate *adj.* educated, informed; intelligent: *Every literate person knows who Shakespeare was.* **ant.** illiterate, unread, unlettered, ignorant.

litter *n.* trash, rubbish: *Please don't throw litter on the streets. vb.* strew, scatter, disorder: *The park was littered with candy wrappers after the children left.*

little *adj.* **1.** small, tiny, wee, minute: *This little book has more information in it than many large ones.* **2.** brief, short: *There's only a little time left before my plane leaves. adv.* slightly: *Aren't you even a little hungry?* **ant.** *adj.* **1.** large, big, huge. **2.** long, extended.

live¹ *vb.* **1.** abide, reside, dwell: *I am going to live in India when I grow up.* **2.** exist, be; survive: *No animal —including man—can live without any water at all.*

live² *adj.* **1.** alive; surviving: *My grandmother used to go visiting carrying a live white mouse on a gold chain. There were only two live victims found after the crash.* **2.** energetic, active; unrecorded: *There's live entertainment this weekend at the movie theater.*

lively *adj.* **1.** active, live, vigorous, spry, nimble, quick: *Jack's grandmother is pretty lively for a woman of 92.* **2.** gay, animated, spirited: *That certainly was a lively dance you did last night.* **ant.** slow, dull, sluggish.

living *n.* livelihood; support: *How does that fellow make his living? I've never seen him work.*

load *n.* burden, weight; cargo, shipment, delivery: *That's quite a load you're carrying. I've ordered another load of coal for the winter. vb.* weight, burden; lade: *We* *loaded the luggage into the car. Don't load me up with so many packages.*

loan   *n.* advance; credit: *I asked the bank to approve a loan of $1,000 for my new car.* *vb.* lend, advance: *Can you loan me a dollar till Tuesday?*

lobby   *n.* vestibule, foyer, anteroom, entry, entryway: *Please wait for me in the hotel lobby.*

locate   *vb.* **1.** find, discover, unearth: *I haven't been able to locate a copy of the book you asked for.* **2.** situate, site, place: *I've been planning to locate the new factory along the river.*

location   *n.* site, situation, locate, spot, place, area, neighborhood: *The top of that hill would be a fine location for your new home.*

lock¹   *n.* tress, braid, plait: *Betty's golden locks flowed down to her shoulders.*

lock²   *n.* latch, hasp, bolt, padlock: *I have nothing that anyone would want, so I don't keep a lock on the door.* *vb.* latch, padlock, bolt, fasten: *Lock the door carefully after I leave and don't let anyone in.*

lodge   *n.* **1.** cottage, cabin, hut; chalet: *The prince had a hunting lodge in the mountains.* **2.** club, society: *There was a meeting of our lodge every Tuesday at the local restaurant.* *vb.* **1.** room, stay, reside, abide, board, dwell: *I've been lodging with my aunt while looking for a job.* **2.** settle, fix, put: *Trying to get the pencil out of the rifle barrel, my finger became lodged in the hole.*

lofty   *adj.* **1.** tall, high, towering: *A lofty skyscraper can be seen as you approach the city.* **2.** exalted, elevated: *His lofty ideas of himself annoyed everyone.* **3.** proud, scornful, haughty: *She's much too lofty to have anything to do with us.* **ant. 1.** lowly, low.

logical   *adj.* reasonable, rational, sensible: *It's logical to assume that you will annoy someone if you insult him.* **ant.** irrational, crazy.

lone   *adj.* sole, alone, solitary; apart, separate, separated: *A lone cowboy rode along the trail.*

lonely   *adj.* lonesome, alone; lone: *I feel so lonely when you go away for more than a day.*

long¹   *adj.* extensive, lengthy, extended: *I have never seen a piece of spaghetti six feet long. You have kept me waiting for a long time.* **ant.** short, brief, limited.

long²   *vb.* crave, desire, wish: *I long for a tall glass of iced tea.*

long-winded *adj.* dull, boring; wordy: *The senator gave such a long-winded speech that I fell asleep in the middle of it.* **ant.** terse, curt.

look *vb.* **1.** gaze, glance, survey, watch, regard, see, study: *Look at the girl in the window.* **2.** appear, seem: *It looks as if we won't be able to go on our picnic now that it's raining.* **3.** seek, search for: *Please look for your keys yourself.* *n.* **1.** glance, peek, peep, glimpse: *I've only had one look at the page, but I've memorized it.* **2.** gaze, stare; contemplation, study, examination: *The fixed look she gave me made me nervous.* **3.** appearance, expression: *The look in her face when I told her!*

loose *adj.* **1.** unfastened, untied, free, undone: *There's a lion loose from the circus!* **2.** wobbly, insecure, unscrewed, movable: *The arm of the chair is loose.* **3.** baggy, draped, slack: *Now that I've lost all that weight, my trousers are too loose on me.* *vb.* loosen; set free: *Whenever anyone came too close to the property, they would loose the guard dogs.* **ant.** *adj.* **1.** fastened, tied, secure. **2.** firm, secure, steady. **3.** tight, confining.

loosen *vb.* loose, untie, undo, unchain, unfasten: *The man was choking, so I loosened his collar and tie.* **ant.** tighten, tie, secure.

loot *n.* plunder, booty, take: *The bank robbers escaped with the loot.* *vb.* rob, steal, plunder, rifle, sack: *It was the manager of the bank who had looted the customers' accounts.*

lord *n.* nobleman, peer; master, ruler, governor: *The lord of the castle ordered the festivities to begin.*

lore *n.* knowledge, learning, wisdom: *The American Indians were experts in the lore of the forest.*

lose *vb.* mislay, misplace: *I've lost my door key again.* **ant.** find, discover, locate, place.

loss *n.* **1.** damage, injury, hurt: *The insurance was barely enough to cover our losses in the fire.* **2.** want, bereavement, need; misfortune, trouble; death: *The loss of Ben's mother was a loss to us all.*

lost *adj.* **1.** missing, mislaid, misplaced, gone, absent: *The ring, which I thought was lost, turned up in John's soup.* **2.** wasted, spent, misspent, squandered: *The money lost in gambling every year amounts to billions of dollars.*

lotion *n.* balm, salve, cream, liniment: *This hand lotion will smooth out the roughness in a few minutes.*

loud *adj.* noisy, ear-splitting, thunderous, blaring, shrill:

Please don't speak in such a loud voice in the hospital rooms. The loud sound of a car backfiring startled us all. **ant.** soft, quiet, murmuring.

lounge *vb.* loaf, idle, laze: *Stop lounging about the house and go out and get yourself a job!* *n.* **1.** couch, sofa, divan, davenport: *Only two people can sit on this lounge comfortably.* **2.** salon, parlor, lobby: *Let's go into the lounge and wait for Hattie there, where it's more comfortable.*

love *n.* adoration, warmth, devotion, tenderness, liking, friendliness, affection: *How can you compare a person's love for his family with his love of ice cream and candy?* *vb.* worship, adore, treasure, cherish, like: *Darling, when I say I love you, I mean I want to be with you forever.* **ant.** *n.* hate, loathing. *vb.* hate, detest, loathe.

lovely *adj.* attractive, fair, charming, comely, pretty, beautiful, handsome: *The bride was lovely in white lace.* **ant.** homely, ugly, hideous.

lower *vb.* **1.** reduce, decrease, lessen, diminish: *If you don't eat a balanced diet you lower your resistance to disease.* **2.** soften, quiet, turn down: *Please lower the volume of that hi-fi.* **3.** degrade, disgrace, humble: *I wouldn't lower myself to talk to someone who's such a bigot.* **4.** sink; drop: *Martin lowered himself carefully into the hot bath. Lower the leaf of the table gently.* **ant.** **1.**, **2.**, **4.** increase, raise.

loyal *adj.* faithful, true, devoted, dependable; patriotic: *The British ambassador acknowledged that he was a loyal subject of the queen.* **ant.** disloyal, treacherous, traitorous.

loyalty *n.* faithfulness, devotion, fidelity; allegiance, patriotism: *The king rewarded his knights' loyalty with grants of land and castles. It's amazing to see that dog's loyalty to his master.* **ant.** disloyalty, treachery, traitorousness.

luck *n.* fortune, chance, fluke: *It's all a matter of pure luck whether or not you win in the lottery.* **ant.** misfortune.

lucky *adj.* fortunate, favorable, favored, blessed: *Sharon has always been lucky at cards.* **ant.** unlucky, unfortunate.

luggage *n.* baggage, bags, suitcases, valises, trunks: *The customs inspectors will examine the contents of your luggage when you re-enter the country.*

lull *vb.* calm, soothe, quiet: *We were lulled to sleep by the sound of the waves beating on the shore.* *n.* calm, hush, quiet, stillness, silence; pause: *I took advantage of a lull in the activities to steal away unnoticed.*

luminous *adj.* alight, light, lighted, glowing, bright, luminescent, fluorescent: *At night we could see millions of luminous particles in the wake of the boat.*

lump *n.* **1.** bump, protuberance: *I still have the lump on my head where she hit me.* **2.** cube; piece, block: *I have two lumps of sugar in my tea.*

lure *n.* attraction, temptation, bait: *The salesman used the promise of free information service as a lure to sell the encyclopedia.* *vb.* entice, attract, tempt, draw: *The spider attempted to lure the fly to land on its web.*

luscious *adj.* juicy, delicious, delectable: *That Comice pear is the most luscious fruit I've ever eaten.*

lust *n.* **1.** desire, passion, craving, appetite: *It was his lust for money that drove the poor man to commit murder.* **2.** lechery, wantonness: *The dance that Salome did for King Herod was to arouse his lust.*

luster *n.* **1.** sheen, gloss, glister, glitter; brightness, brilliance, radiance: *The luster of the pearls showed up best in candle light.* **2.** fame, glory, repute, honor, distinction: *Although the luster of his accomplishments had won him praise, he was then awarded the Nobel prize.*

luxuriant *adj.* lush, dense, rich, rank: *The luxuriant growth of the jungle was so thick that the sunlight never reached the ground.*

luxurious *adj.* lavish, rich, splendid, deluxe: *The luxurious furnishings in the palace took my breath away.* **ant.** sparse, Spartan, simple, crude.

lyric *n.* words, text, libretto: *I know the lyrics, but the music is unfamiliar to me.*

⁌ M ⁊

macabre *adj.* gruesome, horrible, horrifying, ghastly, grim: *At night, around the campfire, we used to tell macabre tales of the supernatural.*

machine *n.* device, contrivance, engine, motor, mechanism: *This new kind of machine will print a sheet of paper in four colors on both sides at one time.*

mad *adj.* **1.** insane, crazy, mentally ill, deranged: *The composer finally went mad and had to be confined in a hospital.* **2.** angry, furious, enraged, irate, raging: *I'm very mad at Nora for not telling me about Ted's surprise party.* **ant. 1.** sane, rational, lucid. **2.** happy, cheerful, content.

madden *vb.* enrage, infuriate, anger, vex, annoy: *The horses, maddened by the thousands of flies, stampeded into the river.* **ant.** mollify, calm, please.

magazine *n.* **1.** periodical, journal: *Our family subscribes to a lot of nature magazines.* **2.** arsenal, armory: *One of the enemy shells hit our magazine and blew the entire building sky-high.*

magic *n.* sorcery, sleight-of-hand, witchcraft: *The way that rabbit appeared in the silk top hat was magic. adj.* magical: *This is a magic wand that turns into a snake unless I'm holding it.*

magical *adj.* magic, marvelous, miraculous; mystical: *A magical change took place, and the little green frog turned into an ugly princess.*

magician *n.* sorcerer, wizard, witch, warlock, conjuror, enchanter: *The magician made the card disappear, then reappear behind my ear!*

magnificence *n.* splendor, grandeur, luxury: *There are few countries today that can match a British coronation ceremony in magnificence.*

magnificent *adj.* **1.** splendid, luxurious, rich, lavish, grand: *The throne room of the palace is the most magnificent I've ever seen.* **2.** marvelous, wonderful, extraordinary, impressive: *From our bathroom windows we have a magnificent view of the mountains.* **ant.** plain, simple.

magnify *vb.* enlarge, increase: *These glasses magnify the tiny print so that I can read it easily.* **ant.** diminish, reduce.

magnitude *n.* **1.** extent, dimension, measure: *Nobody had any idea of the magnitude of the disaster because all telephones and other communications had been cut off.* **2.** importance, consequence, significance: *The results of the research were of some magnitude for all mankind.*

maid *n.* **1.** maidservant, housemaid, chambermaid, servant: *We left the hotel room early so the maid could clean up and make the beds.* **2.** maiden, girl, young woman, lass: *The shepherd was singing a song to a pretty maid who had brought his lunch.*

maiden *adj.* first, original, earliest: *The Titanic sank on her maiden voyage.*

main *adj.* chief, principal, foremost: *The main problem in building a house over there is that the ground is swampy.* **ant.** secondary, accessory.

maintain *vb.* **1.** keep, continue, keep up, preserve, support: *Despite oppositions, Johnson maintained his leadership of the political party.* **2.** preserve, keep, keep up, renew: *If the town maintained the park in good condition, the people would be able to use it.* **3.** assert, state, hold, declare; claim, contend: *The man whom the police are questioning maintains that he was nowhere near the scene of the crime.* **ant. 1.** discontinue.

maintenance *n.* **1.** support, living, subsistence, bread, livelihood: *On the salary you are paying me I don't even have the bare maintenance I need.* **2.** upkeep, preservation: *This is a delicate machine, and maintenance and repairs are costly.*

majestic *adj.* **1.** royal, kingly, princely, regal, noble, grand, stately: *The star of the play made a majestic entrance and everyone applauded.* **2.** splendid, magnificent: *The decorations in the grand ballroom of the hotel are truly majestic.* **ant. 1.** lowly, base. **2.** squalid.

majesty *n.* dignity, nobility, grandeur: *The majesty of the mountains lay before us.*

major *adj.* greater, larger; important, chief: *The items of major concern are your safety and the ease with which the job can be done.* **ant.** minor, inconsequential.

make *vb.* **1.** fabricate, manufacture, produce, form, build, construct, create: *By using assembly lines, it became possible to make a car in an hour.* **2.** become, develop into: *I think that Barbie would make an excellent class president.* **3.** cause, render; occasion: *The popcorn and hot dogs and soda pop made me ill.* **4.** do, effect, execute, perform, accomplish: *Alan made a bow and the curtain came down at the end of the play.* **5.** compel, cause, force: *Patrick's mother makes him wear the velvet suit with the lace collar whenever they go visiting.* **6.** earn, gain, obtain, acquire, get: *My guess is that as president of the company, Abernathy makes about $25,000 a year.* **7.** reach, arrive at: *I don't see how we can make Chicago in three days if you drive at ten miles an hour all the time.* **8.** appoint, elect, select, assign: *Ernie's father was made head of the town committee on preservation of trees.* *vb. phr.* **1. make believe** pretend, fantasize, imagine: *Let's all make believe that we're sailing across the ocean in a big ship.* **2. make good** repay, compensate, reimburse: *The company had to make good the loss of my wallet.* **3. make it** succeed, triumph: *After working hard for 20 years, Prof. Kelly has finally made it to the top of his profession.* **4. make out** discern, perceive, understand, recognize: *Hubert mumbles so, I can hardly make out what he's saying.* **5. make up a.** create, invent, fabricate: *The students made up a story about the Pilgrims and then put it on as a play.* **b.** compose, form, join, constitute: *Do we have enough people to make up a baseball team?*

malady *n.* illness, sickness, affliction, disease, ailment, disorder: *Oscar has been taken ill with some strange malady that affects his big toe.*

male *adj.* masculine, manly, virile: *She described his dislike of dishwashing as a typically male attitude.* **ant.** female, feminine, womanly.

malice *n.* spite, resentment, viciousness, grudge, bitterness: *I'm sorry! I stepped on your sore foot by accident, not out of malice.* **ant.** benevolence, charity.

mammoth *adj.* huge, colossal, enormous, immense, elephantine, gigantic: *The ancient peoples who lived on Easter Island carved mammoth statues.* **ant.** small, tiny, minuscule.

manage *vb.* **1.** direct, guide, lead, supervise, superintend, control, conduct, administer, rule: *My uncle manages an aircraft factory.* **2.** succeed, arrange, bring about: *I managed to cling to a small tree that saved me from falling off the cliff.* **3.** handle, control, manipulate: *The* *stagecoach driver was able to manage a team of eight horses.* **ant. 1.** mismanage, bungle.

manageable   *adj.* controllable, docile, tractable, willing; obedient: *An animal born in captivity is more manageable than one born in the wild.* **ant.** unmanageable, wild, recalcitrant.

management   *n.* control, supervision, direction, regulation, administration, care: *The management of the company was in the hands of the owner's son.*

manager   *n.* supervisor, superintendent, overseer, executive, director, boss: *If that shop doesn't give me better service next time, I'm going to report it to the manager.*

manner   *n.* way, method, style, fashion, custom: *I don't like the rude manner in which you speak to your teacher.*

manufacture   *vb.* make, assemble, fabricate, construct: *The company manufactures toys in the plant down the road. n.* making, assembly, fabrication, construction, production: *Detroit, Michigan, is the center of automobile manufacture in the world.*

many   *adj.* numerous, abundant, plentiful: *There are many uses for plastic in modern commerce.* **ant.** few.

map   *n., vb.* chart, graph, plan: *This map of New England doesn't include New York State. The survey team was mapping the area using photographs taken from an airplane.*

margin   *n.* edge, rim, border: *The napkins have a colored margin that matches the design of the tablecloth.*

marine   *adj.* maritime, oceanic, nautical: *My brother is studying marine biology at the Scripps Institution.*

mariner   *n.* sailor, seaman: *The bars near the docks are very popular with mariners.*

mark   *n.*   **1.** impression, effect, trace, imprint, stamp, brand: *The teachers at the school have left their mark on their students.* **2.** sign, symbol, emblem, badge: *The king made his mark on the treaty by using his signet ring.* **3.** target, goal: *The first three arrows were wide of the mark, but the last hit the bull's-eye. vb.* **1.** label, tag, price, ticket: *These sweaters were marked $20 yesterday.* **2.** stamp, brand, imprint, identify: *The bookplate marks this book as one of mine.* **3.** note, heed, notice, pay attention to, attend, register: *Mark what I say about these chemicals or you may get hurt. vb. phr.* **1. mark down** reduce *or* cut (a price): *The prices of automobiles have been marked down 10 percent.* **2. mark off** separate, segregate, designate: *These spaces in the parking lot have been marked off for executives' cars.* **3. mark up** increase *or* raise (a price): *These cameras were marked up for only a small profit over cost.*

market *n.* marketplace, mart, supermarket, shop, store, bazaar, stall: *We have to go to the market to do our week's shopping tomorrow.* *vb.* sell, merchandise: *This company has been marketing cosmetics for almost 50 years.*

marriage *n.* **1.** wedding, nuptials: *There aren't many people old enough to remember the marriage of the king.* **2.** matrimony, wedlock; union: *Marriage is a solemn condition, but it can be rewarding for the right couple.* **3.** alliance, association, confederation: *The marriage of the company making toothpaste with the one making toothbrushes worked out very successfully.* **ant.** divorce, separation.

marry *vb.* wed; betroth: *Anyone married to the same person for almost 25 years knows him or her pretty well.*

marsh *n.* swamp, bog, fen, morass, quagmire: *In the spring, the marsh is teeming with young birds and other wildlife.*

marshal *vb.* arrange, order, organize, rank: *The officers marshaled the military forces in readiness for the big battle.*

marvel *n.* wonder, miracle, phenomenon: *The electric light was one of the marvels of the late 19th century.* *vb.* wonder, stare, gape: *The children marveled at how an elephant could dance so gracefully.*

marvelous *adj.* wonderful, miraculous, wondrous, extraordinary, amazing, astonishing, astounding: *The eruption of the volcano was one of the most marvelous things I'd ever seen.* **ant.** commonplace, ordinary, usual.

masculine *adj.* **1.** male: *There is some question as to whether professional basketball is strictly a masculine sport.* **2.** manly, brave, bold, courageous: *Victor is so very masculine that he looks peculiar in a dress.* **ant.** feminine, female, unmasculine.

mask *n.* protection, protector; disguise, camouflage: *You must wear a mask when operating this machinery. The beautiful ladies all wore masks to the ball.* *vb.* conceal, hide, disguise, veil, screen: *I find it difficult to mask my contempt for someone who would strike a person when he's down.*

mass *n.* **1.** pile, heap, quantity, aggregation: *A huge mass* *of building materials was being accumulated near the foundation.* **2.** size, bulk, magnitude, extent: *The mass of the sun is many times greater than that of the earth.* *vb.* gather, amass, accumulate, collect, marshal, assemble: *The armies were massed on the battlefield.*

massacre *n.* slaughter, genocide, killing, butchery, extermination: *Early hunters in the 19th century were responsible for the massacre of millions of American buffalo.* *vb.* slay, murder, kill, butcher, exterminate: *The Nazis were guilty of massacring millions of innocent people.*

massive *adj.* **1.** huge, immense, gigantic, tremendous: *Behind the town was a massive pile of rocks from the last avalanche.* **2.** large, bulky, weighty, ponderous: *A massive rock was balanced on the edge of the cliff, about to topple into the valley below.* **ant. 1.** small, little, tiny. **2.** light, weightless.

mast *n.* spar, pole; post: *Run the flag up to the top of the mast upside down, to show the boat is in trouble.*

master *n.* **1.** expert, maestro, genius: *From what the museum curator could see, this artist was a master with a brush.* **2.** ruler, leader, chief, commander, captain, boss, director, supervisor, superintendent: *In ancient Greece and Rome, slaves assumed the names of their masters.* *vb.* **1.** conquer, overcome, subdue, overpower: *The inexperienced chessplayer was easily mastered by the professional.* **2.** control, dominate: *Philip easily mastered the game of bridge.* *adj.* **1.** major, chief, principal: *The man was a master bridge player.* **2.** expert, skillful, skilled: *My cousin Peter has a license as a master mariner.*

masterful *adj.* domineering, bossy, commanding, dictatorial: *My sister always said she wanted to marry someone who is masterful.*

masterly *adj.* skillful, expert, superb, adroit: *The sailing team captain handles his boat in a masterly manner.* **ant.** clumsy, maladroit, awkward.

mastermind *n.* genius, expert: *Robin is a mathematical mastermind who can solve these problems in seconds.* *vb.* manage, direct, supervise; organize: *The woman who masterminded the bank robbery escaped and now lives in Brazil.*

masterpiece *n.* masterwork, perfection, model: *Da Vinci's paintings were all masterpieces, the products of great genius.*

match *n.* **1.** equal, equivalent, peer: *Stan is very good at tennis, but he's finally met his match in Paul.* **2.** competition, rivalry, contest, sport: *The wrestling match has been postponed.* *vb.* **1.** even, equal, balance, equate: *You can't match that 98-pound weakling with a 400-pound sumo wrestler!* **2.** agree, resemble, harmonize: *I'm sorry to tell you that your green polka-dot tie doesn't match that pink-and-purple shirt.*

matchless *adj.* unequaled, unrivaled, peerless, incomparable: *The acrobat turned in a matchless performance on the parallel bars.* **ant.** unimpressive, ordinary.

mate *n.* **1.** associate, companion, comrade: *The moving man said he'd get two of his mates to help with the piano.* **2.** counterpart, complement: *I cannot find the mate to this shoe.* *vb.* breed: *What would happen if you mated a goat with a bluebottle? You'd get a butterfly!*

material *n.* **1.** substance, matter, stuff; fabric: *We were unable to identify the material of which the flying saucer was made.* **2.** cloth, fabric, textile: *The shop sells material by the yard.* *adj.* **1.** substantial, considerable, important: *The absence of the letter-opener from the desk of the victim is material to the case.* **2.** physical, real, touchable, palpable, tangible: *You cannot discuss the spiritual world in terms of material objects.* **ant.** *adj.* **1.** immaterial, irrelevant. **2.** immaterial, intangible, spiritual.

matter *n.* **1.** substance, material: *The matter of which the universe is composed is almost infinite in its variety.* **2.** subject, affair, business, interest: *We have a matter to discuss before you go to the movies.* **3.** trouble, difficulty: *What's the matter? You look pale.* *vb.* count, signify, mean: *Does it matter whether you paint the table before or after the bookcase?*

mature *adj.* **1.** ripe, aged, ready, seasoned: *When these tomatoes are mature, each will weigh at least a pound.* **2.** adult, full-grown, matured, grown: *The movie my parents saw last night is suitable only for mature audiences.* *vb.* age, ripen, develop: *This tree hasn't matured enough to be transplanted.* **ant.** *adj.* **1.** young, youthful. **2.** immature, innocent, naive.

maybe *adv.* perhaps, possibly: *If it's a nice day tomorrow, maybe I'll go to the beach.* **ant.** definitely, decidedly.

meadow *n.* pasture, field, plain: *We went out into the meadow to pick wildflowers.*

meager *adj.* scanty, sparse, frugal, mean: *The shipwrecked sailors had only meager supplies of food.* **ant.** plentiful, bountiful, ample, abundant.

meal *n.* repast, refreshment; breakfast, dinner, lunch: *The waitress brought our meal and we started to eat.*

mean[1] *vb.* **1.** intend, plan, expect, propose: *What do you mean to do when you arrive in Florida?* **2.** indicate, denote, signify, say, express, suggest: *You ought to know that I say what I mean, and I mean what I say.*

mean[2] *adj.* **1.** unkind, cruel, nasty, rude: *I think it was very mean of you to tell Hortense that her dress is ugly.* **2.** stingy, miserly, tight, selfish: *Scrooge was so mean that he didn't even give his employees a day off at Christmas.* **ant.** **1.** gentle, thoughtful, kind. **2.** generous, openhanded.

mean[3] *n.* average: *Each family has a mean number of 3.2 children.*

meaning *n.* sense, signification, denotation; significance, import, gist: *The meaning of the speech is clearly that we must all pay higher taxes in order to beat inflation.*

means *n. pl.* **1.** wealth, riches, money: *The bank president is a man of means and should contribute more than just a dollar to charity.* **2.** support, agency, resources: *What means can we use to persuade him to give more?*

measure *n.* **1.** extent, size, weight, volume, bulk, dimension, depth, breadth, height, length: *It is difficult to comprehend the measure of the universe because the earth is so small by comparison.* **2.** rule, test, standard, trial: *By some measure, all the students in the class have done rather well.* *vb.* rule, weigh, count, estimate, gauge: *How do astronomers measure the distance from the earth to the nearest star? Not in the same way you measure flour for baking a cake or cloth for making a coat.*

measureless *adj.* limitless, immeasurable, boundless, immense, vast, infinite: *From the surface of Mars we could look into the measureless blackness of space.* **ant.** measurable, ascertainable, figurable.

meat *n.* flesh, lean; food: *Jack Sprat ate only meat—his wife ate only fat.*

mechanic *n.* **1.** machinist: *Only skilled mechanics are permitted to operate these machines.* **2.** repairman: *The auto mechanic said we needed a new carburetor.*

mechanism *n.* machine, machinery, device, tool, contrivance:

In addition to the main engine, there is a small mechanism to control the windshield wipers.

medal *n.* award, decoration, medallion, badge, reward: *Tim's father won the Distinguished Service Medal during the war.*

meddle *vb.* interfere, pry, intrude, snoop: *My mother has a friend who meddles in everyone else's business all the time.*

medicine *n.* medication, drug, remedy, potion, prescription, cure: *Any medicine you take for your cold can't cure it —it can only make you feel better.*

medium *n.* **1.** average; modicum: *There must be some medium between your being either very good or very naughty.* **2.** means, mechanism, factor: *I actually spoke to the President through the medium of one of his assistants.* *adj.* average, median, middling: *The medium-priced suits are on this rack.* **ant.** *n.* **1.** extreme.

meet *vb.* **1.** encounter, come across *or* upon: *I don't think that we have met before.* **2.** converge, connect, join, unite: *This road meets the highway about three miles past that railway crossing.* **3.** settle, satisfy, fulfill, answer, discharge: *I don't know if Hugo has the money to meet his obligations.* **4.** convene, gather, assemble, congregate: *The committee is supposed to meet next week.* **5.** agree, unite: *I'm not sure that we all now meet on these points that we disputed earlier.* *n.* contest, meeting, competition, match: *Our school won both the track meet and the swimming meet easily.* **ant.** *vb.* **1.** miss. **2.** diverge, split. **4.** scatter. **5.** disagree.

melancholy *n.* sadness, gloom, depression: *Since she moved from the country to the city, Janet seems so full of melancholy.* *adj.* sad, gloomy, depressed, downcast, downhearted, blue, unhappy: *The cry of the hoot owl sounds so melancholy—like the howl of the wolf.* **ant.** *adj.* happy, joyful, jubilant.

mellow *adj.* **1.** ripe, mature, cured, aged, full-flavored: *This pear is so mellow I can eat it with a spoon.* **2.** smooth, sweet, melodious: *The mellow sounds of the orchestra filled the room where we were dining.* *vb.* ripen, mature, develop, soften: *This whiskey has mellowed with age.* **ant.** *adj.* **1.** immature, unripened.

melody *n.* tune, air, music, song: *Those words are different, but the melody is an old, traditional one.*

melt *vb.* **1.** liquefy, dissolve: *The ice in my ginger ale has melted.* **2.** fade out, blend, dwindle, vanish, disappear: *As we approached their village, the natives seemed to melt away into the jungle.* **3.** soften, relax: *The giant's heart melted when he saw the children, and he let them play in his garden.* **ant. 1.** harden, freeze, solidify.

memorable *adj.* historic, unforgettable, important, significant: *The time when I was awarded my diploma was a memorable occasion for the whole family.* **ant.** forgettable, passing, transitory.

memory *n.* recollection, remembrance: *After more than ten years, my memory of the conversation is not very accurate.*

menace *n.* threat, warning, intimidation: *That driver is a menace to everyone else on the road.* *vb.* threaten, intimidate, warn: *As I stepped nearer to the gate, a huge dog leaped out and menaced me.*

mend *vb.* **1.** repair, patch, restore, fix: *There's a man down the street who mends broken china.* **2.** improve, recover, recuperate, heal: *Greg's broken arm mended very quickly.* **ant. 1.** ruin, destroy, spoil.

mental *adj.* intellectual, reasoning, thinking: *Ian's mental abilities are extraordinary, but he isn't very good at physical things, like sports.* **ant.** physical.

mention *vb.* refer to, introduce, touch on: *Please don't mention the subject of your leaving to mother.* *n.* reference, remark: *I do seem to remember that the speaker made some brief mention of the other candidates.*

merchandise *n.* wares, stock, goods, commodities: *The shopkeeper said that he doesn't keep that kind of merchandise and would have to order it.* *vb.* sell, promote: *The sales manager suggested merchandising the posters through bookstores.*

merchant *n.* storekeeper, shopkeeper, retailer, trader, dealer; businessman: *Mr. Wozzeck is one of the biggest wine merchants in the world.*

merciful *adj.* kind, compassionate, lenient, forgiving, tenderhearted, kindhearted, sympathetic: *In contrast to his cruel father, the young king was merciful and dealt out justice fairly.* **ant.** unjust, unforgiving, harsh, mean, vengeful.

merciless *adj.* cruel, ruthless, pitiless, savage, hard, hardhearted, unfeeling: *In order to get the truth, the spy* *was to undergo merciless torture.* **ant.** merciful, benevolent, openhearted.

mercy *n.* **1.** compassion, sympathy, pity, consideration, leniency, kindness, pity, tenderness: *The prisoners begged for mercy, and the chieftain allowed them to be released.* **2.** disposal, discretion, disposition: *The poor fly was caught in the web and was now at the mercy of the spider.* **ant.** **1.** cruelty, ruthlessness, pitilessness.

mere *adj.* bare, scant: *I was a mere lad when I was sent off to sea as a cabin boy on a schooner.* **ant.** considerable, substantial.

merely *adv.* barely, hardly, only, simply: *When I offered to carry her packages, I was merely trying to be helpful, and she didn't have to accuse me of trying to steal them.*

merit *n.* worth, value, quality, worthiness: *I think that there is a great deal of merit to the energy conservation plan.* *vb.* deserve, earn, qualify for, be worthy of: *Joe merited that commendation for bravery for saving the girl from drowning.*

merry *adj.* cheerful, cheery, joyful, gay, happy, jolly, joyous, jovial: *We all had such a merry time at the party that we didn't notice it was past midnight.* **ant.** sad, doleful, gloomy.

mess *n.* **1.** untidiness, dirtiness: *Your face is a mess from eating pizza.* **2.** confusion, disorder, muddle, jumble: *I've never seen a mess like the one in Sophie's room—everything's strewn about.* **3.** difficulty, trouble, predicament: *Pete has got himself into a mess with the history teacher again—something about late homework.* *vb.* confuse, muddle, dirty: *It takes an hour to straighten up and clean a room that you mess up in a minute.*

message *n.* **1.** communication, note, letter, memorandum, memo: *The courier carried the message for three weeks through the jungle.* **2.** information, news, word, advice: *I have a message for you from your mother: Don't forget to brush your teeth.*

messenger *n.* courier, bearer, runner, agent: *The messenger ran all the way but arrived too late with the package.*

messy *adj.* dirty, disorderly, disordered, confused, confusing; untidy, sloppy, slovenly: *The teacher wouldn't accept Joan's homework because it was too messy.* **ant.** neat, orderly, tidy.

method *n.* way, technique, manner, approach, means: *By*

*that method, it would take four people three days to
complete the work.*

middle   *n.* center, midpoint, median: *The yogi sat down in
the exact middle of the floor and started to chant. adj.*
center, central, halfway, intermediate: *Bill lives in the
house at this end, John in the one at the other end, and
Betty lives in the middle one.* **ant.** *n., adj.* beginning, end.

midst   *n.* middle, center, thick, heart: *The police chased the
fugitive but he was lost in the midst of the throng.*

might   *n.* power, strength, force: *It would take the might of
a giant to lift the stone from the mouth of the cave.* **ant.**
weakness, frailty, vulnerability.

mighty   *adj.* strong, powerful, muscular: *The blacksmith was
a mighty man who could bend a steel bar with his bare
hands.* **ant.** weak, frail.

migrate   *vb.* move, resettle; immigrate, emigrate: *The United
States was settled by people who migrated from Europe.*
ant. remain, stay, settle.

mild   *adj.* **1.** calm, gentle, temperate, pleasant: *After a
bitter cold winter, New England experienced a mild
spring.* **2.** amiable, kind, compassionate, peaceful, calm:
Tom is known to have a mild disposition. **3.** bland,
soothing: *This is a sharp, not a mild, cheese.* **ant. 1.**
stormy, turbulent. **2.** violent, excitable, hot-tempered.

mind   *n.* **1.** intellect, brain, intelligence, reason, understanding, sense: *Albert Einstein had the mind of a genius.*
2. inclination, intention: *I have a mind to dismiss the
entire class early to go swimming. vb.* **1.** care for, look
after, watch, tend: *Stefanie has a job minding three
children after school.* **2.** pay attention, obey, heed, attend: *When your father tells you to do something, you
had better mind.* **3.** object (to), care (about), dislike:
*Do you mind moving the car a little? You've driven it
onto my foot!*

mine   *n.* **1.** pit, shaft, excavation, lode, vein: *The mine was
rich in coal and could be worked for 25 years.* **2.** source,
mother-lode: *Jim was a mine of information about baseball. vb.* dig, excavate, drill, quarry: *My grandfather
mined silver in Colorado.*

mingle   *vb.* combine, mix, blend: *After sifting the flour,
mingle it with the other ingredients in a bowl.* **ant.** separate, sort.

miniature   *adj.* tiny, small, midget, little, minute: *I dreamed*

*that a white mouse was driving under my bed in a minia-
ture car.* **ant.** outsize.

minimize *vb.* diminish, decrease, lessen, reduce: *A safety
helmet minimizes the effect of a blow on the head in an
accident.* **ant.** maximize, enlarge.

minister *n.* clergyman, pastor, parson, preacher, vicar, pre-
late, curate, chaplain, deacon, cleric, reverend: *Last
Sunday our minister preached a sermon on kindness to
people before kindness to animals.*

minor *adj.* smaller, lesser, secondary, petty, unimportant:
*The department stores no longer consider shoplifting a
minor offense.* *n.* boy, girl, child, youth, adolescent: *No
minors were allowed to attend the movie.* **ant.** *adj.* major.
n. adult, grownup

mint *vb.* coin, punch, stamp, strike: *The government has
stopped minting pure silver coins.*

minute[1] *n.* jiffy, moment, instant, second: *When my wife
says "Wait a minute," I wait an hour.*

minute[2] *adj.* tiny, wee, microscopic, minuscule: *I've never
understood how the fly's minute wings could carry it so
quickly.* **ant.** large, huge, immense.

miraculous *adj.* marvelous, wonderful, incredible, phenom-
enal, extraordinary: *The doctors had given me up for
dead, but, as you can see, I've made a miraculous recovery.* **ant.** ordinary, commonplace, everyday.

mirror *n.* looking-glass, glass; reflector: *I don't always like
what I see when I look in the mirror.* *vb.* reflect: *The
image of the building is mirrored in the pond.*

mirth *n.* glee, joy, gaiety, joyousness, jollity, joyfulness,
merriment, laughter: *The birthday party was marked by
the happiness and mirth of all who came.* **ant.** gloom,
sadness, seriousness.

miscarry *vb.* fail, go wrong: *Our plans for an outing mis-
carried because Edith forgot the food.* **ant.** succeed.

mischief *n.* **1.** prankishness, playfulness, roguishness, ras-
cality: *That red-headed boy is full of mischief—putting
a tack on the teacher's chair!* **2.** trouble, harm, damage,
injury: *The vandals who broke into the school last night
did a lot of mischief.*

mischievous *adj.* prankish, roguish, playful, naughty: *Penny
isn't really a bad child, but she does tend to be mischievous.* **ant.** good, well-behaved.

miser *n.* skinflint, tightwad, Scrooge: *The old miser never* *gave anything to anyone and just sat counting his money, day and night.* **ant.** philanthropist.

miserable *adj.* **1.** unhappy, uncomfortable, wretched, heartbroken: *Ted was miserable when he wasn't chosen to play on the team.* **2.** poor, penniless, needy, poverty-stricken. *The miserable people in other countries have no one to turn to for help but us.* **3.** mean, contemptible, hateful, low, wretched, bad: *What rotten, miserable person has been teasing these animals?* **4.** unlucky, unfortunate, luckless: *I've had a miserable run of cards today—can't seem to win one game.* **ant.** **1.** happy, joyful, content. **2.** wealthy, well-off, prosperous. **3.** noble, honorable. **4.** lucky, fortunate.

miserly *adj.* stingy, tightfisted, pennypinching, cheap, mean; selfish: *That miserly old lady even refused to call in a doctor when she was sick.* **ant.** generous, openhanded, spendthrift, extravagant.

misery *n.* **1.** unhappiness, suffering, anguish, woe, agony, distress: *During the famine I saw almost more misery than I could stand in one lifetime.* **2.** grief, sorrow: *We all tried to console the widow in her misery.* **ant.** **1.** delight, joy.

misgiving *n.* doubt, hesitation, suspicion, mistrust, uncertainty: *My father's misgivings about lending me the family car were confirmed when I had a slight accident.*

mislay *vb.* lose, misplace: *I've mislaid the keys to my house.* **ant.** find, discover.

miss *vb.* **1.** need, want, desire, crave, yearn for: *Danny missed playing baseball in the winter and basketball in the summer.* **2.** drop, fumble, bumble: *Sonia missed the ball completely, even when we threw it gently.* *n.* slip, failure, error, blunder, fumble: *A miss is as good as a mile.*

missile *n.* projectile, shot: *In modern warfare, guided missiles are widely used.*

mist *n.* fog, cloud, haze, steam: *The mist was so thick that we couldn't drive any further.*

mistake *n.* error, slip, fault: *Lester, this homework paper is full of mistakes and you must do it over.* *vb.* misunderstand, misjudge, confuse; misinterpret: *I mistook the reflection of the searchlight on the clouds for a flying saucer.*

mistaken *adj.* wrong, incorrect, confused, misinformed, inaccurate: *Alan was mistaken about whom he had seen down near the beach.* **ant.** correct, right, accurate.

misunderstand *vb.* misinterpret, misjudge, confuse, jumble, mistake: *Tony misunderstood what I said and became very angry for no reason.* **ant.** comprehend, perceive.

mix *vb.* combine, blend, mingle: *When you mix the chemicals together be careful that they not explode.* *n.* combination, blend, mixture: *The people on that island are an unusual mix of natives and immigrants. Use a prepared mix to make this chocolate cake.* **ant.** *vb.* separate, divide.

mixture *n.* **1.** mix, confusion, jumble, hodgepodge; mess: *Your jacket and your trousers are a curious mixture of styles.* **2.** blend, combination: *I made up this mixture so that we could dip bread in it for French toast.*

moan *n., vb.* groan, wail, lament, cry: *I thought I heard someone in the next room give a loud moan. When I went to see what it was, it turned out to be the wind moaning in the chimney.*

mob *n.* swarm, crowd, rabble, throng, horde: *There was a mob of people gathered near the ice-cream vendor.* *vb.* swarm, crowd, throng; riot: *The rock star was mobbed when he left the theater by people seeking his autograph.*

mobile *adj.* movable; free; portable: *The TV station covered the events from a mobile unit.* **ant.** immobile, stationary, fixed.

mock *vb.* scorn, deride, ridicule, tease, jeer: *When the singer came out on stage, the audience mocked him, and he wept.* *adj.* imitation, fake; fraudulent, sham: *Mock turtle soup doesn't taste like the real thing.* **ant.** *vb.* praise, honor, applaud. *adj.* real, genuine, authentic.

mockery *n.* **1.** ridicule, scorn, derision: *Bernard's painting was held up to the mockery of the other students.* **2.** travesty, sham, pretext, pretense: *You have made a mockery of a very serious matter by ridiculing it.* **ant.** praise, admiration.

mode *n.* manner, method, style, technique, practice, way, fashion: *This mode of working while standing at the fireplace is strange to me.*

model *n.* **1.** example, pattern, mold, ideal: *I tried to make a vase, using the one over there as a model.* **2.** copy, imitation, facsimile: *This airplane is an actual, working model of the real thing.* **3.** version, style, design: *This* car is a late model. **4.** mannequin, sitter: *I'd very much like to have you sit as a model for my next painting.* *vb.* **1.** form, shape, mold, fashion, pattern, design: *Dick has modeled a figure out of clay. Sandra tries to model herself after her aunt.* **2.** sit, pose: *Cordelia models for that high-fashion boutique downtown.*

moderate[1] *adj.* **1.** reasonable, average, medium, fair: *The doctor said that a moderate amount of coffee would do me no harm.* **2.** conservative, middle-of-the-road, cautious: *The senators' plans for economic recovery were moderate, not extreme.* **ant. 1.** immoderate, excessive, heavy.

moderate[2] *vb.* **1.** arbitrate, referee, judge, umpire: *The head of the department moderated the debate between the two teams.* **2.** weaken, pacify, lessen, calm, sober, temper: *As the sun sank toward the horizon, the scorching heat of the day was moderated by a cool breeze.* **ant. 2.** intensify, increase, aggravate.

modern *adj.* present-day, up-to-date, recent, novel, new, fresh, modish, stylish: *The Gordons just built a modern home down near the beach.* **ant.** old-fashioned, antique, out-of-date, outmoded.

modernize *vb.* refurbish, refurnish, rebuild, improve, renovate, renew: *We have modernized our kitchen with a refrigerator and electric stove.*

modest *adj.* **1.** demure, decent; prudish: *The British school Diane was sent to was for "modest young ladies from good families."* **2.** humble, moderate, proper, unassuming, retiring: *Harriet was wearing a modest black dress buttoned up to the high neck.* **3.** humble, simple, plain: *Some of our greatest leaders have come from very modest backgrounds.* **ant. 1.** immodest, libertine, loose. **2.** gaudy, outlandish, tasteless, showy. **3.** vain, proud, arrogant.

modesty *n.* humility, simplicity, decency, propriety: *As Carolyn came into the room, we were all struck by her charming modesty.* **ant.** vanity, conceit, pride.

modify *vb.* **1.** change, alter, vary, adjust: *If you expect to remain as a student in this school, Patrick, you'll have to modify your behavior.* **2.** moderate, temper, change, curb: *Since she was elected, I think that the record will show that the congresswoman has modified her views on welfare.*

moist *adj.* damp, dank, humid; muggy, clammy, wet: *The*

basement is so moist and dark that mushrooms grow there.
ant. dry, arid, parched.

moisten *vb.* dampen; wet: *The laundress moistened the clothes before ironing them.* **ant.** dry.

moisture *n.* dampness, wetness, condensation, mist: *On these cold nights, the moisture on the insides of the windows freezes.* **ant.** dryness, aridity.

moment *n.* **1.** instant, jiffy, flash, twinkling: *The receptionist asked me to sit down and wait a moment.* **2.** importance, gravity, seriousness, consequence: *It is of no great moment to me whether you go tomorrow or tonight.*

momentous *adj.* important, serious, consequential, essential: *An event of momentous proportions prevented me from arriving on time.* **ant.** unimportant, trivial, trifling.

monarch *n.* king, ruler, emperor, queen, empress, sovereign: *We all bowed our heads with respect as the monarch entered the room with her retinue.*

money *n.* **1.** coin, cash, currency, bills, notes, specie: *Can you lend me some money to go to the movies?* **2.** funds, capital: *I doubt that the company has the money it needs for expansion.*

monitor *n.* supervisor, director, adviser: *Felix will be the lunchroom monitor for today and will try to keep the children in line.* *vb.* watch, observe, control, supervise: *We were able to monitor the actions of the robot from the control booth.*

monotonous *adj.* boring, dull, tedious, humdrum, tiring, tiresome, wearisome: *Watching a record turning on a phonograph is terribly monotonous. The politicians gave one monotonous speech after another.* **ant.** interesting, fascinating, riveting.

monster *n.* beast, brute, fiend, villain, wretch, demon: *That little monster pulls the wings off butterflies.*

monstrous *adj.* **1.** huge, tremendous, immense, gigantic, enormous: *Arranged around the walls of the cave were monstrous statues of all kinds of imaginary beasts.* **2.** horrible, revolting, shocking, repulsive, hideous, dreadful, terrible: *The guards were known for their monstrous tortures of the prisoners.* **ant. 1.** tiny, diminutive, small, miniature.

monumental *adj.* **1.** huge, enormous, immense, colossal, gigantic: *At the top of the mountain stands a monumental cross.* **2.** significant, important: *The invention of*

the wheel allowed man to make monumental progress.
ant. 1. miniature, tiny. **2.** insignificant, trivial.

mood   *n.* temper, humor, disposition: *Jerry seems to be in a very happy mood today.*

moody   *adj.* temperamental, changeable; short-tempered, irritable, testy, peevish, fretful, spiteful: *I don't want to speak to you if you're so moody—we'll just have an argument.* **ant.** calm, even-tempered, good-natured.

moral   *adj.* upright, honest, ethical, just, good, honorable: *Victoria is one of the most moral people I know—she'd never do anything wrong or questionable.* **ant.** immoral, dishonest, sinful, corrupt.

morale   *n.* spirit, confidence, assurance: *It was decided to give the salesmen a pep talk to improve their morale.*

moreover   *adv.* also, further, furthermore, in addition, besides: *Lenore won first prize in diving; moreover, she won a first in swimming, as well.*

morsel   *n.* bite, tidbit, bit, piece: *The beggar shared his bread by giving a few morsels of it to his dog.*

mortal   *adj.* **1.** human; temporary, perishable, momentary: *Since all men are mortal, they must die someday.* **2.** lethal, deadly, fatal: *The knight received a mortal wound from the sword and lay dying.* **ant. 1.** immortal. **2.** superficial.

mostly   *adv.* generally, chiefly, mainly, for the most part, largely, principally: *Sometimes our dog goes out for walks with us, but mostly he just lies around.*

motion   *n.* movement, change, action: *Because of the breeze, the branches of the trees are constantly in motion.* *vb.* gesture, signal, indicate: *I was about to say something, but Vincent motioned to me to be quiet.* **ant.** *n.* stillness, immobility.

motivate   *vb.* stimulate, move, cause, prompt: *What motivates Dennis to behave the way he does?*

motive   *n.* reason, purpose, idea, cause, ground: *What do you suppose Ed's motive is in telling people I hate ice cream?*

motto   *n.* slogan, byword, catchword; proverb, saying: *The mattress manufacturer's motto is, "We stand behind every product we sell."*

mound   *n.* hill, hillock, pile, heap: *The picnickers left behind a mound of garbage that we cleaned up.*

mount   *vb.* **1.** ascend, climb, go up: *The cowboy mounted his horse and rode away. Frank had to mount a ladder to reach the light bulb.* **2.** rise, increase, ascend: *As the* costs of raw materials mounted, the manufacturers passed them on to the consumer. **3.** prepare, make ready, ready, set up: *The enemy was going to mount an attack at dawn. n.* **1.** horse, steed, charger: *The comical knight rode an old nag as his mount.* **2.** mountain; hill: *Mount Everest is the highest in the world.* **ant.** *vb.* **1., 2.** descend.

mountain *n.* mount, alp, peak; pike, height, ridge, range: *The mountains seemed to rise from the plains in the distance.*

mourn *vb.* lament, grieve, sorrow, bemoan: *David mourned the loss of his pet rabbit.* **ant.** rejoice, celebrate.

mournful *adj.* sad, sorrowful: *We could hear the mournful cry of the wolf.* **ant.** cheerful, joyful, happy.

move *vb.* **1.** advance, proceed, progress, go on; stir, budge, travel, shift; retreat: *As soon as anyone moved, the dogs would begin to growl.* **2.** push, propel, shift: *Please move your chair closer to the table.* **3.** affect, touch, influence: *I was deeply moved by the play. n.* movement, motion, action: *Hilary made a move as if to leave.*

movement *n.* **1.** move, motion, action, activity: *I noticed a slight movement of the door and knew someone was behind it.* **2.** effort, action, crusade: *There was a movement among the students to introduce tennis as a competitive sport.*

muffle *vb.* deaden, soften, quiet, mute: *The thickness of the wall muffled the voices of those in the other room.* **ant.** amplify, louden.

multiply *vb.* **1.** increase; double, triple, treble: *The number of readers of the new magazine multiplied in the beginning.* **2.** reproduce, propagate: *Rabbits multiply very rapidly.* **ant.** decrease, lessen.

multitude *n.* throng, crowd, mass, horde, swarm, mob: *Appearing at last on the balcony, the mayor spoke to the multitude assembled in the square below.*

murder *n.* killing, homicide, assassination; slaughter: *The suspect was accused of the murder of three people whose bodies had been found in his basement. vb.* kill, assassinate, slaughter, slay: *It was found that the killer had murdered the people out of revenge.*

murderer *n.* killer, slayer, assassin: *Until just a few years ago, convicted murderers were executed in most states.*

murmur *n.* mutter, mumble, grumble, complaint; whimper: *A murmur of protest was heard from the audience when the new taxes were announced. vb.* mutter, mumble, grumble; whimper: *The trees murmured under the onslaught of the icy winds.*

mutinous *adj.* rebellious, revolutionary, unruly: *After three weeks in the harsh climate the crew of the whaler was growing mutinous.* **ant.** obedient, dutiful, compliant.

mutiny *n.* rebellion, revolt, uprising: *All of the men who took part in the mutiny were sent back to England in chains.* *vb.* rebel, revolt, rise up: *The crew of the* Bounty *mutinied against Captain Bligh and set him and a few men adrift in a boat.*

mutual *adj.* **1.** reciprocal, alternate: *If you give our employees a discount in your shop, we'll give yours a mutual discount in ours.* **2.** common, shared: *Albert is our mutual friend.*

mysterious *adj.* secret; puzzling, strange: *The mysterious disappearance of Judge Crater has never been resolved.* **ant.** open, direct, obvious.

mystery *n.* strangeness; difficulty; riddle, puzzle: *There is a mystery surrounding the woman who lives in the castle, and we may never know the solution.*

myth *n.* **1.** legend, tradition, fable: *The ancient Greek and Roman myths have still a profound effect on our literature and language.* **2.** lie, prevarication, fiction: *That whole story she told about being an heiress is just a myth.*

N

nag *vb.* annoy, pester, irritate, torment, vex: *Warren's mother is always nagging him about cleaning up his room.* *n.* shrew, pest, nuisance: *Phil's wife is an awful nag.*

naked *adj.* **1.** unclothed, undressed, bare, uncovered, nude: *At night, when it was hot, we used to go swimming naked.* **2.** simple, plain, obvious, unadorned, undisguised: *Jack finally told me that he had done the deed, and that's the naked truth.* **ant. 1.** covered, clothed, garbed. **2.** suppressed, concealed.

name *n.* **1.** title, tag, label, designation: *Just because my first name is George, that doesn't mean my surname is Washington.* **2.** reputation; character: *Rick has made a name for himself as an author of historical novels.* *vb.* **1.** call, title, term, christen, baptize: *We named our first child Ebenezer.* **2.** designate, signify, mention, remark: *By the time he was two, Dan could name all the days of the week and the months.* **3.** elect, nominate, appoint: *We named Betty chairwoman of our committee.*

nap *n.* snooze, forty winks, siesta, doze: *I'm going to have a short nap before dinner.*

narrate *vb.* tell, relate, describe, recount, report: *As we sat close to the fire, the old man narrated a tale from long, long ago.*

narrative *n.* story, tale, account, history, description: *In the old days, before many people could read, history was passed on in the form of narratives recited by poets and storytellers.*

narrow *adj.* **1.** slender, thin, tapering, tapered, tight: *The passageway at the end of the cave was too narrow for me to squeeze through.* **2.** close, precarious, perilous, dangerous: *The driver leaped clear of the wreck just as it burst into flame—a narrow escape!* **ant. 1.** wide, broad.

narrow-minded *adj.* intolerant, closed, bigoted, close-minded, prejudiced, biased: *How can you ever learn anything at all if you're too narrow-minded to listen to others?* **ant.** broad-minded, liberal, tolerant.

nasty *adj.* **1.** disagreeable, unpleasant, foul: *We sometimes get a spell of very nasty weather in February.* **2.** dirty, filthy, foul, disgusting, loathsome, polluted, offensive: *There was a very nasty pool of sewage where the factory dumped its wastes.* **3.** dirty, foul, filthy, obscene, indecent, improper: *How dare you use such nasty language in the classroom?!* **4.** disagreeable, cranky, unpleasant, vicious, ugly: *Manuel has a very nasty temper.* **ant. 1.** pleasant, fair, seasonable. **2.** clean, pure. **3.** proper, decent. **4.** pleasant, even-tempered.

nation *n.* **1.** country, state, realm, kingdom, republic, commonwealth: *Forty nations agreed to sign the treaty.* **2.** people, race, stock, society, tribe: *Most of the great Indian nations of America no longer exist.*

native *adj.* **1.** natural, innate, inborn, inbred, hereditary: *What's the advantage of native intelligence if it isn't turned to practical use?* **2.** local, original: *The cherry tree is not native to North America; it was imported from Japan.* *n.* national, citizen, inhabitant, resident: *I don't come from around here at all—I'm a native of Nebraska.* **ant.** *adj.* **2.** foreign, alien. *n.* stranger, foreigner, outsider.

natural *adj.* **1.** inbred, inborn, innate, inherited, hereditary, original, basic, fundamental: *It's natural for a frightened animal to attack when cornered.* **2.** normal, customary, typical, usual; characteristic: *Instead of trying to act in a particular way, just do what is natural for you.* **ant.** unnatural, alien, contrary.

naturally *adv.* **1.** normally, usually, typically, ordinarily, customarily: *Naturally I expect everyone to respect his parents.* **2.** freely, readily, simply, openly, sincerely: *Please try to behave naturally when you go for the interview: don't put on an act.* **ant. 2.** artificially.

nature *n.* **1.** world, universe: *It's against the laws of nature to expect things to fall upward.* **2.** character, quality, essence: *What is the true nature of water that makes it expand when cooled and contract when warmed?* **3.** sort, kind, variety, character: *I don't understand the nature of your question.* **4.** manner, disposition, personality, character: *I didn't think it was in Mr. Robinson's nature to get upset over small matters.*

naughty *adj.* **1.** disobedient, unruly, unmanageable, insubordinate, mischievous: *Don't be naughty: just do as you are told and behave yourself.* **2.** indecent, improper, rude:

The boys told naughty stories in the locker room after the game. **ant. 1.** good, well-behaved, obedient.

navigate *vb.* guide, steer, pilot: *When we were in the Navy, we learned how to navigate by the stars.*

near *adj.* close, nearby, neighboring, adjoining: *Please sit in the chair nearest you.* **ant.** far, distant, remote.

nearly *adv.* almost, practically: *I'd forgotten that the party was supposed to be a secret and nearly told Bernie.*

neat *adj.* **1.** clean, orderly, tidy, trim; dapper, natty, smart, elegant: *I want this room to be neat when I return or no dessert for a week! Victor is a very neat dresser.* **2.** orderly, well-organized: *The filing cabinets were arranged in neat rows in the office.* **ant. 1.** messy, sloppy, unkempt, disorganized.

necessary *adj.* needed, required, important, essential: *If you live in the country, a car is necessary, even to do the marketing.* **ant.** unnecessary, dispensable, unneeded.

necessity *n.* requirement, essential, prerequisite: *Many of the things we regarded as luxuries only a few years ago are necessities today.*

need *n.* **1.** want, lack, necessity: *I feel the need for a vacation after working so hard for two years.* **2.** requirement, necessity: *The need for energy is increasing all of the time in the industrialized nations.* **3.** poverty, pennilessness, want: *Every Christmas we make a contribution to families that are in need.* *vb.* want, lack, require, miss: *The poor children needed shoes and clothing and food after the flood destroyed their home.*

needy *adj.* poor, poverty-stricken, penniless, destitute: *After so many people were put out of work, there were many needy families in the area.* **ant.** wealthy, well-to-do, affluent, well-off, well-heeled.

neglect *vb.* **1.** disregard, overlook, ignore: *The judge ruled that he had to take better care of the family he had neglected.* **2.** omit, skip, miss: *The speaker neglected mentioning all those who had helped elect him.* *n.* disregard, negligence, inattention: *The soldier was reprimanded by his commanding officer for neglect of duty. The house was suffering from neglect and needed painting and some repairs.* **ant.** *vb.* **1.** care, attend. *n.* attention, concern, regard.

negotiate *vb.* arrange, settle, transact: *The bank negotiated a deal for the property so that we paid only a small fee.*

neighborhood *n.* area, vicinity, section, district, locality, locale: *The value of the property in this neighborhood has been increasing steadily.*

nerve *n.* **1.** courage, boldness, bravery, spirit: *It took a lot of nerve for the American colonists to rebel against Britain.* **2.** effrontery, impudence, rudeness, impertinence: *You have a lot of nerve walking into my home without knocking or ringing!* **ant. 1.** cowardice, weakness, frailty.

nervous *adj.* **1.** restless, excited, agitated: *The threatening phone calls made everyone in town nervous.* **2.** timid, shy, fearful: *Mona was very nervous about her job interview.* **ant. 1.** calm, tranquil, placid. **2.** bold, courageous, confident.

neutral *adj.* **1.** uninvolved, inactive, nonpartisan: *I am going to remain neutral in the argument between Cecile and Roger.* **2.** dull, drab: *The car was a neutral color.* **ant. 1.** partisan, biased.

new *adj.* **1.** novel, fresh, unique, original, unusual. *Ken announced that he'd discovered a new way to bake chicken.* **2.** recent, modern, current, latest: *The new fashions aren't really very becoming to shorter people.* **ant. 1.** old, ancient, usual. **2.** outmoded.

news *n.* information, knowledge, data, report: *What is the latest news from Washington?*

nice *adj.* **1.** pleasant, agreeable, pleasing: *Maria certainly has a nice disposition.* **2.** kind, thoughtful, friendly, cordial: *Be nice to your sister.* **3.** accurate, precise, exact: *People should learn to make a nice distinction between the meanings of words.* **ant. 1.** unpleasant, disagreeable, nasty. **2.** thoughtless, unkind. **3.** careless, inexact.

nimble *adj.* agile, spry, lively, quick: *With a nimble movement, Arthur ducked the arrow as it sped toward him.* **ant.** clumsy, awkward, oafish.

noble *adj.* **1.** honorable, honest, upright, virtuous, dignified: *It is more noble to give than to receive.* **2.** aristocratic, titled, high-born, well-born, blue-blooded: *The man who will marry the princess comes from a noble family.* **ant. 1.** ignoble, base, dishonest. **2.** lowborn.

noise *n.* tumult, uproar, clamor, din, racket, clatter, outcry: *I heard a noise in the next room that sounded like a thousand glasses breaking.* **ant.** quiet, silence, peace.

noisy *adj.* loud, clamorous, tumultuous: *The neighbors next door had a noisy party last night, and I didn't sleep a wink.* **ant.** quiet, silent, peaceful.

nominate *vb.* name, select, choose, propose: *Three people were nominated for the board, and the members are supposed to vote for two.*

nonsense *n.* trash, rubbish, balderdash: *Everyone knows that the moon being made of green cheese is just nonsense.*

nonsensical *adj.* ridiculous, absurd, silly, stupid, senseless: *The idea of putting square wheels on the wagon is nonsensical.*

normal *adj.* **1.** healthy, sound, whole: *The doctor assured me that my eyesight is normal.* **2.** regular, usual, customary, standard, routine: *The normal way to fly from Chicago to New York is to go East.* **ant. 2.** odd, irregular, peculiar.

normally *adv.* usually, customarily, regularly, frequently: *Normally, I stop in for a soda on my way home from school.*

notable *adj.* noteworthy, remarkable, noted, unusual, uncommon, conspicuous, distinctive, distinguished: *The union and management negotiators made notable progress at the bargaining table last night.* *n.* celebrity, personality, stars: *Notables of the stage, film, and television attended the gala dinner.* **ant.** *adj.* ordinary, usual, commonplace.

note *n.* **1.** message, memorandum, memo, record: *The secretary took notes of what the members of the council said.* **2.** notice, heed: *I have taken note of what you said and will act as you suggest.* **3.** eminence, importance, distinction, repute, reputation: *Many people of note wrote letters of congratulations to the President on his birthday.* *vb.* **1.** notice, attend, observe, heed, regard: *The witness testified that he had noted that the back door of the bank was open.* **2.** write down, record, register: *I noted in my diary all of the interesting things that happened to me and my friends.*

noted *adj.* famous, well-known, celebrated, distinguished, famed, notable: *A noted artist was commissioned to paint the portrait.* **ant.** unknown, anonymous.

notice *n.* **1.** sign, poster, announcement, advertisement: *In addition to the notices we posted on the bulletin board, we also placed one in the newspaper.* **2.** observation, attention, heed, note: *Please take notice of the No Smoking signs in the elevators.* **3.** warning, advice, admonition: *The mechanic gave the garage operator one week's notice of his intention to quit.* *vb.* observe, note, heed, regard, pay attention to: *Notice how carefully the painter works on these miniatures.* **ant.** *vb.* ignore, disregard, overlook.

notify *vb.* inform, advise, announce, mention, reveal: *We were notified that if we didn't pay the bill, our phone service would be discontinued.*

notion *n.* idea, fancy, impression, concept, conception: *I had a notion that you might like a chocolate sundae for dessert.*

notorious *adj.* infamous, ill-famed: *You get what you deserve if you play cards with that notorious cheat.*

nourish *vb.* sustain, support, feed, supply: *Phoebe still nourishes the hope that her dream man will come and carry her away.*

nourishment *n.* sustenance, support, food, nutriment: *This plant obtains nourishment from the soil and doesn't need sunlight.* **ant.** deprivation, starvation.

novel *adj.* new, unusual, different, odd, strange: *He's so old-fashioned that he thinks the waltz is a novel dance.*

nuisance *n.* pest, irritation, annoyance, bother: *You made such a nuisance of yourself last night asking every minute when we were going to open the Christmas gifts.*

number *n.* **1.** total, sum, collection, quantity, amount: *A large number of people visit the museum every year.* **2.** numeral, digit, figure: *Pick a number from one to ten but don't tell me what it is.* *vb.* count, total, add, enumerate, compute, calculate; estimate: *Number the desks in this classroom.*

numerous *adj.* numberless, many; infinite: *Numerous people have seen this motion picture.* **ant.** few, scanty.

nurse *vb.* take care of, tend, care for, attend: *When you were sick, wasn't it your mother who nursed you back to health?*

nutrition *n.* food, nutriment, nourishment, sustenance: *The school dietitian is an expert on nutrition and what is good for children.*

⛥ O ⛥

oath   *n.*   **1.** pledge, promise, vow: *I have sworn an oath never to reveal the secret.* **2.** curse, profanity, swearword, curseword: *When the hammer struck his finger the carpenter uttered an oath that I shall not repeat*

obedience   *n.* submission, docility: *My dog went to a school where she was taught obedience.* **ant.** disobedience, rebelliousness.

obedient   *adj.* docile, yielding, respectful, obliging: *Until he was 12, Clark was a very obedient child and did as he was told.* **ant.** rebellious, mutinous.

object   *vb.* protest, disapprove of, complain: *My mother objected when I said I wanted to climb the mountain alone.* *n.* **1.** objective, goal, target, aim: *Our object in staging the rally was to get people to cheer for our football team.* **2.** thing, article, tangible: *The object on the table was a golden statue.* **ant.** *vb.* approve, agree, assent.

objection   *n.* protest, disapproval, doubt: *My only objection to going to the movies was that I wouldn't be able to study for the examination.* **ant.** agreement, assent, concurrence.

objective   *n.* aim, goal, purpose: *Our objective was to reach the border before dawn.* *adj.* fair, just, impartial, unbiased: *Since you are not involved and won't profit either way, perhaps you can give us an objective opinion.* **ant.** subjective, biased.

obligation   *n.*   **1.** requirement, responsibility, duty: *Anyone who is elected to an office should be prepared to assume its obligations.* **2.** contract, agreement: *The company has taken on the obligation to supply clean towels to the school.*

oblige   *vb.*   **1.** require, force, compel: *The arresting officer is obliged by law to read a captive his rights.* **2.** please, serve, favor: *I am very much obliged to you for your kindness.* **ant.** disoblige, free.

obscure   *adj.*   **1.** unknown, inconspicuous: *The best play of the year was written by an obscure playwright.* **2.** hidden, dim, unclear, indistinct: *The sign was too obscure for* *me to read what it said.* **3.** dark, dim, murky, dusky: *The attic was too obscure for reading.* *vb.* screen, veil, hide, conceal, cover: *The car was completely obscured by the bushes.* **ant.** *adj.* **1.** famous, noted, distinguished. **2.** clear, lucid, illumined. **3.** bright.

observance *n.* honoring, keeping; attention: *The observance of Mother's Day in America is now imitated in other countries.* **ant.** omission.

observant *adj.* watchful, alert, keen, vigilant, attentive: *It was observant of Miranda to notice the car parked across the street with the two detectives in it.* **ant.** unobservant, inattentive.

observation *n.* **1.** watching, attention: *Our observation of the cave was rewarded when we saw the bears emerge.* **2.** comment, remark, opinion: *Wendy made the observation that she considered the book very boring.*

observe *vb.* **1.** see, notice, look at, regard, witness, watch: *Observe the way the ameba surrounds its food, then absorbs it with its body.* **2.** honor, keep, celebrate: *The pilgrims observed all religious holidays.* **3.** obey, follow, abide by: *Please observe the No Parking signs.* **ant. 1., 2.** ignore, disregard.

obsolete *adj.* old-fashioned, outdated, outmoded, antiquated: *"Olde" is an obsolete spelling for "old."* **ant.** new, modern, up-to-date, fashionable.

obstacle *n.* block, stop, barrier, interference, obstruction: *The supervisor of the department continually put obstacles in the way of my promotion.* **ant.** aid, support.

obstinate *adj.* stubborn, opinionated, willful, pig-headed, inflexible: *Even when she knows she's wrong, Hope is too obstinate to admit it.* **ant.** pliable, pliant, yielding.

obstruct *vb.* block, stop, hinder, prevent, interfere: *There was a metal box obstructing the chimney, and we found it was full of gold coins.* **ant.** help, further.

obstruction *n.* obstacle, block, blockage, interference, barrier: *There was an obstruction in the road that we couldn't drive around.*

obtain *vb.* get, acquire, gain, procure, secure, attain: *People who had sugar and meat during the war obtained it on the black market.* **ant.** lose, forgo.

obvious *adj.* clear, unquestionable, transparent, plain, unmistakable: *Jimmy's thoughts as he stood looking into the candy-store window were obvious.* **ant.** subtle, hidden, unobtrusive.

obviously *adv.* clearly, plainly, certainly, surely, evidently: *Obviously, if Clara isn't here, she must be somewhere else.*

occasion *n.* **1.** time, occurrence, happening: *The family gave Dad a gold watch on the occasion of his fiftieth birthday.* **2.** opportunity, chance, excuse: *Should the occasion arise, please bring some firewood in from the shed.*

occasional *adj.* irregular, random, sporadic: *The weather report called for occasional rain this weekend.* **ant.** regular, chronic, constant.

occasionally *adj.* now and then, infrequently, seldom, irregularly: *I still visit my grammar-school teacher occasionally.* **ant.** often, regularly.

occupant *n.* resident, tenant, inhabitant: *The firemen evacuated the occupants of the building in less than ten minutes.*

occupation *n.* **1.** trade, profession, business, job, employment: *For many years, my uncle's occupation was as architect for the city.* **2.** seizure, capture: *When the soldiers defending the castle surrendered, the enemy's occupation of the mountain was complete.*

occupy *vb.* **1.** take up, use, fill, hold: *The parents occupied the back half of the seats at the school play.* **2.** obtain, seize, capture: *The invading army soon occupied the city and its suburbs.* **3.** engage, employ, busy, absorb: *Worries about the coming exams occupied Nellie's mind.*

occur *vb.* happen, take place, befall: *What has occurred between last week and this to make you change your mind?*

occurrence *n.* event, happening; incident: *Our family picnic is an annual occurrence.*

ocean *n.* sea, deep, briny, main, Davy Jones's locker: *The oceans cover more than two-thirds of the surface of the earth.*

odd *adj.* strange, unusual, peculiar, queer, weird, extraordinary: *Sylvia's new boyfriend is certainly an odd fellow.* **ant.** ordinary, regular, unexceptional, straightforward.

odor *n.* smell, aroma, scent, fragrance, bouquet, perfume: *The odor of orange blossoms filled the warm evening air.*

offend *vb.* **1.** irritate, annoy, vex, anger, provoke, displease: *Marie was offended at Paul's suggestion that she burn her new hat.* **2.** outrage, insult: *The sight of the concentration camp offended all of us.* **ant. 1.** please, flatter, delight.

offender *n.* culprit, miscreant, criminal, lawbreaker: *The lawyers had no pity for the three-time offender.*

offense *n.* **1.** sin, wrong, transgression, trespass, crime, wrongdoing, misdemeanor: *The policeman said that my offense was smoking in the subway.* **2.** attack, onslaught, assault: *After being on the defense for so long, we finally went on the offense.* **3.** resentment, indignation, anger: *Brodie took offense when we suggested he was too cowardly to ask Alexa for a dance.*

offensive *adj.* **1.** aggressive, attacking: *Our football team then made a number of offensive maneuvers that gained some ground.* **2.** unpleasant, disagreeable, revolting, nauseous, sickening, nauseating, disgusting: *Certainly, most people find the smell of rotten eggs offensive. n.* attack: *Our team took the offensive and we won.* **ant.** *adj.* **1.** defensive, defending. **2.** pleasing, pleasant, agreeable, attractive.

offer *vb.* **1.** present, tender, proffer, submit: *The plan that Bill offered was to be voted on the next day.* **2.** volunteer: *Manuel offered to help with the collection at the school. n.* suggestion, proposal; presentation: *We have received three offers to buy the car.* **ant.** *vb.* refuse, deny. *n.* refusal, denial.

offhand *adj.* casual, informal, impromptu, unprepared: *My offhand guess at the number of pennies in the jar is 3,185.* **ant.** planned, considered, calculated, thought-out.

office *n.* **1.** suite, offices, office building: *I will be working late at the office tonight.* **2.** position, post, situation; occupation: *Janet was planning to run for a political office at the next election.*

officer *n.* **1.** executive, manager, director, administrator: *Rick's father is an officer in the company, and that's how Rick got the job.* **2.** policeman, lawman; sheriff: *During the parade, there was an officer directing traffic at every road.*

offset *vb.* balance, counterbalance, set off, compensate for: *The losses in one department were offset by the profits in another.*

offshoot *n.* branch, by-product: *The factory in our town is just an offshoot of the main company out West.*

offspring *n.* children, descendants, issue, progeny: *The male offspring of the crowned heads of England have always gone to that school.*

off-the-record *adj.* unofficial, restricted, confidential: *After* *the speech, the governor made some off-the-record remarks that couldn't be reported.*

often *adv.* frequently, oftentimes, regularly, usually: *All of us often went to the soda shop after school.* **ant.** rarely, seldom, hardly.

okay, O.K. *adj.* correct, fine, all right: *If that's the way you want it, it's okay with me.* *vb.* approve, allow, authorize: *I had to get the principal's office to okay my absence last week.* *n.* approval, permission: *May I have your okay on this order before I send it out?*

old *adj.* **1.** aged, elderly: *My parents aren't very old.* **2.** used, worn, dilapidated, ragged, faded, broken-down: *There was an old shack in the woods where the boys would meet secretly.* **3.** former, ancient, olden, old-fashioned, antique: *My aunt collects old cigar boxes.* **ant. 1.** young, youthful. **2.** fresh, brand-new.

old-fashioned *adj.* old, antiquated, outmoded, passé: *Bella was wearing one of her enormous, old-fashioned hats.* **ant.** new, up-to-date, fashionable, current, modern.

old-timer *n.* oldster; veteran, master: *The old-timers in town really knew how to herd cattle.* **ant.** newcomer.

omit *vb.* **1.** leave out, exclude, except, bar: *It was decided to omit from consideration in the honor society all those with less than a B average.* **2.** ignore, neglect, overlook: *By mistake, your name was omitted from the list of members.* **ant.** include.

one-sided *adj.* partial, biased, prejudiced, unfair: *If you ask Frank what happened, you will get a very one-sided story.* **ant.** impartial, just.

only *adj.* sole, single, lone, solitary: *When you have no brothers or sisters you are called an only child.* *adv.* merely, just, but, not more than: *It took me only three hours to walk the 12 miles.*

onset *n.* beginning, opening, start, commencement: *The icy winds came down from the north, signaling the onset of winter.* **ant.** end, conclusion, finale.

onward *adv.* forward, ahead: *She stumbled onward a few feet, then fell, an arrow in her back.* **ant.** backward.

ooze *vb.* seep, exude, drip: *The oil oozed from the ground.* *n.* slime, mire, mud: *Many fossils have been found in the ooze at the bottom of the sea.*

open *adj.* **1.** unclosed, uncovered, accessible: *The door was open all night—anyone could have walked in. The jar of jam was left open and became moldy.* **2.** public, free, unrestricted, permitted: *The museum is open to the public on Mondays.* **3.** free, easy, candid; sincere, honest: *Donald was very open about his plans for the next week.* **4.** unoccupied, vacant, unfilled: *The job advertised last week is still open.* *vb.* **1.** start, begin, commence: *The chairman opened the meeting with a short speech of welcome.* **2.** expand, spread, extend: *When Roger opened his fist, I saw the stain on his fingers, proving that he was the culprit.* **ant.** *adj.* **1., 2.** closed, shut, sealed. **3.** private, secretive. **4.** filled, taken. *vb.* **1.** finish, end, stop. **2.** close, clench.

open-handed *adj.* generous, kind, charitable: *Although the old man gave nothing to the organized charities, he was very open-handed when it came to friends.* **ant.** tight-fisted, stingy, mean.

open-hearted *adj.* honest, frank, candid. *It isn't often when a politician will be so open-hearted with his supporters.* **ant.** devious, insincere.

opening *n.* **1.** gap, hole: *The dog escaped from our yard through an opening in the fence.* **2.** beginning, start, commencement: *At the opening of the ceremonies, a huge limousine arrived.* **3.** vacancy, opportunity, chance: *We have an opening for a skilled typist.*

open-minded *adj.* fair, tolerant, liberal, just: *The judge was very open-minded to listen to both sides before commenting.* **ant.** bigoted, intolerant, prejudiced.

operate *vb.* **1.** run, work, use, manage: *Do you know how to operate a printing press?* **2.** run, work, function, perform: *After leaving the service station, the car operated very smoothly.*

operation *n.* **1.** performance, function, action: *The operation of this motor is poor and irregular.* **2.** administration, direction, supervision, handling: *A new executive was brought in to take charge of the operation of the factory.* **3.** surgery: *The operation on my toe will be tomorrow.*

opinion *n.* belief, view, sentiment, idea, viewpoint: *My opinion of that restaurant is that the food is good but the service bad.*

opponent *n.* rival, competitor, contestant, antagonist: *My opponent in the chess finals is a Life Master.* **ant.** ally, colleague, teammate.

opportunity *n.* chance, time, occasion: *Jed explained that he had not had the opportunity to phone to say he'd be late.*

oppose *vb.* resist, battle, combat, withstand, thwart: *The club* *had opposed admitting any minority-group applicants as members.* **ant.** support.

opposite *adj.* **1.** contrary, reverse, different: *Ken turned the car around and drove off in the opposite direction.* **2.** facing: *I walked in and took my place on the opposite side of the courtroom.* **ant. 1.** same, like, similar.

opposition *n.* **1.** antagonism, resistance, defiance, counteraction: *The committee refused to tolerate any opposition to its plans.* **2.** foe, enemy, contestant, adversary, antagonist, competition: *The opposition was led by the congressman from our district.* **ant. 1.** support, help, cooperation.

oppress *vb.* **1.** burden, suppress, crush; persecute: *The people were sorely oppressed under the dictatorship.* **2.** burden, worry, depress: *The father of a large family can often find his responsibilities oppressing.*

oppression *n.* tyranny, injustice, cruelty, persecution: *The oppression of the minorities in that country was so severe that he moved to England.* **ant.** freedom, liberty.

oppressive *adj.* burdensome, difficult, hard; stifling: *The people could no longer stand the oppressive practices of the government, and they revolted. The atmosphere in this room is oppressive without any windows open.*

optimism *n.* hopefulness, confidence: *Thea's father expressed optimism in the outcome of her final examinations.* **ant.** pessimism, doubtfulness, cynicism.

oral *adj.* spoken, uttered, verbal, said, vocal, voiced: *We were asked to give oral, not written, reports.* **ant.** written, printed.

oration *n.* speech, address, sermon, lecture: *The major prepared an oration to be delivered at the dedication of the war memorial.*

orbit *n.* course, path, circuit, lap, revolution: *The planets move in elliptical orbits around the sun.* *vb.* circle, revolve: *The moon orbits around the earth, which orbits around the sun.*

order *n.* **1.** command, direction, instruction, rule: *The sergeant received the order to move the company into the front line area.* **2.** requisition, purchase order; contract: *The shop acknowledged receiving our order for two boxes of stationery.* **3.** goods, merchandise, shipment: *Two weeks afterward, our order arrived in the mail.* **4.** arrangement, classification, system, sequence: *The words in this book are in alphabetical order.* *vb.* **1.** command, direct, instruct: *The police were ordered to investi-*

gate a report of a prowler in the neighborhood. **2.** buy, obtain, request: *That is not the stationery we ordered.*

orderly *adj.* **1.** neat, well-organized, regulated: *In contrast to Mary's room, which is a mess, Anita's is very orderly.* **2.** disciplined, well-organized, well-behaved: *I want everyone to line up and to go into the corridor in orderly fashion during the fire drill.* **ant. 1.** messy, sloppy, undisciplined. **2.** disorganized, haphazard.

ordinarily *adv.* usually, commonly, generally: *Ordinarily, I'd ask you to do the letter over again, but this time I'll let it go.*

ordinary *adj.* **1.** usual, common, customary, regular, normal: *Just do everything in the ordinary way and try to pretend nobody is watching you.* **2.** average, mediocre, everyday, undistinguished: *Although Annette wears fancy clothes for her job in the hotel, she dresses in ordinary clothes during the day.* **ant. 2.** extraordinary, unusual, special.

organization *n.* **1.** formulation, plan, classification: *The experts disagreed on the organization of the information for the files.* **2.** group, association, federation, society, confederation, institute, league, guild, fellowship, brotherhood, syndicate: *The members of the teacher's organization agreed to meet with the school-board officials.*

organize *vb.* **1.** arrange, compose, coordinate, shape, regulate, order, classify: *The office manager asked Ronnie to organize the files.* **2.** establish, found, form, mold: *Ten of us decided to organize a swimming and tennis club.*

organized *adj.* orderly, planned, neat, arranged: *An organized person is not apt to forget things.*

origin *n.* beginning, source, root, cradle, birthplace, rise, start: *Scientists have not been able to pinpoint exactly the origin of man.* **ant.** end, termination.

original *adj.* **1.** first, primary, beginning: *The original settlers of this section of the country were Indians.* **2.** unique, new, fresh, novel, creative: *The invention of the steam engine, by James Watt, was an original idea.* **ant. 1.** secondary. **2.** outmoded, old-fashioned.

originate *vb.* **1.** arise, begin, start: *The idea of coining money originated many centuries ago.* **2.** invent, create, begin: *I wonder who originated the umbrella.*

originator *n.* inventor, creator; discoverer: *The originator of the first sewing machine must have been a genius.* **ant.** imitator, follower.

ornament *n.* decoration, adornment, ornamentation, embellishment: *The old lady was wearing a curious gold ornament on a chain around her neck.* *vb.* decorate, adorn, embellish: *At Christmas, we ornamented the cakes with red and green icing.*

ornamental *adj.* decorative, ornate: *The grating at each window was not for protection, it was purely ornamental.*

outcome *n.* result, end, consequence, upshot: *I had to leave before it was over, so I didn't know the outcome of the game.* **ant.** cause.

outdo *vb.* surpass, excel, beat: *Nancy outdoes all her competitors in gymnastics.*

outfit *n.* gear, clothing, get-up, garb; kit, equipment: *Stephanie arrived at the dance wearing a new outfit of gold lamé. My father was given a whole new fishing outfit for his birthday by the family.* *vb.* equip, supply, provide: *Tim went to a special shop that outfitted him with everything he needed for the hunting trip.*

outgrowth *n.* development, result, effect, product: *Many of our modern laws are an outgrowth of the legal system of ancient Rome.*

outlaw *n.* criminal, badman, bandit; fugitive: *The sheriff cornered the outlaws in the barn and then captured them.* *vb.* prohibit, ban: *The sale of guns may be outlawed in some states next year.*

outline *n.* **1.** edge, border, contour, frame: *If you see it against the sky, you will be able to make out the outline of the jagged cliff in the distance. Draw an outline of the map of the United States.* **2.** plan, sketch, rough, framework: *Nick handed in an outline of the paper he was going to write.* *vb.* draft, sketch, plan, draw: *The playwright outlined the plot of his new musical.*

outlook *n.* **1.** view, viewpoint: *Because Tessie comes from a family that has money, her outlook on saving it is different from mine.* **2.** future, prospect, chance, opportunity: *The outlook for people with a diploma is better than that for those who quit school.*

output *n.* production; productivity, yield: *The average American farm of today has more than double the output that the average farm of a hundred years ago had.*

outrage *n.* affront, offense, insult: *In wartime, soldiers commit outrages on the people whose land they capture.* *vb.* shock, injure, offend: *I was outraged when I learned that Jim had borrowed the car after I had told him not to.*

outrageous *adj.* shocking, offensive, disgraceful, shameful, shameless, gross, contemptible: *If he says that I was with him last night, he's telling the most outrageous lie.* **ant.** reasonable, sensible, prudent.

outset *n.* beginning, start, commencement: *At the outset, I want to declare my innocence of any wrongdoing.* **ant.** end, climax.

outside *n.* **1.** exterior, surface, covering: *The outside of the tin box never hinted that it contained gold and precious stones.* **2.** limit, bounds: *I would guess that, at the outside, 300 students live in that dormitory.* **ant. 1.** inside, interior.

outsider *n.* stranger, alien, foreigner; nonmember: *We never allowed outsiders to attend meetings of our secret club.* **ant.** insider, intimate.

outstanding *adj.* **1.** important, well-known, famous, prominent, conspicuous, leading: *Alan's mother was one of the most outstanding violinists of her time.* **2.** unpaid, overdue, due, owing: *I keep all of the paid bills in this drawer and all of the outstanding ones in the other.* **ant. 1.** ordinary, average.

outwit *vb.* confuse, bewilder, trick, baffle: *Doubling back on his trail, the clever old fox outwitted the hounds, which soon lost the scent.*

overall *adj.* general, complete, comprehensive: *The overall length of the boat is 38 feet.*

overcast *adj.* cloudy, clouded, dark: *Photographs taken on overcast days do not show sharp shadows, as on sunny days.* **ant.** clear, sunny.

overcome *vb.* **1.** conquer, defeat, beat, subdue: *The heavyweight boxer easily overcame any challenger.* **2.** overpower, weaken, overwhelm: *The firemen were nearly overcome by the smoke.* **ant.** submit, yield.

overlook *vb.* ignore, disregard, neglect, miss: *The judge said that he was going to overlook the criminal's past record if he'd promise to stay out of trouble.* **ant.** notice.

overpower *vb.* overwhelm, vanquish, overcome, conquer, subdue, defeat, beat: *The snake easily overpowered the rabbit, which was no match for its speed and strength.* **ant.** surrender.

overrule *vb.* repeal, revoke, disallow, override, nullify, cancel: *The Supreme Court overruled the finding of the lower court and found the defendant not guilty.*

oversight *n.* error, overlooking, omission, blunder, neglect, fault: *Through an oversight, the report cards weren't sent out on time.*

overtake *vb.* catch, reach; pass: *Although the horse had had a poor start, before the finish line it had overtaken every other horse and won the race.*

overthrow *vb.* overpower, defeat, conquer; upset, overturn: *The army succeeded in overthrowing the government so quickly that no one was hurt.* *n.* defeat, collapse, fall: *The overthrow of the king was being plotted by spies in another country.*

overwhelm *vb.* **1.** defeat, overcome, crush, overpower: *The tiny force defending the palace was quickly overwhelmed by the army.* **2.** bury, cover: *When the dikes broke, the waters flooded through the streets, overwhelming the town.*

own *vb.* possess, have, hold: *Everything that I own in the world could fit into a large suitcase.*

❧ P ❧

pace   *n.*   **1.** step: *Take three paces to the right, then one to the left, and dig there for the buried treasure.* **2.** gait, rate; velocity: *Anne was typing only three letters an hour and was asked to increase her pace.*

pacific   *adj.* peaceful, calm, peaceable, tranquil, quiet; gentle: *Jan has a very pacific disposition and rarely seems upset. If you had ever seen the Pacific Ocean during a typhoon, you would wonder why it was named "pacific."* **ant.** turbulent, excited, roiled.

pacify   *vb.* calm, quiet, tranquilize, smooth, lull: *Although Ben was furious at being insulted, we succeeded in pacifying him after a few minutes.* **ant.** upset, excite, disturb.

pack   *vb.*   **1.** stow; prepare: *Pack your suitcase right away —we're off for a holiday this afternoon.* **2.** cram, ram, crowd, stuff, compress: *Those sardines are packed in the can almost as tightly as people on a subway train during rush hour.* *n.* **1.** bundle, package, parcel, load: *Each hiker carried a pack on his back.* **2.** crowd, herd, gang, mob, group: *A pack of people was huddled around the speaker in the park. The pack of wolves had attacked the sheep during the night.*

package   *n.* bundle, parcel, pack, packet, load: *The package was weighed at the post office and insured for $50.* *vb.* containerize, crate, box, bottle: *The perfume comes packaged in a leakproof container.*

packet   *n.* package, bundle: *The mailman delivered a small packet of letters this morning.*

pact   *n.* agreement, contract, compact, arrangement, deal, settlement, treaty, bargain: *There is a trade pact between our two countries.*

pad   *n.*   **1.** cushion, wadding; stuffing, filling, padding: *If you keep this pad under your sprained knee it will make you more comfortable.* **2.** block; bundle: *The detective made notes on a small pad of paper.* *vb.* cushion: *This fragile vase should be carefully padded for shipping.*

paddle   *n.* sweep, scull; oar: *The first thing you did wrong was to lose the canoe paddle overboard.*

pageant *n.* spectacle, exhibition, show, display, extravaganza: *Every year at Christmas our school puts on a pageant.*

pain *n.* **1.** distress, suffering, misery, ache, pang, torment, agony: *Harold kept on running in spite of the pain of his sprained ankle.* **2.** anguish, misery: *Betty's decision to live away from home caused her parents much pain.* *vb.* hurt, harm, distress, ache: *My mother's arthritis pained her a great deal.* **ant.** *n.* **1.** comfort, ease. **2.** delight, joy.

painful *adj.* agonizing, aching, inflamed, sore, throbbing: *That punch in the nose must have been very painful.* **ant.** soothing.

painstaking *adj.* careful, exacting, scrupulous: *The miniature model of the car was made with painstaking attention to detail.* **ant.** careless, slipshod.

pair *n.* couple; brace, team: *A pair of horses drew the carriage.* *vb.* match, mate, couple, join: *The teacher paired us off and we marched out of the room two abreast.*

pal *n.* buddy, chum, friend, sidekick: *I went bowling last night with a couple of pals of mine.*

pale *adj.* **1.** white, ashen, colorless, wan, pallid: *Before it becomes warm enough to go sunbathing and get tan, everyone looks pale.* **2.** dim, faint: *The bedroom is being painted pale blue.* *vb.* whiten, blanch. *Grover paled when he was told he'd been seen taking the book from the shelf.* **ant.** *adj.* **1.** ruddy, flushed. **2.** dark, bright.

pamper *vb.* baby, coddle, spoil: *Parents sometimes pamper a child so much that he thinks he can have anything he asks for.*

pamphlet *n.* brochure, booklet, leaflet: *Many political pamphlets were published in England during the 18th century.*

pang *n.* pain, hurt, throb: *I got a sudden pang in my leg, as if from a muscle cramp.*

panic *n.* alarm, fear, dread, fright, terror: *When they saw and smelled the fire, the horses' panic was so great they stampeded.* *vb.* terrify, frighten, alarm: *The civilians were panicked by the scream of the bombs dropping nearby.* **ant.** *vb.* calm, soothe, tranquillize.

pant *vb.* puff, gasp, wheeze: *Jack came panting up the hill with Jill.*

pantry *n.* storeroom, larder, cupboard, scullery: *We went from the kitchen into the pantry to make the sandwiches.*

paper *n.* **1.** newspaper, journal: *Have you read the paper today?* **2.** document, record, proof: *When you apply for a job, you should bring all the necessary papers with* *you.* **3.** article, report, essay: *Only invited scholars read their papers at the international meeting.*

parade *n.* march, procession, review; pageant: *Today is the annual St. Patrick's Day parade.* *vb.* march, walk, strut: *The pretty girls were always parading on the boardwalk along the beach.*

paradise *n.* **1.** heaven: *Many people believe that if they're good, they'll end up in paradise when they die.* **2.** utopia: *We spent our holiday on what was promised in the travel brochure would be a tropical paradise.*

parallel *adj.* similar, corresponding, like, resembling: *Our thinking has been parallel on the subject of liberty for many years.* *n.* **1.** equal, match, counterpart: *As a scientist, George has no parallel in this country.* **2.** similarity, likeness, resemblance, correspondence: *It isn't accurate to draw a parallel between 20th-century rulers and those of the 16th century.* *vb.* resemble, correspond to, match, equal: *My experience parallels yours when it comes to service in the army.* **ant.** *adj.* divergent.

paralyze *vb.* deaden, benumb, numb: *When it saw the snake, the rat was paralyzed with fear.*

parcel *n.* package, bundle, packet: *The department stores deliver parcels free of charge within a certain area.*

pardon *n.* excuse, forgiveness; amnesty, acquittal, exoneration: *The governor refused to give pardons to the criminals convicted of major crimes.* *vb.* excuse, forgive, acquit, exonerate: *On his birthday the king pardoned all his political opponents still in jail.* **ant.** *vb.* condemn, sentence.

pare *vb.* **1.** peel, skin: *I know how to pare an apple so that the skin comes off in one long, curly piece.* **2.** diminish, reduce, cut, trim, crop, shave: *The finance committee is meeting to see if the operating budget can be pared down a bit.*

part *n.* **1.** portion, piece, section, fraction, fragment: *Since I helped to pay for it, part of that apple pie should go to me.* **2.** share, allotment, participation, interest: *If everyone does his part, we shall be finished much sooner.* **3.** role, character: *Philip played the part of Macbeth.* *vb.* **1.** divide, split, break up, disconnect: *The curtains parted to reveal a striking stage set. We had to part at the gate because only passengers were allowed beyond it.* **2.** depart, go, leave, quit: *It is late, and I must part from this house to go home.* **ant.** *n.* **1.** whole, entirety.

partial *adj.* **1.** incomplete, unfinished, undone: *I made a partial payment toward the car.* **2.** prejudiced, biased, one-sided, unfair, unjust: *The umpires and referees in sports should not be partial to one team or the other.* **ant. 1.** entire, complete, comprehensive.

participate *vb.* share, partake, join; engage in: *The coach planned that everyone should participate in sports.*

particle *n.* bit, spot, grain, speck, shred, scrap: *A particle of sand or grit flew into my eye. There's not a particle of truth in that story.*

particular *adj.* **1.** special, specific, distinct: *This particular bed was slept in by George Washington.* **2.** careful, especial, special, finicky, finical: *Suzanne is very particular about the people she associates with.* **3.** notable, exceptional, remarkable, unusual: *This is a very particular painting and should fetch a great sum at the auction.* *n.* detail, point, item, feature: *The report on the condition of the playground was correct in every particular.*

partisan *n.* follower, disciple, supporter, backer: *After the government was overthrown, its partisans continued to fight.* *adj.* partial, biased, prejudiced: *The senator was known to play partisan politics on issues involving national defense.*

partition *n.* **1.** division, separation, distribution: *The allies agreed to the partition of Germany after the war.* **2.** divider, screen, separator, barrier, wall: *A new partition was installed dividing the office in half.* *vb.* divide, separate, apportion: *The ranch was partitioned among the heirs of the cattle baron. We ought to partition off a section of the cellar for a workshop.* **ant.** *n.* **1.** joining, unification.

partner *n.* associate, colleague, participant: *My partner in the new business is an expert engineer.*

party *n.* **1.** group, gathering, company, crowd: *Every Wednesday a party of theatergoers would travel into town in a chartered bus.* **2.** block, faction, body, organization: *You don't have to join a political party to vote in the election, unless it's a primary.*

pass *vb.* **1.** go, move, proceed, continue: *Have you seen an orange kitten pass this way?* **2.** disregard, bypass, ignore: *The manager passed over George when it was time to consider promotions.* **3.** circulate, spend: *The counterfeiter succeeded in passing some phony $20 bills in town.* **4.** go by *or* away, end, terminate, cease, expire:

The day of the horse and buggy has passed. **5.** enact, legislate, establish, approve, okay: *The Senate passed the new tax bill.* **6.** exceed, surpass: *California has passed New York in population.* **7.** spend, while away, fill: *I passed the time waiting for the train in reading a book.* *n.* **1.** gorge, ravine, canyon, gap, defile: *The army reached the mountain pass before dawn and launched an attack immediately.* **2.** permit, admission, permission, ticket: *You will need an official pass to visit the rocket factory.* **3.** toss, throw, hurl: *Namath threw a forward pass that was caught by a teammate.* **ant.** *vb.* **2.** consider, notice, note.

passable *adj.* acceptable, satisfactory, adequate, tolerable, fair: *I would call Jordan a passable executive.* **ant.** exceptional, extraordinary, superior.

passage *n.* **1.** paragraph, section, text: *The speaker read a passage from* Moby Dick *and then discussed its meaning.* **2.** passing, transition, movement: *The passage of time seems so slow when you are waiting for someone.* **3.** passageway, corridor, hall: *The Congressmen were interviewed by the press in the passage outside the conference room.* **4.** journey, voyage, trip, crossing, tour: *When he was just a boy, my grandfather worked for his passage from England to America as a cabin boy.*

passenger *n.* rider, commuter, traveler; tourist, voyager, traveler: *The New York subways carry millions of passengers daily. When he retired, Captain Williams sailed around the world just to see what it was like to be a passenger.*

passion *n.* **1.** emotion, feeling, zeal, rapture, excitement: *The passion Victoria had for the women's lib movement sometimes made her say things she didn't mean.* **2.** love, desire, affection, liking, fondness, enthusiasm: *My mother has a strong passion for all of her nine children.* **ant.** indifference, apathy, coolness.

passionate *adj.* emotional, excited, impulsive, zealous, enthusiastic, earnest, sincere: *The political leader gave a passionate speech, trying to win labor to his cause.*

past *adj.* **1.** gone, over, finished, done, done with: *The days when you could buy a hot dog for a nickel are past.* **2.** former, preceding, prior: *The past president of the class is still a member of the student council.* **3.** recent, preceding: *In the past few days nobody has seen Joan at school. n.* **1.** antiquity, old times, the (good) old days,

days of yore, yesterday: *It always seems as though everything was better in the past.* **2.** experiences, former life, secret life: *She may be old now, but that author had quite an exciting past.* **ant.** *adj.* **1.** ahead. **2.** present, future. *n.* **1.** present, future.

pastime *n.* amusement, recreation, entertainment; hobby: *David collects stamps as a pastime, not professionally.*

patch *n., vb.* mend, repair: *My jacket has a patch over each elbow. Do you think that the tailor can patch my torn trousers?*

patent *n.* protection, copyright, control, permit: *Dick's mother has a patent on a new kind of rocket fuel.* *vb.* license, limit, copyright: *Some of the strangest devices you have ever seen have been patented in America.*

path *n.* walk, way, trail, track, footpath, lane, pathway, walkway: *The path leading from the street to our front door is bordered by flower beds.*

pathetic *adj.* pitiable, pitiful, moving, touching: *The half-drowned kitten looked so pathetic that we had to take it home and care for it.*

patience *n.* **1.** calmness, composure, passiveness, serenity, courage: *Our teacher's patience came to an end when Evelyn started to giggle again.* **2.** endurance, perseverance, persistence: *It takes a great deal of patience to stand in line for four hours to buy a ticket to a concert.* **ant.** **1.** impatience, restlessness, impetuosity.

patient *adj.* **1.** persistent, untiring, persevering: *If you'll be patient, the dentist will be with you in a few more moments.* **2.** resigned, submissive: *As Tom grew older, he became more patient with other people's faults.* **3.** calm, serene, quiet, unexcited, unexcitable, self-controlled, unruffled, unshaken: *The old pony was very patient when children wanted to ride him. After years of patient research, the scientists finally perfected the medicine.* *n.* invalid, case, inmate: *Danny was a patient in the hospital for a week after he broke his leg.*

patrol *vb.* guard, watch; inspect: *Three armed sentries are assigned to patrol the factory at night.*

patron *n.* **1.** customer, client, purchaser, buyer: *The first patrons arrive at the restaurant at 6:30 for breakfast.* **2.** supporter, benefactor, backer, philanthropist: *The patrons of the arts center have contributed millions of dollars to its support.*

patronize *vb.* **1.** buy at, support: *We always patronize our* *local shops.* **2.** condescend, stoop, talk down to: *The department head didn't like the new clerk because he spoke to her in a patronizing way.*

pattern *n.* **1.** model, guide, template, example, original: *Penny was building a model car, using a Rolls Royce as a pattern.* **2.** design, decoration, figure: *The dress has a beautiful pattern but I don't like the way it fits.* *vb.* model, copy, follow, imitate: *The capital buildings of many states are patterned after the capitol in Washington.*

pause *n.* hesitation, rest, wait, interruption, delay, break, intermission, recess: *After a short pause for a sip of water, the speaker went on to discuss the habits of lions in the wild.* *vb.* hesitate, rest, wait, interrupt, break, delay, recess: *You ought to pause to think before replying to that question.* **ant.** *n.* continuity, perpetuity. *vb.* continue, perpetuate.

pay *vb.* **1.** settle, remit, discharge: *I have very few bills to pay this month.* **2.** compensate, recompense, reward, return: *Phil's new job pays him $2.50 an hour.* *n.* payment, salary, wage, wages, fee, income: *How much is your pay per month?*

peace *n.* **1.** quiet, serenity, calm, peacefulness, tranquillity: *Every time I spend a day in a big city, I yearn for the peace of the countryside.* **2.** pact, treaty, truce, accord, armistice: *Do you remember the date of the Peace of Westphalia? A peace agreement was signed in Geneva this week.* **ant.** agitation, upheaval, disturbance.

peaceable *adj.* peaceful, gentle, mild, calm, friendly, amiable, pacific: *The neighboring Indian tribes had always been peaceable until the white man came along.* **ant.** hostile, warlike, aggressive.

peaceful *adj.* peaceable, quiet, calm, serene, tranquil: *It's very peaceful to spend a week fishing in a mountain stream.* **ant.** disrupted, agitated, riotous.

peak *n.* **1.** top, summit, point, crest: *We could see the peaks of the Rocky Mountains from our hotel room in Denver.* **2.** top, maximum, pinnacle: *Prices on the stock market reached their peak for the year today.* **ant. 2.** base, bottom.

peculiar *adj.* **1.** unusual, odd, strange, unfamiliar, uncommon, queer, outlandish, curious: *The camel is a very peculiar animal.* **2.** characteristic, special, unique, exclusive: *A love of eucalyptus leaves is peculiar to the koala,* *which looks like a teddy bear.* **ant. 1.** ordinary, regular, unspecial.

peculiarity *n.* characteristic, distinctiveness: *We noticed the peculiarities of Oscar's behavior but didn't think they were serious enough to comment on.*

peddle *vb.* hawk, vend, sell: *The beggar was peddling shoelaces and pencils outside the theater.*

pedestrian *n.* walker, stroller: *Pedestrians should cross streets only at the corners. adj.* ordinary, common, everyday, dull, commonplace: *The comedian told some very pedestrian jokes that weren't funny at all.* **ant.** *adj.* unusual, fascinating, extraordinary, special.

pedigree *n.* family, descent, ancestry, parentage, line, lineage: *The pedigree of this prize collie goes back through eight generations of champions.*

peek *n., vb.* peep, peer, glimpse, look: *We got a peek at what they were doing without their seeing us. Close your eyes and count to 20—and no peeking!*

peel *n.* skin, rind, peeling: *I slipped on a banana peel and everyone laughed when I fell down. vb.* skin, strip, pare: *My uncle can peel an orange so that the skin comes off in one piece.*

peep *vb., n.* cheep, chirp, squeak: *The baby chicks peeped constantly when they were awake. I don't want to hear a peep out of you after you get into bed.*

peer[1] *n.* **1.** equal, parallel, match, rival: *As a high-jumper, Kim has no peer.* **2.** nobleman, lord: *The peers of the British realm are listed in this book.*

peer[2] *vb.* peek, peep, glimpse; scrutinize, examine: *The old lady peered at me closely, trying to see if I was someone she knew.*

pen *n.* enclosure, cage, coop, sty: *Domestic animals like chickens and pigs are often kept in pens.*

penalize *vb.* punish; dock: *In the wrestling match, Dick was penalized points for clasping his hands around his opponent.*

penalty *n.* punishment; forfeit; fine: *The penalty in England for stealing bread was once death by hanging. In basketball, the penalty for holding is two free shots for the other team.*

penetrate *vb.* **1.** pierce, enter, bore, hole: *The bullet penetrated the wall just an inch away from my head.* **2.** permeate, spread, seep: *The smoke from the fire pene-*

trated all the rooms, and we had to have everything cleaned.

penetrating *adj.* **1.** piercing, boring, puncturing, sharp, acute: *We were quite surprised that such a young person could have such a penetrating mind.* **2.** keen, shrewd, sharp, acute, intelligent, sharp-witted: *Sadie has a penetrating observation to offer concerning the course in physics.*

peninsula *n.* point, neck, spit, headland: *At high tide, much of the peninsula is under water.*

penniless *adj.* poor, poverty-stricken, needy, destitute: *The old miser wouldn't have anything to do with the penniless beggars who followed him, asking for money.* **ant.** rich, wealthy, well-off, prosperous.

people *n.* **1.** human beings, humans, persons, beings: *Many people have moved from the country to the cities.* **2.** race, nation, tribe, clan, family: *How many people live in America today? A primitive people was found recently, living in the Philippine Islands.* *vb.* populate: *Australia was originally peopled by the Aborigines, long before the white man came.*

perceive *vb.* **1.** see, discern, notice, observe, distinguish, make out: *It is very difficult to perceive the differences between the monarch and the viceroy butterflies.* **2.** understand, comprehend, grasp: *I cannot perceive the purpose in your trying to swim across the channel.*

perception *n.* understanding, apprehension, comprehension: *Everyone's perception of the events leading up to the fight was different.*

perceptive *adj.* discerning, sharp, acute, observant: *It was very perceptive of Alexa to note that the man's coat was buttoned the wrong way in the photo.*

perfect *adj.* **1.** faultless, excellent, flawless, pure, ideal: *The acrobat's style was perfect.* **2.** complete, finished, whole: *The Preamble to the Constitution says that one of its main purposes is to "form a more perfect union" among the states.* **3.** complete, utter, total: *He might have told you he was my brother, but he was a perfect stranger to me.* **4.** exact, precise, sharp, correct: *The two pieces of ancient sculpture turned out to be a perfect match.* *vb.* complete, achieve, finish, accomplish: *No one has yet been able to perfect a perpetual-motion machine.* **ant.** *adj.* **1.** imperfect, flawed, second-rate.

perform *vb.* **1.** do, carry out, accomplish, achieve, complete: *With a little coaxing, Harry would perform the trick of walking on his hands.* **2.** present, act out, give, produce: *The children performed the play on an outdoor platform in the park.*

performance *n.* presentation, offering, exhibition, appearance: *There will be two performances of the play on Wednesdays and Saturdays and none on Sundays.*

performer *n.* actor/actress, entertainer: *Stan was understudy to some of the leading performers in the theatrical company.*

perfume *n.* **1.** scent, essence; toilet water, cologne: *Every Mother's Day I give my mother a bottle of perfume.* **2.** odor, scent, fragrance, smell, aroma: *The perfume of the orange blossoms filled the night air.*

perhaps *adv.* maybe, possibly, conceivably: *If the children will be home for Christmas, perhaps we can have a big party.* **ant.** definitely, absolutely.

peril *n.* danger, hazard, risk: *This insurance policy will cover you against such perils as falling apples, finding sharp bones in bananas, and heat waves in winter.* **ant.** security, safety.

perilous *adj.* dangerous, risky, hazardous, unsafe: *The climbers were making a perilous descent down the face of the cliff.* **ant.** safe, secure.

period *n.* **1.** time, interval, term; era, age, epoch: *My uncle spent a brief period in the navy. The 15th to 17th centuries were a period of exploration and migration.* **2.** course, cycle; timing: *The period of the day is marked by the revolution of the earth on its axis.*

perish *vb.* die, expire; pass away, depart: *More than 100 animals perished in the circus fire.*

permanent *adj.* **1.** enduring, lasting, stable, continuing, long-lived, persisting, persistent; perpetual, everlasting: *Dick's father was given a permanent appointment to the school board. Stainless steel is a more permanent material than aluminum for building.* **2.** unchanging, unaltered, unchanged, constant, unvarying, invariable: *Because of the accident, Tim has a permanent scar on his arm.* **ant.** passing, temporary, inconstant, fluctuating.

permission *n.* consent, leave; freedom, liberty: *Please ask the teacher's permission to leave the room. Permission to speak freely is given by the Constitution—but that does not mean you can say anything you like.*

permit *vb.* allow, let, tolerate, suffer: *No one is permitted* *to talk during class. n.* license, permission, authorization: *Only members of the faculty have permits to park in that area.* **ant. vb.** forbid, prohibit, disallow.

perpendicular *adj.* vertical, upright, standing: *Three perpendicular posts won't be enough to support the fence in the wind.* **ant.** horizontal.

perpetual *adj.* unceasing, continuing, continuous, continual, everlasting, permanent, constant, eternal, ceaseless, undying: *Jim's perpetual whistling is very annoying. This perpetual clock never needs winding.* **ant.** intermittent, inconstant, fluctuating.

perplex *vb.* confuse, puzzle, mystify, bewilder: *Donna was completely perplexed by the algebra problem. The controls of a modern jet plane are a perplexing array of buttons, switches, levers, and knobs.*

persecute *vb.* oppress, torment, ill-treat, maltreat, victimize, abuse: *Minorities in many countries suffer persecution for no reason.*

persevere *vb.* endure, persist, last, continue: *If you work hard and persevere, you have an excellent chance of succeeding in anything you undertake.* **ant.** lapse, desist, discontinue, stop.

persist *vb.* persevere, continue, remain, endure: *Jane persisted in her claim that she had done nothing wrong by borrowing the book without permission.* **ant.** stop, desist.

person *n.* human, human being, individual, personage, someone, somebody: *Three unknown persons broke into the office at night and stole the typewriter.*

personal *adj.* **1.** private, secret: *Linda revealed many personal things about herself that I wouldn't repeat to anyone.* **2.** individual, special, particular: *My personal opinion is that each one of us ought to do what he does best.* **ant. 1.** public, general.

persuade *vb.* **1.** influence, induce, convince: *Peter persuaded me to try to get a job for the summer holidays.* **2.** urge, coax, prompt: *You don't have to persuade Anne to eat everything on her plate.* **ant. 1.** dissuade, discourage.

persuasive *adj.* convincing, influential, winning, alluring, compelling, stimulating: *I must admit that your arguments for finishing my schoolwork are very persuasive.* **ant.** unconvincing, dubious.

pest *n.* nuisance, irritation, irritant, annoyance, tease, bother: *Why must you be such a pest about my keeping my room neat?*

pester   *vb.* annoy, irritate, vex, trouble, harass, torment, tease, bother, worry: *Please don't pester me while I'm trying to study.*

pet   *n.* favorite, darling: *Eunice is the teacher's pet. vb.* fondle, caress, baby: *Phoebe had great fun at her aunt's house where she petted the new kittens.*

petition   *n.* request, application, appeal, solicitation, entreaty: *Most of the neighbors signed the petition for saving the trees along the streets. vb.* request, apply, appeal, solicit, entreat: *The students got together to petition the teachers to give them less homework.*

petty   *adj.* **1.** unimportant, trivial, insignificant, paltry, trifling: *The young man arrested last night had committed a large number of petty crimes, like shoplifting.* **2.** stingy, mean, miserly: *Some people are very generous to themselves but very petty when it comes to others.* **ant. 1.** grand, vital, significant. **2.** generous, bighearted.

phantom   *n.* specter, ghost, apparition: *The old man swore that he had seen a phantom who haunted the ghost town. adj.* unreal; imaginary: *He insisted that the ghost was a phantom cowboy who had been killed in a gunfight.*

phase   *n.* **1.** stage, period, state: *The Neanderthal was thought to be an early phase in the development of modern man.* **2.** aspect, side, view, condition: *Each phase of the project should be handled by the person who knows most about it.*

phenomenon   *n.* **1.** happening, occurrence, fact, incident: *The fish that climbs trees in Borneo is a very strange phenomenon.* **2.** marvel, wonder: *Anyone who can balance himself on only one finger is truly a phenomenon.*

physical   *adj.* **1.** bodily, corporeal, corporal: *I get a complete physical examination once a year.* **2.** real, material, natural: *Man cannot fly—it's a physical impossibility.* **ant. 1.** mental, spiritual.

pick   *vb.* **1.** choose, select: *I was picked to represent our class at the annual spelling bee.* **2.** gather, harvest, reap, collect, pluck: *Every autumn our family goes to an orchard where for a small fee you can pick all the apples you want.* **3.** steal, rob: *My pocket was picked while I was in the bus. n.* choice, selection; best, choicest: *When Josie's dog had puppies, we were allowed the pick of the litter.*

picture   *n.* **1.** painting, drawing, photograph, illustration: *I love the pictures in my family album.* **2.** image, likeness, representation: *Jean is the picture of health.* **3.** description, account: *Try to give us a picture of the events of last Saturday.* **4.** movie, motion picture, film: *We used to go to the pictures every Wednesday evening.* *vb.* **1.** describe, represent: *In his story, the writer pictured a world where there was no evil.* **2.** imagine, conceive of: *Can you picture yourself winning the Miss America contest?*

piece *n.* quantity, unit, section, portion, part: *How many pieces of candy did Betty eat last night?*

piecemeal *adv.* partially, gradually: *Instead of telling us the whole story at once, we had to drag the details out of George piecemeal.* **ant.** entire, whole, complete.

pierce *vb.* **1.** stab, perforate, puncture: *Once you pierce the skin of the sausage with a fork, all the juices and fat run out.* **2.** affect, rouse, touch, move, excite, thrill: *Cory's sad story about the death of her cat pierced our hearts.*

pile *n.* heap, collection, accumulation: *There's a pile of dirty clothes in the corner of your room and I want it taken away.* *vb.* heap (up), collect, accumulate, amass, assemble: *Please ask the men to pile that firewood near the woodshed. How could you have piled up so many traffic tickets in one day?*

pilgrim *n.* traveler, wanderer: *The knights met many pilgrims who were on their way to the holy land.*

pilgrimage *n.* tour, journey, trip, expedition: *I make an annual pilgrimage to the small town in Maine where I was born.*

pillar *n.* column, shaft, support, prop: *The roof of the ancient temple is held up by 24 marble pillars.*

pillow *n.* cushion, pad, bolster: *Sometimes, if your back is sore, it helps to sleep without a pillow.*

pilot *n.* aviator; steersman, helmsman: *My uncle was a fighter pilot in the Air Force. That's nothing; my father is a pilot on a transatlantic 747.* *vb.* steer, guide: *A man who knows the harbor waters was brought aboard to pilot the ocean liner up to the pier.*

pin *n.* **1.** fastening, fastener, clip, peg: *A wooden pin was used to hold the door shut.* **2.** brooch, tiepin, stickpin, tietack: *Sandy's mother wore a diamond pin to the opera last night.* *vb.* fasten, fix: *After we finished the ice cream, we all played Pin the Tail on the Donkey.*

pinch *vb., n.* nip, squeeze: *Why do grownups all like to* *pinch children's cheeks? The pinch of these tight new shoes is more than I can stand.*

pioneer *n.* pathfinder, explorer, guide; pilgrim, homesteader: *The spread westward of American civilization was due chiefly to the early adventurous pioneers.*

pious *adj.* devout, religious, reverent: *A pious man, the farmer never overlooked his morning and evening prayers.* **ant.** impious, irreligious, profane.

pirate *n.* buccaneer, corsair, privateer, freebooter, plunderer: *Some books make pirates seem romantic, when in fact they were killers and thieves.* *vb.* steal, rob, plagiarize: *The novel sold very well in America, and soon it was pirated for publication in Taiwan.*

pistol *n.* gun, handgun, automatic, revolver, six-gun, six-shooter; weapon: *In England, the police do not carry pistols except under special conditions.*

pit *n.* hole, cavity, hollow, well, excavation: *In India they used to catch tigers alive by digging a huge, deep pit and covering it with leaves so that the animal would fall into it without seeing it.*

pitch *vb.* **1.** set up, establish: *We pitched camp near the river.* **2.** throw, toss, fling, hurl: *It was John's turn to pitch and he knew how to throw a curve.* **3.** plunge, rock: *The huge ship was pitching like a matchbox in the typhoon.* *n.* **1.** throw, toss, hurl, cast: *At the carnival we paid ten cents a pitch to see if we could get the rings around the bottles.* **2.** slant, angle, incline, grade: *In countries where it snows a lot, the roofs of the houses have a very steep pitch.*

pitcher *n.* jug, ewer: *Mother put a pitcher of milk on the table.*

pitfall *n.* trap, deadfall, snare: *There are many pitfalls on the road to happiness.*

pitiful *adj.* pitiable, pathetic, distressing, heart-rending: *The vicious crocodile, now caught in the trap, gave out with a pitiful cry.*

pitiless *adj.* unpitying, merciless, unmerciful, ruthless, mean, cruel, hard-hearted, stony-hearted: *The pitiless head-masters of many schools in Victorian England beat their students regularly.* **ant.** kind, kindly, gentle.

pity *n.* sympathy, compassion, charity, mercy, tenderheartedness, softheartedness: *I feel so much pity for the animals in zoos that I want to set them free.* *vb.* feel for, sympathize (with), commiserate (with): *Pity the poor children* *elsewhere in the world, many of whom have nothing to eat.* **ant.** *n.* cruelty, pitilessness, vindictiveness.

place *n.* **1.** space, plot, region, location, area, spot: *There's a place I know where the sun always shines and the swimming is marvelous.* **2.** job, situation, duty, employment, position: *Bill got a new place in another company as manager of the personnel department.* **3.** residence, home, house, dwelling: *I love your new place, Anna! Too bad you can't afford to furnish it! vb.* **1.** put, set, arrange, locate: *Place your hands on top of the table, palms up.* **2.** hire, engage, appoint: *We placed three new people in the advertising department this month.* **3.** identify, connect: *I know that face, but I just can't place it.*

plague *n.* **1.** pestilence, Black Death, epidemic: *The plague in Europe in the Dark Ages killed about one quarter of the population.* **2.** trouble, vexation, nuisance, irritation: *A plague of locusts destroyed almost the entire crop. vb.* trouble, vex, annoy, irritate, pester: *Financial troubles always plagued this family.*

plain *adj.* **1.** simple, undecorated, unembellished, ordinary, unadorned: *Sophie was wearing a plain black dress with a shocking pink collar and cuffs.* **2.** homely, unattractive: *Zeke married a plain girl whom he'd met in Oklahoma, but she soon became a movie star.* **3.** clear, understandable, unmistakable, obvious: *I made it quite plain that Sue would not go out with anyone who drank or smoked.* **4.** candid, blunt, outspoken, frank, open, honest, sincere: *If you don't mind some plain speaking, I'd like to know why you arrived home so late. n.* plateau, mesa, prairie, steppe, savanna, tundra: *The central plains of the United States are extensive farming areas.* **ant.** *adj.* **1.** fancy, elaborate, ornamented. **2.** pretty, beautiful, comely. **3.** disguised, hidden, unclear.

plan *n.* **1.** plot, procedure, scheme, design, method: *Donald outlined his plan for selling the school yearbook to local merchants.* **2.** drawing, floor plan, rendering, map, chart, diagram: *When I checked the plan of the building I found the hidden passageways. vb.* plot, scheme, design, arrange, contrive: *The engineers planned to build the plant near the river. If it's sunny on Saturday, we plan a picnic in the park.*

plane *n.* **1.** level: *If you are going to be rude, then the plane of this conversation is too low for me.* **2.** airplane, aircraft, airliner: *Tony just got off the plane from London.*

plastic *adj.* **1.** pliant, supple, moldable, pliable, flexible: *Clay is a plastic substance that can be shaped into many forms.* **2.** synthetic: *Plastic surfaces may not be as attractive as natural ones but they're easier to clean.*

platform *n.* **1.** dais, stage, pulpit: *The primitive theater was nothing more than a raised platform on which the actors stood.* **2.** policies, principles: *The politicians met to work out the party platform for the coming elections.*

play *n.* **1.** show, drama, performance, theatrical: *Each year at Christmas our class put on a play for the rest of the school.* **2.** amusement, sport, entertainment, recreation, game, pastime: *There is a time for work and a time for play, and play comes after work.* **3.** fun, frolic, jest: *A pun is a play on words.* *vb.* **1.** act, perform, present, represent, impersonate: *Randy played the part of the grandfather in our melodrama.* **2.** sport, frisk, romp, caper, frolic: *After school was over, we all went out to play on the beach.* **3.** compete, participate, contend: *My brother taught me how to play chess.* **4.** perform (on): *I have a piano, in case anyone knows how to play. Can you play the harmonica?* *vb. phr.* **play ball** collaborate, cooperate: *If we can get the teacher to play ball, maybe we'll have shorter homework assignments.* **play down** de-emphasize, minimize, belittle: *If I were you, I would play down my experience as a pickpocket.* **play up** emphasize, stress: *You ought to play up your good points, like your ability to draw.*

plaything *n.* toy, game, gadget, trinket: *Put away your playthings and straighten out your room. Philip didn't realize it, but they were using him as their plaything and taking advantage of his good nature.*

plea *n.* **1.** appeal, request, entreaty: *Ted's plea for fair treatment by his teammates was sincere.* **2.** excuse, apology, answer, reply: *My only plea for having given George the rifle was ignorance.* **3.** defense, pleading, case: *The lawyer entered a plea of not guilty for his client.*

plead *vb.* **1.** beg, entreat, appeal: *Sonia pleaded with her captors to let her go.* **2.** answer, declare, present: *The man pleaded guilty to driving on the wrong side of the road.*

pleasant *adj.* **1.** enjoyable, nice, agreeable, pleasurable, satisfying, satisfactory, adequate, acceptable: *We had a pleasant visit with my cousin, but it could have been much more fun.* **2.** affable, agreeable, charming, mild, amiable, friendly, personable, courteous: *Fred's a pleasant enough fellow, but he's not my best friend.* **ant.** horrid, disagreeable, sour, nasty, difficult.

please *vb.* **1.** gratify, satisfy: *It pleases me to think of my parents' getting a good rest from work.* **2.** desire, choose, wish: *You may do as you please about going to the concert.* **ant.** **1.** displease, annoy, vex.

pleasing *adj.* pleasant, agreeable, charming, delightful, engaging: *Doris has a pleasing manner that everyone likes.* **ant.** irritating, annoying.

pleasure *n.* **1.** delight, satisfaction, enjoyment, gladness, happiness, joy, well-being, gratification: *Stefan gets a great deal of pleasure out of spending a day with his grandchildren.* **2.** luxury, indulgence: *His pleasures are his greatest weakness.* **ant.** **1.** pain, discomfort, torment. **2.** obligation, duty, responsibility.

pledge *n.* promise, agreement, commitment, oath: *Ronnie gave his pledge to abide by the rules of the club if he became a member.* *vb.* promise, agree; swear, vow: *Timothy has pledged to help out at home after school.*

plentiful *adj.* abundant, bountiful, fullness, fruitful, copious: *The pioneers thanked God for a plentiful harvest during the first year.* **ant.** scarce, rare, scanty.

plenty *n.* abundance, fullness, fruitfulness, bounty, plentifulness: *If you examine what those in other countries have, America is the land of plenty.* **ant.** need, want, scarcity.

plight *n.* difficulty, predicament, dilemma, situation, state, condition: *Consider the plight of the orphan, who has no family to love him.*

plot *n.* **1.** plan, scheme, design, intrigue, conspiracy: *Some think that the oil shortage is the result of an international plot.* **2.** story, theme, outline, thread: *The acting in the movie was marvelous, but there was very little plot.* *vb.* plan, scheme, design, contrive, conspire: *The prisoners spent six months plotting their escape.*

pluck *vb.* snatch, pull, jerk, yank: *You have to pluck the feathers out of a chicken before cooking it, not after.* *n.* courage, bravery, nerve, boldness, determination, spirit: *It takes pluck to admit it when you've done something wrong.*

plug *n.* stopper, cork, bung: *She pulled out the plug and* *let all the water out of the bathtub. vb.* stop (up), obstruct: *The rust inside the pipes plugged up the whole system.*

plump *adj.* chubby, fat, stout, portly, fleshy: *Esmeralda has become quite plump from eating candy and drinking soda.* **ant.** slim, thin, skinny.

plunder *vb.* rob, pillage, sack, ravage, strip, raid, loot: *The conquering armies plundered the city till nothing of value remained. n.* **1.** booty, loot, spoils: *The soldiers needed many wagons to carry off their plunder.* **2.** pillage, robbery, sacking, sack: *The plunder of Troy lasted two months.*

plunge *vb.* **1.** submerge, dip, immerse: *I plunged my burnt finger into the cool water.* **2.** dive, jump, rush: *Davey plunged into the river to try to save the drowning girl. n.* leap, dive, jump: *We all took a plunge into the swimming pool before dinner.*

poem *n.* verse, poetry, lyric: *"Evangeline" is one of the longest poems in the English language.*

poetry *n.* verse; meter; rhyme: *My brother-in-law writes poetry that doesn't rhyme.*

point *n.* **1.** locality, position, location, spot: *Don has reached a point in his life where he doesn't want to waste time any more.* **2.** aim, object, intent, purpose, idea: *The point of my story is to show that you cannot afford to be dishonest.* **3.** meaning, import, drift: *You don't get the point of the joke, do you?* **4.** cape, ness, promontory: *We stood out on the point, near the lighthouse, watching the boats sail past. vb.* **1.** indicate, show, designate: *The boy pointed to the place in the wall where the man had disappeared.* **2.** direct, guide, head, lead, steer; aim: *I pointed the canoe homeward to arrive before sundown. Don't ever point a gun at anyone!*

poise *n.* **1.** self-control, control, assurance, composure, dignity, carriage: *Suzanne, although she's only 14, has the poise of a 21-year-old.* **2.** balance, steadiness, equilibrium: *That acrobat on the high wire has unbelievable strength and poise. vb.* balance; hesitate: *The diver poised on the edge of the high platform before diving into the pool.* **ant.** *n.* **1.** indelicacy, coarseness, boorishness, ineptitude. **2.** awkwardness, instability, uncertainty.

poison *n.* venom, virus, toxin, bane: *Children should never be allowed to touch or use poison of any kind. The spitting cobra can project its poison more than 20 feet. vb.*

infect, contaminate, pollute: *Exhaust fumes from cars poison the atmosphere in large cities.*

poke *n., vb.* stab, thrust, jab, punch: *When I teased Peter, he gave me a poke in the ribs. Don't poke that broom handle into the hornets' nest.*

policy *n.* tactic, strategy, procedure, approach, system, rule, management: *The government followed a policy that allowed employees to retire as early as 55 years of age.*

polish *vb.* **1.** shine, brighten: *When you've finished making the beds, you may polish the silver.* **2.** refine, finish: *The president polished his speech while he was on his way to the meeting.* *n.* **1.** gloss, shine, sheen, luster, brightness: *The furniture has such a high polish that you can see yourself in it.* **2.** refinement, finish, elegance: *The lady has excellent taste and polish.* **ant.** *vb.* **1.** dull, tarnish.

polite *adj.* courteous, thoughtful, mannerly, considerate, cordial, respectful: *One should always be polite to his elders.* **ant.** rude, discourteous, uncivil.

pollute *vb.* contaminate, dirty, befoul, taint: *The waters near large cities are usually polluted by sewage wastes.* **ant.** clean, purify, clarify.

ponder *vb.* weigh, consider, study, reflect, deliberate, think, contemplate: *I have spent many hours pondering over the best way to bring up children.*

poor *adj.* **1.** impoverished, poverty-stricken, needy, indigent, destitute, penniless, hard up: *There are many more poor people in India than in all the western countries combined.* **2.** bad, substandard, faulty, inferior, worthless: *The machinery made in this factory is of such poor quality that no one wants it.* **3.** unfortunate, unlucky, doomed, luckless, unhappy, miserable, pitiful, pitiable: *After the man's wife went away, the poor fellow just didn't know what to do.* **ant.** **1.** rich, wealthy, well-heeled, prosperous. **2.** good, excellent. **3.** lucky, fortunate.

popular *adj.* **1.** well-liked, well-thought-of, approved, accepted, favorite, celebrated, admired, famous: *Jack Benny was once one of the most popular comedians in America.* **2.** common, general, familiar, ordinary, current, prevailing: *The popular view of the scholar is of someone out of touch with the world, buried in books.*

populous *adj.* thronged, crowded, teeming, dense: *Tokyo is one of the most populous cities in the world.*

porch *n.* veranda, patio: *On warm summer evenings, the* *family used to sit out on the porch, greeting friends who came to visit.*

port   *n.* harbor, haven, anchorage, refuge: *As all sailors know, any port is welcome in a storm.*

portable   *adj.* movable, transportable; handy: *Putting a handle on top of this TV set isn't enough to make it portable —I can't even lift it!*

portion   *n.* **1.** share, part, allotment, quota, section, segment: *The city receives only a portion of the taxes paid to the state by its residents.* **2.** serving: *Tom ate three portions of apple pie with ice cream after that big dinner.* *vb.* apportion, allot, distribute, deal out: *The profits from the sale were portioned out to us.*

portly   *adj.* **1.** dignified, grand, impressive, majestic: *The countess was a portly dowager in her seventies who was crazy about hot dogs.* **2.** corpulent, stout, fat, heavy, obese: *The man buying that green suit ought to choose a darker color because he's so portly.* **ant. 2.** slim, thin, slender.

portrait   *n.* picture, likeness, representation; painting: *A portrait of Alexander Hamilton hangs in the National Gallery.*

portray   *vb.* represent, depict, picture: *The painting portrayed a man riding a horse. Penelope portrays a very old lady in the school play.*

pose   *vb.* **1.** model, sit: *When Janet was a student, she made money posing for fashion ads.* **2.** pretend, feign, act: *Donald posed as an expert on computers, but he'd never even seen one.* **3.** assert, state, set forth: *Getting an elephant for a pet poses the problem of how to feed it.* *n.* posture, position, attitude: *If you take a pose so that your face is in the light, I can get a much better photograph.*

position   *n.* **1.** location, place, station, spot, locality, site: *The position of that building causes it to block our sunlight during the summer.* **2.** condition, situation, state, status: *What is the postmaster's position in a small community compared with that in a large city?* **3.** job, employment, place, situation, office, occupation: *Raquel just got a very good position in the printing company.* **4.** posture, pose, deportment, bearing: *Your telling my wife about that party we attended has put me in an awkward position. For how long can you maintain that* *position of standing on one leg?* **5.** belief, view, attitude, opinion: *My position is that the teachers ought to be paid as much as the government can afford.* *vb.* place, situate, put, locate: *The painting must be carefully positioned in the frame for the best effect.*

positive *adj.* **1.** clear, definite, sure, certain, direct, unmistakable: *We gave the tourists positive directions on how to get there, but they got lost.* **2.** sure, certain, definite, obstinate: *Betty was positive that Jim had said to meet him at 8:00 o'clock.* **3.** practical, real; beneficial: *I want to see some positive effects before I approve another test of this plane.* **ant. 1., 2.** unsure, dubious, mixed-up, confused. **3.** negative, adverse.

possess *vb.* **1.** have, own, hold: *Everything Tim possesses can fit into his one small knapsack.* **2.** occupy, control, hold: *This small country possessed many colonies rich in natural resources. Dave was possessed by a fit of laughter.*

possession *n.* **1.** ownership, occupancy, custody: *The sheriff disputed our possession of the vacant house in the woods.* **2.** property: *That fountain pen is one of my prized possessions.*

possible *adj.* practical, practicable, doable, feasible: *It's possible that Sonja won the Olympic gold medal for pole vaulting, but it isn't very probable.*

post *n.* **1.** shaft, column, pole, pillar: *We built a bird house and put it on top of a tall post in the garden.* **2.** job, position, office: *Donna's father was appointed to an important post in the embassy.* **3.** position, station, location: *The sentry didn't leave his post to investigate the eerie noises.* **4.** fort, camp, base: *The soldiers from the nearby post came into town on Saturday nights to have a good time.* *vb.* **1.** mail: *The letter I posted last evening in New York arrived in Dubuque this morning.* **2.** assign, station, position: *There were two guards posted at the gate.*

postpone *vb.* delay, defer, put off: *The coach's decision about who was going to play in the big game was postponed till after exam week.*

pot *n.* saucepan, kettle, vessel: *That pot won't be big enough for cooking all the spaghetti.*

potent *adj.* powerful, strong, mighty; influential, convincing, effective: *Penicillin is a potent medicine. The president gave some potent arguments for higher taxes in his speech.* **ant.** impotent, weak, powerless, feeble.

potential *adj.* **1.** possible; likely: *Ken is a potential mem-*

ber of the varsity swimming team. **2.** latent, hidden, dormant: *The potential energy of the hydrogen atom is unbelievably great.* *n.* potentiality, capacity, ability: *Renee has good potential as a soprano.*

pouch *n.* sack, bag; container: *Johnny Appleseed always carried with him a pouch filled with apple seeds.*

pound *vb.* beat, strike, hit: *The senator kept pounding on his desk with his shoe.*

pour *vb.* flow: *The water pours from that spout into the barrel every time it rains.*

poverty *n.* **1.** need, want, indigence, destitution, distress, pennilessness: *Many of Dickens' characters lived in the worst of poverty in 19th-century England.* **2.** scarcity, lack, scantiness, scarceness: *Comic books may be fun to read sometimes, but they suffer from a poverty of expression.* **ant. 1.** wealth, richness, comfort. **2.** abundance, fruitfulness.

power *n.* **1.** ability, capability: *It isn't within my power to grant you permission to stay home from school.* **2.** force, energy, strength, might, vigor: *It takes a lot of power to hit a baseball over the fence for a home run.* **3.** authority, command, control, rule, sovereignty: *When the Democrats came into power, they passed many laws dealing with restoring a healthy envrionment.*

powerful *adj.* **1.** strong, mighty, potent: *The blacksmith was a huge, powerful man who could lift an anvil with one hand.* **2.** influential, effective, convincing: *The FBI is a powerful arm of law enforcement of the U.S. government.* **ant. 1.** weak, powerless. **2.** ineffectual.

practical *adj.* possible, workable, doable, achievable, attainable: *The most practical way to get the job done is to hire qualified people to do it.* **ant.** impractical, visionary.

practice *n.* **1.** habit, custom, usage, tradition: *Breaking a bottle over the bow of a ship at its launching is a well-established practice.* **2.** operation, action, performance: *Your theory sounds fine, but how can it be reduced to practice?* **3.** exercise, drill, repetition: *Practice makes perfect.* *vb.* **1.** exercise, drill, repeat: *If you practice, they may let you play the piano in the school orchestra instead of the kazoo.* **2.** observe, follow, pursue: *You should practice what you preach.* **3.** do, exercise, work at; function: *My uncle practices medicine in Kalamazoo.*

practiced *adj.* skilled, adept, expert, able: *Sophie is a practiced violinist.* **ant.** inept.

prairie   *n.* grassland, plain, steppe, savanna: *It took the pioneers many days to cross the prairie in covered wagons, which were also called "prairie schooners."*

praise   *vb.* commend, laud, applaud, admire, celebrate: *Fran's dog was very pleased when she praised him for doing a trick correctly.* *n.* commendation, compliment, approval, kudos: *Praise from one's friends is often more valued than praise from one's parents.* **ant.** *vb.* disapprove, condemn, criticize. *n.* criticism, negation.

pray   *vb.* beseech, beg, entreat, supplicate, importune: *It makes no difference how hard you pray or whom you pray to, only studying hard will help you pass that examination.*

prayer   *n.* request, appeal, entreaty: *Do you say your prayers before going to bed each night?*

preach   *vb.* moralize, lecture, teach; urge: *Tony's grandfather preached in the midwest, trying to make sinners reform.*

precaution   *n.* forethought, care, foresight, prudence: *As a precaution, you should always close the cover of a matchbook before striking a match.*

precedence   *n.* priority, preference: *What others wish should sometimes take precedence over what you wish to do.*

precedent   *n.* example, criterion, model: *Allowing Cory to go home early may set a precedent that will prove hard to follow.*

precious   *adj.*   **1.** valuable, costly, priceless, expensive, dear: *Jewelers today have only fake jewelry in their shop windows: the precious jewelry is kept in the safe.* **2.** beloved, dear, cherished, favorite: *The memory of the masked ball is so precious to Phoebe that she'll never forget it.*

precipice   *n.* cliff, bluff, crag: *The car hung, balanced at the edge of the precipice above the valley below.*

precipitate   *adj.* sudden, swift, hasty, speedy: *We had to make a precipitate decision, for the tree was about to fall.* **ant.** considered, gradual.

precipitous   *adj.* steep, abrupt, sharp: *At the end of the trail, the explorers came to a precipitous wall of rock, 1,000 feet high.*

precise   *adj.*   **1.** definite, exact, well-defined: *The pirates gave me a precise description of where I could find the buried treasure.* **2.** rigid, stiff, inflexible, careful, severe:

Only precise adherence to the rules is tolerated in this school.

precisely *adv.* exactly, specifically: *From her tone of voice, we could tell that the teacher meant precisely what she said.*

precision *n.* exactness, accuracy, correctness: *The navy flyers kept the fighter planes in formation with amazing precision.*

predicament *n.* quandary, dilemma: *Here was a predicament!: If I wanted a hot dog, I had to give up my ice cream.*

predict *vb.* foretell, prophesy, forecast: *No one can predict the future.*

prediction *n.* prophecy, forecast: *Have you heard the weather prediction for tomorrow?*

predominant *adj.* prevalent, dominant, prevailing: *The predominant majority has voted that all children should get free passes to the movies.* **ant.** secondary, accessory.

predominate *vb.* outweigh, prevail, rule: *The votes in favor of taking a vacation in the mountains predominated over those favoring a beach holiday.*

preface *n.* introduction, foreword, prelude, preliminary, preamble, prologue: *To find out what an author has in mind, it's a good idea to read the prefaces of books.* *vb.* precede, introduce, begin: *The speaker prefaced his remarks with some jokes that put everyone at ease.*

prefer *vb.* favor, select, elect, fancy: *I prefer chocolate ice cream to vanilla.*

preference *n.* choice, selection, option, election, decision, pick: *If I were to have a preference, I should like to move second at checkers.*

prejudice *n.* favoritism, bias, partiality, unfairness: *He has a strong prejudice against people who make up their minds without weighing both sides of the question.* *vb.* influence, convince, bias, warp: *If everyone claims to be prejudiced in favor of peace, why do we have wars?*

preliminary *adj.* preparatory, introductory: *Before you start recording the program, I'd like to make some preliminary remarks.* *n.* introduction, preface, prelude: *Now that the preliminaries are over, let's get down to business.*

premature *adj.* untimely, early, unexpected: *Because of my premature return home from the theater, I surprised a burglar in the cellar.* **ant.** timely.

preoccupied *adj.* distracted, absorbed, inattentive, meditative: *Irene was too preoccupied to notice that the train had already passed her stop.* **ant.** alert, aware, conscious.

prepare *vb.* ready, arrange, plan (for): *The two brothers had prepared dinner as a surprise for their mother.*

prescribe *vb.* direct, designate, order: *The doctor prescribed two of these tablets every four hours.*

presence *n.* **1.** attendance: *Samuel's presence at the meeting will be important to its success.* **2.** nearness, vicinity, closeness: *Please don't use such language in my presence.* **3.** bearing, personality, appearance: *The king of Madagascar was a man of tremendous presence.* **ant. 1.** absence.

present¹ *adj.* **1.** existing, current; being: *The present membership of the club is 25.* **2.** here, attending; near, nearby: *If you hear your name called, please answer "Present."*

present² *vb.* **1.** give, donate, grant: *The retiring employee was presented with a gold watch.* **2.** introduce, acquaint: *May I present my cousin, Ebenezer Gluck?* **3.** show, display, exhibit, offer, furnish: *Please present your tickets to the person at the door to the theater.* *n.* gift, donation, gratuity, tip, largess: *Toby received more presents for his birthday than anyone I know.*

presently *adv.* soon, shortly, right away, directly, immediately: *The doctor will see you presently.*

preserve *vb.* **1.** keep, maintain, conserve, save: *Preserve your energy for the next race.* **2.** can, conserve, cure, salt, pickle: *All of the vegetables we don't eat fresh we preserve and eat during the winter.* **ant. 1.** squander, waste, use.

press *vb.* **1.** push: *Press the button and the elevator will come.* **2.** squeeze, compress: *After the grapes have been pressed, the skins and pulp are used to make brandy.* **3.** embrace, hug, clasp: *Suzie pressed the shivering kitten to her bosom.* **4.** iron, smooth, finish, mangle: *Do you think you can press this skirt for me?* **5.** urge, insist on: *If I press you, would you be able to buy something for me if you go to the city?* **6.** push, crush, crowd: *So many people pressed into the subway car that I could hardly breathe.* *n.* **1.** pressure, urgency: *The press of business is so great that I cannot plan a holiday from the city.* **2.** the Fourth Estate; journalists, reporters, newspapermen: *The president gave a full briefing to the press before going into the meeting.*

prestige *n.* reputation, importance, influence, weight, distinction; renown, fame: *Sandra's father and mother have a great deal of prestige in the community.*

presume *vb.* suppose, assume, believe, take for granted: *Since you're wearing your bathing suit, I presume you are going swimming.*

presumption *n.* supposition, assumption, guess: *Your presumption that I am going out just because you see me wearing a hat happens to be false.*

presumptuous *adj.* impertinent, bold, impudent, fresh, rude, arrogant, forward: *It was very presumptuous of you to comment on the teacher's hairdo.*

pretend *vb.* **1.** imagine, make believe: *Let's pretend that you are a knight and I a damsel in distress.* **2.** falsify, fake, simulate, feign: *Don't try to pretend that you didn't know you were absent from school yesterday.*

pretense *n.* **1.** deceit, falsification, fabrication: *Tom made a pretense of trying to appear innocent.* **2.** lie, falsehood, deception: *Your story about going to the movies was nothing but pretense.*

pretentious *adj.* ostentatious, show-off, gaudy: *I still say that wearing an academic cap and gown to his daughter's grammar-school commencement was very pretentious.* **ant.** humble, simple.

pretty *adj.* attractive, comely, fair; lovely, beautiful: *Willie used to be such a pretty child.* **ant.** plain, homely, ugly.

prevail *vb.* **1.** predominate: *The minimum wage that now prevails is $2.50 per hour for most workers.* **2.** succeed, win, triumph: *Even though the forces of evil may seem to have the upper hand, in the end good will prevail.* **ant. 2.** lose, yield.

prevailing *adj.* current, common, habitual, general, regular, steady, universal: *The prevailing opinion among the strikers was to accept the company's offer. In the Caribbean, the prevailing winds are from the east.*

prevalent *adj.* common, prevailing, widespread, extensive: *After the earthquake, looting of shops was prevalent in the city.* **ant.** rare, infrequent.

prevent *vb.* block, stop, thwart, halt, check, interrupt, obstruct, retard, hinder, slow, deter, inhibit: *I was prevented from entering the building by the police.* **ant.** help, abet, allow.

previous *adj.* prior, earlier, former: *The colonel's previous order was to attack, but he has now decided to retreat.* **ant.** later, following, subsequent.

prey   *n.* victim: *The rabbit was easy prey for the bobcat.*
vb. **prey on,** victimize; seize, raid: *There was a band of
thugs in the hills that preyed on the villages for food.*

price   *n.* cost, charge, expense, value: *The price of food in
Britain has risen almost 25% in the past months. vb.*
value, rate: *We shall have to price all these goods before
putting them out for sale.*

pride   *n.* **1.** conceit, vanity, arrogance, self-importance, egotism, pretension: *John is so swelled up with pride over
his new job that I think he'll burst.* **2.** self-respect, satisfaction: *Stephanie has too much pride to ask her family
for money, so she works.* **3.** enjoyment, fulfillment, satisfaction: *Dick takes so much pride in his vegetable garden
each summer.* **ant. 1.** humility, humbleness.

primarily   *adv.* chiefly, mainly, essentially, firstly, originally:
This book is intended primarily for young people. **ant.**
secondarily.

primary   *adj.* **1.** chief, main, principal: *My primary purpose in being here is to help you learn.* **2.** first, earliest,
prime, original: *Our primary consideration should be
the safety of the participants in the race.* **3.** elementary,
basic, fundamental, beginning; grammar: *Primary-school
education usually lasts for six years.* **ant. 1., 2.** secondary.

prime   *adj.* **1.** primary; first; chief: *The prime effect of
education is to teach understanding rather than just
knowledge.* **2.** best, top-grade, superior, excellent: *I wish
I could bite into a prime sirloin steak, medium-rare,
right this minute. vb.* ready, prepare: *I wasn't primed
to leave tonight and need a day or so to get my things
together.*

primitive   *adj.* **1.** prehistoric, primeval: *In primitive societies, the men went out to hunt and the women stayed
home.* **2.** uncivilized, uncultured, unsophisticated, simple,
rough, rude, brutish: *Why is it that so many children
today have such primitive table manners?* **ant. 2.** cultured, sophisticated, cultivated.

principal   *adj.* chief, main, leading, prime, first, essential,
primary: *The principal problem lies in selecting the
right people to do the job. n.* chief, head, leader; headmaster, dean: *The board of education appointed a new
principal to the high school.* **ant.** *adj.* secondary, accessory.

principle   *n.* **1.** rule, standard, law: *The cafeteria operates
on the principle of first come, first served.* **2.** theorem,

law, axiom, proposition: *Democratic government was founded on the principle that all men have equal rights.*
3. honesty, uprightness, virtue, goodness: *My father was a man of very high principles.*

print *vb.* **1.** issue, publish; reissue, reprint: *We printed 2000 copies of the yearbook.* **2.** letter, block-print: *Please print your name legibly at the top of the sheet of paper.* **3.** develop; enlarge: *I had the pictures printed on glossy paper.* *n.* **1.** mark, fingerprint, sign: *The detectives found three identifiable prints on the door leading to the bedroom.* **2.** type, letters, printing: *Make sure you read the fine print at the end of the contract before signing it.* **3.** copy, lithograph, picture, photograph, etching, engraving: *The New York Public Library has a fine collection of prints by famous artists.*

prior *adj.* earlier, sooner, preceding: *I'm sorry I can't come to your party, but I have a prior engagement.* **ant.** subsequent, later.

prison *n.* jail, penitentiary, stockade, brig: *The convicted criminal was sentenced to 15 years in prison.*

private *adj.* **1.** personal, individual; special, particular: *What I have in my bank account is my own private business.* **2.** secret, confidential, hidden: *The congressman made his views known in a private communication to this reporter.* **ant. 1.** public, general.

privilege *n.* freedom, liberty, permission, right, advantage: *What gives Manny the privilege to turn in his homework late every week?*

prize *n.* reward, award, premium, bounty, bonus: *The company gives a yearly prize for the best suggestion made by an employee.* *vb.* value, esteem; estimate, rate: *Don's judgment is highly prized by the directors of the company.* **ant.** *vb.* undervalue, disregard.

probable *adj.* likely, presumable: *It's very probable that Ken will receive the mathematics award this year.*

probe *vb.* examine, investigate, inquire, scrutinize, explore: *The committee was established to probe campaign donations.* *n.* examination, investigation, inquiry, scrutiny, exploration: *The probe of senators' bank accounts revealed nothing of an illegal nature.*

problem *n.* **1.** difficulty, predicament, dilemma: *A problem has arisen in connection with my tax refund, causing a month's delay.* **2.** question; puzzle, riddle: *I couldn't do the last problem on the math exam.*

procedure *n.* operation, conduct, management, process, method, system: *What procedure should I follow to apply for an income tax refund?*

proceed *vb.* **1.** move ahead *or* on, go on, progress, continue: *Let us now proceed to the next house and interview the people there.* **2.** result, issue, spring, emanate: *The next step in the operation will proceed from the last one.* **ant. 1.** withdraw, retreat.

proceedings *n. pl.* record, account, annal, document: *The proceedings of the annual meeting were published in a large volume.*

proceeds *n. pl.* income, reward, intake, profit, return, yield: *Tom puts the proceeds from his investments into a savings bank.*

process *n.* course; procedure, method, system, operation: *In the process of saving the puppy, I lost my glasses. The scientist developed a new process for refining iron ore.* *vb.* treat, prepare: *George's father is the man who invented the technique for processing wood into paper.*

procession *n.* parade, cavalcade, train: *I sat in the doctor's waiting room, watching a procession of people go in ahead of me.*

proclaim *vb.* announce, advertise, declare, publish. *The president has proclaimed the week beginning June 9 as National Prune Week.*

proclamation *n.* announcement, declaration; promulgation: *The dictator issued a proclamation saying that everyone must be off the streets by 9:00 pm.*

procure *vb.* get, obtain, win, secure, gain, acquire: *You should be able to procure that book at your local public library.*

prod *vb.* nudge, goad, push, jab: *The cattle move a lot faster when prodded by a jolt of electricity.*

produce *vb.* **1.** bear, bring forth, yield, supply, give: *A ewe rarely produces twin lambs.* **2.** create, make, originate, generate, occasion, bring about, give rise to, cause: *The utility company produces energy from an atomic reactor.* **3.** show, exhibit, present, display, demonstrate: *The judge said that we had to produce proof of damages in order to have a valid suit.* *n.* product, production, fruits, crops, harvest: *We buy all the produce for the restaurant directly from the farmers to ensure freshness.*

product *n.* **1.** result, outcome, output, produce: *The product of all that hard work is my not worrying about* *earning a living in my old age.* **2.** goods, stock, commodity, merchandise: *American shops once refused to sell any products manufactured in Germany.*

productive *adj.* fertile, fruitful, rich; creative: *The soil on our farm is no longer productive. Patrick's productive imagination is always yielding new ideas for projects.* **ant.** wasteful, useless.

profess *vb.* declare, state, avow: *Ricky professes to know more about chemistry than the teacher.*

profession *n.* occupation, calling, vocation, employment: *Medicine, law, and teaching are professions but carpentry, plumbing, and boatbuilding are trades.* **ant.** avocation, hobby, pastime.

profit *n.* **1.** gain, return, earnings: *If I buy something for $10, sell it for $20 and have expenses of $5, my profit is $5.* **2.** advantage, benefit, gain, improvement: *I can't see any profit in continuing this dispute.* *vb.* gain, benefit, improve, better: *It doesn't profit you to say bad things about others.* **ant.** *n.* **1.** loss, debit. *vb.* lose.

profitable *adj.* gainful, beneficial, favorable, productive, useful, lucrative: *Even a fool knows that buying dear and selling cheap is not profitable. The corner grocery store was profitable enough to support the entire family.*

profound *adj.* deep, solemn, serious; wise, knowing, knowledgeable, intelligent, learned: *There is a profound difference between effort and success. The professor gave such a profound speech that no one understood it.* **ant.** shallow, superficial.

program *n.* schedule, record, plan, calendar, agenda: *There was a full program of activities for the three-day meeting.*

progress *n.* advance, advancement, movement, improvement, development: *The doctor was pleased to see that I was making considerable progress toward recovery.* *vb.* advance, improve, proceed, develop: *If Frank continues to progress in his studies, he may graduate early.* **ant.** *n.* regression. *vb.* regress, backslide.

prohibit *vb.* **1.** forbid, disallow, ban: *The fire laws prohibit smoking in elevators.* **2.** prevent, obstruct, stop, hinder: *A sprained ankle prohibits Jane from walking any faster.* **ant.** **1.** allow, permit. **2.** help, encourage.

prohibition *n.* ban, prevention, restriction, embargo: *The authorities issued a prohibition on the import of cigarettes.* **ant.** permission, allowance.

project *n.* **1.** plan, proposal, outline, scheme, design: *Your* *project for the new shopping center must pass the zoning board for approval.* **2.** activity, homework: *The children are going to construct a model Indian village as a homeroom project.* *vb.* **1.** propose, plan, outline, design, scheme: *How much time do you project will be required to clear the land for the building?* **2.** cast, throw: *The image from the film was projected onto the screen.* **3.** protrude, bulge, extend: *The corner of the table projects too far to allow the door to be closed.*

prolong *vb.* lengthen, extend, increase: *If you prolong the schedule one more day we shall miss the plane.*

prominent *adj.* **1.** well-known, famous, noted, notable, noteworthy, important, eminent, distinguished, leading, celebrated: *A prominent scientist had been invited to give our commencement address.* **2.** noticeable, obvious, conspicuous: *The error in the statistics was too prominent to be ignored.* *ant.* insignificant, unimportant.

promise *n.* assurance, pledge, oath, vow, word: *The manager gave his promise that our new dishwasher would be repaired.* *vb.* pledge, vow, assure, swear: *You promised that we could go to the movies if we finished all our homework.*

promote *vb.* **1.** advance, further, support, help, aid, assist: *To promote the sale of the vacuum cleaners, the store offered a week's free trial.* **2.** raise, elevate, advance: *Vickie was so proud when her father was promoted to foreman of the whole factory.*

prompt *adj.* timely, punctual: *The fireman's prompt action saved the lives of three elderly ladies. Please try to be more prompt at the dinner table.* *vb.* **1.** urge, arouse, incite: *Your reminder prompted me to phone to ask if you could come to dinner.* **2.** hint, suggest, propose, mention: *I don't need you to prompt me about buying flowers for my mother's birthday.* *ant. adj.* laggardly, tardy, late.

pronounce *vb.* **1.** utter, proclaim, announce: *The minister said, "I now pronounce you man and wife."* **2.** articulate, utter, enunciate: *When he was about nine, Eugene had difficulty pronouncing the letter "L."*

pronounced *adj.* definite, clear, noticeable: *There is a pronounced difference between parsnips and turnips.* *ant.* indistinguishable, minor, unnoticeable.

proof *n.* **1.** evidence, demonstration, testimony, confirmation: *The man accused of the crime offered proof that* *he was 1,000 miles away when it was committed.* **2.** test, trial: *The proof of the pudding is in the eating. adj.* protected, impenetrable, impervious: *This thick plastic is proof against bullets.*

proper *adj.* **1.** suitable, correct, fitting, just: *I think that making children who write on walls clean them off is proper punishment.* **2.** polite, well-mannered, decent: *When she's around grown-ups, Natalie is always very proper.*

property *n.* **1.** belongings, possession, possessions, effects: *Please remove all personal property from your lockers at the end of the school term.* **2.** land, real estate, acreage, tract: *My uncle just bought a large piece of property in Kansas.*

prophecy *n.* prediction, augury: *Your prophecy that I would fail my Latin course didn't come true—I got an A.*

prophesy *vb.* predict, foretell, divine, augur: *The fortuneteller prophesied that we would be wealthy by Christmas.*

prophet *n.* oracle, fortuneteller, forecaster, seer, clairvoyant, soothsayer: *If you predict sunshine and we have a hurricane, I'd say you're a pretty poor prophet.*

proportion *n.* **1.** relation, comparison, balance: *You must be careful to mix the ingredients in the correct proportion or you won't get an edible cake.* **2.** part, section, share, piece: *What proportion of the interest in the company do you think the investors have? vb.* adjust, balance, arrange: *The club members proportioned the work among themselves.*

proposal *n.* **1.** offer, suggestion: *I think we ought to accept Ted's proposal and let him donate space for the sale.* **2.** program, scheme, plan: *The company accepted our proposal, and we'll soon have the contract to build the ship.*

propose *vb.* **1.** present, offer, tender, recommend, suggest: *The union proposed a settlement that would give each employee a 20% raise.* **2.** plan, intend, expect, mean: *How do you propose to climb up the face of a sheer cliff 500 feet high?*

prospect *n.* **1.** expectation, anticipation: *Your job prospects won't be very good if you don't complete your education.* **2.** buyer, candidate: *Dan's father will be entertaining two business prospects at dinner tonight. vb.* search, explore, dig: *Last summer we went prospecting for gold, but we didn't find any.*

prospective *adj.* proposed, planned, hoped-for: *Susan's pro-*

*spective employer phoned to say that the job had been
filled.*

prosper *vb.* succeed, thrive, rise, flourish: *During the summer, George's business prospered, and he was able to
buy a new truck.* **ant.** wane, fail.

prosperous *adj.* wealthy, well-off, rich, thriving, flourishing,
well-to-do: *There are many prosperous businessmen who
live in our community.* **ant.** poor, impoverished.

protect *vb.* shield, guard, defend: *If you want to live alone
in a city apartment, you should get a dog to protect
yourself.*

protection *n.* **1.** guard, security, shield, safety: *The shed
provided protection against the rain. That small dog
won't give you much protection against burglars.* **2.**
assurance, safeguard: *You don't carry enough insurance
to provide protection in case of illness.*

protest *n.* objection, complaint; opposition, disagreement:
*Our protest against the way children were treated had
no effect on our parents.* *vb.* object, complain: *If you
didn't protest about the conditions here, no one would
do anything to improve them.* **ant.** *n.* approval, assent.
vb. approve, assent.

proud *adj.* **1.** prideful, egotistical, conceited, vain: *Vickie
is too proud to admit that she sometimes gets help with
her homework.* **2.** arrogant, haughty, self-important,
snooty: *The people next door are too proud to have
anything to do with us.* **3.** honorable, high-minded, dignified: *We respect the proud heritage of America.*

prove *vb.* **1.** show, demonstrate, confirm, verify, affirm: *If
that ring is pure gold you'll have to prove it to me.* **2.**
test, examine, try: *Now that you have the answer, prove
it by substituting that value in the formula.*

proverb *n.* saying, adage, maxim, byword: *"A penny saved
is a penny earned" is a good proverb, in spite of inflation.*

proverbial *adj.* well-known, common, general: *Scrooge's
stinginess is proverbial.*

provide *vb.* supply, furnish, equip, give, bestow: *The army
provides you with a uniform when you join—you don't
have to buy one.*

provision *n.* arrangement, condition: *Provision was made in
our agreement in case one of us failed to keep the
bargain.*

provisions   *n. pl.* store, supplies, stock: *We have enough provisions to last us only till the end of the week.*

provoke   *vb.*   **1.** bother, vex, irritate, annoy, irk, anger, enrage: *Don't provoke me any more or I won't let you go to the game on Saturday.*   **2.** cause, occasion, bring about: *The articles in the newspaper provoked many senators to vote for the antipollution bill.*

prowl   *vb.* slink, sneak, lurk: *The police caught a man prowling around behind our house last night.*

prudence   *n.*   **1.** carefulness, care, caution, tact: *By remaining silent on the war issue, Tom exercised good judgment and prudence.*   **2.** wisdom, judgment, foresight, common sense: *Don showed prudence in not asking the teacher a lot of silly questions.* **ant.** rashness, recklessness, foolishness.

prudent   *adj.*   **1.** wise, discreet, careful, sensible: *You should be more prudent in what you say to others lest you hurt their feelings.*   **2.** provident, reasonable: *When I want advice on prudent investments, I ask someone who knows.* **ant.** **1.** rash, reckless, foolish, foolhardy.

pry   *vb.* peep, peer, peek, meddle: *You're always prying into other people's affairs.*

public   *n.* society, people: *The public has a right to know about the workings of government. adj.* **1.** common; governmental, municipal, civil, federal: *This is a public park and I have every right to be in it.* **2.** free: *I went to a public high school.* **ant.** *adj.* private.

publish   *vb.*   **1.** issue, distribute, bring out: *During his career, Alfred published many worthwhile works of literature.*   **2.** announce, declare, proclaim, disclose, reveal, publicize: *The state lottery commission publishes the winners' names each week.*

pull   *vb.* drag, draw: *You seldom see a horse pulling a wagon any more. vb. phr.* **pull apart** separate, divide: *The referee couldn't pull the wrestlers apart.* **pull away** leave, depart: *Just as I arrived, I saw the train pulling away.* **pull down** wreck, destroy, raze: *The company is going to pull down the old factory.* **pull off** remove: *I pulled off my burning clothes and dived into the water.* **pull out** leave, depart: *The bus pulls out at midnight.* **pull through** survive, recover: *James has had a serious illness, but the doctor said he'll pull through all right.* **pull up** stop: *I pulled up at the traffic light, waiting for it to change to* *green. n.* **1.** wrench, jerk; haul, tow: *I gave a hard pull and the handle came off.* **2.** *Informal.* influence, weight: *David's father has a lot of pull in this town.*

punctual *adj.* prompt, timely, on time: *Please try to be punctual in arriving for work in the morning.* **ant.** tardy, late, laggardly.

punish *vb.* discipline, chasten, castigate, reprove, lecture, scold: *The worst feeling is being punished for something you didn't do.* **ant.** reward.

pupil *n.* student, learner; undergraduate: *My Latin class has only three pupils in it.*

purchase *vb.* buy, obtain, get, acquire, procure: *We drove into the village once a week to purchase groceries and other supplies. n.* buying, shopping, acquisition: *Ernest made two purchases in the hardware store.*

pure *adj.* **1.** unmixed, genuine, simple, undiluted: *This sweater is made of pure wool.* **2.** spotless, untainted, clean, uncontaminated, unpolluted: *The spring gave abundant pure water.* **3.** innocent, good, chaste, virtuous: *The priest led a completely pure existence.* **ant. 1.** adulterated, mixed. **2.** dirty, foul, tainted. **3.** immoral, licentious.

purely *adv.* completely, entirely, totally: *Fred's comment was purely intended to be complimentary, not sarcastic.*

purpose *n.* **1.** intention, intent, object, end, aim, objective, goal: *My purpose in life is to help people learn as much as possible about the English language.* **2.** use, application: *What is the purpose of this device? n. phr.* **on purpose** intentionally, deliberately: *You stepped on my toe on purpose!*

pursue *vb.* follow, chase, hound, track: *The police pursued the fugitive through three states.*

pursuit *n.* chase, hunt: *The pursuit of the fox led us deep into the forest.*

push *vb.* **1.** force, shove, thrust: *Kim pushed a pencil through the hole in the wall.* **2.** press, shove: *The crowd pushed me right back onto the train I had just left.*

put *vb.* **1.** place, set: *Please put the tray down on the table.* **2.** attach, establish, assign: *Don't put too much emphasis on how much money your friends have.* **3.** express, state, say: *It wasn't so much what George said as how he put it that was so clever. vb. phr.* **put aside** save, keep: *My mother always put a little money aside for a rainy day.* **put away 1.** save, set aside, store: *I had a little bit put away for your birthday.* **2.** commit: *That* *crazy old man ought to be put away.* **put down** defeat, repress: *You really put that fellow down when he tried to insult you.* **put off 1.** delay, postpone: *Don't put off till tomorrow what you can do today.* **2.** disconcert: *Stanley was put off by the rude way the hotel manager spoke to him.* **put on 1.** don; dress, attire: *Please don't put on your purple shirt with the green trousers.* **2.** pretend, fake, feign: *Don't put on airs with me, young man.* **3.** stage, produce, present: *The Royal Shakespeare Company is putting on* Macbeth. **put out 1.** extinguish, douse: *Put out that match!* **2.** discomfort, inconvenience: *I hope it won't put you out if I stay for tea.* **3.** extend, offer: *Sam put out his hand and I shook it warmly.* **4.** eject; discard: *Don't forget to put out the garbage after dinner.* **put through** effect, achieve, do: *The lawmakers put through the new tax bill.* **put up 1.** preserve; can, smoke, pickle: *We put up tomatoes and beans every year.* **2.** erect, build, construct: *I hope they put up a new movie theater nearby.* **put up with** endure, stand, tolerate, suffer: *I can't understand how you can put up with Deirdre's constant complaining.*

puzzle *n.* confusion, question, riddle, problem: *It's a puzzle to me how your cousin, who is so lazy, can keep his job.* *vb.* confuse, perplex, bewilder, mystify: *I was puzzled by your comment, but now I understand what you meant.*

⋹ৡ Q ৡ⋼

quaint *adj.* **1.** strange, unusual, odd, curious, uncommon: *Tourists often commented on the quaint customs of the people in town.* **2.** old-fashioned, antiquated, antique, picturesque: *My aunt still makes quilts using those quaint old stitches.* **ant. 1.** common, commonplace, ordinary.

quake *vb.* tremble, shake, quiver, shudder: *The leaves of the aspen tree quake in the slightest breeze.* *n.* earthquake, temblor: *The mild quake yesterday rattled the doors and windows in my neighborhood.*

qualify *vb.* **1.** suit, fit, befit: *The interviewer told Rosette that she didn't qualify for the job.* **2.** limit, restrict, change: *Instead of making a general statement, you ought to qualify your remarks.*

quality *n.* **1.** attribute, property, characteristic, character, trait, feature: *A good doctor has the quality of sympathy in his basic nature.* **2.** grade, rank, status, condition: *What is the quality of a European education?*

quantity *n.* amount, extent, mass, bulk, measure, number: *Can you estimate the quantity of pennies in the jar and win the prize?*

quarrel *n.* argument, dispute, disagreement, difference, spat, tiff, fight: *The quarrel between my brother and me arose because he wanted me to stay home while he went to the movies.* *vb.* argue, dispute, disagree, differ, squabble, bicker, spar, fight: *Our children seldom quarrel about anything.*

quarrelsome *adj.* edgy, testy, irritable, peevish, snappish, disagreeable: *Stewart has a tendency to be quarrelsome, which gets him into many unnecessary arguments.* **ant.** even-tempered, genial.

queer *adj.* odd, peculiar, unusual, extraordinary, uncommon: *People sometimes do the queerest things, like flag-pole sitting.* **ant.** ordinary, conventional, usual.

quench *vb.* satisfy, slake: *That sweet soda can't really quench your thirst.*

query *n.* inquiry, question: *If you have a query about the assignment, please ask your teacher.* *vb.* inquire, question,

268

ask: *Don't query me about physics and chemistry, I'm the Spanish teacher.*

quest   *n.* search, journey, hunt: *The quest for the Holy Grail was the source of many medieval romances.*

question   *n.*   **1.** query, inquiry: *Timmy, if you have a question, please raise your hand.* **2.** doubt, uncertainty: *There has been some question about whether John could visit us.* *vb.* **1.** query, ask, inquire, interview: *The police questioned the man closely.* **2.** doubt; suspect: *How dare you question my honesty?* **ant.** *n.* **1.** answer, solution. *vb.* **1.** answer, reply, respond.

quick   *adj.*   **1.** rapid, swift, fast, speedy: *Walter plays a lot of tennis and is very quick on his feet.* **2.** impatient, abrupt, hasty, curt: *You must learn not to be so quick with people who aren't as intelligent as you.* **3.** prompt, ready, immediate: *The quick answer to your question is "No," but I should explain that more fully.* **ant.** **1.** slow, sluggish. **2.** patient.

quiet   *adj.*   **1.** silent, still, soundless, mute: *Please be quiet in the library.* **2.** tranquil, peaceful, calm, restful: *The patient was finally quiet after a restless night.* *vb.* **1.** silence, still, hush, mute, soften: *You'd better quiet down or the neighbors will complain.* **2.** calm, cool, relax, pacify, subdue: *Though Father was extremely angry at first, we quieted him with our explanation of how the fender had been scraped.* *n.* silence, stillness, peace, peacefulness, calm, calmness: *You could hear a pin drop in the quiet.* **ant.** *adj.* **1.** noisy, loud, boisterous. **2.** perturbed, anxious, fitful.

quit   *vb.*   **1.** leave, depart, vacate: *You should seriously reconsider before deciding to quit school.* **2.** stop, cease, discontinue: *Quit teasing Anne about having red hair.* **3.** resign, leave: *After 25 years without a promotion, Bill quit.*

quite   *adv.*   **1.** rather, somewhat: *I was quite annoyed when the boys hit a baseball through my window.* **2.** completely, entirely, wholly: *If you have quite finished talking, I should like to say something.*

quiver   *vb.* shake, quake, tremble, shudder, shiver, vibrate: *Every time a truck goes by, I feel the house quiver.*

R

race¹ *n.* **1.** contest, competition, run, meet, match: *When Mel entered the race, he had no idea he would win.* **2.** stream, course: *The race under the mill was strong enough to turn the paddle-wheel. vb.* **1.** run, compete, contend: *Phil wasn't allowed to race on Saturday because of his sore ankle.* **2.** hurry, run, speed, dash, hasten: *We raced to finish our homework before the noon deadline.* **ant.** *vb.* **2.** dawdle, linger, dwell.

race² *n.* family, kind, strain, breed, people, nation, tribe, stock: *The Mongolian race developed in Asia.*

rack *n.* framework, frame, bracket: *Hang your clothes on the rack alongside the door.*

racket *n.* noise, hubbub, disturbance, fuss, uproar, din, tumult: *The chickens in my neighbor's yard make a terrible racket every morning.*

radiant *adj.* bright, shining, beaming, brilliant: *In my dream, a radiant halo surrounded the head of the angel.* **ant.** dim, lusterless, dark.

radiate *vb.* emit, spread, shed, diffuse, irradiate: *Peter radiates good will everywhere he goes. The sun radiates light and warmth.*

radical *adj.* **1.** basic, fundamental, essential: *We shall have to make radical changes in our plans if we can't use the hall.* **2.** extreme, thorough, revolutionary: *The radical element in the organization has been warned about the disturbances.*

rag *n.* dishrag, dishclout, wiper, remnant; cloth: *Polish the silverware with a clean rag.*

rage *n.* **1.** anger, fury, wrath: *The director's rage at the news that his screen credit had been omitted was huge.* **2.** fad, fashion, craze, vogue, mania: *Except for a few diehards, the hula-hoop rage has passed. vb.* **1.** fume, rant, rave, storm: *When he found that the dog had eaten his dinner, Father raged about the house for an hour.* **2.** storm, overflow; burn: *The hurricane raged all about us. The fire raged out of control for three hours.*

ragged *adj.* torn, tattered, shredded, worn: *I wish you wouldn't wear that ragged sweater when you visit your aunt.*

raid *n.* **1.** attack, assault, invasion: *The commandos planned a raid on the submarine base.* **2.** arrest; seizure: *Aunt Martha was caught in the police raid of the gambling casino.* *vb.* attack, assault, invade, maraud: *The ammunition dump was raided last night.*

rail *n.* fence, railing, bar: *They raised the rail a notch higher and the horse couldn't jump over it.*

rain *n.* drizzle, sprinkle, shower, rainstorm, deluge: *I hope the rain keeps up—up in the sky, that is!*

raise *vb.* **1.** lift, elevate, hoist: *Please raise your hand if you wish to speak in class.* **2.** rear, bring up; cultivate: *My mother raised 12 children. Mr. Green raises corn on his farm.* **3.** rouse, awaken, excite: *Our hopes were raised when we spied a sail.* **4.** increase; enlarge: *Your salary will be raised by 10 percent next week.* *n.* increase, rise: *A raise in salary might not cover my expenses.* **ant.** *vb.* **1.** lower. **4.** decrease, lessen, reduce. *n.* decrease, reduction, cut.

ramble *vb.* amble, stroll, saunter, wander, walk: *We rambled through the meadow looking for wildflowers to pick.* *n.* stroll, walk: *Let's take a ramble along the beach.*

random *adj.* chance, haphazard, unplanned, unscheduled, irregular, casual: *Frank picked one random number and won $250 in the lottery.* **ant.** particular, specific, special.

range *n.* **1.** extent, expanse, area, limit: *Shelly was interested in a very narrow range of subjects.* **2.** pasture, grassland, plain: *The cattle were turned loose to feed on the range.* *vb.* **1.** vary, change: *The weather in our area ranges from bad to awful.* **2.** wander, travel, roam, rove, stray: *The prince ranged far and wide, through many lands, seeking adventure.*

rank *n.* grade, level, order, class, standing, degree: *Morris achieved a high rank among the officers in the company.* *vb.* arrange, order, sort, classify: *Eugene ranks at the top of his group.* *adj.* **1.** wild, dense, luxuriant, lush, vigorous, abundant: *The vegetation was so rank we could barely make our way through it.* **2.** smelly, putrid, offensive, foul, rotten: *A rank odor emanated from the sewer.*

ransom *n.* deliverance, release; compensation: *The child's ransom was earned when the family swore not to pursue*

the kidnaper. $50,000 is what they wanted for ransom.
vb. redeem: *I ransomed my car from the garage by pay-*
ing the repair bill.

rap *n.* knock, blow, thump: *Every time he played a wrong*
note, the piano teacher gave him a rap on the knuckles.
vb. **1.** knock, cuff, thump, whack: *When you get there,*
rap three times and ask for Joe. **2.** (*slang*) discuss, talk
(over): *We were rapping about sports all evening.*

rapid *adj.* quick, swift, speedy, fast: *Lenore gave a rapid*
response to the question. **ant.** slow, sluggish, halting.

rapture *n.* joy, bliss, ecstasy, delight: *Marie experienced such*
rapture whenever she saw an Elvis Presley movie!

rare *adj.* **1.** unusual, uncommon, scarce, infrequent: *Good*
diamonds are expensive because they are rare. **2.** excellent, fine, choice, matchless: *The museum has a collection*
of rare paintings by 16th-century artists. **3.** underdone,
undercooked, red: *I enjoy eating a rare steak.* **ant. 1.**
common, ordinary, usual, everyday.

rascal *n.* **1.** villain, scoundrel, rogue, trickster, swindler,
scamp: *The rascal told me one story and you another*
about how much money he needed. **2.** imp, mischief-
maker: *That little rascal ate all the cookies.*

rash[1] *adj.* thoughtless, hasty, hotheaded, foolhardy, reckless:
If you think before you act, you can avoid doing many
rash things. **ant.** considered, thoughtful, prudent.

rash[2] *n.* eruption, eczema, dermatitis: *You know you have*
measles when you see a red rash on your chest.

rate *n.* **1.** pace, speed, velocity: *Alexa worked at a fast*
rate and finished everything in one day. **2.** price: *What*
is the long-distance telephone rate on weekends from
here to London? **3.** proportion, ratio: *The rate of increase*
in school dropouts was disappointing. vb. **1.** price, value:
The dresses in this shop are rated too much over their
cost. **2.** rank, grade, evaluate: *Jeannette is rated as one*
of the top students in the school.

ration *n.* allowance, portion: *During the Second World War,*
everyone was entitled to his ration of meat, butter, sugar,
and other foods. vb. apportion, parcel out, distribute: *The*
food was rationed out carefully among the marooned
sailors.

rational *adj.* **1.** sensible, reasonable: *The only rational way*
for us to find a new leader is to elect one. **2.** sane, clearheaded, normal: *People who really believe that the moon*

is made of green cheese are not rational. **ant.** **2.** irrational, insane, crazy.

rave *vb.* **1.** rant, rage, storm: *The king raved on about how his generals were plotting against him.* **2.** praise, laud: *Mrs. Johnston was raving about the new hairdresser in town.*

raw *adj.* **1.** uncooked, undone: *I love to eat raw carrots.* **2.** unprocessed, untreated, rough, unrefined: *The factory takes raw materials and converts them into finished products.*

ray *n.* beam: *The sun's rays penetrated the dusty windows of the old house.*

reach *vb.* **1.** arrive at, get to, come to: *We didn't reach home till after dark.* **2.** stretch, extend: *I could just reach up to the top of the door.* *n.* extent, distance, range, scope: *The criminals fled to Brazil, beyond the reach of the law.*

react *vb.* respond, reply, answer: *When Harriet was rude her mother reacted by cutting off her allowance.*

reaction *n.* response, result, reception: *My reaction to higher taxes is to give up my job and move to the country.*

readily *adv.* promptly, quickly; easily: *The newspaper editor responded readily to my letter.*

ready *adj.* **1.** prepared, done, arranged, completed: *The roast will be ready in an hour.* **2.** quick, prompt, skillful: *Whenever anyone said anything, the comedian was able to provide a ready wisecrack.* *vb.* prepare, arrange: *He readied himself to go out to dinner.*

real *adj.* true, actual, genuine, authentic: *Some people believe that Shakespeare's real name was Bacon.* **ant.** false, counterfeit, sham, bogus.

realize *vb.* **1.** actualize; perfect: *We realized a profit of $3 on the sale of the chair.* **2.** understand, be aware of, appreciate, recognize: *Do you fully realize whom you are speaking to?*

really *adv.* actually, truly, honestly: *Do you really think you'll be able to come to the party?*

realm *n.* **1.** kingdom, domain: *The queen's realm extended from one sea to the other.* **2.** area, domain, sphere, province, department: *In the realm of surgery, Dr. Franklin has no equal.*

reap *vb.* harvest, cut, gather, mow, pick: *The men were reaping the melon crop.* **ant.** sow, plant, seed.

rear[1]   *n.* back; rump, posterior: *At the rear of the house stood an old car. Hugo was struck in the rear with the paddle. adj.* back: *The rear window of the car was all fogged up.* **ant.** *n.* front.

rear[2]   *vb.* **1.** raise, bring up: *The little girl had been reared in a convent.* **2.** lift, raise, elevate; rise: *The horse reared on its hind legs.* **3.** build, construct, erect: *The shed could be reared by two men in one afternoon.*

reason   *n.* **1.** purpose, motive, cause, object, objective, aim: *What was your reason for phoning me at midnight?* **2.** explanation, excuse: *I have already given you two good reasons why you should study hard.* **3.** judgment, understanding, intelligence, common sense: *The decision is a matter of reason, not of opinion.* **4.** sanity: *The poor fellow painting the grass green seems to have lost his reason. vb.* **1.** argue, justify: *You cannot reason with an angry man.* **2.** conclude, suppose, assume, gather, infer: *I reasoned that the team that came in first won the race.*

reasonable   *adj.* **1.** sensible, rational, logical: *As a reasonable person, you must know that no family can survive on $20 a week.* **2.** moderate, bearable: *I think that $500 is a very reasonable price for that car, considering its condition.* **ant.** **1.** irrational, insane. **2.** outrageous.

rebel   *n.* revolutionary, mutineer, traitor: *The rebels attacked the president's mansion last night. vb.* revolt, defy, overthrow: *The peasants rebelled when told that there wouldn't be enough to eat.*

rebuke   *vb.* upbraid, chide, reproach, scold: *The teacher rebuked Peter for talking during an examination. n.* reprimand, reproach, scolding: *After the first rebuke from their parents, the children never again went near the cliff.* **ant.** *vb., n.* praise.

recall   *vb.* **1.** remember, recollect: *I recall having met you at last year's party.* **2.** retract, withdraw: *The auto company recalled all cars of the model that had faulty brakes. n.* memory, recollection, remembrance: *Vincent has total recall and can remember everything that ever happened.*

receive   *vb.* **1.** accept, get, acquire, come by, obtain: *I received my copy of the magazine today.* **2.** entertain; greet, welcome: *The ambassador is receiving guests in the front hall.* **ant.** **1.** give, offer.

recent   *adj.* late, up-to-date, new, novel: *A recent article in the newspaper gave a lot of information about Ghana.* **ant.** old, out-of-date, dated.

reception   *n.* party, gathering: *We went from the ceremony at the church directly to the wedding reception.*

recess[1]   *n.* hollow, niche, dent, opening, cranny, nook: *The golden idol was concealed in a narrow recess in the cave.* *vb.* hollow, indent: *I carefully recessed a shallow pocket in the floor where I hid the jewel.*

recess[2]   *n.* respite, rest period, rest, pause, break: *The children were allowed to buy milk and cookies during the recess.* *vb.* break, rest, pause: *The legislature has recessed for the Easter holiday.* **ant.** *vb.* convene, gather.

recipe   *n.* formula, instructions: *Have you tried that new recipe for chocolate cake?*

recite   *vb.* repeat; report, list: *Each student was asked to memorize a poem to recite in class the next week. Abner was able to recite the names of all of the U.S. presidents in chronological order.*

reckless   *adj.* thoughtless, careless, rash, wild: *Ned's uncle was arrested for reckless driving.*

recognize   *vb.* **1.** recollect, recall, know: *I recognized the bank teller as the man I had seen in the movie theater.* **2.** acknowledge, admit: *I recognize your authority to order me about, but I don't like it.*

recollect   *vb.* remember, recall: *I recollect seeing you in Ohio last summer, now that you mention it.* **ant.** forget.

recommend   *vb.* **1.** commend, praise, approve: *I recommended Brad for the job.* **2.** advise, counsel, suggest: *The board has recommended that a new school be built on the hill.* **ant. 1.** disapprove, veto.

reconcile   *vb.* **1.** unite, bring together, mediate: *The couple were reconciled after the misunderstanding.* **2.** adjust, adapt, settle: *Leon and Debbie have reconciled their differences and are friends again.*

record   *vb.* write, enter, register: *The clerk recorded every transaction in the ledger.* *n.* **1.** history, chronicle, account: *The record shows exactly how each member of Congress voted on every issue.* **2.** disk, recording: *I bought a lot of new records yesterday.* **3.** document, archive, register, annal: *The records of births and deaths were destroyed in the fire.*

recover   *vb.* **1.** regain, retrieve, redeem, salvage, recapture: *I recovered my balance after I tripped.* **2.** improve, better; heal, mend, convalesce: *The economic situation is bound to recover by the end of the year. Father has recovered completely from his illness.*

recreation *n.* amusement, entertainment, diversion, enjoyment, fun: *After studying all day, what do you do for recreation on weekends?*

recruit *n.* beginner, trainee; draftee, volunteer: *The new recruits were issued uniforms that didn't fit.* *vb.* draft, select, induct, enlist: *We were able to recruit seven people to join the navy last week.*

reduce *vb.* **1.** lessen, diminish, decrease: *I wish they would reduce the price on that dress I saw in the window.* **2.** lower, degrade, downgrade: *Since Al's father lost his job, the family has been in reduced circumstances.* **ant. 1.** increase, enlarge, swell. **2.** elevate, raise.

refer *vb.* **1.** direct; recommend, commend: *At the town hall I was referred to the motor vehicle office for my new license.* **2.** concern, regard, deal with, relate: *The word "energy" refers to any kind of power.* **3.** mention, suggest, touch on, hint at: *What do you suppose the doctor was referring to when he suggested I lose some weight?*

referee *n.* umpire, arbitrator, arbiter, judge: *The boxing referee took a very long time counting up to ten.* *vb.* umpire, arbitrate, judge: *On Saturdays, my father enjoys refereeing soccer games.*

reference *n.* **1.** direction; allusion, mention: *Your mother made reference to my dirty shirt, so I'd better change for dinner.* **2.** regard, concern, relation, respect: *You'd better not say anything in reference to Anne's going out with Morton.*

refine *vb.* **1.** improve, clarify: *My summer job certainly refined my ideas on how restaurants are run.* **2.** clean, purify: *Refined gold is almost 100% pure.*

refined *adj.* cultivated, polite, courteous, well-bred, civilized: *Bob's parents are such refined people.* **ant.** rude, coarse, brutish.

reflect *vb.* **1.** mirror; reproduce: *The strange face was reflected in the window of the shop.* **2.** think, ponder, cogitate, consider, deliberate, contemplate: *If you reflect on your experience a little, you'll realize that you are responsible for your own actions.*

reflection *n.* **1.** image, appearance, likeness: *I could see my reflection in the highly polished table top.* **2.** deliberation, consideration, study, meditation: *After some reflection, Len decided that he'd better go to the library after all.*

reform *n.* change, betterment, correction, improvement: *The new candidates campaigned on the promise to bring about governmental reforms.* *vb.* change, improve, better, correct: *The criminal promised to reform, so he was released on parole. We must reform the way we are mailing our magazine.*

refrain *vb.* stop, cease: *You should refrain from eating candy before dinner or you'll kill your appetite.*

refresh *vb.* renew, exhilarate, invigorate: *I felt completely refreshed after a cold shower.* **ant.** tire, exhaust.

refreshment *n.* snack; food, drink: *How about some kind of refreshment while waiting for me to change my clothes?*

refuge *n.* safety, shelter, protection: *We sought refuge from the storm in a cave that was close by.*

refuse[1] *vb.* turn down, deny, disallow, decline: *The teacher refused us permission to be a day late turning in our assignments.* **ant.** accept, allow.

refuse[2] *n.* garbage, waste, rubbish, trash: *The town used to dump refuse into the river, but that's against the law now.*

regard *vb.* **1.** look at *or* upon, consider, estimate: *Philip always regarded his brother as a better tennis player.* **2.** attend, respect, honor, value: *I regard very highly your ability to get along well with so many people.* *n.* **1.** reference, relation, concern: *With regard to your summer cottage, would you rent it to us this year?* **2.** respect, concern, estimation, esteem: *I hold the English professor in very high regard.* **3.** concern, thought, care: *Toby has no regard at all for his mother's feelings.*

regardless *adj.* despite, notwithstanding, aside (from); besides: *Regardless of your own feelings, don't you think we ought to bring a gift? I think we ought to invite Oscar, regardless.*

regime *n.* government, management, direction, administration: *Under the new regime, foreign visitors must register at the police station.*

regimented *adj.* orderly, ordered, rigid, controlled, disciplined: *The routine in some military academies is very regimented.* **ant.** free, loose, unstructured.

region *n.* area, place, locale, territory: *The northern region fell under the control of the invaders in a few weeks.*

register *n.* **1.** record; catalog: *All transactions were entered in the register daily.* **2.** list, book, record, roll: *Every* *hotel guest must sign the register. vb.* enroll, record; enter, list, catalog: *Please register for your classes before the beginning of the school year.*

regret *vb.* lament, bemoan, feel sorry about, be sorry for: *I sincerely regret having hurt your feelings, but I didn't do it on purpose. n.* sorrow, remorse, concern, qualm, scruple, misgiving, contrition: *My regret at having to leave before the end of the summer was heartfelt.*

regular *adj.* **1.** usual, customary, habitual, normal: *My regular routine gets me to the office at about 8:30 in the morning.* **2.** steady, uniform, even, systematic, orderly: *I could hear his regular breathing from the room next door.* **ant. 1.** irregular, odd, unusual.

regulate *vb.* **1.** govern, control, direct, manage, legislate: *The government doesn't regulate prices in a free economy like ours.* **2.** adjust, set: *Please regulate the heat in this room so that we don't freeze and boil alternately.*

regulation *n.* **1.** law, rule, statute: *There's a city regulation against parking in a bus stop.* **2.** management, direction, supervision, rule, order, control: *The Customs Service in the U.S. comes under the regulation of the Department of the Treasury.*

rehearse *vb.* practice, repeat; train: *Our class has to rehearse the play we're presenting to the rest of the school.*

reign *n.* rule, dominion, sovereignty; power: *How long was the reign of Henry VIII? vb.* rule, govern: *Queen Elizabeth II is the reigning monarch of the United Kingdom.*

reject *vb.* **1.** refuse, deny: renounce: *I don't know why my application was rejected, unless I misspelled something.* **2.** discard, expel, throw out *or* away: *The inspector rejected the radio as faulty.* **ant.** accept.

rejoice *vb.* delight; celebrate, enjoy: *When we heard that our team had won, we rejoiced. The people rejoiced in their newly found leader.*

relate *vb.* **1.** tell, report, narrate, recount, describe: *I shall relate to you everything that took place at the haunted house.* **2.** connect, associate, compare: *How do the angles of a triangle relate to one another?*

relation *n.* **1.** connection, association, relationship, similarity: *The relation between cause and effect is sometimes difficult to understand.* **2.** relative, kinsman: *I spent last week visiting some relations in Arkansas.*

relative *adj.* **1.** proportional; dependent: *The people in that house live in relative luxury compared with us.* **2.**

in regard to, about: *Relative to your request for permission to go to the movies, the answer is still no.* *n.* kinsman, relation: *The orphan had no living relatives.*

relax *vb.* **1.** loosen, slacken, let go: *The shark relaxed its hold on the raft, allowing it to drift away.* **2.** repose, recline, unwind, rest: *When my father comes home from work, he likes to relax for a while, reading the newspaper.* **ant. 1.** tighten, increase, intensify.

relaxation *n.* ease, comfort, rest: *Many people recommend the kind of relaxation you get sleeping on a waterbed.*

release *vb.* **1.** let go, relinquish, set loose, free, liberate, set free: *Stefanie released me from the promise I made not to tell anyone. I found a knife and cut through the ropes, releasing the prisoner.* **2.** let out, publish, proclaim, announce: *The company finally released the story about the president's award.* *n.* **1.** freedom, liberation: *After his release from prison, the ex-convict was able to find a decent job through the help of some friends.* **2.** publicity, announcement, proclamation: *The release was distributed to every major newspaper in the state.*

reliable *adj.* trustworthy, dependable: *I need a reliable car that won't break down every week. Tom is completely reliable and has shown up for work every day without fail.* **ant.** unreliable, erratic, eccentric.

relief *n.* **1.** ease, comfort: *The new medicine brought me some relief from the leg pains.* **2.** aid, assistance, support, help: *The relief plans for the poor have not yet been approved.*

relieve *vb.* **1.** ease, comfort, soothe, lessen: *That massage relieved the tension I felt.* **2.** spell, replace: *The new watchman relieved Bill at midnight so that he could go home early.*

religion *n.* faith, belief; persuasion: *Mohammedanism is a religion chiefly of the Middle East.*

religious *adj.* **1.** pious, devout, devoted, reverent, holy, faithful, godly: *Porter's family is very religious and goes to church every Sunday.* **2.** strict, rigid, exacting, conscientious: *Religious observance of the rules will keep you out of trouble.* **ant. 1.** irreligious, impious. **2.** lax, slack, indifferent.

relish *n.* **1.** satisfaction, enjoyment, delight, appreciation, gusto: *Nicole ate the vegetables with such relish—yet, I thought she didn't like them.* **2.** condiment: *I like relish on my hot dogs.* *vb.* enjoy, like, appreciate: *Vincent* *relishes the idea of baking his own bread.* **ant.** *n.* **1.** distaste, disfavor.

reluctant *adj.* unwilling, hesitant, disinclined, loath: *Harold was reluctant to go to the party because he didn't know any of the other guests.* **ant.** ready, eager.

remain *vb.* stay, continue, linger: *Sally remained after everyone else had left.* **ant.** depart, leave, go.

remainder *n.* residue, leftover, rest: *After the best part of the lumber is used for furniture, the remainder is sold as scrap.*

remark *vb.* say, mention, comment, state, note, observe: *Imogene remarked that she liked Sophie's new dress.* *n.* comment, statement, observation: *Your remark about Teddy's nose was really very unkind.*

remarkable *adj.* unusual, special, extraordinary, noteworthy, uncommon: *Don's recovery from his operation has been truly remarkable.* **ant.** average, ordinary, commonplace.

remedy *n.* cure, medicine, relief, medication: *In the old days, people thought that snake oil was a good remedy for almost any ailment.* *vb.* cure, correct, improve: *The town tried to remedy its budget problem by raising taxes.*

remember *vb.* **1.** recall, recollect: *I never can remember my cousin's telephone number.* **2.** memorize, retain, know by heart, keep *or* bear in mind: *I remember every word of a poem I learned when I was three years old.* **ant.** forget.

remembrance *n.* **1.** recollection, recall, memory: *My remembrance of the incident is nothing like yours.* **2.** keepsake, souvenir, memento: *I keep the remembrances of my visit to Canada in a small brass box.*

remit *vb.* **1.** pay; send, forward: *Please remit $2 with your order.* **2.** pardon, forgive, excuse, overlook: *The governor remitted the convict's sentence, and he was released.*

remittance *n.* payment: *Your remittance of $9.52 was received in yesterday's mail.*

remnant *n.* remainder, remains, residue, rest: *After the pattern had been cut from the fabric, the remnants were given to the children for making dolls' clothes.*

remodel *vb.* reshape, remake, rebuild, renovate, redecorate; change, modify: *We remodeled our kitchen last year and installed new appliances.*

remote *adj.* **1.** distant, far off *or* away: *Stanley went to a remote island off Maine in order to complete his book.*

2. slight, unlikely, inconsiderable: *You don't have even a remote chance of winning the lottery.* **ant. 1.** near, nearby, close.

remove *vb.* **1.** doff, take off: *Please remove your hat when you enter a building.* **2.** transfer, dislodge, displace, take away, eliminate: *The rotten stump was removed from the garden, leaving a big hole.* **3.** eliminate, kill, murder, assassinate: *The gang leader had removed all those who opposed him.*

render *vb.* **1.** make, cause to be *or* become: *Thirty families were rendered homeless by the flood.* **2.** do, perform; supply, offer: *Norbert rendered us a great service by fetching the groceries from the market.* **3.** present, offer, give, deliver: *The electric company renders a bill at the end of each month.*

rendition *n.* version, interpretation: *The school orchestra's rendition of the symphony was almost professional.*

renounce *vb.* **1.** give up, abandon, leave, abdicate, forsake, forgo: *The hermit renounced all worldly goods and went to live in a cave.* **2.** disown, reject, deny: *When my aunt married a man her father didn't like, he renounced her.*

renown *n.* fame, repute, reputation, glory, distinction, prestige: *Reggie's mother is a poet of great renown.* **ant.** anonymity, obscurity.

rent *n.* rental, payment: *How much rent do they pay for the shop?* *vb.* lease, let, hire: *We don't rent our house, we own it. Let's rent a car for the weekend.*

repair *vb.* mend, patch, restore, renew, adjust: *The painting was repaired so that you couldn't see the damage at all.* *n.* **1.** patch: *I can see where the repair was made in this glass.* **2.** reconstruction, rehabilitation, rebuilding: *This old house is in need of repair.*

repeal *vb.* cancel, abolish, end: *The higher court repealed the action of the lower court.* *n.* cancellation, abolition, end: *The repeal of prohibition put all of the bootleggers out of business.*

repeat *vb.* **1.** reiterate, iterate, restate: *I've already told you three times, and I shall not repeat it again.* **2.** redo, remake, reproduce: *Don't repeat your performance of last week—it was awful.* *n.* repetition, redo, remake: *All the TV programs during the summer are repeats.*

repel *vb.* **1.** repulse, check, rebuff: *The small force at the fort repelled the attacks all day long.* **2.** refuse, reject, decline, discourage: *Frances repelled all friendly advances* *when she first came to town.* **3.** revolt, revulse, offend, nauseate: *The smell of the marigold repels insects.* **ant. 3.** attract, lure.

repulsive   *adj.* repellent, offensive, horrid: *The war movie had a number of repulsive scenes that made me sick.*

reputation   *n.*   **1.** repute, name, standing: *Your reputation as an expert on fossils is excellent. If you are unfriendly, you may get a bad reputation.* **2.** fame, renown, distinction, prominence, prestige: *The doctor's reputation for success in treating arthritis has spread far and wide.*

request   *n.* petition, question, appeal, entreaty: *Your request for a leave of absence has been approved. vb.* ask, appeal, petition, entreat, beseech: *We requested 500 towels for the gym, and they sent us 500 trowels!*

require   *vb.*   **1.** need, want, demand, order: *Each student is required to bring his book to class.* **2.** call for, demand, need: *You will require diesel fuel to run the boat engine.*

requirement   *n.*   **1.** need, demand, necessity: *What requirements should you provide for when you go camping?* **2.** condition, prerequisite, provision: *There is no requirement that an applicant have experience for the job.*

rescue   *vb.* save, set free, liberate, release, ransom, deliver: *The firemen rescued eight children from the burning building. The knight rescued the beautiful princess from the castle dungeon. n.* liberation, release, ransom, deliverance, recovery: *The mountain climbers survived the rescue.* **ant.** *vb.* abandon.

research   *n.* study, scrutiny, investigation: *Research has shown that women live longer than men. vb.* study, scrutinize, investigate, examine: *Scientists are constantly researching the causes of major diseases.*

resemblance   *n.* similarity, likeness: *Any resemblance to real persons, living or dead, is a coincidence.*

resemble   *vb.* take after, look like: *David doesn't resemble his father at all.*

resentment   *n.* bitterness, displeasure, indignation: *Charley's feeling of resentment came from the unfair way he had been treated.*

reserve   *vb.* save, keep, hold, maintain: *I reserve some of my money for a rainy day. Please ask the restaurant to reserve a table for four at 8 o'clock.* **ant.** squander, waste.

reside   *vb.*   **1.** abide, dwell, live, stay: *Where are you residing now?* **2.** lie, abide: *Early scientists believed that* *the key to a person's health and personality resided in the fluids of the body.*

residence *n.* **1.** home, abode, dwelling: *The 25-room residence down the street was sold last week to a young couple.* **2.** stay, sojourn: *Because of my residence abroad, I don't pay taxes in America.*

resign *vb.* quit, abdicate, leave, abandon: *I resigned from my job last week.*

resolute *adj.* resolved, firm, determined, set, decided: *Dan was resolute in his decision about letting the children come home after dark.* **ant.** wavering, irresolute, vacillating.

resolution *n.* **1.** resolve, determination: *I thought that Alexa had shown remarkable resolution in the performance of her work.* **2.** statement, decision, recommendation, verdict, judgment: *The committee has approved the resolution that we allow women to join the club.*

resolve *vb.* **1.** determine, settle, conclude, decide, confirm: *The students finally resolved to plan a picnic for the following Saturday.* **2.** solve; explain: *Politicians have been unable to resolve the energy problem.* *n.* intention, purpose, resolution, determination: *Our firm resolve to return kept up our spirits.*

resort *n.* **1.** hotel, lodge, motel, vacation spot: *There are many winter resorts in the Caribbean.* **2.** relief, recourse, refuge: *Leaping across the chasm was the fugitive's only resort to avoid his pursuers.* *vb.* turn to, apply to, go to, use, employ: *Food was so scarce that the shipwrecked crew resorted to eating leaves and berries.*

resource *n.* reserve, store, supply, source: *The building of the Alaska pipeline was believed to destroy many natural resources.*

respect *n.* **1.** admiration, regard, honor, esteem, approval: *I have the greatest respect for your abilities.* **2.** particular, regard, detail, point, feature: *In many respects, I find John the most suitable person for the job.* **3.** reference, connection: *With respect to your wanting to go to the movies, you have our permission.* **4.** concern, consideration: *You should have more respect for your elders.* *vb.* honor, esteem, revere: *I respect your opinion, even though I disagree with you.* **ant.** *n.* **4.** disrespect, disregard.

respectable *adj.* **1.** acceptable, proper, decent, respected:

The president of the bank ought to be a respectable citizen. **2.** fair, passable, presentable: *I think that coming in second is a pretty respectable showing in a national contest.* **ant. 1.** disreputable, unsavory.

respectful *adj.* polite, courteous, well-bred, well-behaved, well-mannered: *Violet is a sweet, respectful child.* **ant.** rude, impertinent, flippant.

respond *vb.* reply, answer; acknowledge: *I wrote to Betty six weeks ago, but she hasn't yet responded.*

response *n.* reply, answer, acknowledgment: *I have had no response to my advertisement in the Sunday paper.*

responsible *adj.* **1.** accountable, answerable: *Who is responsible for writing this on the blackboard?* **2.** chargeable, culpable: *The man responsible for the accident has been identified.* **3.** able, reliable, capable, trustworthy, upstanding, honest: *Do you consider yourself a responsible member of the community?*

rest[1] *n.* **1.** repose, relaxation, inactivity, quiet, ease: *The doctor told my mother that she needed a rest after all that hard work this winter.* **2.** immobility, motionlessness, standstill: *The wheel came to rest on the number 17, and I had won $25.* *vb.* **1.** relax, lounge: *I have a cousin who does everything backwards: he works for two weeks, then rests up for the other 50.* **2.** lie, lean, depend, hang: *Our decision for the picnic schedule will rest on the weather report.*

rest[2] *n.* remainder, residue, surplus, excess: *After I have eaten everything I want, the rest goes to my dog.*

restful *adj.* quiet, peaceful, calm, tranquil: *Our cottage near the lake is the most restful place I know.* **ant.** disturbed, upsetting, tumultuous, agitated.

restless *adj.* nervous, jumpy, fidgety, unquiet, restive: *I'm so used to getting a lot of exercise that I get restless when I have to sit at a desk all day.* **ant.** calm, tranquil, peaceful.

restore *vb.* **1.** return, replace: *Please restore that book to the shelf where you found it.* **2.** renew, repair, renovate, mend: *The antique clock has been restored to its original condition.* **3.** reinstate, re-establish, reinstall: *After his military service, Len was restored to his old job at the press.*

restrain *vb.* control, check, hold, curb: *I just couldn't restrain my enthusiasm and leapt up, applauding.*

restraint *n.* control, self-control, reserve, constraint: *Even* *though you may get angry and feel like shouting, you should exercise restraint.*

restrict *vb.* limit, confine, restrain: *The manager's authority is restricted to the advertising department.*

result *n.* effect, outcome, consequence: *As a result of your misbehavior, the entire class will have to remain after school.* *vb.* arise, happen, follow, issue: *The return of the watch resulted from the ad in the paper.* **ant.** *n.* cause.

resume *vb.* continue, restart, reassume, recommence: *After each interruption, the speaker patiently tried to resume his talk.*

retain *vb.* **1.** hold, keep: *Retain the ticket stub when you enter the theater.* **2.** remember, recall: *Do you retain any of the poems you memorized as a child?* **3.** hire, employ, engage: *We retained a lawyer to look after our interests.* **ant. 1.** free, release.

retaliate *vb.* revenge, repay, return, avenge: *After I ate all of my brother's candy, he retaliated by hiding my shoes.*

retard *vb.* delay, hold back, slow, hinder, check, obstruct: *The strike retarded production of the new passenger planes.* **ant.** advance, speed.

retarded *adj.* backward, slow, behindhand; slow-witted, dull, stupid: *Every community should have classes or a school for retarded children who can learn at their own speed.* **ant.** advanced, quick.

retire *vb.* **1.** leave, part, withdraw, retreat: *The knights retired from the battlefield in order to regroup their forces.* **2.** resign, leave: *In our company, anyone who reaches the age of 70 must retire.* **ant. 1.** advance, attack.

retiring *adj.* shy, withdrawn, modest, reserved: *Because Minnie has a retiring personality, she seldom runs for election to the Student Council.* **ant.** bold, impudent, forceful.

retort *vb.* reply, respond, snap back, answer, rejoin: *"You know what you can do with your baseball bat!" Tom retorted angrily.* *n.* reply, response, answer, rejoinder: *Don't be so rude and don't give me any of your nasty retorts!*

retreat *vb.* retire, leave, withdraw, depart: *Soundly defeated, the regiment retreated to the safety of the fort.* *n.* **1.** departure, retirement, withdrawal: *In the face of the huge numbers of the enemy, the battalion's retreat was expected.* **2.** shelter, hideaway, refuge: *I bought a small retreat up in the hills.* **ant.** *vb.* advance.

return *vb.* **1.** go back, come back: *I returned home at midnight.* **2.** bring *or* take back: *When will you return the lawnmower you borrowed last summer? n.* restoration, restoring; deliverance: *The return of their lands to the American Indians is long overdue.*

reveal *vb.* disclose, communicate, tell, divulge, publish, announce, publicize, broadcast: *Rick and Norma revealed that they had been secretly married for a year.* **ant.** conceal, hide.

revenge *n.* vengeance, reprisal, repayment, retaliation: *Steve would get his revenge for Don's taking his bike by flattening the tires. vb.* avenge, repay, retaliate: *We'll revenge the insults to our team by beating them in the championship.*

revenue *n.* income, take, profit, receipts, proceeds, return: *The manager explained that his store had the greatest revenues of any in the chain.*

revere *vb.* venerate, respect, admire: *The mayor of our town is much revered for his fairness on all issues.* **ant.** despise.

reverence *n.* respect, homage, veneration: *I regard successful men and women with great reverence.*

reverent *adj.* respectful, honoring: *When you enter a place of worship, you should have a properly reverent attitude.* **ant.** disrespectful, impious.

reverse *adj.* opposite, contrary: *Why are the handlebars of your bicycle in reverse position? n.* **1.** opposite, contrary: *Bill said he would disapprove the action, but he did the reverse.* **2.** back, rear: *The coin has Washington on the front and an eagle on the reverse.* **3.** defeat, misfortune, catastrophe: *The army suffered one reverse after another when fighting the partisans. vb.* **1.** invert, transpose, turn: *The middle letters of the sign were reversed, so it read "LAIDES," which means "ugly people" in French.* **2.** repeal, revoke, overthrow: *The Supreme Court reversed the lower court ruling.*

review *vb.* **1.** re-examine, restudy, study: *I reviewed the plans for the new theater and made a few changes.* **2.** criticize, survey, inspect: *The new novel was reviewed in last Sunday's newspaper. n.* **1.** examination, study: *The review of the city's budget is scheduled for next week.* **2.** criticism, critique, judgment, opinion: *The movie at the local theater received a very bad review in the press.*

revise *vb.* alter, change, improve, amend, correct, update:

Please revise this paper and hand it in again next Monday. A revised edition of the dictionary contains many new words.

revive *vb.* **1.** renew, refresh, reanimate, rejuvenate, reawaken: *The book about the war revived people's interest in the Civil War period.* **2.** recover, rewake: *That 15-minute nap before dinner revived me completely.* **ant. 2.** tire, exhaust, enervate.

revolt *vb.* **1.** rebel, mutiny, rise up: *The peasants revolted in England in the 14th century.* **2.** disgust, nauseate, repel, sicken: *The sight of the injured at the train wreck revolted me and I was unable to help.* *n.* **1.** revolution, rebellion, mutiny, uprising: *The revolt of the masses in Russia took place in 1917.* **2.** disgust, revulsion, aversion, loathing: *What a feeling of revolt the sight of a dead animal gives me!*

revolution *n.* **1.** revolt, rebellion, uprising, overthrow, mutiny: *The French Revolution followed soon after that in America.* **2.** turn, cycle, rotation, spin, orbit: *The earth makes one revolution about the sun each year, and one revolution on its axis each 24 hours.*

revolve *vb.* turn, rotate, spin, cycle, circle: *Above the center of the dance floor, a mirrored ball revolved, glittering like a jewel as the spotlights reflected from it.*

revolver *n.* pistol, six-shooter, six-gun, gun: *The policeman fired his revolver into the air as a warning.*

reward *n.* prize, award, recompense, pay: *As a reward for saving the dog from the river, Dirk received a medal from the humane society.* *vb.* compensate, pay: *If you are good to people, you will be rewarded by their being good to you.*

rhyme *n.* **1.** verse, poem, poetry: *Putting the lesson in rhymes made it easier to learn.* **2.** similarity in sound: *Children are fascinated by stories told in rhyme, whether by Mother Goose or Dr. Seuss.*

rich *adj.* **1.** wealthy, well-off, well-to-do, affluent: *The big house on the hill is owned by the richest man in town.* **2.** abundant, bountiful, plentiful, fruitful, fertile: *The farmers will have a rich harvest this year.* **ant. 1.** impoverished, poor. **2.** scarce, unproductive, scanty.

rid *vb.* clear, free, shed, eliminate: *It was the Pied Piper who rid the town of Hamelin of its rats.* *adj.* clear, free, delivered: *I'm happy to be rid of that awful cold I had last week.*

riddle *n.* problem, puzzle, question, mystery: *How he managed to escape from that locked room is a riddle to me.*

ride *vb.* **1.** journey, tour, motor, drive: *We rode through the jungle on the back of an elephant.* **2.** drive, manage, guide, control: *Don't ride your bicycle on the wrong side of the road.* **3.** drift, float, go: *There was no opposing it, so I just rode along with the crowd during the election.*

ridicule *vb.* mock, deride, taunt, tease: *Don't ever ridicule anyone because he's different—he may be much better, too.* *n.* mockery, derision, burlesque, satire: *The writers held the politicians up to ridicule until they resigned.* **ant.** *n.* respect, praise.

ridiculous *adj.* nonsensical, farcical, absurd, laughable, ludicrous, comic, preposterous: *Painting that elephant pink is the most ridiculous prank you've ever done. The beautiful girl looked ridiculous wearing a false beard and mustache.* **ant.** sensible, sound.

right *adj.* **1.** correct, factual, accurate, true: *The calculation is right, but you have the wrong answer.* **2.** good, just, honest, upright, lawful, moral: *I know that you want to do what is right.* **3.** proper, suitable, apt, correct: *Phoebe knows which is the right fork to use for her salad.* *n.* **1.** justice, virtue, morality, goodness: *The right shall prevail and evil will be conquered.* **2.** title, claim, privilege: *You have the right to think whatever you like.* *adv.* **1.** properly, correctly, legally, honorably, fairly: *I believe that the reporter didn't get the story right.* **2.** directly, straight, straightaway: *I went right home after school.* **ant.** *adj.* **1.** wrong, incorrect, fallacious.

rigid *adj.* **1.** stiff, unbending, unbendable, unyielding, inflexible: *The leather belt was so rigid that I had to oil it in order to bend it.* **2.** severe, strict, stern, inflexible, harsh: *Why must the principal be so rigid about the rules?*

rim *n.* edge, lip, border, brim: *The rim of that glass is chipped on one side, so be careful with it.*

ring[1] *n.* band, fillet, circlet, loop, circle: *The ring of mushrooms in the forest meant that fairies and elves had been dancing there. Why don't you wear your diamond ring tonight? Because I don't have one.* *vb.* circle, surround, encircle: *The cliffs ringed us round, and escape seemed impossible, until I noticed something.*

ring[2] *vb.* **1.** peal, resound, sound, tinkle, jingle: *The doorbell just rang and I am in the bathtub.* **2.** summon; announce, proclaim: *Please ring this bell for service. Ring out the old year, ring in the new at midnight. n.* tinkle, jangle, peal, jingle: *To this day I can recall the ring of the old school bell.*

riot *n.* disorder, disturbance, tumult, uproar, confusion: *When the police prevented the people from buying flour, there was a riot in which 200 were injured. vb.* rebel, revolt: *The prisoners rioted because there wasn't enough food and clean clothing.*

rip *vb., n.* cut, tear, slit, slash: *The sword ripped through the drapery like a hot knife through butter. Nancy was embarrassed because there was a big rip in her dress.*

ripe *adj.* ready, mature, developed, grown, aged: *If it isn't fairly soft, that avocado is ripe enough to eat.* **ant.** immature, ungrown.

ripen *vb.* mature, age, develop, mellow: *These watermelons are best when they have ripened on the vine.*

ripple *vb.* ruffle, wave: *A light breeze rippled the surface of the pond. n.* wavelet, wave: *Tim threw a pebble in the lake and watched the ripples spread from the center.*

rise *vb.* **1.** arise, get up; wake, awaken: *We rose at dawn to watch the animals drink at the watering hole.* **2.** ascend, mount, arise, climb: *The string broke, and Dottie's balloon rose up into the summer sky.* **3.** prosper, flourish, advance, thrive, succeed, progress: *After marrying the boss's daughter, Bill rose rapidly in the company. n.* **1.** increase, addition, enlargement: *A rise in the cost of labor is soon followed by a rise in the cost of living.* **2.** ascent, climb: *The rocket's rise from the launching pad was noisy and swift.*

risk *n.* peril, danger, hazard, chance: *I don't think that the glory of having climbed the mountain is worth the risk of getting killed trying. vb.* chance, hazard, imperil, endanger: *Would you risk your life to run into a burning house to rescue a dog?*

risky *adj.* dangerous, chancy, perilous, hazardous, unsafe: *Investing all your money in a company that makes buggy whips is risky to say the least.* **ant.** safe, secure.

rival *n.* competitor, contestant, antagonist, opponent: *My rival in the boxing match is about 50 pounds heavier than I. vb.* compete, contest, oppose: *Your beauty rivals that of the rose. adj.* competing, opposing, opposed, competitive: *A rival suitor won the hand of the fair maiden.*

river *n.* stream, brook, creek, tributary: *This river has some* *of the biggest salmon in the northwestern United States.*

road *n.* way, roadway, street, avenue, highway, thoroughfare, boulevard, drive, turnpike, pike, parkway: *Take this road until you come to a traffic light; then turn left and go up the hill.*

roam *vb.* wander, ramble, rove, range: *With an hour to wait before the movie started, we just roamed around the neighborhood.*

roar *vb.* bellow, cry, shout, yell, bawl: *When the tiger became caught in the net, it roared until the jungle seemed to shake.*

rob *vb.* steal, pilfer, rifle, sack, pillage, plunder: *When I returned home, I found that someone had robbed my hi-fi set.*

robbery *n.* theft, pillage, plundering, burglary, thievery: *The police caught the burglar and he was sent to jail for robbery.*

rod *n.* pole, bar, wand, staff, pike, stick, baton, billy: *A steel rod from the truck's cargo was driven right through the wall in the accident.*

rogue *n.* rascal, criminal, outlaw, scamp, scoundrel, villain: *My grandfather had a reputation along the Mississippi as a gambler and a rogue.*

role *n.* part, character; task, function: *Theodora was selected for the leading role in the play. What role do temperature and dampness play in catching cold?*

roll *vb.* **1.** turn, revolve, spin, rotate, whirl: *A huge rock came rolling down the hill.* **2.** wind, tie, wrap: *Please roll up that cord so we can use it again.* **3.** flatten, press, level, smooth: *The baker rolled out the dough before cutting it to make cookies. n.* **1.** bun; bread: *After eating two buttered rolls, I was no longer hungry.* **2.** list, register, roster: *Please read the roll so we can tell if everyone is here.*

romance *n.* **1.** love affair, affair, enchantment: *The entire court knew that the queen was carrying on a romance with the butler.* **2.** novel, story, tale: *Romances were always very popular reading.*

romantic *adj.* unpractical, extravagant, exaggerated, fantastic, wild: *Penny dreamed she would someday meet a romantic lover who would sweep her off her feet.* **ant.** realistic, down-to-earth.

room *n.* **1.** chamber, enclosure: *We have an extra room if you'd like to stay over a few days.* **2.** space: *There was* *room for one more person in the elevator.* vb. lodge, stay, reside: *Dave rooms with a nice family who have a large house right near the college.*

root *n.* cause, origin, basis, reason: *Some people think that money is the root of all evil.*

rosy *adj.* **1.** pink, reddish: *At dawn, the sky became all rosy just before the sun came up.* **2.** fresh, healthy, ruddy: *After a week at the seashore, we all returned home in rosy condition.* **3.** cheerful, happy, bright, promising, optimistic: *Everything is beginning to look rosy again.*

rot *vb.* spoil, decompose, decay, mold, putrefy: *The fruit will begin to rot on the trees if it isn't picked soon.* *n.* decay, mold: *There was some rot in one of the planks of the boat, and we had to replace it.*

rotate *vb.* **1.** turn, revolve, spin, orbit: *The lazy Susan rotates in the center of the table and everyone can help himself to pickles and relishes.* **2.** alternate, take turns: *Instead of your dealing the cards all evening, why don't we rotate?*

rotten *adj.* **1.** moldy, decayed, spoiled, decomposed, putrid, tainted: *Food kept without refrigeration soon becomes rotten.* **2.** corrupt, immoral, dishonest, deceitful: *The government of the town had become rotten through bribery and greed.* **ant. 1.** fresh.

rough *adj.* **1.** uneven, unpolished, irregular, bumpy: *The rough surface of the furniture would have to be sandpapered before painting.* **2.** coarse, impolite, unpolished, rude, crude, unrefined: *The farmer's rough manners made no difference to us because he was so kind.* **3.** stormy, wild, violent, disorderly, turbulent: *The sea was beginning to get very rough, and we knew a storm was coming.* **4.** uncomfortable, inconvenient: *Life among the pioneers was very rough.* **5.** unfinished, hasty, crude, vague: *I saw a rough draft of the article before it was rewritten.* **ant. 1.** smooth, sleek. **2.** suave, sophisticated.

roughly *adv.* about, approximately, nearly: *There were roughly 212 million people in America 200 years after its independence.*

round *adj.* **1.** circular, curved, spherical: *That serving platter isn't round, it's oval.* **2.** arched, bowed, rounded: *The top of the tree is round now that it has been trimmed.* **3.** approximate, rough: *In round figures, I'd say 50 people came.* *adv.* circularly, around: *The merry-go-round went round and round.* *prep.* enclosing, encircling,

circling: *The costume called for her to wear a heavy steel collar round her neck.* *n.* routine, series, succession, cycle, course: *The doctor makes his rounds in the hospital every day, visiting each patient in turn.*

roundabout *adj.* indirect, devious: *Why don't you come right out and say what you mean instead of talking in a roundabout way?* **ant.** direct, straightforward.

rouse *vb.* **1.** awaken, waken, wake up: *I was roused at 4 o'clock in the morning to stand watch on the ship.* **2.** stir up, excite, stimulate: *The band played a rousing march.*

rout *vb.* scatter, defeat, conquer, overcome: *The enemy was completely routed by the attack from all sides.* *n.* flight, defeat, retreat: *When reinforcements arrived from the fort, the attackers were put to rout.*

route *n.* track, way, course, road, path: *The route across the fields is safer than the one through the forest.*

routine *n.* way, method, system, habit: *I generally follow the same routine every day, arising at seven and retiring by eleven.* *adj.* habitual, customary, usual: *The routine technique for frying an egg calls for melting the butter first.* **ant.** *adj.* uncommon, rare, unusual.

row[1] *n.* series, rank, file, array, order: *The commanding officer marched past a long row of soldiers who stood at attention.*

row[2] *n.* quarrel, spat, squabble, disturbance: *Whenever my cousin threatened to move out of the house, there would be a big family row.*

royal *adj.* regal, majestic, noble, sovereign, ruling, imperial; kingly, queenly, princely: *The royal scepter is carried in all of the processions.*

rub *vb.* scour, scrape; shine, polish: *Rub the table surface with sandpaper till it's smooth.*

rubbish *n.* **1.** waste, garbage, litter, debris, trash: *Please take the rubbish out when you leave.* **2.** nonsense, drivel, balderdash: *If she thought before speaking, maybe Mabel wouldn't talk such rubbish.*

rude *adj.* impolite, crude, unmannerly, uncivil, ill-mannered, coarse, impudent, impertinent: *I don't want anyone in my house who is so rude as to spit on the floor.* **ant.** courteous, polished, cultivated.

ruffle *vb.* disturb, disarrange, disorder, rumple: *The pages of the book were ruffled by so many children's having read it.* *n.* frill, trimming: *There was an old-fashioned* *dress in the museum with white lace ruffles at the collar and cuffs.*

rug *n.* carpet, floor-covering: *Please vacuum the rug after you've dusted the room.*

ruin *vb.* **1.** spoil, destroy, demolish, wreck: *Barbie's hairdo was ruined in the rain.* **2.** bankrupt, beggar, impoverish: *My grandfather was ruined when the company in which he had invested went broke.* *n.* **1.** rubble, wreck: *The grass grew among the few walls of the ruin that still stood.* **2.** destruction, devastation, decay, disintegration, dilapidation: *The ruin of the beautiful ancient Greek temples has deprived us of much architectural knowledge.*

rule *n.* **1.** order, ruling, law, regulation, guide: *If you want to get along with a minimum of trouble, follow the rules.* **2.** control, government, dominion, domination: *The islands off the coast don't come under the rule of the king.* *vb.* **1.** govern, control, manage, lead, conduct, direct: *The king ruled the country with an iron hand.* **2.** decree, decide, judge: *The magistrate ruled that the defendant should receive a trial by jury.*

ruler *n.* **1.** leader, governor, commander, chief: *The ruler of the tribe wore a feathered costume and had a bone through his nose.* **2.** foot rule, yardstick: *Put the ruler alongside this edge of the cabinet and tell me how long it is.*

ruling *n.* decision, decree, judgment: *The ruling was handed down by the Supreme Court that everyone must be given equal opportunity for education.*

rumor *n.* gossip, hearsay: *That news about your winning an Oscar was just a rumor, I guess.*

run *vb.* **1.** speed, hurry, hasten, race: *The man just snatched my purse and ran away.* **2.** compete, contest, oppose: *We all knew that the mayor was going to be a candidate for senator if his wife would allow him to run.* **3.** operate, function, work, go: *My car hasn't run properly since the accident.* **4.** pass; ferry: *The train runs only once a day. The boat runs between here and the island all the time.* **5.** stretch, lie, extend, reach: *This railway line runs from here right up the river to the state line.* **6.** flow, stream, pour: *The tears came running down Anne's cheeks.* *n.* **1.** sprint, dash, rush: *After a ten-minute run, I finally caught the train.* **2.** series, sequence; spell, period: *I've had a run of bad luck at cards lately.* *vb. phr.* **1. run away** escape, elope, flee:

The children ran away after breaking a window. **2. run down** hunt, seize, catch: *The bloodhounds ran down the escaped convicts in a nearby swamp.* **3. run into a.** crash, collide: *The two bicyclists ran into each other head on.* **b.** meet, encounter: *Guess whom I ran into at the movies last night.* **4. run out** lose, dissipate: *I ran out of money while on vacation and had to borrow from friends.* **5. run up** incur: *I ran up a large phone bill last month.*

rural *adj.* rustic, pastoral, backwoods, country, farm, agricultural: *The rural parts of the nation were just beginning to be electrified.* **ant.** urban, citified.

rush *vb.* run, hasten, speed, hurry, dash: *I rushed to the phone but the person who called hung up.* *n.* haste, hurry: *Dick came into the house in a rush—he'd forgotten his keys.* **ant.** *vb.* linger, tarry.

⋙ S ⋘

sack *n.* bag, sac, pouch: *We used to carry the coal in an old potato sack.*

sacred *adj.* holy, hallowed, divine, consecrated: *Everyone should treat a church as a sacred place.* **ant.** blasphemous, profane.

sad *adj.* **1.** unhappy, downhearted, sorrowful, depressed, dejected, melancholy, glum, downcast, gloomy, cheerless: *Mimi's kitten is lost—that's why she looks so sad.* **2.** saddening, discouraging, dismal, tragic: *I was just sitting down to dinner when they phoned with the sad news about grandpa.* **ant.** happy, joyous.

safe *adj.* **1.** protected, secure: *I ran down the street and didn't feel safe till I'd locked the house door behind me.* **2.** reliable, trustworthy, dependable: *Do you think that a hamburger stand might be a safe investment? n.* vault, strongbox, safety deposit box: *We don't keep important papers around the house but in the safe down at the bank.* **ant.** *adj.* **1.** dangerous.

safeguard *n.* protection, guard, shield: *That new lock on the door should be an excellent safeguard against a thief's breaking in.*

sag *vb.* droop, fail, weaken: *I could feel myself sag under the weight of the couch and asked the movers for help.*

sake *n.* **1.** reason, purpose, motive: *The lieutenant said he would carry the flag for the sake of the regiment.* **2.** benefit, welfare, advantage: *For whose sake are you wearing that flannel shirt on such a hot day?*

salary *n.* wage, pay, compensation, payment: *Dave found he could earn a higher salary if he changed jobs and worked for the boatyard.*

saloon *n.* bar, cocktail lounge, pub: *In the good old days, you could tell it was summer when the saloons went on half doors.*

salute *vb.* greet, welcome, receive: *When Lord Flimsy went to his club, his friends all saluted him with much respect.*

salvation *n.* rescue, deliverance; release: *Grasping that root as I fell off the cliff proved to be my salvation.*

same *adj.* identical, equivalent: *Susan was very unhappy that another girl was wearing the same dress as she.*

sample *n.* example, specimen, token: *The company was giving away free samples of soap and cologne.* *vb.* test, taste; examine, inspect: *Would you care to sample some of this ham I just baked?*

sanction *n.* **1.** permission, authority, authorization, support, approval: *You have the principal's sanction for putting on a musical festival at Christmas.* **2.** ban, embargo, penalty, punishment: *The Arab nations made sanctions against the countries that supported their enemies.* *vb.* approve, authorize, allow, permit, support: *Does your mother sanction that kind of behavior in public?*

sane *adj.* rational, sound, normal, balanced, reasonable: *The criminal was found to be sane and had to stand trial for robbing the old man.* **ant.** insane, irrational, crazy.

sanitary *adj.* clean, disinfected, hygienic, purified: *The gas stations along the road have sanitary washrooms that are safe to use.* **ant.** dirty, unclean, fouled, soiled.

sap *vb.* exhaust, weaken, drain, undermine: *That bout I had with a virus last month sapped my strength completely, and I felt as weak as a kitten.*

satisfaction *n.* **1.** pleasure, contentment, gratification, enjoyment: *My father got considerable satisfaction from my having made the varsity football team.* **2.** payment, repayment, amends: *The refugees demanded satisfaction from the Germans after the war, and many of them got it in the form of pensions.*

satisfactory *adj.* sufficient, okay, all right, adequate: *Victor seems to be making satisfactory progress in school.* **ant.** unsatisfactory, poor.

satisfy *vb.* **1.** fulfill, meet, gratify: *Will you be able to satisfy the camp's requirements for a swimming instructor?* **2.** cheer, comfort, please: *Jane's mother wasn't satisfied till she heard that the children had arrived safely.*

saunter *vb.* amble, wander, stroll, walk: *A well-dressed young man sauntered up to me and asked for $10 to have dinner.*

savage *adj.* **1.** wild, uncivilized, uncultivated, rough, rugged, crude, natural: *Before the pioneers moved westward the savage wilderness had never seen man's footprint.* **2.**

cruel, heartless, fierce, ferocious: *The man was the victim of a savage attack on his way home that evening.* n. aborigine, cannibal, native, barbarian: *The painted savages had begun their dance at the fire.* ant. adj. 1. tame, cultivated.

save vb. 1. rescue, free, liberate; preserve, salvage: *The fireman saved three people from the burning building.* 2. preserve, keep, reserve; hoard: *I managed to save $2 a week from the money I earned mowing lawns.*

say vb. speak, utter, remark, state, declare: *I don't think your mother heard what you said.*

scale n. 1. balance, steelyard: *Our bathroom scale makes you think you're five pounds lighter than you are.* 2. gradation, range; ratio, proportion: *The people who do hard physical work are seldom paid on the same scale as office workers.* vb. climb, mount: *The two men scaled the wall and ran away.*

scan vb. 1. glance at *or* over: *I only scanned the material and I don't remember what it says.* 2. examine, study: *After scanning the data carefully, the analyst was ready with his report.*

scandal n. disgrace, disrepute, shame, dishonor: *The political scandal was so embarrassing that the mayor resigned and moved to another city.*

scanty adj. sparse, scarce, meager, inadequate, insufficient: *The food was becoming scanty as the family became poorer and the prices increased.* ant. plentiful, abundant.

scarce adj. rare, sparse, scanty, insufficient: *The high price of certain items, like gold and plantinum, comes from their being scarce.* ant. common, usual.

scarcely adv. hardly, barely: *I had scarcely walked in the door when it began to pour outside.*

scare vb. frighten, shock, startle: *You certainly scared me when you jumped out from behind that door!*

scarf n. kerchief, babushka: *In this cold weather you ought to wear a scarf on your head.*

scatter vb. spread, sprinkle, disperse: *The farmer scattered seeds along the furrows dug in the earth.* ant. gather, collect, assemble.

scene n. view, display, exhibition, spectacle: *The scene that lay before us as we stood at the top of the mountain will never be forgotten.*

scent n. 1. odor, smell, fragrance, aroma, perfume: *The*

scent of roses filled the morning air. **2.** trail, spoor, track: *A bloodhound's sense of smell is so strong that he can follow a week-old scent.*

schedule *n.* timetable, program, plan, calendar: *According to the schedule, the train from Chicago should have been here ten minutes ago. vb.* plan, program, list: *My English class is scheduled for ten o'clock every morning.*

scheme *n.* **1.** plan, plot, design, program: *I have worked out a scheme that will allow me to have a library study period before my history class.* **2.** plot, intrigue, conspiracy: *The secret service discovered a scheme to assassinate the president. vb.* plan, plot, intrigue, contrive: *The town government was so corrupt that every politician was scheming against every other politician.*

scholar *n.* student; savant, wise man, sage; teacher, professor: *As a scholar in the humanities, the professor had written many famous books on English literature.*

scoff *vb.* mock, belittle, deride, ridicule: *They scoff at scars who never felt a wound. The children scoffed at my story about finding a monster in the school basement.*

scold *vb.* reprove, berate, reprimand, criticize, censure, blame: *Dad scolded me for coming home late for dinner.*

scope *n.* range, reach, extent: *The broad scope of the study of the population included everyone.*

scorch *vb.* char, burn, singe: *The laundry scorched the sleeve of my shirt when they ironed it.*

score *n.* **1.** record, tally, reckoning: *According to the score, the home team is winning. The coach asked me to keep score.* **2.** rating, mark: *Dick received the highest score in the class.* **3.** account: *I have a score to settle with Dorothy because of what she has been telling people about me. vb.* record, tabulate, count: *Brenda scored the highest of all the students in the math test.*

scorn *n.* contempt: *Betty turned up her nose to show her scorn for anyone who cheated on an exam. vb.* **1.** despise, hate: *All our friends scorned people who were dishonest.* **2.** refuse, ignore, spurn, reject: *I scorned his offer to behave because I knew he'd do the same thing again.*

scour *vb.* scrub, clean, wash: *Diane used powder to scour the baking pan.*

scourge *n.* **1.** affliction, plague: *Lack of adequate food is the scourge of many countries.* **2.** whip, lash: *The slave-driver lay about him with a leather scourge, beating all within his reach. vb.* punish, chastise, afflict; torment:

In the old days, criminals were scourged in public by beating with a cat o' nine tails.

scowl *vb., n.* glare, frown, glower: *The teacher scowled at anyone who gave a wrong answer. The old man looked unpleasant because of the scowl on his face.*

scramble *vb.* **1.** mix, blend, combine: *I had scrambled eggs for breakfast.* **2.** hasten, scurry; clamber, climb: *When the announcement came to abandon ship, the passengers scrambled into the lifeboats.*

scrap *n.* **1.** piece, part, fragment, crumb, rag: *Please pick up every scrap of paper you can find.* **2.** junk, waste, trash: *Vincent's uncle is a dealer in metal scrap. vb.* junk, discard, abandon: *I should have scrapped that car months ago—it's not safe to drive any more.*

scrape *vb.* scour, rub; scratch: *Every spring we scrape the paint off the bottom of our boat and put on a fresh coat.*

scratch *vb., n.* scar, scrape: *I scratched my finger with that saw, so I'll put some iodine on it. My mother was angry when she saw the scratch on the table. n. phr.* **from scratch** from the beginning, from the outset: *You'll have to start from scratch if you want that paint job to turn out well.*

scream *vb., n.* shriek, cry, yell, screech: *We heard a woman scream so we called the police. When she saw that someone had walked in her flowerbed, my aunt let out a scream.*

screech *vb., n.* scream, shriek, yell, cry: *The owl screeched in the darkness, and we huddled together. When Anne saw us get off the plane, she gave a screech of joy and ran toward us.*

screen *n.* cover, protection, separation, partition: *An ornate screen divided the room in two. vb.* shield, conceal, hide; separate, partition: *The bookcase screened the other side of the room from my view.*

script *n.* **1.** handwriting, hand, penmanship, writing: *The old man wrote his letters in a beautiful, ornate script.* **2.** book, scenario, lines, text: *Maureen didn't know her part because, she said, she'd lost her script on the bus.*

scrub *vb.* scour, wash, cleanse, clean: *Don't scrub my clothes so hard—you're wearing them out.*

scrutinize *vb.* examine, study: *The detectives scrutinized every inch of the room, looking for a clue to the murderer.*

search *vb.* explore, examine, investigate, scrutinize, inspect:

We searched everywhere but couldn't find a trace of the stolen tarts. n. exploration, examination, investigation; quest, hunt: *The search for the kidnapped heir goes on.*

secede *vb.* withdraw, resign, quit: *Do you know how many states seceded from the Union in 1861?*

secret *adj.* hidden, concealed, unknown: *My brother and I used to talk a secret language. n.* confidence; mystery: *If you can keep a secret, I'll tell you where Ma has hidden the chocolate.* **ant.** *adj.* open, public.

sect *n.* denomination, group, segment, faction: *Which sect of the Protestant church does your family belong to?*

section *n.* sector, part, segment, division, subdivision; share: *I had two sections of an orange for breakfast. What section of town does Blanche live in?*

secure *adj.* **1.** firm, tight, fast, fastened, stable, fixed: *"The lifeboats are all secure, Captain," reported the seaman.* **2.** safe, protected, defended: *We felt secure, huddled in the warm cabin round the fire.* **3.** assured, self-assured, confident, resolute: *I envy Barbie when she applies for a job—she always seems so secure. vb.* **1.** fasten, fix, tighten: *Please secure the door when you go out.* **2.** obtain, procure, acquire: *The officer ordered the seamen to secure a supply of diesel fuel for the launch.* **3.** protect, defend, guard: *The fort will be secured from attack when the cavalry arrives.* **ant.** *adj.* **1.** loose, free. **2.** endangered.

sediment *n.* dregs, lees, grounds, residue: *I hate drinking coffee that has sediment at the bottom of the cup.*

see *vb.* **1.** observe, perceive, look at, descry, behold, regard, examine, study, view, eye, notice: *I can see a small red barn or boathouse across the river, but it's too far to see if anyone is near it.* **2.** understand, comprehend, recognize, appreciate: *Yes, I see what you mean about Louis.* **3.** learn, determine, find out, ascertain: *Please see who's at the door.* **4.** experience, undergo, suffer: *I've seen a lot of life in just a few years.* **5.** escort, attend, accompany: *I'll see you to your limousine, madam.* **6.** think, deliberate, ponder: *I'll see about that matter at another time.*

seek *vb.* search for, look for: *The dog came sniffing up to us, seeking his master.*

seem *vb.* appear, look: *That man seems to be lost; perhaps you can help him.*

seize *vb.* **1.** grab, grasp, clutch: *The thief tried to seize the woman's handbag, but she held it tight and he ran off.* **2.** capture, take: *After a siege of 40 days, the attackers finally seized the castle.* **ant. 1.** release, loosen.

seldom *adv.* rarely, not often, infrequently, scarcely: *We seldom see Harvey any more.*

select *vb.* choose, pick, prefer: *In a supermarket you can select the fruit you want by yourself. adj.* special, chosen, choice, preferred, selected, picked, elite: *The select troops became the king's personal bodyguard.*

selfish *adj.* self-centered, greedy, mingy, stingy, mean, miserly: *Selfish people seldom have really good friends.*

sell *vb.* vend, trade, barter, market, retail, merchandise: *She sells seashells by the seashore; the seashells that she sells are seashore shells.*

send *vb.* dispatch, transmit, forward, convey, ship, mail: *The manufacturer wrote that he had sent the goods by truck.*

senior *adj.* older, elder; superior: *The senior senator from Montana made a four-hour speech about sheep.* **ant.** junior, minor.

sensation *n.* **1.** sense, feeling, sensibility, perception, sensitiveness: *The dentist gave me a shot when he filled the cavity, and I have no sensation in my lower lip.* **2.** excitement, thrill, stimulation: *The new rock group was an overnight sensation.*

sensational *adj.* thrilling, startling, exciting, marvelous, superb, spectacular: *My closest friend has just written what will probably be a sensational bestseller.*

sense *n.* **1.** sensation, feeling, perception: *The doctor asked me if I had any sense in my left leg.* **2.** understanding, reasoning, intellect, judgment, wit, common sense, brains: *I don't know what's the matter with Sadie, but she hasn't the sense she was born with!* **3.** insight, awareness, consciousness: *Have you no sense of honor or of loyalty? vb.* perceive, feel, discern, appreciate: *I sensed someone near me, even though I had heard nothing and couldn't see in the darkness.*

sensible *adj.* reasonable, rational, common-sensical; responsive; responsible: *I am pleased that Don is sensible enough to want to complete school.* **ant.** foolish.

sensitive *adj.* **1.** sore, tender, delicate: *The end of my finger is still sensitive where I burned it yesterday.* **2.**

touchy, tense, nervous: *Donald is very sensitive on the subject of the marks he got in school last year.* **3.** perceptive, keen, receptive: *Bob has very sensitive hearing.*

sentiment   *n.*   **1.** feeling, attitude, opinion: *Roger never let his sentiments be known about the loss of his aunt.* **2.** tenderness, emotion: *The movie was so full of sentiment that even the adults cried.*

separate   *vb.*   **1.** divide, disconnect, split, break up: *We finally separated the two fighting dogs.* **2.** isolate, segregate: *The boys and the girls are separated in our school.* *adj.* **1.** separated, apart, divided, detached: *We were able to keep the dogs and the cats separate.* **2.** distinct, different: *Please sort the nuts and the bolts into separate containers.* **3.** independent: *Victor's mother and father have decided to lead separate lives.*

sequence   *n.* order, succession, series, arrangement: *Please put these words into alphabetic sequence.*

serene   *adj.* peaceful, quiet, calm, tranquil: *The lake was again serene after the storm had passed.* **ant.** agitated, turbulent, stormy.

series   *n.* order, sequence, succession: *Fourteen cars were damaged in a series of rear-end collisions on the freeway last night.*

serious   *adj.*   **1.** grave, earnest, sober, solemn: *I think you ought to have more fun and try to be less serious.* **2.** important, critical: *Disobeying the school rules is a serious matter.* **ant. 1.** frivolous, jocular, light.

servant   *n.* domestic, attendant, retainer; butler, valet, manservant, footman; maidservant, maid: *Many of the large houses are now closed down because people no longer wish to work as servants.*

serve   *vb.*   **1.** attend, wait on: *The waitress came over to our table and asked, "May I serve you?"* **2.** assist, help, aid: *The soldier re-enlisted in order to serve his country.*

session   *n.* meeting, sitting, gathering: *1975 marked the 93rd Session of the Congress of the United States.*

set   *vb.*   **1.** put, place, position, pose, station: *You can set the table down near the window.* **2.** assign, appoint, fix, settle, establish, determine: *If you will set a time when we are to meet, I shall be there.* **3.** harden, solidify, thicken, congeal, jell: *The cement will set overnight.* **4.** rate, price, value: *The discount at the sale was set at 20 percent.* *vb. phr.* **set apart** separate, segregate: *The children who refused to behave were set apart from the* *others.* **set aside** save, reserve: *The man in the shop has set aside a transistor radio for me till I have the money to pay for it.* **set back** slow, retard, hinder, delay: *Our original schedule was set back six weeks by a fire at the factory.* **set down** write, record: *Each student should set down his own ideas for where we have the picnic.* **set forth** begin, start: *The Pilgrims set forth on their journey from Plymouth.* **set free** liberate, release, free: *We took the fawn into the forest and set it free.* **set off 1.** detonate, touch off, explode: *The children are not allowed to set off the fireworks by themselves.* **2.** embark, start out: *I like to set off on a car trip early in the morning.* **3.** contrast, offset: *The red necktie sets off the pale pink shirt very well.* **set out** begin, start, commence: *There were ten people at the inn who had set out from London that morning.* **set up** establish, found: *The children set up a business to sell lemonade during the hot summer.* **set upon** or **set on** attack: *The stagecoach was set upon by robbers as soon as it left town. n.* **1.** collection, assortment; kit: *The stamp collector has a complete set of first-day covers. Do you have a chemistry set?* **2.** group, company, clique, circle: *I don't like the set that Margie is going with these days. adj.* **1.** stubborn, obstinate, determined: *The old man was dead set against any new ideas.* **2.** settled, firm, unchanging: *Agnes's father is very set in his ways, isn't he?*

settle *vb.* **1.** agree upon, establish, decide: *I think we ought to be able to settle who is going to clean the erasers.* **2.** pay, satisfy: *The insurance company settled the claim in two weeks.* **3.** locate, lodge, reside, abide: *The Mormons settled in Salt Lake City.* **4.** sink, subside: *The ground under the new house settled, creating cracks in the walls.*

sever *vb.* cut; divide; split: *Before cutting the log for firewood, Tim severed the branches from it.* **ant.** join, connect.

several *adj.* a few, some, a couple, a handful: *Several people have asked me if I know you.*

severe *adj.* **1.** cruel, strict, harsh, rigid, firm, unyielding: *The principal of our school is a severe disciplinarian.* **2.** difficult, harsh, unpleasant: *An especially severe winter has made our fuel bill much higher.* **3.** violent, dangerous: *The severe storm knocked down power lines all over the state.* **ant.** **1.** lenient, easygoing. **2.** mild.

sew   *vb.* stitch; mend: *Mother sewed up a hole in my sock.*

shabby   *adj.* ragged, worn, threadbare: *Van's uncle loved to wear a shabby old raincoat to the office.*

shack   *n.* hut, hovel, shed, shanty: *The hunter lived alone in a shack in the woods.*

shade   *n.* **1.** shadow, darkness, gloom, dusk: *In the shade, I was unable to see who it was.* **2.** tint, color, hue: *That shade of blue goes with your eyes very well. vb.* **1.** darken, blacken: *If you shade that part of the drawing, it will look more natural.* **2.** screen, conceal, cover, block: *I shaded the sun from my eyes with my hand.*

shaggy   *adj.* woolly, hairy, uncombed, unkempt: *Tom received a shaggy dog for Christmas from his parents.*

shake   *vb.* quiver, tremble, quake, shiver, shudder: *The tiny kitten was shaking with the cold on our doorstep, so we took it inside.*

shame   *n.* **1.** embarrassment, humiliation: *A feeling of shame came over me when I realized that Suzie had overheard me talking about her sister.* **2.** disgrace, dishonor: *The soldier's court martial brought shame to the entire platoon. vb.* **1.** humiliate, humble, abash, mortify: *Tony was shamed into admitting that she had taken all the cookies out of the jar.* **2.** disgrace, dishonor, humble: *Should a teacher be shamed by a student who misbehaves?* **ant.** *n.* **2.** pride, honor.

shameful   *adj.* disgraceful, humiliating, dishonorable, scandalous: *I think it shameful the way your aunt gossips with everyone about everyone else's personal affairs.*

shameless   *adj.* unashamed, unembarrassed; bold, brazen, insolent, impudent: *The girls who pose for the photos in that magazine are absolutely shameless.* **ant.** modest, demure.

shape   *n.* **1.** form, figure, outline; appearance: *That swimming pool is in the shape of a question mark.* **2.** mold, frame, form, pattern, cast: *The clay hardened into the shape of the container where it is kept. vb.* form, fashion, model; mold, cast: *Try to shape this block of wood to resemble an apple.*

share   *n.* portion, part, ration, allotment: *You have already eaten your share of the pie. vb.* **1.** participate, partake: *Everyone who does his work can share in the rewards.* **2.** divide, distribute, apportion: *I think you ought to share the candy among you equally.*

sharp   *adj.* keen, acute, cutting, fine: *The guide's hunting*

knife has such a sharp edge that he can shave with it.
ant. blunt, dull.

shatter   *vb.* shiver, break, burst: *The baseball went through Mrs. Maloney's window and shattered it.*

shawl   *n.* scarf, stole: *The old lady bundled the woolen shawl around her shoulders to keep warm.*

sheer   *adj.*   **1.** transparent, thin, see-through; clear: *The model was wearing sheer stockings.*   **2.** utter, simple, absolute: *Your story about the frog turning into a prince is sheer nonsense.*   **3.** steep, abrupt: *We were faced with a sheer rocky cliff that no one could climb.*

sheet   *n.* layer, leaf; film, coating: *Put a sheet of paper over the top of the jar before sealing it. There's a sheet of ice on the roads tonight, so be careful.*

shelter   *n.* protection, haven, sanctuary: *We sought shelter from the storm by crouching in a cave.* *vb.* protect, shield, harbor, guard: *The farmer sheltered many fugitives who escaped from the chain gang.*

shield   *n.* guard, defense, protection, shelter: *We had to plant a row of trees alongside the house as a shield from the icy winds.* *vb.* guard, defend, protect, shelter: *The magician gave Bobby a coat that would shield him from the harmful rays of the villain's raygun.*

shift   *vb.* move, change, transfer: *The foreman shifted three men from the factory to the warehouse. The wind, which had been from the south, shifted to the north.* *n.*   **1.** move, change, transfer: *My shift to another job in the company meant I would earn more money.*   **2.** turn, spell, period: *I work the day shift but I used to work nights.*

shimmer   *vb.* shine, glimmer, glisten, gleam: *The moonlight was shimmering on the lake as we finally put out the campfire and went to sleep.*

shine   *vb.*   **1.** gleam, beam, glisten, glimmer, shimmer, glow, radiate: *The sun shone every day of our holiday.*   **2.** polish, brush, buff: *I shined my riding boots in preparation for the horse show competition.* *n.* gloss, luster, radiance, polish: *My face was reflected in the shine of the chrome on the car.*

shiny   *adj.* glossy, polished, bright, glistening: *The furniture is shiny because someone waxes it once a week.* **ant.** dull, lusterless.

shipshape   *adj.* neat, clean, Bristol-fashion: *The chief petty officer told the seamen to put everything into shipshape order.* **ant.** messy, sloppy.

shiver *vb.* **1.** quake, tremble, quiver, quaver, shudder, shake: *We stood on the corner, shivering in the cold, waiting for the school bus.* **2.** shatter, break, burst: *The mirror shivered into a thousand splinters when the bullet struck it.* *n.* shudder, tremble: *A shiver ran down my spine when I thought of the way the kitten had been killed.*

shock *n.* **1.** blow, clash, collision, impact: *The shock of the huge truck striking the wall broke all the windows in the house.* **2.** disturbance, upset, agitation: *The shock at the news of her son's death was too much for the mother to bear.* *vb.* **1.** surprise, stagger, astound, stun, startle, bewilder: *The parents were shocked when they saw the X-rated film.* **2.** horrify, outrage, offend, revolt, appall: *The world was shocked to discover what had been going on in the Nazi death camps.*

shore *n.* beach, coast, seaside, seacoast: *When the boat neared the shore, two of the three men in it jumped out and waded in to meet us.*

short *adj.* **1.** brief, concise, abbreviated, condensed, curtailed, terse, abridged: *The movie is short—it lasts only 20 minutes.* **2.** slight, little, undersized, scanty: *The string is too short to go around the package even once.* **ant. 1.** long, lengthy. **2.** tall.

shorten *vb.* **1.** cut, curtail, abbreviate, abridge: *The article is good, but it has to be shortened to fit into the space in our magazine.* **2.** take in, lessen, reduce: *The dressmaker had to shorten my sister's skirt by three inches.* **ant.** lengthen.

short-handed *adj.* understaffed: *During the summer, with many people away on holiday, we are often short-handed.*

shortsighted *adj.* **1.** nearsighted, myopic: *The optometrist said that I was shortsighted and needed glasses.* **2.** thoughtless, unthinking, unimaginative: *It was quite shortsighted of you not to have foreseen your mother's displeasure at the ink on the carpet.*

shout *n., vb.* yell, roar, bellow: *Jimmy gave a shout when I stepped on his toe. "Ouch!" he shouted.*

shove *vb., n.* push, jostle: *The conductor shoved a few more people into the subway car. If you give the wagon a good shove, it will roll down the hill by itself.*

shovel *n.* spade: *Tom picked up the coal shovel and started to stoke the furnace.*

show *vb.* **1.** display, present, exhibit: *I have already shown you all the books I have on the subject of gardening.* **2.**

indicate, note, point: *Show me the way to go home.* **3.** explain, reveal, tell: *I wish you would show me how to do that trick with the disappearing mouse.* **4.** prove, demonstrate: *If you expect me to believe your story about the purple banana, you'll have to show me.* **5.** guide, usher, lead: *The man in the green uniform will show you to your seats. vb. phr.* **show in** conduct, lead, direct: *Please show Mr. Gilbert in.* **show off** brag, boast: *Every time the teacher looks at him, Oscar shows off.* **show up** **1.** arrive, appear, turn up, surface: *Ten o'clock is no time to show up for school!* **2.** expose, belittle, discredit: *The experienced pianist did not like being shown up by his own pupil. n.* **1.** presentation, exhibit, exhibition, display: *Mother and I went to a flower show yesterday.* **2.** drama, play, musical: *Where are we to meet after the show?*

shred *n., vb.* tatter; mince: *After the fight, Moran's shirt was in shreds. I like shredded carrots in my salad.*

shrewd *adj.* **1.** cunning, sly, crafty, tricky: *Putting a tack on the teacher's chair was not a very shrewd move, Moriarty.* **2.** clever, ingenious, intelligent: *My father is a very shrewd investor, and many businessmen seek his advice.*

shriek *vb., n.* scream, screech, yell, howl: *Mother shrieked when she saw the bloody bandage on my arm. We were very frightened when we heard a piercing shriek at midnight.*

shrill *adj.* sharp, piercing: *The train whistle was so shrill that it hurt my ears.* **ant.** muted, muffled.

shrink *vb.* **1.** contract, diminish, dwindle, shrivel: *If you wash that shirt in hot water, it will shrink two sizes.* **2.** recoil, withdraw, flinch, retreat: *Dick shrinks from any responsibility you try to give him.* **ant.** **1.** swell.

shudder *vb., n.* shiver, tremble, shake, quiver: *I shuddered at the thought of going out into the bitter cold. The dog gave a violent shudder, making the rain from his coat fly everywhere.*

shun *vb.* avoid, evade, elude: *I can't help the feeling I have that George is shunning me.*

shut *vb.* close; lock, seal: *Please shut the door when you leave.* **ant.** open.

shy *adj.* timid, bashful: *Liza used to be very shy, but now she talks freely to everyone.* **ant.** bold, self-confident, brazen.

sick *adj.* ill, unwell, ailing, unhealthy, infirm: *Irena was sick in bed for only one day in the past ten years.*

side *n.* **1.** face, surface: *A cube has six sides.* **2.** opponent, foe, rival: *Which side are you for, the one with the green helmets or the one in the white? adj.* secondary, indirect; unimportant: *The main issue is the kind of postal service we are getting; the cost of a stamp is a side issue.*

siege *n.* blockade: *The castle was under siege for six months before it finally gave up.*

sieve *n.* strainer, colander, screen, riddle: *After the mixture is passed through a sieve to separate out the coarser parts, you cook the remainder for two hours.*

sight *n.* **1.** vision, eyesight: *Bill's sight requires him to wear eyeglasses.* **2.** view, spectacle, scene, display: *The trained porpoises leaping through the air together are quite a sight.* **3.** eyesore: *My mother told me that my room was a sight and that I must clean it up at once.*

sign *n.* **1.** symbol, token, indication, suggestion, hint: *Those black clouds on the horizon are the sign of a coming storm.* **2.** signal, clue: *The dog gave no sign that it would bite. vb.* authorize, approve, confirm: *Please sign the contract on the dotted line.*

signal *n.* sign, beacon, flag: *What kind of signal did Paul Revere receive from the Old North Church tower?*

significance *n.* importance, weight, moment: *I didn't understand the significance of the teacher's remarks until many years later.*

significant *adj.* important, meaningful, vital, crucial, critical: *The significant part of the speech by the principal was applauded by the audience.* **ant.** unimportant, insignificant, trivial.

signify *vb.* **1.** indicate, show, signal, communicate: *The policeman signified his permission to cross the street by a smile and a nod.* **2.** mean: *What do you suppose those strange hand movements signify?*

silence *n.* **1.** quiet, stillness, noiselessness, soundlessness, hush: *After the noise and bustle of the city, I really enjoy the silence and serenity of the country.* **2.** muteness, speechlessness: *Silence is golden, but speech is silver.* **ant.** **1.** noisiness, clamor, racket.

silent *adj.* **1.** quiet, noiseless, soundless, still, hushed: *I dived down into the lake, down into its silent depths.* **2.** mute, speechless, uncommunicative: *My father was silent on the subject of where we were going for our holiday.*

ant. 1. noisy, clamorous. **2.** talkative, communicative.

silly *adj.* senseless, foolish, stupid, ridiculous, witless, thimble-witted: *I want to be serious and you keep on acting in that silly way, giggling all the time.*

similar *adj.* like, resembling, alike: *A teaspoon and a soup-spoon are similar, but not identical. Your shirt is similar to mine.* **ant.** different, dissimilar.

similarity *n.* likeness, resemblance: *I see the similarity between our ideas, but there are still many differences.*

simple *adj.* **1.** uncomplicated: *Addition and subtraction are parts of simple arithmetic.* **2.** clear, understandable, plain: *I cannot give you a simple explanation of why plants are green.* **3.** easy: *That was a simple history exam.* **ant. 1.** complicated, complex. **2.** difficult, abstruse. **3.** demanding.

sin *n.* trespass, transgression, wickedness: *The seven deadly sins are pride, anger, covetousness, lust, gluttony, envy, and sloth.* *vb.* trespass, transgress: *Daisy sinned by wishing she had a dress like Margo's.*

sincere *adj.* **1.** honest, open, candid, faithful, trusty, trustworthy: *Don is a sincere friend.* **2.** genuine, real, true: *Mabel shed sincere tears for her lost puppy.*

sincerity *n.* honesty, openness, candor, frankness: *I believed everything you told me because you spoke with such sincerity.*

single *adj.* **1.** one, lone, sole, solitary: *A single man stood on the beach, looking out toward the horizon.* **2.** unmarried, unwed, unattached: *The party at the club next week will be for single people only.* **3.** individual, private: *I reserved a single room at the hotel.*

singular *adj.* **1.** remarkable, unusual, extraordinary, rare, uncommon, exceptional: *Shooting the rapids in a two-man canoe is a singular experience.* **2.** strange, odd, peculiar, queer, eccentric, curious: *The mating dance of certain birds is very singular.*

sink *vb.* descend, fall, drop: *He let go the life preserver and sank like a stone in the deep water.*

sip *vb.* taste, drink: *You should sip the hot lemonade slowly.* *n.* taste, swallow, drink: *May I have a sip of your ginger ale?*

site *n.* location, place, position: *We selected a flat, grassy site to pitch our tent.*

situation *n.* **1.** location, site, locale, placement, position: *The situation of the house gives it magnificent views in* *three directions.* **2.** condition, state, circumstances: *In the present situation, it may not be easy to find a job after school.*

size *n.* dimension, extent, measurement: *If the size of the desk is greater than the space where you want to put it, it won't fit.*

sketch *n.* drawing, picture: *Here is a rough sketch of my home.* *vb.* draw, outline, represent: *In art class, the students were asked to sketch a model of a monkey.*

skill *n.* ability, talent: *Richard plays the piano with great skill.*

skillful *adj.* skilled, accomplished, expert, adept, proficient: *It takes a skillful artist to capture a person's character in a portrait.* **ant.** inept, clumsy, awkward.

skin *n.* covering, outside, peel, shell, rind: *This lemon has a thick skin.* *vb.* peel, pare; flay: *Skin these grapes for me, would you? The cruel pirate gave the man twenty lashes, almost skinning him alive.*

skinny *adj.* thin, scrawny, gaunt, raw-boned: *Would you believe that this beautiful movie star was once a skinny little girl?* **ant.** heavy, hefty, fat.

slack *adj.* **1.** loose, lax, limp: *Let the jumprope hang slack, so that it touches the ground at the center.* **2.** lazy: *Tim is very slack about getting his work done.* **3.** slow, inactive, sluggish: *Summer is the slack period in our business.* **ant. 1.** taut, stiff, rigid. **3.** active, busy.

slang *n.* dialect, jargon: *"Shavetail" was American army slang for a second lieutenant.*

slant *vb.* lean, incline, slope, tilt: *The roof slants down on this side to let the snow slide off easily.* *n.* **1.** incline, slope, pitch: *We came to a steep slant in the road, and the car would go no further.* **2.** angle, approach: *I got a new slant on you when I heard you give a speech in the assembly.*

slash *vb.* **1.** slit, cut, gash: *The recipe says to slash the roast in several places with a sharp knife and to insert garlic in the slits.* **2.** reduce, lower, cut: *Prices on clothing were slashed after Christmas.* *n.* slit, cut, gash: *There were three slashes in my car tire.*

slaughter *vb.* kill, butcher, massacre, slay: *The buffalo were rounded up in the Old West and slaughtered by the millions.* *n.* killing, butchery, butchering, massacre: *We must do something to prevent the continued slaughter of wildlife.*

slave *n.* serf, bondsman, bondservant: *The ancient Greeks used to make slaves of the people they conquered in war.*

slay *vb.* kill, murder, slaughter, assassinate: *With one blow of his sword the knight slew his attacker.*

sleep *n., vb.* rest, repose, slumber, nap, snooze, doze: *I had only five hours' sleep last night. If you sleep too little, you're tired the entire next day.*

slender *adj.* slim, trim, slight, thin: *We keep slender in our family by getting plenty of exercise, plenty of sleep, and by not overeating.* **ant.** heavy, fat, overweight.

slide *vb.* slip, glide, skid, skim: *We used to have fun sliding down the snowy hills on an old board if we had no sled.*

slight *adj.* **1.** small, sparse, scanty, spare: *It takes only a very slight amount of insecticide to kill a fly.* **2.** insignificant, unimportant, trivial: *Irena has a terrible temper and gets angry at the slightest thing.* *vb.* ignore, disregard, snub, scorn: *I felt slighted because I wasn't invited to the dance.* **ant.** *adj.* **1.** large, enormous, huge. **2.** major, significant. *vb.* flatter, compliment.

slim *adj.* **1.** slender, thin, slight; lank: *Sophie looks quite slim now that she has lost 20 pounds.* **2.** small, unimportant, insignificant, weak, scanty, slight: *Ben stands a very slim chance of winning if he has to play chess with Ed.*

slip *vb.* **1.** slide, glide; shift: *I was about to slip off the edge of the cliff when a strong hand caught me and hauled me to safety.* **2.** err, blunder: *I slipped when I gave away your secret.* *n.* error, mistake, blunder: *Your telling my father about where we went yesterday was an unfortunate slip.*

slit *vb.* cut, slash: *With one stroke, I slit open the fish.* *n.* cut, slash, slot, tear: *The slit in the evening dress started at the hem and went up above the knee.*

slogan *n.* motto, catchword: *"Tippecanoe and Tyler, too!" was the slogan of John Tyler's presidential campaign.*

slope *vb., n.* incline, slant: *The lawn behind my house slopes down to the river. The trees on that slope are all bent by the wind.*

slow *adj.* **1.** unhurried, gradual, leisurely: *The slow pace of life in the country is more to my liking than the hectic activity of a big city.* **2.** late, delayed, behindhand: *My watch is five minutes slow.* **3.** dull, boring, tedious: *The play was very slow—I fell asleep.* *vb.* retard, hinder, obstruct, slacken: *We slowed down when we came to the curve.* **ant.** **1.** fast, quick. **2.** fast, ahead.

slumber *n., vb.* sleep, rest, doze; rest, repose: *Nothing can disturb Della's slumber. My father slumbered on, despite the noise of the firemen, ambulances, and police.*

slump *n.* decline, descent, drop, fall; depression: *Prices were in a slump at the Stock Exchange this week. vb.* sink, decline, descend: *George slumped in his chair when Bob told him he couldn't go to the movies with him.*

sly *adj.* cunning, crafty, secretive, wily, foxy: *Harvey pulled a sly trick on me when he listened in on my phone conversation.*

small *adj.* **1.** little, tiny, miniature: *The watch was so small I could hardly see the face.* **2.** unimportant, insignificant, minor, trivial: *Whether you go to the theater or not is a small matter to me.* **ant. 1.** large, big, enormous.

smart *adj.* clever, intelligent, bright: *Donald was smart enough to get straight A's in school. vb.* sting, hurt, burn: *That iodine smarts when you put it on an open cut.* **ant.** *adj.* stupid, slow, dumb.

smash *vb.* break, crash, crush, demolish: *The car was badly smashed in the accident. n.* crash, shattering: *I heard the smash of a pane of glass and thought it was a burglar.*

smear *vb.* **1.** rub, spread, wipe: *Please wash up before dinner: your hands are smeared with grease.* **2.** slander, libel, defame: *After he was smeared for his connection with the building scandal, the Mayor could not win re-election.*

smell *vb.* scent, sniff, detect: *I can smell turkey roasting, and it's making me hungry. n.* **1.** scent, odor, aroma, bouquet: *The smell of orange blossoms filled the air.* **2.** odor, stench, stink: *I can't stand the smell of dead fish.*

smile *n.* grin: *I can see the smile on your face when you think about an ice cream sundae. vb.* grin, beam: *Uncle Bill smiled when I handed him his birthday gift.* **ant.** *n., vb.* scowl, frown.

smooth *adj.* even, level, flat, unwrinkled: *There was no wind, and the lake was as smooth as glass. After he shaves, my father's cheek is so smooth! vb.* level, even, flatten, iron: *Doris smoothed down the sheets on the bed before putting on the blankets.* **ant.** *adj.* rough, uneven.

smother *vb.* stifle, asphyxiate, suffocate: *We were almost smothered by the thick blanket of smoke from the fire.*

snare *n.* trap, net: *We set snares for the fox that was eating our chickens. vb.* trap, catch, capture: *Dave built a large cage in which he hoped to snare a raccoon.*

snarl *vb.* growl: *The dog snarled at the letter carrier.*

snatch *vb.* seize, grab, grasp: *Dorothy just snatched the apple out of my hand and ran away with it.*

sneak *vb.* slink, skulk, steal: *Roger sneaked in when no one was looking and stole a pie.*

sneer *vb.* scorn, scoff, mock, jeer, taunt: *Don't sneer at my swimming records unless you can do better.* *n.* jeer; disdain: *With a sneer, Victor dismissed my attempt at drawing a plan for our new clubhouse.*

snub *vb.* slight, insult; rebuke: *Mary was upset when her friends snubbed her at the party just because she had a shabby dress.* *n.* slight, insult, humiliation: *We all felt the snub when we weren't invited to dinner at the country club.*

snug *adj.* **1.** cozy, sheltered, comfortable: *We built a snug den in our house, with a fireplace and comfortable chairs.* **2.** close-fitting, trim, tight: *Don't you think that those trousers are a little snug around the hips?*

soak *vb.* drench, wet, steep, saturate: *You'll have to soak that cloth in bleach overnight to remove the stain.*

soar *vb.* fly, glide: *High above us, the hawk soared in circles, his wings motionless.*

sob *vb.* lament, cry, weep: *The little boy was sobbing because some bigger boys had taken away his ball.*

sober *adj.* **1.** clear-headed, moderate: *Whenever my grandfather has to drive a car, he doesn't drink and stays sober.* **2.** serious, solemn, grave: *The funeral service for the comedian was the only sober occasion he had ever been associated with.* **ant. 1.** drunk, inebriated, fuddled. **2.** frivolous.

sociable *adj.* social, friendly: *All of the people at the party were very sociable.*

social *adj.* **1.** group, human, common: *The social problems in the city included welfare, unemployment, and other important matters.* **2.** friendly, sociable, genial, polite: *All of our neighbors are very social, and we see one another quite often.*

society *n.* **1.** community, civilization, nation: *Society's problems, like having enough food for everyone, cannot be solved easily or quickly.* **2.** club, organization, association, circle, fraternity: *My mother is a member of two professional medical societies.* **3.** association, companionship, company: *I enjoy the society of other people and spend a lot of time with my friends.*

soft *adj.* **1.** flexible, pliable, pliant; elastic: *This clay is soft enough now for you to mold a figure out of it.* **2.** smooth, velvety, satiny: *My kitten's fur is so soft!* **3.** quiet, low, gentle: *The girl was singing in a soft voice.* **ant. 1.** hard, rigid.

soil *n.* earth, loam, dirt: *You'll need more soil to plant that flower in such a large pot. vb.* dirty, stain, spot: *Badly soiled clothes should be allowed to soak for a while before washing.*

sole *adj.* alone, single, only, solitary: *The only person who came to hear the concert was a sole woman who sat in the balcony.*

solemn *adj.* **1.** serious, sober, grave: *The graduation ceremony was a solemn occasion for all of the students.* **2.** formal, serious, dignified: *The president gave a solemn speech about the state of the nation.* **ant. 1.** cheerful, happy, gay.

solicit *vb.* request, seek, pray, beg, beseech: *The candidate visited many homes, soliciting votes in the coming election.*

solid *adj.* **1.** firm, compact, hard, dense: *The handball was made out of solid rubber.* **2.** three-dimensional: *A solid piece of wood was used as a lever to open the door.* **3.** unmixed, plain: *My new shirt is solid red.* **ant. 1.** loose.

solitary *adj.* isolated, lonely, deserted; sole, only, single: *A solitary tree was outlined at the top of the hill.*

solution *n.* answer, explanation: *I was the only one with the correct solution to the daily math problem.*

solve *vb.* answer, unravel, explain: *The detectives found the clues and fingerprints and were able to solve the crime.*

somber *adj.* **1.** serious, sober, grave, gloomy, dismal: *The sun hasn't shone for so many days that I am in a very somber mood.* **2.** dismal, mournful, sad, melancholy: *The funeral was a somber event.* **ant. 1.** happy, cheerful, gay.

sometimes *adv.* occasionally, now and then: *Sometimes I like to drink ice-cream sodas and sometimes I don't.* **ant.** always, invariably.

soothe *vb.* calm, pacify, comfort, quiet: *I really prefer soothing music to rock 'n' roll.* **ant.** disquiet, upset, unnerve.

sordid *adj.* foul, dirty, filthy, unclean: *The poorer people in the town live in the most sordid surroundings.*

sore *adj.* aching, painful, hurting, tender, sensitive: *My finger is still sore where I caught it in the door yesterday. n.*

cut, bruise, burn, wound, injury: *I have a sore on my knee where I scraped it playing baseball.*

sorrow *n.* sadness, gloom, depression, grief, misery, anguish: *One of my great sorrows is that I never studied to be a doctor.* *vb.* mourn, grieve, lament: *Sonia tried to console the sorrowing family.*

sorrowful *adj.* sad, aggrieved, unhappy, melancholy, depressed, mournful: *The teacher gave us the most sorrowful news this morning: the school mascot had run away.*

sorry *adj.* regretful, apologetic: *I'm sorry if I hurt your feelings, for I didn't mean to.* **ant.** happy, glad.

sort *n.* kind, variety, type: *What sort of a dog did you get for your birthday? a poodle? a spaniel?* *vb.* separate, classify, arrange, order: *Please sort these words into alphabetical order.*

sound[1] *n.* noise; din, racket: *The silence was so great that we could hear the sound of a pin drop.* *vb.* echo, resound: *The fire alarm sounded throughout the building.*

sound[2] *adj.* **1.** secure, safe, uninjured, unharmed, whole, healthy, hardy: *We returned home during the storm, safe and sound.* **2.** trustworthy, reliable; sensible: *I think we can rely on Philip's judgment to be sound.*

sour *adj.* **1.** acid, tart: *Those lemon candies are so sour they make my mouth pucker up.* **2.** bad-tempered, unpleasant, touchy, cross, cranky: *That old man certainly has a sour disposition—he doesn't like anyone or anything.* **ant.** **1.** sweet. **2.** good-natured, sunny, benevolent.

source *n.* origin, beginning: *The source of this stream is a spring high in the mountains.*

sovereign *n.* ruler, lord; monarch, king, queen, emperor, empress: *Queen Elizabeth II is the sovereign of Great Britain.* *adj.* supreme, chief, principal: *Freedom of speech is a sovereign right of the American people.*

space *n.* area, location, room: *Please put the desk into the open space against that wall.*

spacious *adj.* roomy, large: *The children were given a spacious bedroom in the new house.* **ant.** cramped, small, narrow, confined.

span *n.* extent, spread: *This history book covers a span of four centuries.* *vb.* extend, reach, cross: *The bridge spans the river about a mile north of here.*

spare *vb.* **1.** save, set aside *or* apart, reserve: *The bank* *president was able to spare just 15 minutes to talk with our class.* **2.** save; forgive; show mercy to: *Because the robber was a great musician, the king spared his life.* *adj.* extra, additional, unoccupied: *I think we can find a spare tennis racket that you can borrow for today.*

sparkle *vb.* **1.** shine, glisten, glitter, twinkle: *The sea sparkled in the bright sunlight.* **2.** bubble, effervesce: *I like sparkling water with my dinner.* *n.* **1.** shine, glitter, twinkle: *The sparkle of the glasses caught my eye.* **2.** spirit, liveliness, brilliance: *Valerie's personality lent sparkle to the party.*

speak *vb.* say, utter: *You should never speak evil of a person behind his back.*

special *adj.* **1.** exceptional, unusual, extraordinary, different, particular: *We have reserved this jewelry for our special customers only.* **2.** distinct, certain, unusual: *I have made special plans to spend this weekend in the country.* **ant. 1.** average, ordinary.

specialist *n.* expert, authority: *We hired a specialist to examine our horse because the regular veterinarian wasn't sure what was wrong with him.*

specific *adj.* definite, particular, distinct, precise: *Is there any specific reason why you want me to wear my red socks to your party?* **ant.** general, nonspecific.

specify *vb.* designate, name, define: *The teacher specified which children were to be assigned to do extra work.*

specimen *n.* sample, example, model, type, pattern: *The doctor took a blood specimen from my finger in order to test it for a corpuscle count.*

speck *n.* bit, spot, mite: *There's a speck of dust on your white shirt.*

spectator *n.* watcher, viewer, observer, onlooker: *At the tournament, one of the golf balls struck a spectator on the arm.* **ant.** participant.

speculate *vb.* guess, consider, surmise, view, suppose, theorize. *You can't speculate about the date of the signing of the Declaration of Independence—you either know it or you don't.*

speech *n.* **1.** talk, address, oration, lecture, sermon: *The senator gave a speech on the steps of the town hall.* **2.** utterance, articulation, diction, accent, pronunciation, enunciation: *From your speech I can tell that you come from Texas.*

speed *n.* **1.** rapidity, swiftness, haste: *I could see that the* *girl hadn't eaten for several days by the speed with which she gulped her food.* **2.** velocity: *Light travels at a speed of 186,000 miles per second.*

spend *vb.* **1.** pay, expend, disburse: *I spent much too much for that necktie.* **2.** use up, consume: *I wish you wouldn't spend so much time watching television.* **ant. 1.** save, hoard.

sphere *n.* **1.** ball, orb, globe: *In nature, many objects have the form of a sphere.* **2.** area, environment, domain: *In my sphere of work, one must study for many years to become an expert.*

spin *vb.* **1.** turn, revolve, whirl, rotate, twirl: *Every spring we used to spin our tops and try to do tricks with them.* **2.** narrate, tell, relate: *At night, the old men would get together around the fire to spin tales of long ago.*

spine *n.* backbone, vertebrae: *When the chalk squeaks on the blackboard it sends shivers up my spine.*

spineless *adj.* weak, feeble, limp; cowardly: *I don't want to name the spineless fellow who has been frightening the little girls in school.* **ant.** strong, brave, courageous.

spirit *n.* **1.** mood, attitude, outlook, feeling: *I've been in very low spirits since my older brother went away to college.* **2.** vitality, liveliness, energy: *It takes a lot of spirit for an invalid like Betsy to remain cheerful.* **3.** angel, fairy, devil, elf, sprite, goblin, demon: *In the old days, many people believed in evil spirits and blamed them for their own mistakes.* **4.** ghost, phantom, specter: *That house—the deserted one—is inhabited by spirits.* **5.** meaning, intention, intent: *There is often a difference between the letter of the law and the spirit of the law.*

spirited *adj.* animated, excited, active, lively, energetic, vigorous: *We were having a spirited argument about politics when my mother joined in.* **ant.** lazy, indolent, sleepy.

splendid *adj.* **1.** magnificent, brilliant, gorgeous, sumptuous, elegant, luxurious: *The king ordered the craftsmen to create splendid furnishings for the palace.* **2.** excellent, superb, superior: *That's a splendid painting of the Grand Canal in Venice.*

splendor *n.* magnificence, grandeur, display, brilliance: *The splendor of the civilization of ancient Greece may never be seen again.*

splinter *n.* sliver, chip, piece, fragment: *Be careful with that board or you'll get a splinter in your finger.* *vb.* split, shiver: *The glass splintered into a thousand pieces when it dropped on the floor.*

split *vb.* divide, break, cleave: *Let's split the candy bar among the three of us. If you hammer a wedge into the crack in that log, it will split easily.* *n.* crack, opening: *The split in my skirt is right along the seam.*

spoil *vb.* **1.** damage, ruin, destroy: *I left my painting out in the rain and it's completely spoiled. You have spoiled your chances for a good mark in the course by failing the exam.* **2.** rot, mold, molder, ruin: *If you leave milk out of the refrigerator too long it will spoil.*

spokesman *n.* representative, agent: *A spokesman was asked to act for the company because the president was out of town.*

spontaneous *adj.* natural, voluntary, unconscious, unplanned: *Lending Jimmy your skates was a spontaneous act of friendship.* **ant.** studied, cautious.

sport *n.* **1.** entertainment, pastime, game, athletics, play, recreation: *I play chess for sport, not for money.* **2.** mockery, jest, joke, ridicule: *You are making sport of me when you say I'm the greatest singer you've ever heard.*

sporting *adj.* fair, considerate, sportsmanlike: *Big game hunters seldom give their quarry a sporting chance.*

spot *n.* **1.** mark, blemish, blot, stain, flaw, speck: *I wouldn't go near Peter—he has spots all over his face.* **2.** place, location, site: *We have built our new home in a beautiful spot right near the lake.* *vb.* **1.** mark, stain, blot, spatter: *You've splashed the tomato juice everywhere and have spotted the clean tablecloth.* **2.** locate, find: *I spotted you in the school photograph even though it was taken years ago.*

spout *vb.* squirt, spurt: *The lava could be seen spouting out of the volcano from 20 miles away.* *n.* nozzle, tube: *The water comes out of the green spout and the milk out of the white one.*

spray *n.* spatter; splash: *There was a fine spray of cologne from the top of the bottle.* *vb.* sprinkle, spatter, splash: *I sprayed the roses with a fluid that would keep off the bugs.*

spread *vb.* **1.** distribute; disperse: *The icing must be spread evenly over the top of the cake before serving.* **2.** open, unfurl, unroll, unfold: *I helped to spread the sails on the lawn so they could dry in the sun.* **3.** scatter: *The news* *about the fire spread throughout the town.* n. jam, jelly, preserve, conserve: *I like to put a spread on hot toast after it has been buttered.*

spring   vb.   **1.** leap, bound, jump: *I sprang to my feet when the teacher entered the room.* **2.** start, begin, arise, originate: *Rick's eagerness to help with the cooking springs from his wish to be closer to the food.* n. **1.** leap, jump, bound: *With one leap the cat was out of the door and scurrying down the hall.* **2.** fountain; origin, source: *This stream is fed by a spring in the mountains.*

sprinkle   vb. scatter, spread, strew: *Sprinkle the pancake lightly with powdered sugar.* n. scattering, rain: *We were getting wet in the sprinkle that came from the garden hose.*

spry   adj. lively, nimble, quick, alert, agile, energetic: *Mrs. Robinson is very spry for someone of 75.* ant. inactive, lethargic.

spur   n. goad; stimulus: *The will to win is a spur to athletes to do their very best in competitive sports.* vb. goad, stimulate, urge: *The thought of a good meal and a warm fire spurred Nicholas on through the snow toward home.*

stab   vb. pierce, gore, stick, spear; knife, bayonet: *I stabbed the marshmallow with a pointed branch and toasted it over the fire. Caesar was stabbed by Brutus' dagger.*

stable   adj. steady, firm, sturdy, steadfast, solid: *The platform wasn't very stable, and I thought it might give way at any moment.* ant. unstable, shaky.

stack   n. pile, mound, heap, mass: *There's a big stack of firewood out in back if you want to make a fire.* vb. pile, heap, accumulate: *Please try to stack those stones more neatly the next time.*

staff   n.   **1.** stick, pole, club: *Little John always carried his staff with him and used it as a weapon.* **2.** employees, personnel, help, crew: *The company has a skilled staff of 35 people at the main office.*

stage   n.   **1.** platform, scaffold, frame: *The masons were standing on a stage 40 feet off the ground to finish the wall.* **2.** theater, boards: *When I was younger, I wanted to go on the stage, but I couldn't act well enough, so now I'm a star on television.* **3.** phase, step, period: *The project has reached a stage where we need more people right away.* vb. produce, direct; present, put on: *Our school staged the musical comedy* The Boy Friend *this year.*

stagger *vb.* **1.** sway, totter, reel, falter: *Here comes Freddie, staggering down the street as if he'd been hit on the head.* **2.** vary, alternate; zigzag: *If you could stagger your working days and your days off, you could get some rest.*

stain *n.* **1.** spot, blemish, blot, mark: *There's a big stain on your collar—it looks like blood.* **2.** disgrace, dishonor, smirch, blot: *It will take many weeks of very good behavior, Roberto, to clear up that stain on your record.* *vb.* **1.** spot, blot, mark: *You've stained the tablecloth with ketchup!* **2.** tint, dye, color: *The cabinetmaker stained the wood a very dark mahogany.*

stair *n.* stairway, flight of stairs, staircase, steps: *The guest closet is under the stairs.*

stake *n.* **1.** post, stick, pole, pale, picket, rod: *The hunters tied the goat to a stake in the clearing to act as bait for the tiger.* **2.** wager, bet: *The stakes are too high for me to play poker with those men.* **3.** interest, concern: *I bought a stake in that silver mine in Colorado, but I lost everything.*

stale *adj.* **1.** old, spoiled, dry; inedible: *We break up any stale bread we have and feed it to the birds.* **2.** uninteresting, flat, dull, trite: *We had to sit through dinner listening politely and laughing whenever Bill told another of his stale jokes.* **ant. 1.** fresh, new.

stalk *vb.* follow, dog, pursue, shadow, track, hunt: *Have you ever stalked a tiger in the jungles of India?*

stall *vb.* stop; hesitate, postpone, delay: *My car keeps stalling in the middle of traffic. Stop stalling about coming to a decision!*

stammer *vb.* stutter, falter, hem and haw: *Stop stammering and tell me where you've hidden the key!*

stamp *vb.* **1.** trample, crush: *Our guests stamped all over our newly seeded lawn and ruined it completely.* **2.** brand, mark, imprint: *Ellie stamped her name all over my shirt and I can't wash it out.* *n.* die, block, seal: *My father gave me a rubber stamp with my name and address on it.*

stand *vb.* **1.** rise, arise, stand up: *Please stand when the band plays the national anthem.* **2.** remain, stay: *My original instructions still stand.* **3.** tolerate, endure, abide, bear: *I can't stand listening to rock 'n' roll all day long.* *n.* **1.** position, attitude, opinion: *Your stand on the issue is that anyone who goes out on strike ought to be fired.* **2.** table, platform: *The vase was knocked off that wooden stand in the corner.* **ant.** *vb.* **1.** lie, recline, repose.

standard   *n.*   **1.** measure, gauge, example, model, criterion: *The problem is that no one knows the standard for judging right from wrong because it depends on each situation.* **2.** banner, pennant, flag, emblem, symbol: *In the ancient Roman army, the man who carried the legion's standard was very important.* *adj.* basic, typical, approved, official, regular: *Light bulbs are manufactured in a few standard sizes to fit sockets.* **ant.** *adj.* unusual, irregular, special.

standpoint   *n.* viewpoint, position, attitude: *From the standpoint of the British, the American Revolution was a skirmish started by a few revolting colonists.*

staple   *adj.* principal, main, chief, necessary, essential: *Bread and butter are staple foods in most diets.*

stare   *vb.* gaze: *It's very uncomfortable to have someone just staring at you for no reason.*

stark   *adj.* **1.** absolute, utter, complete, sheer: *The stark truth is that your son did chop down the cherry tree, Mrs. Washington.* **2.** harsh, severe, rough, grim: *The stark countryside was uninviting during the winter, especially.*

start   *vb.* **1.** begin, commence, initiate: *I wish you hadn't started Grandpa off on his storytelling—now he'll never stop.* **2.** jump, jerk; twitch: *Oh! You made me start! I didn't know anyone was here.* *n.* **1.** beginning, commencement, initiation, outset, onset: *Just before the official start of the baseball season, Thomas was always the first one to take out his ball and mitt.* **2.** shock, surprise: *You gave me quite a start, peering in the window wearing that spooky mask!* **3.** lead, head start, advantage: *I have a start on the rest of the class because I've already read this book.*

startle   *vb.* surprise, shock, agitate, alarm: *I was startled to learn that although Columbus, an Italian, is credited with discovering America, it was the Spanish queen, Isabella, who financed the voyage.*

state   *n.* **1.** nation, country: *What were once colonies in Africa have mostly all now become independent states.* **2.** condition, status; situation: *The doctor told us that the state of the family's health is excellent.* *vb.* declare, say, assert, express; tell: *For the second time in one hour, Mornie stated why she had come to see the show.* *adj.* public; governmental; federal, national: *We often go camping in a state park.*

stately *adj.* grand, dignified, imposing, elegant, impressive, majestic, magnificent: *Lady Thistlebottom was a stately woman who lived in a stately mansion.* **ant.** mean, base, squalid.

statement *n.* announcement, declaration, assertion: *The senator has already made a statement to the press that he is innocent of accepting a bribe.*

station *n.* depot, post; terminal: *The police station is open 24 hours a day. I got on at the bus station in Cleveland. vb.* place, position, put, locate: *The colonel stationed eight men to stand guard duty last night.*

status *n.* **1.** state, condition: *What is the status of your report? Do you expect to complete it soon?* **2.** rank, position, standing: *The social status of a teacher is much higher in Europe than in America.*

statute *n.* law, rule, ruling, ordinance: *There is a statute in this state against operating a retail store on Sundays.*

stay *vb.* **1.** remain, rest, tarry, linger: *Please stay where you are for a moment.* **2.** remain, continue: *When I was in the Army, I stayed a Private the entire 18 months.* **3.** delay, check, hinder, halt, hold: *The governor stayed the execution of the convicted murderer because new evidence had been discovered. n.* **1.** stop, hindrance, check, halt, delay: *On Christmas Eve, a stay of execution saved six men who were to die the following week.* **2.** brace, support; rope, line, shroud: *When the stay snapped, the mast broke in two and we radioed for help.* **ant.** *vb.* **1.** go, leave, depart.

stead *n.* place: *In whose stead will you go to the party?*

steady *adj.* **1.** even, regular, stable, unremitting: *A steady rain fell all evening and till noon the following day.* **2.** firm, steadfast, reliable: *We need a steady hand at the helm if this boat is to sail across the Atlantic.* **3.** firm, solid, stable: *That little table—the wobbly one—isn't steady enough for the typewriter.*

steal *vb.* **1.** pilfer, rob, shoplift, embezzle: *Binks stole a dog biscuit and ran out into the yard to eat it.* **2.** sneak, prowl: *Dressed in black from head to toe, the thief silently stole down the hall toward the strongroom.*

stealthy *adj.* secret, sly, furtive: *The robber gave a stealthy signal to his accomplice, who quickly subdued the guard.* **ant.** open, direct, obvious.

steep *adj.* sheer, perpendicular: *The expert mountain climbers were moving up the face of a steep cliff.* **ant.** gradual.

steer *vb.* guide, navigate, direct, drive: *The pirate steered the ship so that it was headed straight for the reef.*

stem *n.* trunk; stalk: *The stems of the plants were so thick I couldn't cut through them with my ax.* *vb.* **1.** arise, originate: *The smog stems from the car exhausts.* **2.** stop, check, hinder, halt: *We must do something to stem the tide of crime in the area.*

step *n.* **1.** pace, stride: *All those who want to go to the movies should take one step forward.* **2.** action, move, measure: *It was essential that we take steps to make certain the house was locked up.* **3.** stage: *What's the next step in the process?* *vb.* walk, move, come, go: *Please step this way if you want to watch the sea lions being fed.*

stern *adj.* strict, severe, harsh, hard, rigid, unyielding: *Our English teacher was very stern toward students who didn't do their homework.* **ant.** lenient, forgiving.

stew *n.* goulash, ragout: *Mother made lamb stew for dinner.* *vb.* simmer, seethe, boil: *You have to stew this kind of meat for three hours before you can chew it. You may say that Donald's not upset, but he's stewing about something.*

stick *n.* twig, stalk, branch, staff, rod, pole: *I poked a wooden stick through a hole in the fence and something grabbed the other end of it.* *vb.* **1.** stab, pierce, puncture, spear, gore: *Get some iodine—Gary has a splinter stuck in his finger.* **2.** catch, adhere, hold, cling: *Chewing gum was stuck to the bottom of my shoe.* **3.** remain, abide, stay, persist: *No matter what you say, I'll stick by you.*

stiff *adj.* **1.** rigid, unbendable, inflexible, firm, solid, hard: *My mittens were frozen stiff, and I couldn't get them off.* **2.** cool, cold, unfriendly: *Anne's mother gave me a very stiff reception when I visited her.* **3.** severe, harsh, strong: *Ten years is a very stiff sentence.* **ant.** **1.** limp, lax. **2.** warm, hospitable. **3.** lenient.

stifle *vb.* smother, suffocate, strangle, choke: *It's so hot in here that I'm about to stifle. The children stifled their laughter when the teacher's toupee fell off.*

stigma *n.* mark, stain, blot, blemish: *The soldier's capture for desertion left a permanent stigma on his record.*

still *adj.* **1.** motionless, stationary: *Please be still while I try to bandage your finger.* **2.** tranquil, peaceful, calm, serene: *The room was so still you could hear a pin drop.* *conj.* but, nevertheless, however; besides: *I realize that you have a job; still, you ought to continue your studies.*

vb. **1.** silence, quiet, hush: *The crowd had to be stilled so that we could hear the speaker.* **2.** calm, soothe, pacify: *My fears for Ruth's safety weren't stilled until I learned that she'd arrived at her home.* *n.* stillness, quiet, calm, hush: *Only a dog's barking broke the still of the night.*

stimulate *vb.* arouse, activate, excite, urge, animate; invigorate: *Jan is stimulated by an icy cold shower every morning.*

stingy *adj.* miserly, mean, tightfisted, penny-pinching, cheap, selfish: *Mr. Scrooge was so stingy that he wouldn't give water to a man dying of thirst.* *ant.* generous, openhanded, giving.

stir *vb.* **1.** mix, agitate: *Adele puts five spoons of sugar into her coffee and then doesn't stir it.* **2.** arouse, rouse, stimulate; move: *The President's patriotic speech really stirred his listeners.*

stock *n.* supply, store: *The shop bought an ample stock of decorations for sale before Christmas.* *vb.* store, supply, keep, carry: *The salesman told me that they don't stock every size of shoe in that style.*

stoop *vb.* bend, lean, bow, crouch: *The beggar stooped and picked up the coins thrown to him.*

stop *vb.* **1.** cease, discontinue, conclude, end, finish, quit: *I wish you'd stop calling me Bill: my name happens to be George.* **2.** halt, stay, pause: *When I heard footsteps behind me I started running and didn't stop till I was safe at home.* **3.** obstruct, hinder, hold: *Stop that man! He stole my purse!* *n.* **1.** halt, end: *You must put a stop to copying your homework from others.* **2.** stay, delay, halt: *The train makes a stop at Essex to let off passengers.*

store *n.* **1.** shop, market: *If you go to the store, please bring back a quart of milk.* **2.** supply, reserve, stock, deposit: *There is a large store of food in the company's warehouse.* *vb.* stock, save, bank: *If you store eggs too long they'll spoil.*

storm *n.* tempest; gale, thunderstorm, tornado, hurricane: *In the middle of the storm, all of the lights went out when the house was struck by lightning.* *vb.* **1.** rage, rant: *Father went storming about the house because he couldn't find his slippers.* **2.** attack, besiege, assault: *The army of the black knight stormed the castle for six weeks.*

story[1] *n.* **1.** tale, narrative, anecdote: *Grandpa used to tell us funny stories at bedtime.* **2.** lie, fabrication, fib: *You* *have to learn not to tell such stories or no one will believe you when you tell the truth.*

story² *n.* level, floor: *The house we live in has three stories, including the attic.*

stout *adj.* **1.** fat, obese, overweight, plump, heavy, portly: *If you make fun of someone who is stout, you might hurt his feelings.* **2.** strong, sturdy: *They tied up the prisoners with some stout twine and then called the police.* **ant. 1.** slim, thin, skinny, lean. **2.** flimsy.

straight *adj.* **1.** direct, uncurving: *The straight part of this road continues for about a mile.* **2.** honest, upright, honorable, moral: *The mayor is one of the straightest people I know.* **3.** orderly, correct: *Please try to keep your room straight. adv.* directly: *You must come straight home from school today for your piano lesson.* **ant.** *adj.* **1.** crooked, twisted.

strain *vb.* **1.** stretch, tighten: *We strained the rope trying to pull the car out of the ditch.* **2.** injure, harm, sprain: *Bend at the knees to lift something heavy or you'll strain your back.* **3.** filter, screen, sift: *Strain the tea before serving it.*

strainer *n.* sieve, colander, filter: *Pour the soup through the strainer to remove any small chicken bones.*

strait *n.* **1.** channel, passage: *Do you know where the Strait of Magellan is? I don't.* **2.** difficulty, trouble, distress, crisis: *The family has been in dire straits since Pinky's father lost his job.*

strange *adj.* **1.** odd, peculiar, unusual, curious, extraordinary, queer, bizarre: *A small man, wearing strange, silvery clothes, stepped out of the washing machine.* **2.** foreign, unfamiliar, exotic: *A strange odor lingered in the room after our mysterious visitor left.*

stranger *n.* foreigner, alien, outsider, outlander: *Whenever we see a stranger in our town, we try to make him feel right at home.* **ant.** friend, acquaintance.

strap *n.* belt, strip, band, thong: *The leather strap around my suitcase broke, so I now use a piece of rope.*

strategy *n.* management; technique, approach, tactics: *We must think up a proper strategy for persuading the teacher to let us out of class early.*

stray *vb.* wander, rove, roam: *The horse broke its tether and strayed off into the woods. adj.* lost, strayed: *The dog was trained to find and return stray sheep to the farm.*

stream *n.* **1.** brook, run, creek, rivulet, river: *In the winter,* *the stream near our house froze over.* **2.** flow, rush, torrent: *A stream of abuse from the audience greeted the dishonest politician when he rose to speak.* *vb.* flow, rush, pour, gush: *Tears streamed down the girl's face.*

street *n.* road, way; avenue, boulevard: *The street in front of our house in the city is paved with cobblestones.*

strength *n.* **1.** power, vigor, might: *Sally's father showed off his strength by crushing a brick with his bare hands.* **2.** durability, soundness: *For its weight, aluminum has remarkable strength.* **ant. 1.** weakness, frailty.

strenuous *adj.* energetic, forceful, vigorous, active, determined: *The boys made a strenuous effort to move the fallen tree from the road.*

stress *vb.* emphasize, accent, accentuate: *The minister said that he couldn't stress the importance of honesty enough.* *n.* **1.** emphasis, accent, weight, importance: *In my day, the stress was on a classical and literary education.* **2.** pressure, strain: *The stress on the cable was too great, and it gave way.*

stretch *vb.* **1.** extend, elongate, lengthen: *The rope cannot be stretched to go around the package twice.* **2.** expand, spread, extend: *I can't wear that sweater because it's stretched out of shape.* **ant.** contract, shrink.

strict *adj.* stern, unbending, inflexible, stiff, harsh: *There are strict laws about parking in the city during the day.* **ant.** lenient, easygoing.

strife *n.* conflict, disagreement, discord, difference, quarrel, unrest: *There have been few travelers to that part of the world because of the strife among the countries.* **ant.** peace, tranquillity, concord.

strike *vb.* **1.** hit, smite, beat: *The detective knocked the man down by striking him on the jaw with his fist.* **2.** attack, assault: *The commandos strike at dawn.* **3.** impress, affect, overwhelm: *I was struck by the similarity between the two books.* *n.* walkout, sit-down; slowdown: *The entire staff went out on strike for longer hours and less pay.*

strip *vb.* **1.** undress, disrobe: *The doctor's nurse told me to strip for the examination.* **2.** uncover, peel, remove: *That test was as easy as stripping the skin from a banana.* *n.* band, piece, ribbon: *I cut a strip of cloth 2 inches wide and 10 inches long to use as a bandage.*

strive *vb.* try, attempt, endeavor: *I was striving to reach the man in the quicksand with a branch.*

stroke *n.* **1.** blow, knock, tap, rap: *The huge man knocked down the tree with one stroke of his ax.* **2.** achievement, accomplishment, feat: *Starting a restaurant in the country was a stroke of genius.* *vb.* caress, pet: *The vet stroked the dog to calm it.*

stroll *vb., n.* walk, amble, ramble, saunter: *The robber casually strolled into the bank. We went for a stroll along the river before dinner.*

strong *adj.* **1.** powerful, mighty, brawny, muscular: *The man in the circus is strong enough to pick up an elephant.* **2.** solid, resistant, unbreakable: *The glass in the windshield is almost strong enough to resist the blow of a hammer.* **3.** sharp, spicy, hot; aromatic: *The flavor of this dish is strong enough—don't add any more pepper.* ant. **1.** feeble, weak. **2.** fragile. **3.** bland, tasteless.

structure *n.* framework, construction, arrangement: *The structure as designed by the engineers will be strong enough to withstand an earthquake.*

struggle *vb.* fight, strive, oppose: *The two men struggled for possession of the gun.* *n.* **1.** fight, encounter, clash, battle, conflict: *At the end of the struggle thousands lay wounded on the battlefield.* **2.** effort, exertion: *It's a struggle getting up on time every day.*

stubborn *adj.* obstinate, unyielding, inflexible, rigid, unbending, stiff, pig-headed: *If you're going to be stubborn about doing everything yourself, you may never learn a better way.*

student *n.* pupil; scholar: *The students in our school have great respect for the teachers.*

studio *n.* workshop, workroom: *Have you ever visited an artist's studio?*

study *n.* attention, examination, research: *The committee decided that much study must be given to the question of where the new library was to be built.* *vb.* examine, investigate; consider, weigh: *I have to study for the test tomorrow. We ought to study the problem before giving a reply.*

stuff *n.* **1.** substance, material: *What kind of stuff do they make plastic out of?* **2.** cloth, fabric, textile: *The king's throne room was hung with gold-embroidered stuffs.* *vb.* ram, fill, pack, cram: *I stuffed rags in the cracks to keep out the cold.*

stumble *vb.* trip; lurch: *I stumbled going down the steps and almost fell down.*

stun *vb.* **1.** knock out: *I was temporarily stunned when the baseball struck me on the head.* **2.** astonish, surprise, shock, amaze, astound: *Ike was stunned when they told him that he'd won the gold medal.*

stupid *adj.* dumb, dull, half-witted, thimble-witted, witless, simple-minded, idiotic: *Crossing the road without watching for traffic is a stupid thing to do.* **ant.** intelligent, smart, bright, quick.

sturdy *adj.* rugged, strong, well-built, stout: *Although the flagpole bent in the wind it was sturdy enough not to break.* **ant.** frail, flimsy.

style *n.* **1.** kind, sort, type: *What style of shoe were you looking for?* **2.** elegance, chic, smartness: *Alexa's mother has a great deal of style, no matter what she does or wears.*

subdue *vb.* **1.** defeat, conquer, beat, overcome: *The people, without arms for defense, were quickly subdued by the advancing army.* **2.** lower, reduce, soften, tone down: *The mourners talked in subdued voices at the funeral.*

subject *n.* **1.** topic, theme: *On what subject should I write the essay for the English class?* **2.** subordinate, dependent: *The people were considered subjects of the queen.* *adj.* **1.** depending, dependent: *Subject to your approval, we'd like to plan a picnic for the class.* **2.** subordinate, inferior: *The subject people of the world have come a long way toward independence.* *vb.* **1.** dominate, influence, control, tame, subdue, suppress: *Because of you, we were caught and subjected to punishment.* **2.** expose: *Why must I be subjected to constant abuse just because I have red hair?*

submerge *vb.* dip, sink, submerse: *The submarine submerged to avoid being spotted by the planes.* **ant.** rise, surface.

submit *vb.* **1.** yield, surrender: *The few soldiers remaining finally submitted when the fort was bombed.* **2.** offer, tender: *Our class submitted a plan to the principal for cleaning up the grounds.* **ant.** **1.** resist, fight.

subordinate *adj.* inferior, lower: *Ken was able to get only a job subordinate to the department head.* *n.* worker, assistant, inferior: *Beth is a subordinate of Mrs. White's in the company.* *vb.* lower, demean, reduce: *You ought to learn to subordinate your desires to those of the entire group.* **ant.** *adj.*, *n.* superior.

subsequent *adj.* following, later, succeeding: *A subsequent ruling by the zoning commission denied the permit for a restaurant on the lakefront.* **ant.** previous, preceding.

subside *vb.* sink, lower; diminish: *The land subsided and the foundation of the house was destroyed. My eagerness to see the boy punished subsided with each passing day.* **ant.** erupt, arise.

subsidy *n.* grant, support, aid: *The foundation could not carry out the research without subsidies from wealthy citizens.*

substance *n.* **1.** material, matter, stuff: *This dress is made out of some strange synthetic substance.* **2.** essence: *Tom presented the substance of his argument but no one agreed with him.*

substantial *adj.* **1.** considerable, large, sizable: *The lawyer received a substantial fee for defending the rich man's son.* **2.** real, actual, tangible: *The police have substantial reason to believe that the fire was not accidental.* **3.** wealthy, influential: *My uncle is a substantial member of this community, I'll have you know.* **ant. 1.** trivial, unimportant.

substitute *n.* replacement, surrogate, stand-in: *I'm not good enough to be a regular player, but I'm a substitute.* *vb.* replace, exchange, displace: *Rick was sent in to substitute for Bill when Bill broke his leg.*

subtle *adj.* indirect; suggestive: *There are subtle differences between the totalitarianisms of communism and of fascism.* **ant.** obvious, overt.

subtract *vb.* reduce, diminish, deduct, lessen: *When you subtract 13 from 26 you get 13.* **ant.** add.

succeed *vb.* **1.** thrive, prosper, flourish: *Fred has succeeded very well in business.* **2.** follow, ensue; replace: *We were having such a wonderful time that the succeeding days meant nothing. Mr. Kensington succeeded Mr. Kew as chairman of the garden committee.* **ant. 1.** fail, flop. **2.** precede.

success *n.* prosperity, advance, luck: *The principal of the school wished each student every success in the future.* **ant.** failure.

successful *adj.* lucky, fortunate, prosperous, triumphant, victorious, favorable: *Mr. Rodgers had a very successful business trip to Europe.*

succession *n.* series, course, sequence: *Let me describe for you the succession of events that led up to our leaving town with the police after us.*

successive *adj.* consecutive, sequential, serial: *The successive earthquakes did more damage than the original shock.*

sudden *adj.* unexpected, swift, abrupt, unforeseen: *The sudden blizzard found us without snow-removal equipment.*

suffer *vb.* **1.** undergo, experience, endure: *You must have suffered terrible pain from the burns.* **2.** allow, permit, let: *Why should I suffer these people to come to me with their complaints?*

sufficient *adj.* enough, adequate: *I think we have a sufficient amount of air to last us for one hour.*

suffix *n.* ending: *One meaning of the -ed suffix in English is to indicate the past tense.* **ant.** prefix.

suggest *vb.* offer, propose, recommend, hint: *I suggested that they might try putting out the fire with sand, since water was unavailable in the desert.*

suggestion *n.* hint, proposal, advice: *The teacher liked my suggestion that everyone in the class start his own project.*

suitable *adj.* fitting, apt, becoming, proper: *I don't think that blue jeans and a tee shirt are suitable attire for this French restaurant.* **ant.** inappropriate.

sullen *adj.* **1.** silent, moody, bitter, sulky: *Try to say something to cheer up Bob this morning—he seems so sullen.* **2.** dismal, sad, gloomy, somber: *These sullen winter days are very depressing.* **ant.** **1.** cheerful, cheery, jovial.

sultry *adj.* hot, oppressive, close, stifling: *It was another one of those sultry, 90-degree days, so we all went swimming.*

sum *n.* amount: *There is no need for you to keep on giving such small sums of money to me.*

summary *n.* outline, digest, synopsis, abstract, précis: *Please let me have a summary of the book in just 250 words.* *adj.* brief, concise, short, compact, condensed: *A summary report of what happened at the meeting should be on my desk now.*

summit *n.* top, peak, crown: *After three hours of climbing, we stood at the summit of the mountain.* **ant.** base, bottom.

summon *vb.* call, invoke, convoke, invite: *We were summoned to the director's office at 9 a.m. the next day.* **ant.** dismiss.

sundry *adj.* various, several: *We found sundry items of interest in the dresser drawers in the attic.*

superb *adj.* wonderful, splendid, marvelous, extraordinary, superior, excellent, magnificent, fine: *The turtle soup at this restaurant is superb.*

superintendent *n.* supervisor, manager, director, overseer, administrator: *After 20 years, my uncle was made superintendent of the factory.*

superior *adj.* better, greater, finer: *One can easily see that this painting is of superior workmanship. n.* boss, employer, supervisor: *Each worker must have his time sheet signed by his superior.* **ant.** *adj., n.* inferior.

supervise *vb.* oversee, direct, manage: *If the children had been properly supervised, the accident wouldn't have happened.*

supplement *n.* addition; complement; extension: *The Sunday newspaper costs more because of all the supplements. vb.* add, extend, complement: *Tim supplements his allowance by working in a shop after school.*

supply *vb.* provide, furnish, stock: *The dealer who supplies our grocer with vegetables raised his prices again. n.* store, stock, inventory, quantity: *Our supply of pencils is running low, so please order some more.*

support *vb.* **1.** bear, hold up, sustain, prop: *That flimsy chair cannot support the weight of an adult.* **2.** maintain, sustain, finance: *How can Oscar support his family on so little money?* **3.** back, assist, aid, promote: *I shall support your candidate in the next election.* **4.** strengthen, corroborate, verify, substantiate: *The confession of the thief was supported by the evidence of his fingerprints at the scene. n.* **1.** brace, prop, stay: *I hope that these supports will hold in a windstorm.* **2.** help, aid, assistance: *We need all the support we can get in the fight against disease.* **3.** provider, breadwinner, backer: *Tessie is the sole support of her mother.*

suppose *vb.* **1.** assume, presume: *Suppose you are walking down a lonely street in the middle of the night: would you be scared?* **2.** believe, think; judge: *I suppose you're right about not trusting Philip to get here on time.*

suppress *vb.* subdue, overpower: *The suppressed minorities are making their voices heard more and more.*

supreme *adj.* best, highest, greatest: *The supreme achievement of his life was having chewed an oyster instead of swallowing it whole.*

sure   *adj.*   **1.** certain, positive, confident, convinced: *Are you sure that Marcy said to meet her in the middle of the highway at rush hour?* **2.** reliable, steady, trustworthy, unfailing: *A sure way to make someone angry with you is to punch him in the nose.* **3.** firm, stable, solid, safe: *My footing on the icy steps was far from sure, and I soon slipped and fell.* **4.** fated, destined, unavoidable, inevitable: *If you insult her again, she's sure to slap your face.*

surface   *n.* exterior, outside, covering, cover: *The surface of the sun has a temperature of millions of degrees.*

surge   *vb.* swell, heave, grow: *The tidal wave surged upward on the land, destroying everything in its path.* **ant.** ebb, wane, diminish.

surmise   *vb.* think, judge, suppose, assume, believe, presume, suspect: *I surmised, from seeing your red face and from your jumping up and down, that you are excited about something.* *n.* guess, thought: *It was your surmise that the sun would rise.*

surpass   *vb.* exceed, pass, outdo, outstrip, excel: *In speed, Robbie surpassed all of the competitors; but his style was poor.*

surplus   *n.* excess, remainder: *There will be a surplus of wheat in this year's harvest.* *adj.* extra: *All surplus money will be added to the picnic fund.*

surprise   *vb.* **1.** amaze, astound, astonish, startle: *I was surprised to see George wearing a green dress—he looks so much better in blue.* **2.** catch, startle: *The teacher surprised three students hiding in the supply closet.* *n.* amazement, shock: *The enemy took us by surprise and we surrendered.*

surrender   *vb.* yield, submit, give up: *Twenty thousand soldiers surrendered at the end of the battle.* **ant.** resist.

surround   *vb.* encircle, circle, girdle: *The trunk of the tree was surrounded by a yellow ribbon.*

survey   *vb.* examine, scan, view, inspect: *Before moving into the territory, we carefully surveyed every inch of it.* *n.* **1.** examination, inspection: *A survey of the area yielded no information.* **2.** poll: *In a recent survey, more people were found to be parents than anybody else.*

survive   *vb.* remain, persist, live, continue: *Despite lack of food and water, the castaways survived for almost a week.* **ant.** fail, die, succumb.

suspect   *vb.* **1.** doubt, mistrust, distrust, disbelieve: *The police suspect the three men who were seen loitering near* *the bank.* **2.** suppose, presume, assume: *I suspect that Bob may be late because his car won't start. n.* defendant: *The suspect was seen leaving the scene of the crime. adj.* suspicious, suspected, questionable, doubtful: *Spending large amounts of money after a robbery makes certain people suspect.* **ant.** *vb.* **1.** know, believe, trust.

suspend *vb.* **1.** hang; dangle: *The flag was suspended from the rafters in the gymnasium.* **2.** postpone, defer, withhold, delay, interrupt: *The trial was temporarily suspended when a juror became ill with the flu.*

suspicious *adj.* **1.** distrustful, suspecting, doubting, doubtful, dubious, suspect, questioning, skeptical: *I was suspicious of Anne when she said she had memorized the entire telephone directory.* **2.** questionable, suspect, irregular, unusual: *There was a suspicious-looking person lurking near the back door.*

sustain *vb.* **1.** support, bear, carry, uphold: *That flimsy pole cannot sustain the weight of the entire roof.* **2.** support, maintain, keep: *Our hopes were sustained by the sounds of digging from the other side of the cave-in.* **3.** undergo, endure, suffer; bear: *The injuries sustained in the accident were all minor, and everyone was sent home.* **4.** support, ratify, approve: *The findings of the lower court were sustained by the Supreme Court.*

swallow *vb.* eat, gulp, gorge: *It wasn't easy to swallow 23 hot dogs in the contest. n.* gulp, mouthful: *Take a swallow of water to help you to stop coughing.*

swamp *n.* bog, quagmire, fen, marsh, morass: *Keep away from the swamp if you want to avoid a dangerous area. vb.* deluge, overcome, flood: *After Sadie's singing debut, she was swamped with requests to sing out of town (by the neighbors).*

swarm *n.* horde, throng, mass, host: *A swarm of insects hovered over the picnic table. vb.* throng, crowd: *The fans swarmed around the football players after the game.*

sway *vb.* **1.** wave, bend, swing: *The palm trees swayed gently in the tropical breeze.* **2.** influence, persuade, impress: *The judge refused to be swayed by appeals to sympathy.*

swear *vb.* **1.** vow, declare, state, assert, vouch, vouchsafe: *The prisoner swore that he had never eaten a raw egg in his life.* **2.** curse, blaspheme: *We don't allow students to swear in this school.*

sweat *vb.* perspire: *Physical labor under that hot sun makes* *you sweat. n.* perspiration: *The sweat ran down from my forehead into my eyes, stinging them.*

sweeping *adj.* general, comprehensive, broad, all-embracing, all-inclusive: *I'd say that your comment that all teenagers are naughty is too sweeping to be true.*

sweet *adj.* **1.** sugary, honeyed: *That Turkish candy is too sweet for me.* **2.** fresh, clean, pure, unsalted: *We got sweet water from the well.* **3.** pleasant, melodious, tuneful, musical, harmonious, mellow: *Nicole has a very sweet singing voice.* **4.** charming, agreeable, pleasant, attractive: *Our parrot has a sweet disposition and would never bite anyone.* **ant. 1.** sour, bitter. **3.** discordant, harsh. **4.** irritable, nasty, irascible.

swell *vb.* grow, increase, enlarge, expand: *The balloon swelled as we continued to pump air into it.* **ant.** shrink, diminish.

swift *adj.* fast, quick, rapid, speedy, fleet: *"I am a swift runner," said Tom slowly.* **ant.** slow, sluggish, laggardly.

swindle *vb.* cheat, bilk, cozen, defraud, trick, deceive, con: *I was once swindled out of $100 in the Spanish handkerchief game.* *n.* fraud, deception, trickery: *The company's guarantee is nothing more than a swindle to sell you the tiger.*

swing *vb.* sway, rock, wave: *There was Tarzan, swinging from a vine, with Cheetah jabbering away on the ground.*

switch *vb.* change, shift, turn: *I am switching my support to the Democratic party in the next election.*

sympathetic *adj.* compassionate, considerate, tender, kind: *You must learn to be more sympathetic to the feelings of other people.* **ant.** unsympathetic, intolerant, indifferent.

sympathy *n.* feeling, sentiment, compassion, understanding: *Your sympathy for our problems is sincerely appreciated.*

symptom *n.* sign, indication, mark: *Red spots on your chest are not a symptom of dandruff.*

system *n.* procedure, arrangement, plan, order, scheme: *It is important that you devise a system for disposing of the ashes from the furnace.*

systematic *adj.* organized, orderly, regular, methodical: *The most common systematic way for arranging information is alphabetical order.* **ant.** random, irregular.

T

tackle *n.* gear, equipment, rigging, apparatus: *What kind of tackle would be used to raise a car from a dock onto a ship?* *vb.* **1.** seize, grab, down, catch, throw: *The runner was tackled near the center of the field.* **2.** undertake, try: *If they pay him enough, Jack will tackle any assignment they give him.*

tact *n.* judgment, sense, diplomacy, prudence: *Telling someone that he has bad breath requires a lot of tact.*

tactful *adj.* diplomatic, considerate, sensitive, skillful: *Try to be more tactful when talking to employees about something they've done that's wrong.* **ant.** tactless, unfeeling.

tactics *n. pl.* strategy, plan, approach: *What will be the most successful tactics to make the enemy surrender?*

tag *n.* label, sticker: *According to the tag on this dress, it is two sizes too small for you.* *vb.* mark, label: *All the tagged items are reduced in price for our annual sale.*

take *vb.* **1.** grasp, hold, catch, seize: *They took the puppy from us because we couldn't keep it in the passenger section.* **2.** win, capture, seize, acquire: *After a two-hour battle, the pirates took the treasure ship. You take first prize.* **3.** pick, choose, select; prefer: *Take a number from one to ten; double it; then add the original number.* **4.** guide, conduct, lead, escort, bring: *Who is going to take the children to school today?* **5.** remove, steal, lift, shoplift, rob: *Somebody took my left shoe.* **6.** record, note, write, register: *Have you hired a secretary who can take shorthand?* **7.** require, need, demand: *But it doesn't take two hours to wash your hair!* **8.** charm, attract, engage, bewitch: *I must admit that I am very much taken with Fiona.* **9.** purchase, buy, pay for: *I'd like to take one dozen of the red ones and two dozen of the blue.* *vb. phr.* **take after** resemble: *You certainly take after your mother, Sophie.* **take away** deduct, subtract: *Take 6 away from 11 and you're left with 5.* **take back 1.** reclaim, recover, regain: *The French took back all the conquered land after the war.* **2.** retract, recall, deny: *You had better take back those things you said!* **take down** lower, remove: *The* *teachers made us take down the poster for the cooky sale.* **take in 1.** include, embrace: *When you say "mammal," that ·doesn't take in birds and snakes.* **2.** deceive, dupe, fool: *You certainly were taken in by that fellow who sold you a comb without teeth.* **3.** welcome, shelter, receive, accept: *My ma won't let me take in every stray dog or cat.* **4.** shorten, reduce, lessen: *The tailor took in all my clothes when I lost 25 pounds.* **5.** understand, comprehend: *Marcia took in everything I said but didn't even smile.* **take it 1.** assume, understand, accept: *I take it that you don't like eating raw eggs.* **2.** endure, survive: *I guess that Merrill just can't take it.* **take off 1.** doff, remove: *You'll have to take off all your clothes if you expect to take a bath.* **2.** deduct, subtract, take away: *The owner offered to take off another 10 percent if I pay the freight.* **3.** leave, depart, go: *The bus driver just took off and left us standing in the street.* **take on 1.** employ, hire, engage: *We took on 23 more people at the plant last month.* **2.** undertake, assume. *I think that with his job after school and on weekends, Peter has taken on more than he can handle.* **3.** assume, acquire: *After not having seen another person for so long, Jim took on a lean, mean look.* **take out 1.** extract, remove: *The dentist said he had to take out my last baby tooth.* **2.** entertain, escort, date: *Are you old enough to take out girls?* **take over** seize, capture: *A gang from the other side of town took over our clubhouse.* **take to** enjoy, like, favor: *My new watchdog takes to strangers in the friendliest way.* **take up 1.** start, begin, commence: *Don't you think that it's a little late to take up hang gliding at the age of 83?* **2.** occupy, consume: *All of my days are taken up with going to school or working afterwards.*

tale *n.* story, anecdote: *My father always tells the same old tale when we get together at Christmas.*

talent *n.* skill, ability, gift, aptitude: *Bob has great talent for playing the kazoo.*

talk *vb.* **1.** speak; communicate: *Betty says she doesn't want to talk with you.* **2.** confer, discuss, consult: *I think you ought to talk it over with someone before making a decision.* *n.* **1.** speech, communication: *I admire your capacity for talk.* **2.** gossip, rumor: *There's talk around town that you were seen with lemon meringue pie on your face the night before the pie-eating contest. Just practicing, I guess.*

tall *adj.* high, big: *As the value of the land increases, we tend to build taller buildings.* **ant.** short, low.

tame *adj.* **1.** domesticated, docile, mild, broken: *Civilization began when man learned how to make animals tame.* **2.** dull, uninteresting, unexciting, flat, empty, boring: *Life must be pretty tame for you now that the war is over.* *vb.* domesticate, break: *It takes a lot of patience to tame a wild animal.* **ant.** *adj.* **1.** wild.

tangle *vb.* knot, twist, confuse, snarl: *You've tangled the kite string in the branches of the tree.*

tap *vb.* rap, pat, strike, hit: *If you tap the ball gently, it will roll into the hole and you'll win.* *n.* **1.** rap, pat, blow: *A slight tap on the door or window and the dog will start barking.* **2.** faucet, spigot: *Turn off the tap when you finish washing.*

tape *n.* strip, ribbon: *Please let me have a piece of tape from that roll.* *vb.* **1.** bind, tie, fasten; bandage: *It was only a sprain, so the doctor taped my wrist.* **2.** record: *Brad taped the entire show and now can play it back any time he wants to hear it.*

taper *n.* candle: *We lit a taper and the room sprang into light.* *vb.* decrease, narrow, lessen: *A cone has a circular base and a side that tapers to a point.*

tardy *adj.* late, slow, overdue, behindhand: *If any of you are tardy to class any more, the teacher will report you.* **ant.** prompt, punctual.

target *n.* goal, objective, object, aim: *Our target is to raise $100 for the team uniform fund.*

tariff *n.* tax, levy, duty, rate: *There is a tariff of 10 percent on all imported items.*

tart *adj.* acid, sour; sharp, biting, cutting: *Lemons are very tart. Victoria's tart comment about my hat was not at all welcome.* **ant.** sweet, sugary.

task *n.* job, duty, chore: *Ben must do some tasks before he may go out to the movies.*

taste *vb.* **1.** sip, try, savor, sample: *Have you tasted Mrs. O'Neill's apple pie?* **2.** experience, undergo: *Only someone who has never tasted war could want to go into battle.* *n.* **1.** flavor, savor: *I don't like the taste of prune juice in my milk.* **2.** appreciation, discernment, discrimination, judgment: *That sign is in very bad taste.*

taunt *vb.* tease, annoy, bother, pester; mock, jeer, ridicule, make fun of: *Why must you continue to taunt me just because I wear short pants?*

tavern *n.* bar, cocktail lounge, café, pub: *During the winter, we used to meet at the tavern to trade sailing stories and have a beer or two.*

tax *n.* tariff, levy, duty, rate: *Connecticut has a 7 percent sales tax on everything except food. vb.* **1.** assess: *A government should not tax its citizens without giving them a voice in running the country.* **2.** strain, burden, encumber, load, overload: *The work taxed her so much she fell ill.*

taxi *n.* taxicab, cab: *"Please call me a taxi." "All right. You're a taxi!"*

teach *vb.* instruct, train, educate, inform, tutor: *Schools ought to teach students English before they reach college.*

teacher *n.* instructor, tutor, lecturer, professor: *The teachers in our school are very kind and helpful to students who don't understand everything easily.*

teamwork *n.* cooperation, collaboration: *If we apply teamwork, we'll finish the job much sooner.*

tear¹ *vb.* rip, split, rend, divide: *My father is so strong that he can tear a telephone book in half. n.* rip, split, rent: *There's a tear in my coat that I have to sew up.*

tear² *n.* drop, teardrop: *A tear ran down Penny's cheek when she peeled the onion. vb.* water: *The pollution in the city air makes my eyes tear.*

tease *vb.* irritate, annoy, pester, bother, vex, harass, harry: *Do not tease the animals.*

technical *adj.* technological, industrial, mechanical; specialized: *Operating a typewriter is simple, but repairing one is a technical skill.*

technique *n.* method, system, approach, routine, procedure: *Scientists have developed a new technique for treating certain diseases.*

tedious *adj.* tiring, tiresome, dull, boring, wearisome: *Driving two hours a day to and from school can become very tedious.* **ant.** interesting, engaging, exciting.

teem *vb.* swarm, abound: *The teeming mass of people in the downtown area is surprising to someone from the country.*

tell *vb.* **1.** relate, narrate: *Please tell us a bedtime story.* **2.** inform, advise, explain: *Can't you tell me where you live?* **3.** reveal, disclose, divulge, declare: *Doesn't Philip ever tell the truth?* **4.** determine, discern, discover: *I can't tell whether the car is blue or green in this dim light.* **5.** command, order, bid: *You tell Harvey that he'd better get to work on time or he won't have a job.*

temper *n.* **1.** mood, disposition, temperament, nature, humor: *Ellie seems to be in a bad temper this morning.* **2.** self-control, patience: *Edward loses his temper over very unimportant things.* *vb.* **1.** moderate, soothe, soften, pacifv: *If you want to get along with people, you must learn to temper your outbursts.* **2.** anneal: *The first swords were made from tempered steel in Toledo, Spain.*

temperament *n.* disposition, nature, temper: *The miser in the castle had a very unpleasant temperament.*

temperamental *adj.* moody, irritable, touchy, testy, sensitive: *Just because you sing opera, that doesn't mean you have to be so temperamental.* **ant.** serene, unruffled.

temperate *adj.* moderate, controlled, restrained, cool, calm: *If you are not involved personally, you can regard the problem in a much more temperate manner.*

tempest *n.* storm; tumult, commotion, turmoil: *As the tempest raged outside, we stayed near the fire, nice and snug.*

temporary *adj.* passing, short-lived, short, fleeting, momentary: *We made a temporary stop for repairs and then drove on.* **ant.** permanent, everlasting, fixed.

tempt *vb.* lure, allure, entice, seduce, attract, invite: *I certainly am tempted to go to the dance when you say that Carol will be there.*

tend *vb.* guard, look after, care for, take care of: *Who was left at home to tend Grandma?*

tendency *n.* inclination, trend, leaning, disposition: *Sharon has always shown a tendency toward fat.*

tender[1] *adj.* **1.** delicate, soft; fragile: *That's the most tender steak I've ever eaten.* **2.** loving, gentle, affectionate, sympathetic: *I received a very tender note from a friend when I became ill.* **3.** sensitive, sore, painful: *My arm is still tender where I banged it last week.* **ant.** **1.** tough, chewy. **2.** unfeeling, cruel.

tender[2] *vb.* offer, proffer, present, propose: *The company tendered a bid of $10,342 to complete the road work.* *n.* offer, proposal: *A tender of $15,000 has already been rejected.*

tenderfoot *n.* beginner, novice, amateur, apprentice: *The other fellows laughed to see the tenderfoot trying to mount the horse over its tail.*

tenderhearted *adj.* sympathetic, softhearted, kind, merciful:

Mandy is so tenderhearted she would care for a sick mosquito! **ant.** hardhearted, cruel.

tense *adj.* stretched, strained, tight; excited, nervous: *My arm was tense from carrying so many books. Bill was tense from lack of sleep.* **ant.** relaxed, lax.

term *n.* **1.** word, expression, phrase, name: *"What is the term for someóne who is too lazy to do any homework?" "Dummy."* **2.** period, interval; semester, session: *What is the term of your agreement? Will you be returning to school next term?*

terminate *vb.* end, stop, cease, close, finish, conclude: *The school year terminates with final examinations.* **ant.** begin, commence, start.

terrible *adj.* horrible, awful, horrifying, dreadful, terrifying: *The earthquake has done terrible damage in Guatemala.*

territory *n.* area, region, province, section: *The salesmen each covered his own territory within the state.*

terror *n.* horror, dread, fear, fright, panic, alarm: *Until the mad killer was caught, everyone in town was living in terror.*

test *n.* trial, examination, exam, quiz: *We are going to have a math test tomorrow.* *vb.* quiz, examine: *Are we going to be tested on what was taught today?*

testify *vb.* warrant, depose, state, witness: *Patrick testified that he had been robbed at knifepoint by the defendant.*

text *n.* book, textbook, manual: *We have to buy a new text next year.*

thankful *adj.* grateful, obliged, appreciative: *Gerry was thankful that Sarah had cooked dinner for him.*

thaw *vb.* melt, liquefy, dissolve: *The ice thawed in the warm weather. You have to thaw out the frozen food before eating it.* **ant.** freeze, solidify.

theft *n.* robbery, thievery, stealing, larceny, burglary; pillage, plunder: *The theft yielded the criminals only sixty-two cents.*

theme *n.* **1.** subject, topic, thesis, argument, point: *The main theme that ran through the speech was that we must be good to each other.* **2.** composition, paper, essay, report: *I have to write a theme for English class, and I don't know what to write on.*

theory *n.* hypothesis, guess, assumption, explanation: *I have a theory that the earth is really a cube, but no one agrees.*

therefore *adv.* consequently, hence, so, then, accordingly: *I am breathing; therefore, I must be alive.*

thick   *adj.*   **1.** dense, solid: *The crowd was so thick that I was unable to get through.* **2.** heavy, compact, syrupy, viscous: *The oil was quite thick and coated everything with a black goo.* **ant. 1.** thin, slim. **3.** watery.

thief   *n.* robber, burglar, criminal: *A thief stole the knocker off our front door.*

thin   *adj.*   **1.** narrow, slim, lean, slender; sparse, meager, scanty: *Carolyn looks thin after losing 20 pounds. That's a pretty thin excuse for being late—you couldn't find a sock?* **2.** watery, weak, light: *The soup is so thin here that they seem to make it by boiling a pot of water with only one noodle in it for flavor.*

think   *vb.*   **1.** consider, contemplate, reflect, meditate: *I have been thinking about going on vacation, but I cannot decide where.* **2.** judge, deem: *Don't you think that Mr. Carson is an excellent teacher?* **3.** suppose, assume, believe: *I think that you'll want to go to the movies when you find out what's playing.*

thirst   *n.* desire, appetite, craving, longing: *The students in this class have an unusual thirst for knowledge.*

thorn   *n.* barb, nettle, spine, prickle, bramble: *These roses have very sharp thorns, so be careful when handling them.*

thorough   *adj.* complete, careful, thoroughgoing; completed: *Jim did a very thorough job of cleaning the leaves off the lawn.* **ant.** careless, haphazard, slapdash.

thoroughfare   *n.* street, highway, avenue, boulevard, parkway: *The main thoroughfare in our town is called New Street.* **ant.** byway.

thought   *n.*   **1.** meditation, deliberation, contemplation, reasoning, cogitation: *I didn't want to disturb Irena because she was deep in thought.* **2.** concept, idea, belief: *It was Patrick's thought that taking a holiday in Chichicastenango might help him get a good rest.*

thoughtful   *adj.*   **1.** kind, considerate, attentive, courteous, friendly: *Gerry is so thoughtful—he always brings wine when invited to dinner.* **2.** absorbed, pensive, reflective: *When he heard about how difficult it was for uneducated people to get a job, Tom became very thoughtful.* **ant. 1.** thoughtless.

thrash   *vb.* beat, whip, flog, punish, defeat: *Until quite recently, students who misbehaved were thrashed by their teachers.*

threat   *n.* warning; menace: *You cannot scare me with your* *threats about tattling to my mother. The rocks at the mouth of the harbor are a threat to safety for ships.*

threaten *vb.* **1.** warn, menace, caution, forewarn, intimidate: *The bully threatened Percy with a beating if he didn't give him the ball.* **2.** loom: *The black clouds threatened from the west.*

threshold *n.* **1.** doorsill: *It was formerly customary for a husband to carry his bride over the threshold of their new home.* **2.** edge, verge; beginning, start: *I was on the threshold of telling the secret when they stopped torturing me.*

thrift *n.* economy, saving: *Not eating in order to save money is false thrift.*

thrifty *adj.* frugal, sparing, parsimonious, economical, saving: *My grandmother was so thrifty that she saved up every bit of string she could find.* **ant.** spendthrift, prodigal.

thrill *n.* excitement, stimulation, tingle: *We all got a great thrill out of watching our team win the gold medal for swimming.* *vb.* excite, stimulate, rouse, arouse: *The star said that she was thrilled to receive an Academy Award.*

thrive *vb.* prosper, succeed, grow, flourish: *The family business thrived after we moved to Chicago. These plants will thrive only if you don't water them too much.* **ant.** languish, expire, die.

throng *n.* crowd, multitude, swarm, mass, horde: *A throng of people crowded round the plane to welcome the visitor from Yakutsk.* *vb.* crowd, swarm, teem: *Spurred on by favorable reviews, people thronged the theaters to see the film.*

through *adj.* done, completed, over, finished: *In June, school will be through for a few months. Are you through using the sugar?*

throughout *prep.* **1.** everywhere, all through, all over: *We searched throughout the house but couldn't find the cat.* **2.** during: *Throughout the last three days you were begging to go to the movies.*

throw *vb.* toss, hurl, pitch, cast, fling, send: *Throw the ball to me and I'll run with it.* *n.* toss, pitch: *That was a great throw from the outfield to home plate.*

thrust *vb.* push, shove; force: *You don't have to thrust the thing right into my face just because I didn't see it at first.* *n.* push, shove, drive: *With a single, powerful thrust, the native's spear had killed the wild boar.*

thwart *vb.* frustrate, obstruct, stop: *Bill Jackson was* *thwarted in his plan to run for election by not being able to raise the necessary funds.*

tidings   *n. pl.* news, information, word, report: *The messenger brought tidings of a huge sea battle being fought down the coast.*

tie   *vb.* **1.** bind, secure, fasten: *June is a little early to be tying up Christmas packages, isn't it?* **2.** join, connect, knot, link, fasten: *The captive was tied to a stake and the natives danced about him, singing. If you tie these two pieces together, then the cord will be long enough to go round. n.* **1.** cord, string, rope, strap, band, fastener: *I need some kind of a tie to keep these two bundles together.* **2.** cravat, four-in-hand, necktie: *You must wear a tie and jacket to eat in the main dining room of the hotel.*

tight   *adj.* **1.** firm, taut, secure, strong, fast, fixed: *This knot was tied so tight that no one can open it.* **2.** sealed, airtight, watertight, locked, fastened: *I can't open this jar because the cover was screwed on too tight.* **3.** tipsy, high, drunk, intoxicated, inebriated: *Mother got a little tight from drinking champagne at her anniversary party.* **4.** stingy, miserly, niggardly: *Old man Phoebelfinger is too tight to donate any money to charity.* **ant. 1.** loose, slack. **3.** sober.

tilt   *vb.* slope, incline, slant, lean, tip: *You tilted the table when you leaned on it, spilling my milk and cookies onto the floor.*

time   *n.* **1.** period, interval, span, space, term: *The time between spring and autumn is called summer. Don't spend so much time talking on the phone, Mabel.* **2.** rhythm, tempo, beat, measure: *The orchestra then played Beethoven's Eighth Symphony in ragtime. vb.* regulate, gauge, adjust, measure: *The engineers are trying to time the number of pulses per second.*

timetable   *n.* schedule: *The print on this timetable is so small that by the time I make it out I shall have missed my train.*

timid   *adj.* shy, bashful, retiring, coy, fainthearted, diffident, fearful: *Anne-Marie is so timid that she refused to dance with anyone at the school prom.* **ant.** bold, forward, self-confident.

tinge   *vb., n.* tint, color, dye, stain: *We tinged our tee shirts a pale shade of blue. There's a slight tinge of pink in the sky at sunset.*

tint *n., vb.* tinge, color, dye, stain: *These walls need a warm tint in order to set off the color of the carpet. Some older people with white hair tint it bluish.*

tiny *adj.* small, wee, little, miniature: *Just as I said that, a tiny figure leaped out of the box and granted me three wishes.* **ant.** large, huge, enormous.

tip¹ *n.* end, point, peak, top: *That huge mountain is just the tip of the iceberg—most of it is under water.*

tip² *vb.* tilt, upset, knock over: *The canoe tipped, and we both fell into the raging rapids.*

tip³ *n.* **1.** gratuity, gift, reward: *My father gave the waiter a good tip because the service had been so good.* **2.** hint, clue, inkling, suggestion: *The man in the loud checkered suit just gave me a tip on which horse would win the race.*

tire¹ *vb.* **1.** weary, weaken, exhaust: *Since my illness, I tire easily.* **2.** weary, weaken, fatigue, exhaust: *All that exercise tired me.* **ant.** exhilarate.

tire² *n.* wheel, casing: *My bicycle had a flat tire on the way to school today.*

tired *adj.* exhausted, weary, run-down, fatigued, sleepy: *I am so tired from walking around the museum that I could go to sleep standing up.*

tireless *adj.* energetic, active, strenuous, enthusiastic: *Walter was a tireless campaigner for the Republican nominee.*

title *n.* **1.** name, heading, designation: *What is the title of that book?* **2.** ownership, deed, right, claim: *The title to that property is held jointly by my mother and father.* *vb.* name, designate, entitle, call: *I have titled my latest movie, "Murder Done with a Cream Puff."*

toil *vb.* work, labor, slave, sweat: *Think about all those people toiling in the fields to harvest the food that you take for granted.* *n.* work, labor, drudgery, effort, exertion: *After ten hours of toil, I just want to eat and go to sleep.* **ant.** *vb.* relax, loll.

token *n.* sign, mark, sample: *Ben gave Betty a bracelet as a token of his feeling for her.*

tolerant *adj.* considerate, patient, liberal, impartial: *Our teacher is sometimes too tolerant of our misbehavior in class.* **ant.** intolerant, biased, bigoted, prejudiced.

tolerate *vb.* permit, allow, authorize, stand, condone: *The school will not tolerate students' smoking anywhere on the grounds or in the buildings.*

tone *n.* **1.** sound, noise: *At the tone, the time will be ex-*

actly noon. **2.** manner, mood, expression: *Sheldon's voice reflected the angry tone of the argument.*

tool *n.* utensil, implement, instrument, device: *I'd like to repair this watch, but I haven't the proper tools for doing so.*

top *n.* **1.** peak, summit, tip, pinnacle: *From the top of that mountain you can see for many miles.* **2.** cap, cover, lid: *I've lost the top of the toothpaste tube.* *vb.* excel, surpass, outdo, exceed, beat, better: *Ted topped his earlier performance in this week's swimming meet by five seconds.* **ant.** *n.* **1.** bottom, base.

topic *n.* subject, issue, theme: *The topic we shall discuss today is, "Should children under ten be allowed to stay up till midnight?"*

torment *vb.* annoy, vex, pester, harass, harry, torture, distress: *Peter was tormented by the worry that he'd miss the train if he waited for Letitia.* *n.* torture, agony, anguish, misery: *I can't describe the torment I went through until I learned you were safe.*

torrent *n.* downpour, flood, deluge: *When the dam cracked, a torrent of water was let loose onto the town below.*

torture *n.* torment, anguish, misery, pain, cruelty: *The soldiers used torture to make the captive tell where the guns were hidden.* *vb.* torment, hector, abuse: *Stop torturing me by talking about water here in the middle of the desert.*

toss *vb.* **1.** throw, pitch, hurl, cast: *Larry easily tossed the paper into the waste basket across the room.* **2.** pitch, turn, stir, move, tumble: *I tossed all night and couldn't have slept more than one hour.*

total *adj.* entire, whole, complete, full: *The total number of students who volunteered to help clean up was six.* *n.* sum; entirety: *What is the total of this column of figures?* *vb.* add: *Would you please total the number of times you were late or absent?*

totter *vb.* reel, stagger, falter: *There goes old Mrs. Grundy, tottering down the street.*

touch *vb.* **1.** feel, handle, finger: *Please do not touch the paintings.* **2.** affect, move, concern: *We were all touched by the story of the orphan who had found a home.* **3.** mention, refer to, treat, discuss: *The speaker touched on the subject of cheating on exams and Zeke looked nervous.* *n.* **1.** contact: *The very touch of her hand makes me tingle all over.* **2.** hint, trace, suggestion: *This soup* *needs a touch more pepper.* **3.** skill, knack, ability, talent: *That clock cabinet shows the touch of a master craftsman.*

touching *adj.* moving, effective, tender: *Seeing Billy hugging his puppy was a touching scene.*

touchy *adj.* sensitive, jumpy, nervous, testy, short-tempered, irritable: *Women's rights is a touchy question in some countries. You needn't be so touchy, just because I dropped your lunch on the floor!* **ant.** calm, collected.

tough *adj.* **1.** strong, hard: *This shoeleather is so tough it will last forever.* **2.** leathery, inedible, sinewy: *This steak is as tough as shoeleather.* **ant. 1.** weak, vulnerable. **2.** tender.

tour *vb.* travel, visit: *Our whole family will be touring the country this summer in our new car.* *n.* trip, excursion, voyage, journey: *I once took a tour of all the monuments in Washington, D.C. Are you going on a tour of the Colorado river?*

tournament *n.* contest, tourney, match, competition: *Boris is likely to win the chess tournament again this year.*

tow *vb.* pull, drag, draw, haul: *Isn't it amazing how that small tugboat can tow that enormous string of barges?*

town *n.* village, hamlet, municipality, community: *We live in the country, where the nearest town is 20 miles away.*

toy *n.* plaything, game: *It's time to put away your toys and come in to have dinner.* *vb.* play, trifle: *Sadie was just toying with my emotions: she really loved Arthur.*

trace *n.* sign, mark, hint, suggestion, vestige: *You can taste just a trace of rust in this water. I couldn't find the slightest trace of her in the entire building.* *vb.* track, hunt, pursue, follow: *The detective traced the thief's movements the night of the robbery.*

track *n.* **1.** mark, sign, trail, trace, spoor: *The tracks of the raccoon were plainly visible in the snow.* **2.** trail, path, road, route, way: *We went far from the beaten track to find these blueberries.* *vb.* **1.** trail, pursue, trace, hunt, follow, dog: *The police tracked the fugitive through the wilderness till they caught him.* **2.** trail, carry, drag: *Now you've tracked mud all over the clean floor!*

tract *n.* region, area, district, territory: *A huge tract of land has been set aside for wildlife conservation.*

trade *n.* **1.** commerce, business, dealing, traffic; enterprise: *Trade between the countries has become competitive.* **2.**

occupation, livelihood, craft, profession: *Where do you think Phil learned the harness-making trade?* **3.** barter, swap, exchange: *What do you want in trade for that baseball?* *vb.* barter, exchange, swap: *I'll trade my bat for your baseball.*

tragedy *n.* misfortune, unhappiness, misery: *The tragedy of Ophelia's sickness is that she would improve if she could afford to buy the medicine.*

tragic *adj.* sad, unfortunate, miserable, depressing, mournful, melancholy: *You've heard about the tragic death of Moira's kitten, haven't you?* **ant.** comic.

trail *vb.* **1.** drag, draw: *Phoebe came in, trailing her fur coat on the floor just to show off.* **2.** pursue, track, trace, follow: *The dogs trailed the fox to the woods and then lost the scent.* *n.* **1.** path, track: *Here comes Peter cottontail, hopping down the bunny trail.* **2.** scent, spoor: *The bloodhounds picked up the trail of the escaped convict and began to howl.*

train *vb.* teach, drill, prepare, tutor, educate: *My uncle trained me to dive from a 50-foot tower when I was nine.*

trait *n.* feature, quality, characteristic: *Edwin has all the traits one looks for in someone who wants to study medicine.*

traitor *n.* betrayer, turncoat, spy: *The traitor was caught selling secrets to the enemy.*

tramp *vb.* march, stamp, trample, stomp: *Vickie came into the house quite angry and tramped up the stairs to her room.* *n.* vagabond, vagrant, hobo, bum, gypsy: *Three tramps jumped off the freight train just as it entered the city.*

trample *vb.* stomp, crush, squash: *The children had trampled down all the newly seeded grass.*

tranquil *adj.* peaceful, calm, undisturbed, quiet: *Only the harsh cry of the jackal broke the tranquil silence.* **ant.** disturbed, upset, agitated.

transaction *n.* negotiation, deal, settlement: *The government has approved the transaction for buying oil from Kuwait.*

transfer *vb.* **1.** shift, move, transport: *All of these boxes must be transferred to another warehouse today.* **2.** assign, reassign, change: *The author has transferred all his rights to the book to his wife.* *n.* change, move, shift: *The transfer of ownership of the boat will be completed when we receive payment.*

transform *vb.* change, convert: *In a wink, the prince was transformed into a green frog.*

transmit *vb.* send, dispatch, transfer, pass: *The information has been transmitted to every office, all over the world, by cable.*

transparent *adj.* **1.** clear, limpid: *If you can see everything through it, it's transparent, but if it's frosted, we call that translucent.* **2.** clear, obvious, evident, plain: *Billy told so many transparent falsehoods that they call him Billy Liar.* **ant. 1.** opaque.

transport *vb.* carry, transfer, move, shift: *The ore is transported from the mine to the processing plant by ship.*

trap *n.* snare, pitfall, net, deadfall: *We set a trap to catch the animal that has been stealing our corn.* *vb.* ensnare, entrap, net, bag: *Hunters used to trap beavers for their fur, but that's illegal now in most places.*

travel *vb.* journey, voyage, cruise, roam: *After traveling all over Europe, we finally returned home, exhausted.* *n.* traveling, touring: *Travel to foreign countries can be very educational.*

treachery *n.* betrayal, disloyalty, treason: *Assassination of the king was an act of treachery that deserves capital punishment.* **ant.** loyalty, steadfastness.

tread *vb.* walk, step; trample, tramp: *Tread lightly over this broken glass. Some inconsiderate fellow has trod all over our flower garden.* *n.* step, walk: *We sneaked along with catlike tread.*

treason *n.* treachery, betrayal, disloyalty, sedition: *Selling atomic secrets to a foreign government is an example of treason.*

treasure *n.* riches, wealth, abundance: *The pirates were said to have buried their treasure on this beach, but no one has yet found it.* *vb.* guard, prize, value: *Manuel told me that he treasures our friendship above anything else.*

treat *vb.* **1.** handle, act, deal, manage, negotiate: *How do you plan to treat the problem of increased student absences?* **2.** administer, attend, tend, heal: *A doctor knows best how to treat the condition you complain of.* **3.** approach, discuss, process, regard: *The scientists treat UFO sightings with very little respect.* **4.** indulge, entertain, pay for, host: *May I treat you to an ice cream cone?* *n.* present, gift: *Dinner tonight will be my treat.*

tremble   *vb.* quiver, shake, quake, shiver, shudder: *The leaves of the aspen tremble in the slightest breath of air.*

tremendous   *adj.* huge, enormous, gigantic, colossal, great, large: *Looming above us, disappearing into the clouds, was a tremendous beanstalk.*

trench   *n.* ditch, gully, moat, arroyo, gorge, gulch: *A deep trench surrounded the castle and we soon filled it with water for added protection.*

trend   *n.* tendency, inclination, course, drift: *The trend a few years ago was to very short skirts, but that has changed.*

trial   *n.* **1.** test, examination, proof, analysis: *The race that was run yesterday was just a trial to see which cars would qualify.* **2.** suit, lawsuit, litigation, hearing, case, contest: *The defendant is on trial for murder. The trial was moved to another city because of the bad publicity here.* **3.** ordeal, suffering, difficulty: *Since her husband died, Mrs. Corvallis has been through a terrible trial.*

tribe   *n.* clan, race: *Most of the Indian tribes that once lived in America are now gone.*

trick   *n.* **1.** deception, trickery, stratagem, wile, deceit: *Throwing that pebble against the window was just a trick to make the teacher look the other way.* **2.** joke, jest, prank: *The children's putting oatmeal in the coffee was just a trick—they meant no harm.* *vb.* dupe, fool, bamboozle, cheat, swindle, defraud: *Using the old Spanish handkerchief game, they tricked me out of $1,000.*

trickle   *vb.* dribble, drop, drip, seep, leak: *The water trickled through the hole in the tank and ran into the ground.*

trifling   *adj.* unimportant, trivial, insignificant, petty: *Whether you wear a green scarf or a red one is a trifling matter.*

trim   *vb.* **1.** clip, prune, shave, cut, shear: *The gardener trims the hedge about three times a year.* **2.** decorate, adorn, ornament: *Let's trim the Christmas tree tonight.* *adj.* neat, compact, tidy: *Susan does not have what I would call a trim figure.*

trip[1]   *vb.* **1.** stumble: *Marla tripped over the rug and sprawled on the floor.* **2.** err, bungle, blunder, slip: *I tripped on the last five questions and failed the exam.*

trip[2]   *n.* voyage, cruise, excursion, journey, tour: *The fortuneteller told me that I would soon take a long trip.*

triumph   *n.* conquest, victory, success: *After winning the golf tourney, the champion had another triumph to add to* *his list.* *vb.* win, prevail, succeed: *Justice and goodness always triumph over evil in the end, but I can't always wait till the end.* **ant.** *n.* defeat, failure.

trivial *adj.* trifling, unimportant, insignificant, petty, paltry: *Whether you go or not is a trivial matter to me.*

trophy *n.* prize: *Can you believe that Bob won a silver trophy for playing the piano and a gold one for stopping?*

trouble *vb.* **1.** distress, disturb, worry, concern, upset, confuse: *As you can imagine, my mother was a little troubled to learn that I had failed my exam.* **2.** bother, inconvenience: *You needn't trouble to go to the door: I can let myself out.* *n.* **1.** misfortune, difficulty, concern: *Sometimes I think that our watchdog is more trouble than he's worth.* **2.** pains, inconvenience, exertion, effort: *Please don't go to any trouble to make anything special— steak, baked potato, salad and pie à la mode will be fine.*

troublesome *adj.* annoying, irritating: *The new car is just as troublesome as the old one.*

true *adj.* **1.** correct, accurate, valid: *That is a true account of what happened.* **2.** genuine, real, actual, valid, legitimate: *Can you prove that you are the true and rightful heir to the fortune?* **3.** faithful, trusty, steady, staunch, loyal, dependable, sincere: *If you were a true friend of mine, you would come to the rescue at once.*

trust *n.* **1.** confidence, reliance, dependence, faith: *I have always put my trust in my equipment, which is why I haven't had an accident yet.* **2.** hope, faith: *I shall accept your story on trust.* *vb.* rely on, have confidence in, depend on: *Whenever someone says to me, earnestly, "You can trust me," I don't.*

trusted *adj.* reliable, trustworthy, dependable, true, loyal, devoted, staunch: *You are one of my most trusted friends, Judas.* **ant.** untrustworthy.

try *vb.* **1.** attempt, endeavor, strive, essay: *I am trying to tell you, but you keep interrupting.* **2.** test, examine, analyze, investigate, prove: *Let's try this new kind of laundry soap.* *n.* attempt, endeavor, effort: *If you give it the old college try, I'm sure you'll succeed.*

trying *adj.* difficult, annoying, troublesome, bothersome: *My father had a very trying day at the office.*

tug *vb.* yank, pull, jerk: *I tugged hard at his beard, it came off in my hand, and there stood Patrick!*

tumble *vb.* fall; trip, stumble: *When we opened the closet* *door, the contents came tumbling out. James tumbled down the stairs and fell in a heap.*

tumbledown *adj.* decrepit, ramshackle, dilapidated, broken-down, rickety: *There's a tumbledown shack by the railroad track.*

tumult *n.* to-do, ado, confusion, disturbance, commotion, disorder, uproar: *The tumult in the restaurant was caused by a mouse that a customer saw run across the floor.* **ant.** peacefulness, tranquillity.

tune *n.* melody, song, air, strain: *That's the same tune that they played at our wedding.*

turn *vb.* **1.** spin, revolve, rotate: *The wheel continued to turn long after the motor had stopped.* **2.** reverse, change: *Turn to face the wall.* **3.** become, change, transform: *The bitter cold turned the pond to ice overnight.* **4.** send, drive: *They turned me away at the door, saying I was too young.* **5.** sour, spoil, ferment: *The milk has turned, so you'll have to drink your coffee black. vb. phr.* **turn aside** divert, deflect: *The heavy armor turned aside the spears and arrows.* **turn down 1.** lower, decrease: *Please turn down the volume of that hi-fi.* **2.** refuse, deny, reject: *They turned down my application for a promotion.* **turn in 1.** deliver, offer, give: *I turned in my report early this week.* **2.** retire, rest: *I think I'll turn in, it's past my bedtime.* **turn into** change, become: *You can't make a frog turn into a prince by kissing it, you fool!* **turn loose** free, liberate, unchain, release: *I don't want to be around when they turn loose that leopard.* **turn off** stop; close: *Please turn off the machine before you leave. Turn off the cold water.* **turn on** start; open: *Turn on the lights. Turn on the faucet and champagne comes out.* **turn out 1.** turn off. **2.** dismiss, discharge, evict: *The landlord turned us out for not paying the rent.* **turn up 1.** appear, arrive, surface: *When did you turn up in this town?* **2.** find, discover, uncover, learn, disclose: *The newspaper turned up three people who had seen the crime.* **3.** increase, raise: *Don't turn that radio up any further; I can hear it perfectly well. n.* **1.** revolution, rotation, cycle, round: *Let's watch the merry-go-round do one more complete turn.* **2.** change, alteration, turning: *Make a right turn at the corner.* **3.** opportunity, stint: *Why can't I have a turn at shooting the gun?*

turncoat *n.* traitor: *When the evidence was all in, it de-*

veloped that the general himself was the turncoat. **ant.**
loyalist.

tutor *n.* teacher, instructor: *Fred was doing badly in math,
so his parents hired a tutor to help him.* *vb.* teach, instruct, coach, train, guide: *I used to tutor French students
when I was in college.*

twilight *n.* dusk, nightfall: *I'll meet you at twilight behind
the rose bushes.*

twinkle *vb.* scintillate, sparkle, shine: *The stars were twinkling in the sky.*

twirl *vb.* spin, rotate, whirl: *Twirling a baton is a lot harder
than it looks.*

twist *vb.* **1.** intertwine, interweave, braid: *These wires are
so twisted I'll never get them apart.* **2.** contort, distort,
warp: *The steel girders of the bridge were all twisted out
of shape by the fire. Why do you always twist everything
that I say?* *n.* curve, bend, turn: *The road had too many
twists and turns for safety.*

twitch *vb., n.* jerk, shudder: *The dying snake lay there
twitching in the sand. With a sudden twitch, the dog had
released himself from the collar.*

type *n.* **1.** kind, sort, variety: *What type of person would
want to kill birds?* **2.** sample, example, model: *Is this
the type of plum you like to eat?*

typical *adj.* representative, characteristic: *Here, on your left,
you see a typical prefabricated home.* **ant.** atypical, odd.

tyrant *n.* dictator, despot: *Many of the czars of Russia were
terrible tyrants who had people slain for no reason.*

⊰ U ⊱

ugly *adj.* **1.** unsightly, hideous, plain, homely: *If you want to see something really ugly, take a look at a Gila monster in the zoo.* **2.** unpleasant, nasty, vicious, wicked, evil: *There's an ugly rumor going around that Penny was seen going out with Charlie.*

ultimate *adj.* final, last, decisive, extreme: *The ultimate insult was when the skunk let go with that awful smell and I couldn't see anyone for days.*

umpire *n.* referee, arbitrator, judge: *After playing in the big leagues for 20 years, Roger got a job as an umpire.* *vb.* referee, arbitrate, judge: *Can we get your father to umpire the Little League game this Saturday?*

unanimity *n.* agreement, unity, accord: *There was unanimity when the votes were finally counted: 93 to 0 against having a picnic in the rain.*

unassuming *adj.* modest, humble, retiring: *Sharon has the most unassuming manner.* **ant.** vain, showy, pompous, arrogant.

unbroken *adj.* continuous, complete, whole, uninterrupted: *We marched for an unbroken six-hour period to evade the enemy.*

uncertain *adj.* unsure, doubtful, dubious, questionable, indefinite, vague: *It was plain that the man giving us directions was uncertain as to where the house was.* **ant.** certain, positive, unmistakable.

uncommon *adj.* rare, unusual, scarce, odd, peculiar, strange, queer, remarkable, exceptional: *This is an uncommon variety of orchid, according to the botany teacher.* **ant.** usual, ordinary.

uncouth *adj.* vulgar, rude, ill-mannered, discourteous, impolite: *That boy has a very uncouth way of speaking to his elders.* **ant.** civilized, cultivated, cultured.

under *prep.* **1.** beneath, below, underneath: *We crawled under the ledge of rock and were safe till the avalanche stopped.* **2.** following, below, in accordance with: *Under this law, you must always walk on the side of the road facing traffic.* **ant.** **1.** above, over.

353

undercover *adj.* secret, hidden: *Bill's uncle was an undercover agent for the FBI.*

undergo *vb.* experience, endure, tolerate, suffer: *Prisoners of war sometimes undergo terrible hardships, and some never live through them.*

underhand *adj.* secret, sly, crafty, sneaky, stealthy, secretive: *Tattling on a classmate is a very underhand way to get even.* **ant.** open, honest, direct.

understand *vb.* **1.** see, comprehend, grasp, realize: *I understand what you're saying but I can't see why you'd want to squeeze oranges for a living.* **2.** hear, learn: *I understand that some students have been playing with firecrackers.*

undertake *vb.* try, attempt, venture: *The teacher asked which students would undertake the collection of old clothes for the poor.*

unearthly *adj.* strange, foreign, weird, supernatural, ghostly: *We heard an unearthly scream at midnight and ran for our lives.*

unemployed *adj.* jobless, idle, inactive, unoccupied: *In that year, the number of unemployed factory workers was almost 5 percent.*

unexpected *adj.* surprising, sudden, abrupt, startling, unforeseen: *The rainstorm was entirely unexpected, for the weather man had predicted sunshine.* **ant.** expected, predicted, anticipated.

unfeeling *adj.* callous, hard, numb, unsympathetic: *Those who are cruel to animals are unfeeling wretches.*

unhappy *adj.* miserable, sad, melancholy, wretched, distressed: *Are you unhappy that vacation is over and you have to go back to school?* **ant.** happy, joyful, joyous.

unhealthy *adj.* sick, sickly, infirm, diseased: *When the flu was going around, there were many unhealthy people in town.* **ant.** healthy, well, hale.

uniform *adj.* unvarying, regular, unchanging: *The laws controlling firearms are not uniform from state to state.*

unimportant *adj.* trivial, trifling, petty, paltry, insignificant: *It's unimportant to me whether you pass or fail, but your parents might care, and so will you, later on.*

uninteresting *adj.* dull, boring, tiresome, tedious, dreary, monotonous: *That two-year course in furniture-polishing is the most uninteresting one I have ever taken.*

unique *adj.* single, sole, solitary, incomparable: *You have a unique opportunity if you take this job and work hard.* **ant.** common, ordinary, commonplace.

unite *vb.* join, combine, connect, link, associate: *The individual states agreed to unite and to form one central government.* **ant.** divide, separate, sever.

universal *adj.* general, prevailing, prevalent, common: *The universal feeling among the members is that you ought to resign from the club.* **ant.** local, regional.

unkind *adj.* unsympathetic, unfeeling, cruel, unpleasant, harsh: *The principal said some unkind things to the mischievous boys. The winter storms have been unkind to the trees.*

unlawful *adj.* illegal, illegitimate, illicit: *It is unlawful to shoot ducks out of the hunting season.*

unlike *adj.* different, dissimilar: *Unlike the American flag, the flag of Italy is red, white, and green.*

unmerciful *adj.* merciless, cruel, brutal, heartless: *The bully gave the small boy an unmerciful beating for no reason at all.*

unnecessary *adj.* needless, purposeless, pointless, superfluous: *It's unnecessary to tell me that I am wrong—I know it only too well.*

unoccupied *adj.* vacant, empty, uninhabited: *Since Rover ran away, our doghouse has been unoccupied.*

unparalleled *adj.* unequaled, peerless, unique, rare, unmatched: *In an unparalleled move, the senator from a southern state voted for racial desegregation.*

unpleasant *adj.* disagreeable, offensive, obnoxious, repulsive, unpleasing: *I noted an unpleasant odor when I entered the house.*

unqualified *adj.* **1.** unfit, inept, incompetent, incapable: *Unless you can offer a year's experience, you would be unqualified for this job.* **2.** absolute, unquestioned, utter: *After insulting me, you can expect an unqualified "No!" to your request for a good reference.*

unruffled *adj.* smooth, unperturbed, calm, serene, cool: *Thomas was unruffled by the crowd of fans who pressed toward him.*

unruly *adj.* disorganized, unmanageable, disobedient, disorderly: *An unruly group waited outside to shout at the speaker when he left.* **ant.** orderly.

unsightly *adj.* unattractive, ugly, hideous: *That's one of the most unsightly messes I have ever seen—clean up your room!*

unsound *adj.* **1.** weak, flimsy, feeble, fragile: *The foundation of the house is unsound and will collapse in a few months.* **2.** diseased, sick, impaired, unhealthy: *I am sorry to say that we consider your brother to be of unsound mind.* **3.** faulty, invalid, false: *The reasoning in your argument is unsound if you think that people will eat insects.*

untidy *adj.* sloppy, messy, slovenly, disorderly: *It is dangerous to maintain a workshop in such untidy condition.*

unusual *adj.* uncommon, exceptional, strange, remarkable, extraordinary, peculiar, queer, odd: *That is the most unusual animal I have ever seen!*

unwholesome *adj.* unhealthful, unhealthy, poisonous, dangerous: *The air from the Pharaoh's tomb is said to be unwholesome; those who inhale it are supposed to die horribly.*

unwieldy *adj.* bulky, awkward, clumsy: *The couch isn't so heavy, but it's too unwieldy for one person to carry.*

uphold *vb.* support, maintain, back: *I uphold the right of any person to a fair trial.*

upright *adj.* **1.** erect, vertical, perpendicular: *We gradually raised the flagpole till it was upright.* **2.** just, honest, honorable, true: *Bill is one of the most upright members of our community.* *n.* pole, support, prop, column: *Slip that upright under the board to support it while I hold it up in the air.*

uprising *n.* revolt, revolution, rebellion, mutiny: *The prisoners at the jail staged an uprising that took three days to calm down.*

uproar *n.* commotion, disturbance, tumult, disorder, noise: *There was such an uproar from the crowd that I couldn't hear the speaker.*

upset *vb.* **1.** overturn, upend, topple, capsize: *The rowboat was upset in the middle of the lake and we almost drowned.* **2.** disturb, agitate, fluster, bother: *I was upset by the news that you were moving so far away.* *adj.* disturbed, unsettled: *My stomach was upset all morning from eating popcorn all last evening.*

urge *vb.* **1.** force, push, drive, press, prod: *Unless you had urged me, I never should have run for office.* **2.** plead, persuade, beg, implore: *I urge you to finish school first.* **3.**

advise, recommend: *The doctor urged that everyone stop smoking. n.* impulse: *I suddenly got the urge to phone my sister in South America.* **ant.** *vb.* dissuade, discourage.

urgent *adj.* **1.** pressing, immediate: *There is urgent business that prevents my mother from leaving town this week.* **2.** insistent, persistent, demanding: *The urgent ringing of the doorbell finally woke me, and I ran to see who it was.*

usage *n.* **1.** treatment; use: *This puppy has been subjected to bad usage.* **2.** custom, habit, practice, convention, tradition: *Usage has it that men hold open doors for women.*

use *vb.* **1.** employ, utilize: *I use green nail polish only on Tuesdays.* **2.** exhaust, spend, expend, consume: *Why use your energy to do housework?* **3.** exercise, work: *I use my left hand less than my right. n.* **1.** employment, utilization: *The use of certain dyes has been found unsafe for human consumption.* **2.** advantage, profit, point, benefit: *It's no use trying to convince you that the earth is flat.*

usher *n., vb.* guide: *She works as an usher and gets to see all the plays for nothing. He uses a flashlight to usher people to their seats in the dark.*

usual *adj.* customary, ordinary, normal, regular, habitual, accustomed, common: *The usual way of communicating is by calling someone's name, not by throwing a pencil at him.*

utensil *n.* tool, appliance, implement, instrument: *What kind of utensil except a fork could you use to test a chicken to see if it's cooked?*

utter[1] *vb.* say, speak, pronounce, express: *Nicole uttered her first words at the age of nine months (and hasn't been quiet since).*

utter[2] *adj.* absolute, complete, total, unqualified: *Anyone who would cross the street against the light is an utter fool.*

V

vacant *adj.* **1.** unoccupied, empty, uninhabited, untenanted: *The apartment will not be vacant till the end of the month.* **2.** thoughtless, vapid, vacuous, stupid: *In reply to my question, all I got was a vacant stare.* **ant. 1.** full, filled, occupied. **2.** bright, alert, intelligent.

vacation *n.* holiday, rest: *I took a two-week vacation in the mountains.*

vague *adj.* uncertain, indefinite, unsure, obscure: *When I asked him where he was going, I got only a vague reply.* **ant.** specific, unequivocal.

vain *adj.* **1.** useless, worthless, idle, trivial, unfruitful, unsuccessful: *I made a vain attempt to catch the paddle, but it had floated out of reach.* **2.** proud, conceited, self-important, arrogant: *Tim is a vain man who will never admit to being wrong.* **ant. 2.** humble.

valiant *adj.* brave, bold, courageous, heroic, intrepid, dauntless, unafraid, fearless: *Those were valiant soldiers who died for their Queen in distant lands.*

valid *adj.* **1.** sound, logical, well-founded: *Your argument is valid, but I just disagree with you.* **2.** genuine, real, true, actual, authentic, trustworthy: *This painted bowl is a valid example of Etruscan art.*

valor *n.* bravery, boldness, courage, intrepidity, heroism, fearlessness: *This gold medal was awarded to my brother for valor on the battlefield.*

valuable *adj.* **1.** important, worthy: *I have valuable information that I am ready to sell to the highest bidder.* **2.** costly, high-priced: *This necklace is very valuable, even though you paid only $2 at auction.* **ant. 2.** worthless.

value *n.* **1.** importance, worth, merit, benefit: *Anyone who has had any experience has learned the value of an education.* **2.** cost, price: *I asked the salesman about the value of the diamond necklace.* *vb.* **1.** rate, price, appraise, evaluate: *This Persian carpet has been valued at more than $25,000.* **2.** esteem, prize, appreciate: *I value your friendship much more highly than I do the winning of the contest.*

vanish *vb.* disappear, evaporate, dissolve: *The little green man gave a quick nod of his head and vanished into thin air.* **ant.** appear.

vanity *n.* pride, conceit, smugness: *It's Ramona's vanity that makes her spend hours putting on makeup.*

vanquish *vb.* conquer, defeat, beat, overcome, subdue: *The Indians succeeded in vanquishing the pioneers who had tried to kill them.*

vapor *n.* mist, fog, steam; haze, smog: *The vapors rising from the swamp prevented us from seeing across it.*

variable *adj.* changeable, shifting, unsteady: *The weather at this time of the year can be so variable that you'd better take an umbrella.* **ant.** constant, unwavering.

variety *n.* **1.** change, diversity: *For variety, why not have an egg for breakfast instead of just cereal?* **2.** sort, kind, form, class, type: *I am not familiar with this variety of corn, but it's delicious.*

various *adj.* several, divers, sundry, different: *We ought to examine the various ways in which the work can be done.*

vary *vb.* change, alter, diversify: *Irena's mood varies from happy to miserable as often as the weather does. You ought to vary your approach in order to see which is the most successful.*

vast *adj.* extensive, huge, enormous, immense, measureless, unlimited: *The distances between galaxies in outer space are vast.*

vault[1] *vb.* leap, jump, spring: *The runner easily vaulted over the high wall and eluded his pursuers.*

vault[2] *n.* **1.** tomb, sepulcher, crypt, grave, catacomb: *The archeologists unsealed the vault of the Pharaoh, who had died 3,000 years before.* **2.** safe, safety-deposit box: *We keep our valuable papers in a vault at the bank.*

vehicle *n.* conveyance: *What kind of vehicle besides a Jeep could go on this road?*

veil *n.* gauze, mask, film, web: *The mysterious lady wore a dark veil and we couldn't see her features.* *vb.* conceal, hide, cover: *Your veiled threats don't frighten me.*

velocity *n.* speed, swiftness, quickness, rapidity: *Light travels at a velocity of about 186,000 miles per second.*

vengeance *n.* revenge, retaliation: *I shall get my vengeance for their having given me a hotfoot.*

venom *n.* **1.** poison, toxin: *The spitting cobra can shoot its venom into the eyes at a distance of more than 30 feet.*

2. spite, bitterness, hate: *The prisoner spoke of his accomplices with such venom that the police were afraid to release him on bail.*

venture *n.* attempt, risk, chance, test: *The investor wouldn't put his money in a venture like yours.* *vb.* risk, dare, gamble, hazard: *I'd venture to say that we ought to leave before the fight starts. Don't try to venture out in the storm.*

verbal *adj.* spoken, oral, unwritten: *We made a verbal agreement that you would leave town for a week.* **ant.** written, printed.

verdict *n.* decision, judgment, opinion, finding: *Whatever the jury may say, my own verdict is that the defendant is guilty of murder.*

verge *n.* edge, rim, lip, margin, brim, brink: *I was on the verge of telling the real story when Ellie and Bob walked in.*

verify *vb.* confirm, affirm, corroborate: *From the boy's statement, we verified that you couldn't have been at the scene of the crime.*

version *n.* rendering, interpretation, rendition: *Your version of the report doesn't seem to agree with the facts.*

vertical *adj.* upright, perpendicular, erect: *The side of the building isn't quite vertical.* **ant.** horizontal.

very *adv.* extremely, greatly, exceedingly, considerably: *Because you have been such a very good class, the teacher will treat you all to ice cream.*

vessel *n.* **1.** ship, boat, craft: *How many vessels pass through the Panama Canal in a year?* **2.** container: *Certain acids that attack glass are stored in wax vessels.*

vestige *n.* trace, hint, suggestion, token: *After we finished cleaning the floor, there wasn't a vestige left of the paint we'd spilled.*

veto *n.* denial, refusal: *The President's veto was overridden by a unanimous vote of the Senate.* *vb.* deny, refuse, negate, prohibit, forbid: *The school board voted an increase for the teachers, but the town council vetoed the measure.* **ant.** *n.* approval. *vb.* approve.

vex *vb.* bother, pester, annoy, irritate, anger, plague: *The entire class was vexed by Jim's behavior.*

vibrate *vb.* tremble, shake, quake, quiver: *The windows vibrated from the noise of the explosion 35 miles away.*

vice *n.* evil, wickedness, sin, corruption, depravity: *Of his* *many vices, drinking and smoking were so mild as to be like virtues.*

vicinity   *n.* neighborhood, area, proximity: *I never slept well when we lived in the vicinity of the boiler factory.*

vicious   *adj.*   **1.** wicked, evil, bad, sinful, corrupt: *Blackmail is a vicious crime.* **2.** savage, dangerous, cruel: *There's a vicious killer on the loose in Cairo.*

victimize   *vb.* swindle, dupe, cheat, take advantage of, deceive: *The confidence man often victimizes people who are greedy.*

victor   *n.* winner, champion, conquerer: *The victor in the track and field events will be given an unusual prize.* **ant.** loser.

victory   *n.* conquest, success, triumph: *Our victory at the polls was due to the will of the people.* **ant.** defeat.

view   *n.*   **1.** sight, vision: *Suddenly the figure of a huge toad came into view up the road, and we ran.* **2.** vista, prospect, look: *There's a lovely view of the town dump from this picture window.* **3.** thought, opinion, belief, judgment, impression: *Please let me have your views on the subject before tomorrow noon.* *vb.* see, look at, examine, regard, inspect: *The entire class was invited to view the model of the city at the museum.*

vigilant   *adj.* watchful, alert, attentive, observant: *The committee agreed that all citizens must be more vigilant if traffic accidents were to be reduced.* **ant.** negligent, careless.

vigor   *n.* energy, vitality, liveliness, strength: *The new team captain attacked his responsibility with vigor.*

vigorous   *adj.* energetic, strong, active, forceful, powerful: *With a vigorous effort, we managed to reach the top of the mountain.*

vile   *adj.*   **1.** wicked, sinful, base, bad, wretched, evil: *How could you have done such a vile thing as to feed the goldfish to the cat?* **2.** offensive, objectionable, disgusting, revolting, obnoxious: *Simon has some exceedingly vile habits of which failing to bathe is the least.*

village   *n.* town, municipality, hamlet: *There's a pretty little village nestled at the foot of the mountain.* **ant.** city, metropolis.

villain   *n.* scoundrel, brute, rascal, cad, rogue, scamp, devil: *The villain was just about to tie the heroine to the railroad tracks when the narcotics squad arrived.*

violate   *vb.* break, infringe: *You are violating the law against pollution just by smoking.*

violent   *adj.*   **1.** powerful, forceful, strong, forcible: *A violent wind tore the sail to shreds and we were at the mercy of the waves.* **2.** furious, angry, savage, fierce, passionate: *My mother and father have never had a violent argument since they were married.* **ant. 1.** gentle.

virgin   *n.* maiden, maid: *The young virgins danced around the maypole in the rites of spring. adj.* untouched, pure, unused, chaste: *That subject is virgin territory that remains to be explored.*

virtue   *n.*   **1.** goodness, morality, righteousness, honor: *A man of virtue would never treat anyone badly.* **2.** merit, quality, advantage: *This auto has the virtue of getting 36 miles per gallon.*

vision   *n.*   **1.** sight, eyesight: *The optician told me that these glasses would improve my vision.* **2.** illusion, fantasy, apparition, specter, phantom, ghost, spook: *Coming down the old, creaking, dusty stairs was a vision of ugliness that gave me nightmares for years.* **3.** farsightedness, imagination, foresight, keenness: *The mayor had the vision, 20 years ago, to see this town as a great yachting center.*

visit   *vb.* call (on), see, attend: *The lady in the gray uniform comes to visit the wounded soldiers every day. n.* appointment; call: *I had a visit with your aunt last night. Have you made your daily visit to the post office?*

visitor   *n.* guest, caller: *Monica, you have two visitors who have come to see you.*

vital   *adj.* essential, life-and-death, critical: *Getting the injured person to the hospital is a vital matter. It is vital that we move quickly.*

vivid   *adj.* clear, strong, bright: *I have a vivid recollection of having seen you somewhere, but I can't recall where.*

vocal   *adj.*   **1.** spoken, said, oral, uttered: *A vocal insult isn't ever as deeply felt as one in writing.* **2.** outspoken, definite, specific: *If Laura weren't so vocal in her criticism of others, she might be better liked.*

vocation   *n.* career, profession, occupation, calling, employment: *For what vocation does studying postage stamps prepare you?*

void   *adj.*   **1.** meaningless, useless, invalid, worthless: *This document is void unless both husband and wife sign it.* **2.** empty, vacant, unoccupied: *The light snapped on and* *we saw that the room was completely void.* n. space, emptiness: *I haven't eaten since breakfast, and I feel a great void where my stomach is.* vb. cancel, annul, invalidate: *The bank manager voided the check and I wrote another.*

volume *n.* **1.** book, tome: *The first volume of the encyclopedia is free.* **2.** capacity, dimensions: *The volume of the truck was large enough to hold a car.* **3.** quantity, mass, bulk, amount: *We received a huge volume of orders for these prune pits.*

voluntary *adj.* spontaneous, optional, free: *Voluntary gifts to the school fund are always welcome.* **ant.** compulsory, required, forced.

vow *n.* pledge, promise, oath: *I took a vow that I would get to school on time from now on.* vb. pledge, promise, swear: *Imogene vowed that she would never see Eustace after the way he behaved.*

voyage *n.* journey, trip, tour, excursion: *The tiny boat set out for its voyage to faraway lands.*

vulgar *adj.* rude, crude, bad-mannered, unrefined, coarse: *Anyone using vulgar language will be punished.*

≈§ W §≈

wage *vb.* carry on, pursue, conduct, make: *The two countries waged continuous war for almost a century.*

wages *n. pl.* pay, compensation, salary, rate, earnings: *Your wages will be doubled because you saved the company so much money.*

wail *vb.* moan, cry; mourn, bewail, lament: *Stop that wailing, here's your Teddy bear back.* *n.* moan, cry: *I heard a low wail coming from the closet.*

wait *vb.* stay, remain, tarry, linger: *Please wait a few minutes; the doctor will be right with you.* *n.* delay, postponement, pause: *There will be a 20-minute wait while they glue the airplane back together again.*

wake *vb.* **1.** rouse, arouse, awaken, waken: *Please wake me at six o'clock in the morning. I don't usually wake without being shaken hard.* **2.** activate, stimulate: *Wake your sense of taste with this piece of cheese.* **ant. 1.** sleep, doze.

waken *vb.* See **wake.**

walk *vb.* amble, stroll, saunter, step, march, hike: *The bowlegged salesman told me, "Walk this way." "If I could walk that way," I said, "I wouldn't need the chafing powder!"* *n.* **1.** stroll, march, amble: *We had a very nice walk in the garden with Grandpa.* **2.** path, lane, passage: *We met on the walk in front of the house.*

wander *vb.* **1.** rove, roam, ramble: *This poor dog has been wandering all over the neighborhood looking for his master.* **2.** err, digress: *Don't wander so much and try to keep to the point of what you're saying.*

want *vb.* desire, need, require, wish, crave: *Don't you want to grow up to be a big, strong man? What do you want for dinner? Waste not, want not.* *n.* need, requirement, desire: *The fund has been set up for those wants that people cannot afford to fill.*

war *n.* hostilities, combat, battle: *Now that we have won the war, let's see if we can win the peace.* *vb.* battle, fight: *The two warring families have hated one another for three generations.*

warden *n.* guardian, custodian, keeper, guard; jailer, turnkey: *The air-raid wardens used to make sure that no lights were showing at night. That sheriff used to be the warden of the state prison at Pocteluma.*

warm *adj.* **1.** heated, temperate, tepid, lukewarm: *The water was warm but not hot enough for tea.* **2.** eager, enthusiastic, sympathetic: *The teacher was not very warm to the suggestion that we go home early. vb.* heat: *Warm the milk before adding the chocolate.* **ant.** *adj.* **1.** cool, cold, brisk. **2.** indifferent, cool.

warmhearted *adj.* friendly, kind, loving, kindhearted: *We have never received a more warmhearted welcome than in your home.*

warn *vb.* caution, admonish, advise: *The policeman warned the driver not to drive so fast in a congested area.*

warp *vb.* twist, turn, bend, distort: *The top of the table warped badly in the dampness.*

warrant *n.* warranty, pledge, guarantee, assurance: *The financial executive of the bank has given the broker warrants to purchase 10,000 shares of stock. vb.* guarantee, authorize, approve: *I warrant that with his record for lateness, no one will want to hire him.*

warrior *n.* fighter, soldier, combatant: *The two warriors, one in silvery armor, the other in black, faced each other on the battlefield.*

wash *vb.* **1.** clean, cleanse, scrub, rub, launder: *The clothes and the dishes are all washed, and now I need a bath.* **2.** touch, border, reach: *The waves began to wash the bottom of the sea wall as the storm became more severe.*

waste *vb.* **1.** squander, misspend, dissipate, spend, consume: *Don't waste your money on gambling because you can't win in the long run.* **2.** decay, dwindle, decrease, wear, wither: *Bob has wasted away to a shadow of his former self. n.* **1.** consumption, loss, dissipation: *The waste of money last year will be difficult to make up for.* **2.** rubbish, garbage, trash, refuse; effluent: *The waste from the factory is being dumped directly into the river, polluting it so that we can't swim in it. adj.* unused, useless, extra: *We take the waste clean paper and use it for memo pads.*

watch *vb.* **1.** observe, look (at), note, regard, notice: *Watch the way that porpoise leaps out of the water!* **2.** guard, attend, tend, protect: *Will you please watch the baby while I run out to buy some milk? n.* **1.** timepiece, chronometer: *No, I don't have a watch that tells the time—I have to look at it.* **2.** vigil, patrol, shift, duty: *When we sailed from Bermuda, each of us took turns standing three-hour watches.* **3.** guard, sentinel, sentry, watchman: *The midnight watch approached us and demanded the password, which I had forgotten.*

watchful *adj.* attentive, alert, vigilant, careful, cautious, wary: *You have to be watchful at all times if you are a soldier on guard duty.*

waterfall *n.* cataract, cascade: *The highest waterfall in the world is somewhere in South America, I think.*

wave *n.* **1.** undulation, ripple, breaker, whitecap, surf, sea: *The waves in the Banzai pipeline are the best in the world for surfing.* **2.** surge, swell, flow, tide, stream: *A wave of protest followed the prime minister's announcement about imports.* *vb.* flutter, stream, flap: *The flag waved in the slightest breeze.*

waver *vb.* **1.** flicker: *The light wavered and we could hardly see.* **2.** hesitate, deliberate: *Why do you waver over a decision as important as the one you must make?*

way *n.* **1.** manner, method, approach, style, technique, fashion, mode, means, system, procedure: *Which way would you suggest as the best for getting the best work out of a student?* **2.** road, path, trail: *A narrow way leads to the stable in the back.* *n. phr.* **by the way** incidentally: *By the way, did you remember to bring your snowshoes?* **by way of** through, via: *You can get to Aston by way of Clinton.* **make one's way** proceed, succeed, progress: *How can she make her own way in the world without an education?* **under way** going, proceeding, moving, leaving, departing: *We have to be under way before dark.*

wayward *adj.* contrary, stubborn, obstinate, headstrong, disobedient, naughty: *What can one do with wayward children except to put them in an institution?*

weak *adj.* **1.** feeble, frail, fragile, delicate: *The legs of the table are too weak to support your dancing on the top.* **2.** diluted, watery: *This drink is a little too weak for my taste.* **3.** undecided, irresolute, unsteady, wavering: *That poor fellow is so weak that he lets his wife tell him when he's hungry and thirsty.* **ant. 1.** strong, powerful.

wealth *n.* **1.** riches, fortune, property, means, money: *The Grindles' wealth comes from a factory they own that makes rings out of peach pits.* **2.** quantity, abundance, profusion: *There's a wealth of mineral resources at the* *bottom of the sea if we could only find some economical way to get to it.*

wealthy   *adj.* rich, well-to-do, prosperous, affluent: *Mr. Hawks is so wealthy that he could buy a dozen yachts like the one over there.* **ant.** poor, destitute, impoverished, poverty-stricken.

weapon   *n.* arm: *In the old days out west, many people carried a weapon for personal protection.*

weary   *adj.* **1.** tired, exhausted, fatigued: *I'm so weary from that ten-mile hike that I could sleep for a week.* **2.** bored; tiresome, tedious: *Mara was just doing the same old weary tasks.* *vb.* tire, exhaust, fatigue: *The same old routine, day after day, just wearies me.*

weave   *vb.* plait, braid, intertwine, interlace, lace, knit: *Indians used to weave blankets of the most beautiful design.*

web   *n.* cobweb, netting, net, network: *The spider's web glistened in the sunlight when the dew was on it in the mornings.*

wed   *vb.* marry, espouse: *Do you think that Sally will wed Duke?*

weep   *vb.* cry, sob, lament; mourn, bemoan: *Don't weep for that silly man—he got what he deserved for being so foolish as to leave you!*

weigh   *vb.* consider, deliberate, ponder, study: *You really have to weigh the advantages of having the extra money against working for a company like that one.*

weight   *n.* importance, significance, influence: *Your opinion will carry a lot of weight with the other members of the committee.*

weird   *adj.* strange, peculiar, odd, unnatural, eerie: *Some of the people who live in that old house on the hill look pretty weird to me.*

welcome   *n.* greeting, reception: *We always give Dad a warm welcome when he comes home from work.* *vb.* greet, receive: *There is a very attractive young lady to welcome you at the door of the restaurant.*

welfare   *n.* well-being, good, prosperity: *The police are there for your own welfare, not to be unpleasant or frightening.*

well   *adv.* **1.** favorably, satisfactorily, adequately, competently: *I think that Joe does his job very well.* **2.** fully, completely, thoroughly: *You are well rid of that unpleasant wife of yours.* **3.** surely, certainly, undoubtedly: *After that experience, they well know not to try doing such a thing again.* **4.** personally, intimately: *Of course, I* *know that lady very well: she's my mother. adj.* healthy, sound, fit, trim, robust: *Are you sure you're feeling well enough to go out?*

wet *adj.* soaked, drenched; moist, damp, dank: *I am wet to the skin from walking in the rain. In this weather, the laundry stays wet for days. vb.* soak, drench; moisten, dampen: *Don't try to wet the stamp too much, or it won't stick.* **ant.** *adj.* dry, arid, parched.

wharf *n.* dock, pier: *The ship came up to the wharf and the cargo was soon unloaded.*

whine *vb.* moan, cry, whimper, complain: *Stop whining about losing the cap from the toothpaste, you silly girl!*

whip *vb.* thrash, beat, scourge; flog: *The cruel man whipped his dog just to be mean. n.* scourge, cat o' nine tails, cat, lash: *The cowboy carried a nine-foot whip on his saddle, and he could use it better than many men their guns.*

whirl *vb.* spin, rotate, revolve, twirl, reel: *We went whirling about the dance floor while the fiddler played his tune.*

whole *adj.* **1.** entire, complete, undivided, uncut, total: *I can't believe that you ate that whole apple pie by yourself.* **2.** unbroken, undamaged, entire, intact: *I wish I could make a wish and make that window I broke whole again!* **ant.** **1.** part, partial.

wholesome *adj.* healthy, healthful, nourishing, good, nutritious: *Mother was waiting for us with a wholesome dinner—roast turkey with all the trimmings.*

wicked *adj.* evil, bad, sinful, immoral, ungodly, profane, blasphemous: *Throwing a rock through the church window was a very wicked thing to do.*

wide *adj.* broad; extensive: *The car is too wide to fit into the garage. The pioneers reached the wide Missouri in their trek westward.* **ant.** narrow, thin.

width *n.* breadth, extensiveness, wideness: *The width of this desk is about 36 inches. We saw a road of such width that we couldn't believe it was for cars.*

wield *vb.* brandish, handle: *You certainly wield that dueling sword like an expert!*

wild *adj.* **1.** uncontrolled, unrestrained, unruly: *Some of those boys are very wild when they aren't being disciplined by their parents.* **2.** primitive, savage: *There was a wild man at the zoo who they said came from Borneo.* **3.** silly, impetuous, crazy, foolish: *Going over Niagara Falls in a barrel is the wildest stunt I've ever heard of.* **4.** untamed, ferocious, undomesticated: *It's against the law* *to keep a wild animal as a pet in this town.* **ant. 1.** restrained. **4.** tame.

will *vb.* wish, desire: *Do what you will with the sausages, but please don't ruin the eggs.* *n.* **1.** decision, resolution, resoluteness, determination: *Terry has a strong will, and I doubt that you'll convince her to diet.* **2.** choice: *I have come here of my own free will.*

willing *adj.* consenting, agreeing, agreeable; energetic, eager, enthusiastic: *We rounded up some willing workers and soon had the entire area cleaned up.*

wilt *vb.* droop, sag; weaken: *These flowers will wilt if you don't water them. After two days of 96° weather, everyone began to wilt.*

win *vb.* **1.** succeed, gain: *Do you think we can win? If they win this game, we have no chance at the trophy.* **2.** obtain, gain, acquire, get, earn: *If you knock over all the wooden milk bottles with this baseball, you'll win a doll.* **ant.** lose, forfeit.

wind[1] *n.* **1.** air, breeze, zephyr, breath, gust, draught, flurry, puff, blow, gale, hurricane, cyclone, typhoon, tornado: *A man by the name of Beaufort devised a scale for winds from calm to hurricane force.* **2.** hint, suggestion, clue, rumor: *We got wind of what they were planning to do, so we locked every door and window.*

wind[2] *vb.* **1.** crank; coil, screw: *Wind up my clock, please. Wind the tinsel round the Christmas tree.* **2.** wander, meander, weave, twist: *The stream winds around and around before emptying out into the river.*

wise *adj.* **1.** intelligent, sensible, reasonable, sage, judicious: *You would be very wise to keep as far away as possible from that shark.* **2.** learned, knowledgeable, sage; smart: *A wise old man once told me that I should never fail to be loyal to someone and to some idea.* **ant. 1.** foolish, foolhardy.

wish *vb.* **1.** desire, want, long for, crave: *I wish to have you near me always. Betty said to tell you that she wishes for you the best of everything.* **2.** bid, express, tell: *Gentlemen, I wish you a good evening.* *n.* **1.** desire, want, longing, craving, yearning: *I hope that your wish to visit Tegucigalpa comes true.* **2.** order, command, request: *In keeping with your wishes, I shall be home by 10 o'clock, but I'll miss half the party.*

wit *n.* **1.** intelligence, understanding, wisdom: *Tom is pleased that you've had the wit to see things his way.* **2.**

humor, wittiness, drollery: *Della's wit in placing the tack on Vera's chair was what made everyone laugh.* **3.** humorist, comedian, wag: *Now, ladies and gentlemen, I have pleasure in introducing one of our greatest wits— Cosmo!*

witch *n.* sorcerer, sorceress, magician, enchanter, enchantress, warlock: *By the time the people of Salem discovered that the girls they had burned were not witches, it was too late.*

withdraw *vb.* **1.** remove, retract, recall: *I wish you would withdraw my nomination for the presidency.* **2.** retreat, retire, depart, go; secede: *The butler asked for permission to withdraw. On the issue of slavery, several states threatened to withdraw from the Union.* **ant. 1.** place, enter.

wither *vb.* fade, dry, shrivel, decay: *These flowers are all withered from having been without water for a week.*

withhold *vb.* check, repress, keep back, hold back: *You should withhold your comments till the other speakers have finished.*

withstand *vb.* resist, oppose: *The soldiers at the fort withstood the Indians' attack for three days.*

witness *n.* eyewitness, spectator, observer, onlooker: *There were only two witnesses to the events that took place in that locked room.* *vb.* see, observe, watch, perceive, notice: *Did you witness the defendant remove a raw carrot from the holster?*

wizard *n.* sorcerer, magician, miracle-worker, conjuror: *The children finally came face to face with the wizard, who waved his hand and made lightning strike the floor before him.*

woe *n.* grief, sadness, misery, distress, suffering, sorrow, anguish: *The criminal life led by Jesse James was a cause of great woe to his mother.*

wonder *vb.* **1.** question, conjecture: *I wonder if Tim will ever make the varsity hockey team.* **2.** marvel: *All the people wondered at how the escape artist could get out of the trunk.* *n.* amazement, astonishment, surprise: *The children watched the elephant ballet in wide-eyed wonder.*

wonderful *adj.* marvelous, extraordinary, amazing, astonishing, astounding, remarkable: *Everyone thought that we'd had a wonderful time at the marine museum.*

word *n.* term, expression, phrase, utterance: *I just can't find the words to tell you how happy I am to have won the* *lottery.* *vb.* term, express, phrase, articulate: *The speech by the principal was very carefully worded to make sure that all the students understood.*

work *n.* **1.** effort, exertion, labor: *It's too much work to write an essay for school three times a week.* **2.** employment, occupation, job: *Some people have been looking for work for more than six months.* **3.** accomplishment, product, achievement: *An enormous amount of work is turned out by this factory in the course of a week.* *vb.* **1.** labor, toil: *I wish you didn't have to work so hard to make a living.* **2.** operate, run; function, perform: *I don't know how to work this can opener. Does your old car still work as well as it did?*

world *n.* earth, globe; universe: *There will be too many people in the world in a few years for the amount of food available. This valley is our entire world.*

worry *vb.* **1.** fret, fidget, chafe, grieve, agonize: *Don't worry about me; I'll be all right.* **2.** bother, annoy, pester, disturb: *Not knowing where the children are is worrying me.* *n.* anxiety, concern, uneasiness: *Now that Martin is safe in bed I have one less worry.*

worship *vb.* **1.** revere, reverence, venerate, respect, glorify, honor: *Each of us is entitled to worship God in his own way.* **2.** adore, idolize: *All of the girls worship that new rock singer.* *n.* reverence, respect, honor: *The worship of a deity is a very personal thing with most people.*

worth *n.* value, importance, merit: *Can an expert estimate the worth of this diamond? adj.* deserving, meriting: *I must say that I don't think that movie is worth the trip downtown.*

worthy *adj.* worthwhile, deserving, meriting, earning: *Do you really believe that someone who could do such a thing is worthy of your affection and respect?*

wound *vb.* injure, harm, hurt, damage: *Abbie came home wounded from the war. n.* injury, damage, hurt, harm: *Isaac has a wound in his leg from where he was shot by the thief he was chasing.*

wrath *n.* anger, fury, rage: *You cannot imagine Father's wrath when he learned that the car was gone.*

wreck *vb.* ruin, damage, destroy: *The car was wrecked in the accident. The discovery that there was money missing wrecked the banker's career. n.* destruction, ruin, devastation: *The ship had struck a rock, and the wreck could now be seen, stranded on the reef.*

wrench *n., vb.* twist, jerk, tug: *I gave it a strong wrench, and the handle came off. With a sharp movement, Charlie wrenched the gun from the hold-up man's hand.*

wrestle *vb.* grapple, tussle; fight: *The attackers wrestled me to the ground, stole my wallet, and ran away.*

wring *vb.* extract, twist: *Please see if you can wring more water out of this sponge.*

writhe *vb.* squirm, twist: *The man was writhing in agony on the floor.*

wrong *adj.* **1.** incorrect, inaccurate, false: *If you had fewer wrong answers on your exam, you would have passed.* **2.** bad, naughty, improper: *That was the wrong thing to do, and Morris knew that he'd be punished for it.* **3.** improper, inappropriate, unsuitable: *You're wearing your shoes on the wrong feet, you silly boy!* **4.** awry, out of order, amiss: *The thing that was wrong with my watch is that it was overwound.* *adv.* improperly, incorrectly: *You put your sweater on wrong.* *n.* **1.** evil, wickedness, sin: *People often remember the wrong that a person has done rather than the right.* **2.** impropriety, incorrectness: *That poor fellow isn't to blame: he just doesn't know right from wrong.* *vb.* injure, harm, abuse, hurt: *The officer was unjustly accused and he felt he had been wronged.* **ant.** *adj.* **1.** right, correct, accurate. **2.** good, proper.

⋙ Y ⋘

yacht *n.* boat, pleasure craft, sailboat, cruiser: *The million-aires used to go down to Palm Beach in the winter on their yachts.*

yarn *n.* **1.** thread; fiber: *You are using pink yarn to darn my blue socks!* **2.** tale, story, anecdote: *The old man had many yarns he used to tell us when we sat around the stove in the general store.*

yawn *vb.* **1.** gape: *If you had slept enough last night, you wouldn't be yawning so much today.* **2.** gape, open: *A huge, bottomless chasm yawned before us, and Reba almost fell in.*

yearn *vb.* desire, want, crave, long for: *In the evenings, Nancy yearned for someone to talk with.*

yell *vb., n.* shout, scream, holler, roar: *Don't yell at me, I'm doing the best I can. Give Bruce a yell and ask him to join us in a game of volleyball.*

yield *vb.* **1.** produce, bear, supply: *This year's crop will yield only three billion tons of grain.* **2.** give way, surrender, cede, submit, give up: *The strikers would yield in their demands only after the police were withdrawn.* *n.* harvest, return, fruits, produce, crop: *The yield from our investment has been very poor this year. This plant has an annual yield of a huge number of avocados.*

young *adj.* **1.** youthful, immature: *You are too young to see an X-rated movie.* **2.** undeveloped, underdeveloped: *This crop is still too young to be harvested.* **ant. 1.** old, mature, grown.

youngster *n.* lad, youth, stripling, child: *The youngsters in the Police Athletic League program are learning the best of sportsmanship.* **ant.** adult, grownup.

Z

zeal *n.* eagerness, enthusiasm, fervor, passion: *The zeal with which Ezra attacked every job he was given soon earned him a promotion in the company.*

zealous *adj.* ardent, eager, enthusiastic: *Doris is one of the most zealous tennis players at the school.*

zest *n.* spice, relish, tang, gusto: *Fiona writes with such zest about her trip that I know she's having a good time.*

zone *n.* area, region, district, section, belt: *The zone immediately around the plant is off limits to unauthorized personnel.*

zoo *n.* menagerie: *Let's go to the zoo and feed the sea lions.*